Preface

Welcome to "Deep Learning: A Comprehensive Guide," a book meticulously designed to cater to the needs of learners at various stages of their journey into the fascinating world of deep learning. Whether you are a beginner embarking on your first exploration into artificial intelligence or a seasoned professional looking to deepen your expertise, this book aims to be your trusted companion.

Deep learning, a subset of machine learning, has revolutionized the field of artificial intelligence, enabling advancements that were once thought to be the stuff of science fiction. From autonomous vehicles to sophisticated natural language processing systems, deep learning has become the backbone of many cutting-edge technologies. Understanding and mastering deep learning is not just a desirable skill but a necessity for anyone looking to thrive in the modern tech landscape.

What This Book Offers

This book is not just a theoretical exposition but a practical guide designed to provide you with a holistic learning experience. Here's a glimpse of what you can expect:

Structured Content:

Starts with neural network basics and advances to topics like convolutional, recurrent, and generative adversarial networks. Each chapter builds on the previous, ensuring a comprehensive learning journey.

Online Practice Questions:

Each chapter includes practice questions from basic to advanced levels to test and reinforce your understanding.

Videos:

Instructional videos complement the book's content, offering step-by-step explanations and real-life applications.

Exercises and Projects:

Includes exercises and hands-on projects that simulate real-world problems, providing practical experience.

Lab Activities:

Features lab activities using frameworks like TensorFlow and PyTorch for hands-on experimentation with deep learning models.

Case Studies:

Illustrates the application of deep learning in industries such as healthcare, finance, and entertainment, highlighting its transformative potential.

Comprehensive Coverage:

Covers a broad spectrum of topics, from theoretical foundations to practical implementations, latest advancements, ethical considerations, and future trends.

Who Should Use This Book?

This book is designed for:

Students and Academics: Pursuing studies in computer science, data science, or related fields.

Industry Professionals: Enhancing skills or transitioning into roles involving deep learning.

Embarking on the journey to master deep learning is both challenging and rewarding. This book is designed to make that journey as smooth and enlightening as possible. We hope that the combination of theoretical knowledge, practical exercises, projects, and real-world applications will equip you with the skills and confidence needed to excel in the field of deep learning.

Table of Contents

Chapter 1: Introduction to Deep Learning

1.1 What is Deep Learning: Deep learning is a revolutionary subset of machine learning that has gained immense prominence in recent years due to its remarkable ability to solve complex problems and provide unprecedented levels of performance in various domains. It is inspired by the structure and function of the human brain, specifically the interconnected neural networks that facilitate learning and decision making. Deep learning has emerged as a powerful tool for data analysis, pattern recognition, and artificial intelligence applications.

1.1.1 Understanding Neural Networks: At the heart of deep learning are neural networks, which are computational models inspired by the neural connections in the brain. These networks consist of interconnected layers of artificial neurons, each performing a simple mathematical operation on the input data and passing it to the next layer. The layers are organized into an input layer, one or more hidden layers, and an output layer. The term "deep" in deep learning refers to the presence of multiple hidden layers, allowing the network to learn hierarchical features from the data.

1.1.2 Importance of Depth: The depth of neural networks plays a critical role in their effectiveness. Shallow networks with only a few layers might struggle to capture intricate patterns in complex data, while deeper networks can automatically learn and represent intricate relationships within the data. Deep learning models excel at tasks such as image and speech recognition, natural language processing, and even playing strategic games like Go.

1.1.3 Learning from Data: Deep learning models learn from data through a process known as training. During training, the model adjusts its internal parameters based on the provided data and its corresponding target outputs. This adjustment is achieved by minimizing a loss function that quantifies the difference between the model's predictions and the actual targets. Gradient descent, a key optimization technique, is employed to iteratively update the model's parameters in the direction that reduces the loss.

1.1.4 Representational Power: One of the fascinating aspects of deep learning is its capacity to automatically learn representations from the raw input data. Through successive layers of transformations, a neural network can learn to extract relevant features and representations, making it possible to learn complex patterns and abstractions that might be difficult to specify manually.

1.1.5 Deep Learning vs. Traditional Machine Learning: Deep learning differs from traditional machine learning in its ability to automatically learn features from data. In traditional machine learning, feature engineering is a manual and often time consuming process. In deep learning, feature extraction is part of the model's learning process, alleviating the need for extensive manual feature engineering. This makes deep learning particularly suitable for tasks with large and complex datasets.

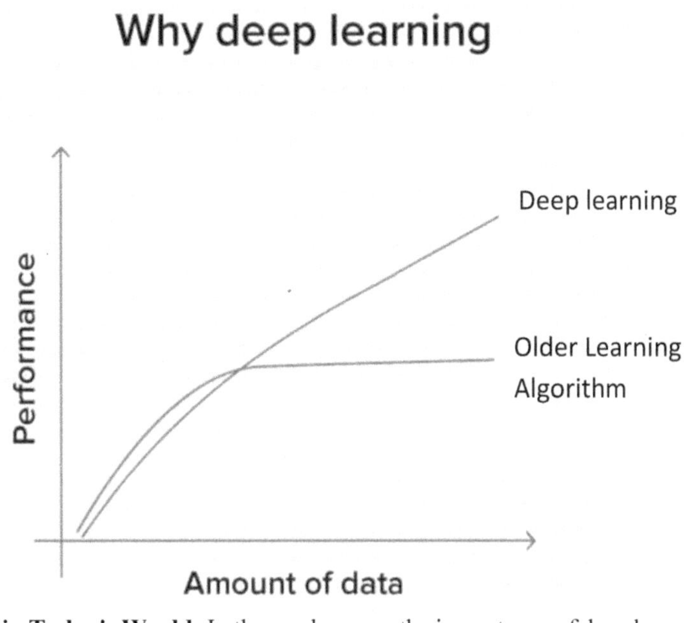

1.2 Importance of Deep Learning in Today's World: In the modern era, the importance of deep learning cannot be overstated. Its transformative impact on various industries and applications has positioned it as a gamechanger in the world of technology and innovation. From healthcare to finance, from entertainment to autonomous vehicles, deep learning has proven its prowess in solving complex problems and pushing the boundaries of what's possible.

1.2.1 Revolutionizing Healthcare: One of the most significant contributions of deep learning is in the field of healthcare. Deep learning algorithms have demonstrated exceptional accuracy in diagnosing diseases from medical images, such as detecting cancerous tumors in radiology scans. Additionally, they can predict patient outcomes, assist in drug discovery, and personalize treatment plans based on individual patient data. The ability to analyze massive amounts of medical data has the potential to revolutionize patient care and medical research.

1.2.2 Transforming Natural Language Processing: Deep learning has brought about a revolution in natural language processing (NLP), enabling machines to understand and generate human language. Applications like language translation, sentiment analysis, chatbots, and voice assistants have become significantly more advanced and accurate due to the deep learning models that underpin them. This has opened up avenues for global communication and seamless human computer interaction.

1.2.3 Enabling Autonomous Systems: Autonomous vehicles are a prime example of how deep learning is shaping the future. Deep learning algorithms process data from various sensors, such as cameras and LiDAR, to enable real time decision making by the vehicle. This technology has the potential to make transportation safer and more efficient, reducing accidents caused by human error and revolutionizing the concept of mobility.

1.2.4 Revolutionizing Entertainment and Creativity: Deep learning has also found its way into the entertainment industry. It powers recommendation systems on streaming platforms, suggesting content that matches users' preferences. Additionally, it has been used to generate art, music, and even movie scripts. The ability of deep learning models to understand and mimic creative patterns is changing how we think about artistic expression and content creation.

1.2.5 Financial Applications: Deep learning has proven its value in the financial sector as well. It's used for fraud detection, algorithmic trading, credit risk assessment, and market analysis. Its ability to process and analyze vast amounts of financial data in real time has the potential to improve decision making and enhance the stability of financial markets.

1.2.6 Scientific Discoveries: Deep learning is accelerating scientific research by aiding in data analysis and pattern recognition. It's used in fields like astronomy, biology, and physics to analyze complex data sets and make new discoveries. For example, it helps in identifying new celestial objects, simulating complex molecular interactions, and analyzing particle collision data in high energy physics.

1.3 Historical Development of Deep Learning: The journey of deep learning from its conceptual roots to its current state as a transformative technology is a fascinating evolution that spans several decades. This chapter explores the historical development of deep learning, tracing its origins, setbacks, breakthroughs, and the factors that led to its resurgence in recent years.

1.3.1 Early Beginnings and Neural Networks: The foundations of deep learning can be traced back to the 1940s and 1950s when the concept of neural networks was first introduced. Pioneers like Warren McCulloch and Walter Pitts proposed mathematical models of artificial neurons, inspired by the workings of the human brain. These early neural network models aimed to simulate basic cognitive processes.

1.3.2 The AI Winter and Setbacks: While the initial enthusiasm around neural networks was promising, the field of artificial intelligence (AI) faced a series of setbacks, often referred to as "AI winters." Funding and interest in AI research declined due to the inability of early neural networks to deliver on their promises. The computational resources available at the time were inadequate to train deep models effectively, leading to a stagnation in the field.

1.3.3 Backpropagation and Revival: In the 1980s, the introduction of the backpropagation algorithm sparked renewed interest in neural networks. Backpropagation, a technique for training neural networks through error backpropagation, made it possible to train deeper networks more efficiently. However, the computational limitations of the era still posed challenges, and deep learning remained a niche area of research.

1.3.4 Emergence of Deep Learning in the 21st Century:

The 21st century saw the renaissance of deep learning, driven by several key factors:

Data Availability: The explosion of digital data created a need for efficient ways to extract insights from massive datasets. Deep learning's ability to automatically learn features from data became highly relevant.

Computational Power: Advances in hardware, including graphics processing units (GPUs) and specialized hardware accelerators, provided the computational power necessary to train deep networks effectively.

Algorithmic Innovations: New techniques, such as dropout regularization and rectified linear units (ReLU), made training deep networks more stable and effective.

1.3.5 Breakthroughs and Milestones:

The 2010s marked a series of breakthroughs in deep learning:

ImageNet Competition: In 2012, a deep convolutional neural network (CNN) named AlexNet won the ImageNet Large Scale Visual Recognition Challenge, significantly advancing the state of the art in image classification.

AlphaGo's Triumph: DeepMind's AlphaGo defeated world champion Go player Lee Sedol in 2016, showcasing the power of deep reinforcement learning and positioning deep learning as a tool for strategic decision making.

1.3.6 Deep Learning Domains and Applications:

With the resurgence of deep learning, its applications expanded rapidly:

Computer Vision: Deep learning models achieved superhuman performance in tasks like object detection, image segmentation, and facial recognition.

Natural Language Processing: Recurrent neural networks (RNNs) and transformer models revolutionized language related tasks, including machine translation and sentiment analysis.

Autonomous Systems: Deep learning played a pivotal role in enabling self driving cars, drones, and robotics through perception and decision making algorithms.

1.3.7 Current State and Future Directions: Today, deep learning continues to evolve, with ongoing research in areas like explainable AI, federated learning, and reinforcement learning. As deep learning becomes more integrated into various industries, the focus is shifting towards addressing challenges related to bias, ethics, and scalability.

1.4.1 Neuron: At the core of deep learning is the artificial neuron, the basic computational unit inspired by the biological neuron. Neurons take inputs, apply a weighted sum, add a bias term, and pass the result through an activation function to produce an output. This output serves as input for subsequent neurons.

1.4.2 Activation Function: An activation function introduces nonlinearity into the neural network, allowing it to model complex relationships in the data. Common activation functions include the sigmoid, tanh (hyperbolic tangent), and rectified linear unit (ReLU). ReLU is particularly popular due to its efficiency and ability to mitigate the vanishing gradient problem.

1.4.3 Layer: Neurons are organized into layers within a neural network. The input layer receives the initial data, the hidden layers process intermediate representations, and the output layer produces the final prediction or result. The depth of a network refers to the number of hidden layers it contains.

1.4.4 Weights and Biases: Weights and biases are the learnable parameters of a neural network. Weights determine the strength of connections between neurons, while biases adjust the output of neurons. During training, the network adjusts these parameters to minimize the difference between predicted and actual outputs.

1.4.5 Feedforward and Backpropagation: Feedforward is the process of passing input data through the neural network to obtain predictions. Backpropagation, short for "backward propagation of errors," is the technique used to update the network's weights and biases by calculating the gradient of the loss function with respect to these parameters.

1.4.6 Loss Function: The loss function quantifies the difference between the predicted outputs and the actual target values. The goal during training is to minimize this loss, typically using techniques like gradient descent. Common loss functions include mean squared error for regression tasks and categorical cross entropy for classification tasks.

1.4.7 Gradient Descent: Gradient descent is an optimization algorithm used to adjust the parameters of a neural network to minimize the loss function. It calculates the gradient of the loss with respect to the parameters and updates them in the opposite direction of the gradient, iteratively improving the model's predictions.

1.4.8 Overfitting and Regularization: Overfitting occurs when a model performs well on the training data but poorly on new, unseen data. Regularization techniques, such as dropout and L2 regularization, help prevent overfitting by introducing penalties for complex models and promoting simpler, more generalized representations.

1.4.9 Hyperparameters: Hyperparameters are settings that determine how a neural network learns. They include parameters like learning rate, batch size, and the number of hidden units in each layer. Proper tuning of hyperparameters is crucial for achieving optimal model performance.

1.4.10 Deep Learning Architectures:

Deep learning encompasses various architectural designs, including:

Convolutional Neural Networks (CNNs): Designed for image analysis, CNNs use convolutional layers to automatically extract features from images.

Recurrent Neural Networks (RNNs): Suited for sequence data like text and speech, RNNs process inputs sequentially and maintain memory of previous steps.

Transformer: A self-attention architecture that excels in tasks involving sequences, such as machine translation and language modeling.

1.5 Project

Unsolved Project

Suppose you're attending a tech seminar and there is a session about deep learning. The speaker explains the concept of deep learning and its importance in today's world. You are interested in understanding the historical development and key concepts of deep learning. Before attending the session, prepare by researching the following: what deep learning is, why it is important in today's world, how it has developed historically, and the key concepts and terminology used in deep learning. This will help you grasp the session better and enable you to ask insightful questions.

1.7 Lab Activity

Unsolved Lab Activity

Create a timeline chart that includes key milestones, significant research papers, and breakthroughs in the field of deep learning.

Exercises

Exercise 1 – Multiple Choice Questions

1. What sets deep learning apart from traditional machine learning?
   a. Manual feature engineering
   b. Dependency on hardware accelerators
   c. Reliance on human decision-making
   d. Utilization of shallow neural networks
2. What is the primary function of an activation function in a neural network?
   a. Determining the number of hidden layers
   b. Adjusting weights and biases
   c. Introducing nonlinearity
   d. Enabling data visualization
3. Which deep learning architecture is best suited for image analysis?
   1. Recurrent Neural Networks (RNNs)
   2. Transformer
   3. Convolutional Neural Networks (CNNs)
   4. Autoencoders
4. What is the purpose of backpropagation in training neural networks?
   a. Calculating the gradient of the loss function
   b. Applying regularization techniques
   c. Adjusting learning rate dynamically
   d. Evaluating the model's performance
5. Which factor contributed to the revival of deep learning in the 21st century?
   a. Decreased availability of data
   b. Limited computational power
   c. Algorithmic stagnation
   d. Advances in hardware and algorithms
6. Which deep learning breakthrough demonstrated the power of deep reinforcement learning?
   a. Alpha Go's victory over a chess grandmaster
   b. ImageNet Large Scale Visual Recognition Challenge
   c. Self-driving car's successful navigation
   d. Stock market prediction accuracy
7. What term describes the phenomenon where a model performs well on training data but poorly on new data?
   a. Under fitting
   b. Regularization
   c. Gradient descent
   d. Overfitting
8. Which deep learning architecture is specifically designed for processing sequences like text and speech?
   a. Transformer
   b. CNN
   c. Autoencoder
   d. RNN
9. What is the role of hyperparameters in a neural network?
   a. Defining the structure of hidden layers
   b. Initializing weights and biases
   c. Tuning the learning rate
   d. Determining the number of training examples
10. What does the term "deep" refer to in deep learning?
    a. The profound insights it provides
    b. The complexity of the activation functions
    c. The presence of multiple hidden layers
    d. The depth of understanding required to implement it
11. How does deep learning differ from traditional machine learning in terms of feature extraction?
    a. Deep learning requires manual feature engineering.
    b. Traditional machine learning uses gradient descent for feature extraction.
    c. Deep learning automatically learns features from data.
    d. Traditional machine learning employs backpropagation for feature extraction

Exercise 2 – True/False

1. The concept of deep learning only emerged in the last decade and has no historical roots in earlier forms of machine learning.
2. Key terminology in deep learning includes concepts such as neural networks, layers, nodes, and weights.
3. The historical development of deep learning shows a progression from simple neural networks to more complex architectures like convolutional and recurrent neural networks.

Exercise 3 – Fill in the blanks

1. The ________________ of deep learning can be traced back to the development of artificial neural networks in the 1940s and 1950s.
2. In today's world, deep learning is crucial for advancements in technologies such as autonomous vehicles, natural language processing, and ________________.
3. Deep learning is a subset of machine learning that focuses on using ________________ to model and understand complex patterns in data.

Exercise 4 - Fill in the blanks with two options

1. The __________ of deep learning in today's world is evident from its applications in various fields such as healthcare, finance, and transportation, highlighting its __________.
2. Deep learning's __________ development can be traced back to the early work on neural networks, leading to significant __________ over the years.
3. Understanding key __________ and __________ is crucial for grasping the foundational concepts of deep learning and its applications.

Review Question

1. What is the fundamental difference between deep learning and traditional machine learning, particularly in terms of feature extraction?
2. Explain the concept of an activation function in a neural network. How does it contribute to the network's ability to model complex relationships?
3. Name two deep learning architectures and describe the types of tasks each architecture excels at.
4. How does backpropagation contribute to the training process of a neural network? What problem does it address?
5. Identify and discuss three key factors that led to the resurgence of deep learning in the 21st century.
6. Describe a specific breakthrough in the field of deep learning that demonstrated its strategic decision-making capabilities. What task did this breakthrough involve?
7. Define the concept of overfitting in the context of machine learning. How can regularization techniques help mitigate overfitting?
8. Compare and contrast the roles of convolutional neural networks (CNNs) and recurrent neural networks (RNNs) in deep learning applications.
9. Explain the importance of hyperparameters in training a neural network. Provide examples of hyperparameters that affect the learning process.
10. How does the depth of a neural network impact its performance? What advantage does a deep network offer over a shallow one?
11. Summarize the significance of deep learning across various industries and applications, illustrating its transformative impact.

Answers

Exercise 1- 1. a, 2. c, 3. c, 4. a, 5. d, 6. a, 7. d, 8. d, 9. c, 10. c, 11. c,
Exercise 2- 1) False, 2) True, 3) True
Exercise 3- 1) historical development, 2) key concepts and terminology, 3) artificial neural networks
Exercise 4- 1) importance, impact, 2) historical, advancements, 3) concepts, terminology

Online Resources

Online Exam Paper:
Link: https://forms.gle/F56gifionbxpDemF8
QR Code:

Chapter 1 Videos Playlist:
Link: https://www.youtube.com/playlist?list=PLzlh_31VWEFrL_MPjYAT4sqgh-ahzjx6o
QR Code:

Chapter 2: Foundations of Neural Networks

2.1 Basics of Neurons and Activation Functions: Neurons and activation functions are the fundamental building blocks of neural networks, forming the basis for information processing and feature extraction. In this section, we'll delve into the basics of neurons and explore various activation functions that enable neural networks to model complex relationships in data.

2.1.1 Neurons: Mimicking the Brain's Functionality: At the core of neural networks are artificial neurons, which are inspired by the way biological neurons in the human brain work. Each artificial neuron takes in multiple inputs, performs a weighted sum of these inputs, adds a bias term, and passes the result through an activation function. The output of the activation function becomes the neuron's output and serves as input to subsequent neurons or the final prediction layer.

2.1.2 Activation Functions: Introducing Non Linearity: Activation functions play a crucial role in neural networks by introducing nonlinearity. Without nonlinearity, neural networks would be limited to representing linear relationships, severely restricting their expressive power. Several common activation functions are used in deep learning:

Sigmoid Function: The sigmoid activation function maps input values to a range between 0 and 1. It's often used in the output layer for binary classification tasks as it produces probabilities. However, the sigmoid function can suffer from the vanishing gradient problem during training.

Hyperbolic Tangent (tanh) Function: Similar to the sigmoid, the tanh function maps inputs to a range between 1 and 1. It's zero centered, which helps alleviate the vanishing gradient problem to some extent. Tanh is used in certain scenarios, but it still has limitations with vanishing gradients for deep networks.

Rectified Linear Unit (ReLU): ReLU is a widely used activation function that returns the input for positive values and zero for negative values. It's computationally efficient and helps mitigate the vanishing gradient problem for deep networks. However, it can also suffer from the "dying ReLU" problem where neurons can get stuck in a state of not firing during training.

Leaky ReLU and Parametric ReLU: To address the dying ReLU problem, variations like Leaky ReLU allow a small gradient for negative inputs, preventing the neuron from becoming inactive. Parametric ReLU takes this idea further by making the slope of the negative part a learnable parameter.

Exponential Linear Unit (ELU): ELU is another variant of ReLU that tries to combine the best of both worlds by having a smooth curve for negative values and an exponential increase for positive values. This helps with the dying ReLU problem and can lead to faster convergence during training.

2.1.3 Choosing an Activation Function: The choice of activation function depends on the problem at hand and the architecture of the neural network. ReLU and its variants are often preferred due to their simplicity and ability to alleviate the vanishing gradient problem. However, it's important to consider factors like model convergence, gradient behavior, and the potential for exploding gradients in very deep networks.

2.2 Structure of Artificial Neural Networks: The structure of artificial neural networks (ANNs) is a critical aspect that determines their ability to learn and generalize from data. In this section, we'll delve into the key components that define the architecture of ANNs, including layers, connections, and the flow of information through the network.

2.2.1 Layers: Organizing Neurons:

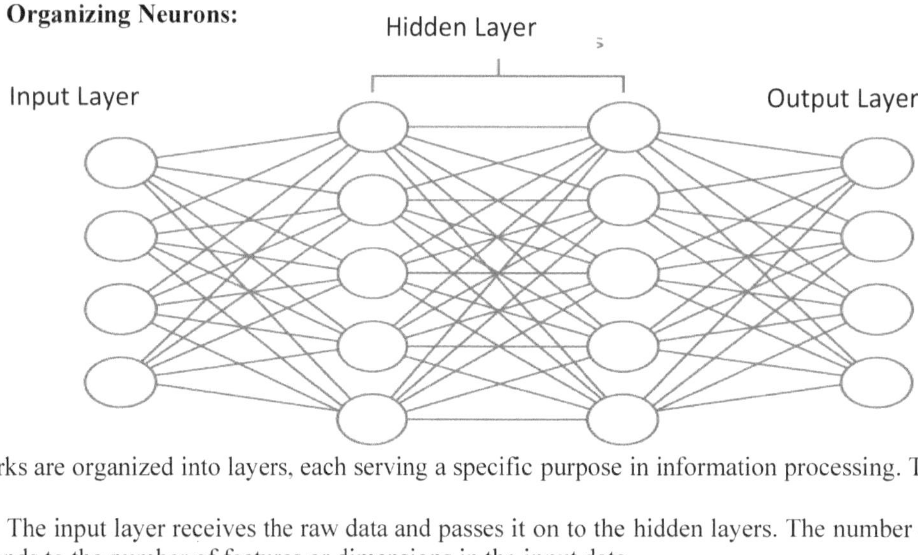

Neural networks are organized into layers, each serving a specific purpose in information processing. The three main types of layers are:

Input Layer: The input layer receives the raw data and passes it on to the hidden layers. The number of neurons in the input layer corresponds to the number of features or dimensions in the input data.

Hidden Layers: Hidden layers process and transform the input data using weighted connections and activation functions. The depth of a network refers to the number of hidden layers it contains. Deep networks have multiple hidden layers that allow them to learn complex hierarchical features.

Output Layer: The output layer produces the final prediction or output of the network. The number of neurons in the output layer depends on the nature of the task, such as binary classification, multiclass classification, or regression.

2.2.2 Connections: Weighted Information Flow: Connections between neurons carry information in the form of weights. Each connection has an associated weight that determines the strength of the signal being transmitted. During training, these weights are adjusted to optimize the network's performance.

2.2.3 Neuron Connectivity: Feedforward and Feedback: In a typical feedforward neural network, neurons are organized in layers, and information flows only in one direction, from the input layer through the hidden layers to the output layer. This one way flow is known as feedforward propagation. Feedforward networks are commonly used for tasks like classification and regression.

Recurrent Neural Networks (RNNs) introduce feedback connections that allow information to loop back to previous layers. This makes RNNs suitable for sequence data, where the order of input elements matters. RNNs have a memory like capability that enables them to maintain context over time, making them valuable for tasks like natural language processing and time series analysis.

2.2.4 Fully Connected Layers: Dense Layers: In a fully connected layer, also known as a dense layer, each neuron is connected to every neuron in the previous and subsequent layers. This dense connectivity enables the network to learn complex relationships but can lead to a high number of parameters, potentially causing overfitting if not properly regularized.

2.2.5 Architectural Considerations:

When designing the architecture of a neural network, several considerations come into play:

Number of Hidden Layers and Neurons: Determining the depth and width of the network depends on the complexity of the task and the available data. Deeper networks can capture more intricate patterns, but they might also require more data to avoid overfitting.

Activation Functions: Choosing the right activation functions for each layer is crucial. ReLU and its variants are often preferred due to their effectiveness in deep networks.

Regularization Techniques: Techniques like dropout and L2 regularization can be applied to prevent overfitting, especially in deep networks.

Output Layer Activation: The activation function in the output layer depends on the task. For binary classification, sigmoid activation is common, while soft max is used for multiclass classification.

2.3 Forward Propagation and Backpropagation: Forward propagation and backpropagation are two fundamental processes that underpin the learning process in neural networks. In this section, we'll explore how these processes work together to enable networks to learn from data and improve their performance over time.

2.3.1 Forward Propagation: Making Predictions: Forward propagation, also known as feedforward propagation, is the process by which input data is processed through the network to produce predictions or outputs. It involves passing the input data through the layers of the network, computing weighted sums, applying activation functions, and generating predictions at the output layer.

The steps of forward propagation are as follows:

Input data is passed into the input layer neurons.

Neurons in subsequent layers calculate weighted sums of their inputs and apply activation functions to produce outputs.

This process continues layer by layer until the output layer is reached.

The final output of the network is the predicted result.

2.3.2 Loss Function: Measuring Prediction Error: After forward propagation, the predicted output is compared to the actual target value using a loss function. The loss function quantifies the difference between the predicted and actual values, indicating how well the model is performing on the task.

2.3.3 Backpropagation: Updating Weights: Backpropagation is the process of adjusting the weights and biases of the network based on the error calculated by the loss function. It involves calculating the gradient of the loss function with respect to the network's parameters and using this gradient to update the weights in a way that reduces the loss.

The steps of backpropagation are as follows:

Compute the gradient of the loss function with respect to the output layer's activations.

Backpropagate this gradient through the network, layer by layer, using the chain rule of calculus. Calculate the gradients of the loss with respect to the weighted sums and activation outputs of each neuron.

Use the calculated gradients to update the weights and biases of the network using an optimization algorithm like gradient descent. The weights are adjusted in the direction that minimizes the loss.

2.3.4 Gradient Descent: Optimizing Weights: Gradient descent is the optimization algorithm used to update the weights and biases of the network during backpropagation. It iteratively adjusts the parameters in the direction of the steepest descent of the loss function, aiming to reach a point of minimum loss.

There are variations of gradient descent, such as stochastic gradient descent (SGD), minibatch gradient descent, and adaptive algorithms like Adam, each with its own advantages in terms of convergence speed and robustness.

2.3.5 Iterative Learning Process: Forward propagation and backpropagation form an iterative learning process. The network's parameters are updated based on the gradients computed during backpropagation, and this process is repeated for multiple iterations or epochs. As the network continues to update its weights, it gradually improves its ability to make accurate predictions on the given task.

2.4 Overfitting and Regularization Techniques: Overfitting is a common challenge in machine learning and deep learning, where a model learns to perform exceptionally well on the training data but fails to generalize to new, unseen data.

Regularization techniques are employed to mitigate overfitting and enhance the model's ability to generalize. In this section, we'll explore the concept of overfitting and delve into various regularization techniques.

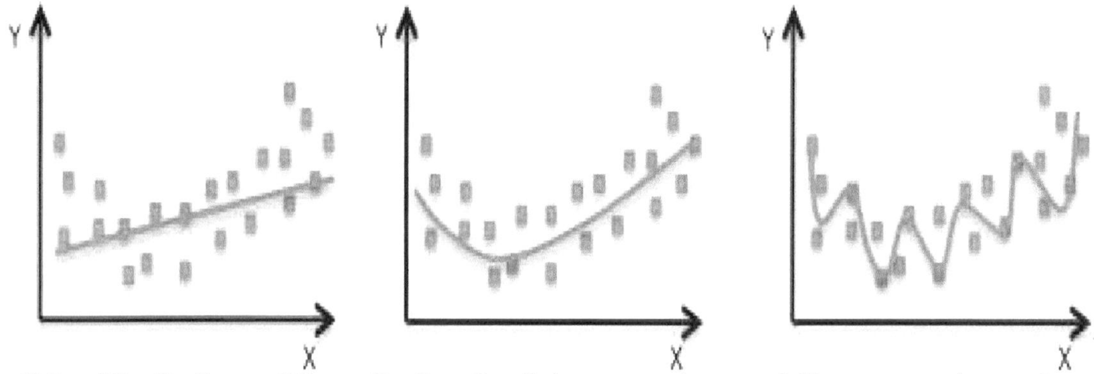

2.4.1 Overfitting: The Challenge of Generalization: Overfitting occurs when a model becomes overly complex and captures noise or random fluctuations in the training data instead of the underlying patterns. This leads to poor performance on new data because the model has not learned meaningful representations and cannot generalize well.

Signs of overfitting include a significant difference between training and validation/test performance, a model that performs well on training data but poorly on new data, and erratic behavior in the loss curve during training.

2.4.2 Regularization: Balancing Complexity: Regularization techniques aim to strike a balance between model complexity and the ability to generalize. They add constraints to the learning process, discouraging the model from fitting the noise in the training data and promoting simpler representations.

2.4.3 L2 Regularization (Ridge Regression) : L2 regularization, also known as Ridge regression, adds a penalty term to the loss function proportional to the sum of squared weights. This encourages the model to distribute the weight values more evenly across different features and prevents any one feature from dominating the others. It effectively reduces the magnitude of the weights and prevents overfitting.

2.4.4 L1 Regularization (Lasso Regression) : L1 regularization, or Lasso regression, adds a penalty term to the loss function proportional to the sum of the absolute values of the weights. Unlike L2 regularization, L1 regularization can drive some weights to exactly zero. This can lead to feature selection, as irrelevant features may have their weights reduced to zero, resulting in a simpler and more interpretable model.

2.4.5 Dropout: Randomly Deactivating Neurons: Dropout is a regularization technique specific to neural networks. During training, dropout randomly deactivates a fraction of neurons (dropout rate) in each layer. This prevents individual neurons from relying too heavily on specific input features and encourages the network to learn more robust and generalized representations.

2.4.6 Early Stopping: Preventing Overtraining: Early stopping is a simple regularization technique that involves monitoring the model's performance on a validation set during training. When the validation performance starts to degrade, training is stopped early to prevent the model from overfitting further. This technique relies on the assumption that a model's performance on the validation set reflects its performance on new data.

2.4.7 Cross Validation: Evaluating Generalization: Cross validation is a technique for assessing a model's performance on unseen data. It involves splitting the dataset into multiple subsets for training and validation, iteratively training the model on different subsets and evaluating its performance. This provides a more robust estimate of a model's generalization ability.

2.4.8 Choosing the Right Regularization: The choice of regularization technique depends on the problem at hand, the complexity of the model, and the available data. L2 regularization is a common starting point due to its effectiveness in preventing overfitting. L1 regularization and dropout can be valuable additions, especially for more complex models and deep networks.

2.5 Project

Unsolved Project

Suppose you're working on a project that involves building and training a neural network. To achieve the best results, you need to understand the basics of neurons and activation functions, the structure of artificial neural networks, the processes of forward propagation and backpropagation, and techniques to prevent overfitting. Before starting, study the following: the role of neurons and activation functions in neural networks, how artificial neural networks are structured, how forward propagation and backpropagation work to train the model, and different regularization techniques to avoid overfitting. This preparation will help you design and train an effective neural network model.

2.6 Lab Activity

Unsolved Lab Activity

Write a report that explains the components of a multi-layer neural network, including input layers, hidden layers, and output layers. Use diagrams to illustrate the architecture.

Exercises

Exercise 1 – Multiple Choice Questions

1. What is the primary function of an artificial neuron in a neural network?
   a. Applying an activation function
   b. Processing and transforming input data
   c. Calculating the gradient of the loss function
   d. Maintaining memory of previous steps
2. Which term describes the process by which artificial neurons take in inputs, perform a weighted sum, add a bias, and pass the result through an activation function?
   a. Backpropagation
   b. Gradient descent
   c. Feedforward propagation
   d. Regularization
3. Why is nonlinearity introduced through activation functions in neural networks?
   a. To simplify computations
   b. To ensure linear relationships
   c. To enable modeling of complex relationships
   d. To reduce the number of neurons needed
4. Which activation function maps input values to a range between 0 and 1 and is commonly used for binary classification tasks?
   a. Hyperbolic Tangent (tanh)
   b. Rectified Linear Unit (ReLU)
   c. Sigmoid function
   d. Exponential Linear Unit (ELU)
5. What problem can the sigmoid activation function encounter during training?
   a. Vanishing gradient problem
   b. Exploding gradient problem
   c. Underfitting issue
   d. Overfitting issue
6. How does the Leaky ReLU activation function differ from the standard ReLU?
   a. Leaky ReLU is zero-centered.
   b. Leaky ReLU returns zero for negative inputs.
   c. Leaky ReLU has a smooth curve.
   d. Leaky ReLU prevents vanishing gradients.
7. Which activation function combines a smooth curve for negative values with an exponential increase for positive values?
   a. Sigmoid function
   b. Hyperbolic Tangent (tanh)
   c. Exponential Linear Unit (ELU)
   d. Parametric ReLU
8. Why is the choice of activation function important when designing a neural network?
   a. It determines the number of hidden layers.
   b. It affects the speed of forward propagation.
   c. It influences the model's ability to generalize and learn.
   d. It determines the output range of the network.
9. What is the primary goal of regularization techniques in neural networks?
   a. To increase model complexity
   b. To fit the training data exactly
   c. To balance model complexity and generalization
   d. To emphasize noisy features in the data
10. Which regularization technique involves randomly deactivating a fraction of neurons during training to promote robustness?
    a. Early stopping
    b. L2 regularization
    c. Dropout
    d. L1 regularization
11. What does early stopping as a regularization technique involve?
    a. Preventing the model from training for too long
    b. Stopping training once the loss reaches zero
    c. Adding noise to the training data
    d. Adjusting the learning rate dynamically

Exercise 2 – True/False

1. Regularization techniques such as L2 regularization and dropout help prevent overfitting in neural networks.
2. Neurons in artificial neural networks use activation functions to introduce non-linearity into the model.
3. The structure of an artificial neural network includes layers of neurons, where each layer is connected to the next.

Exercise 3 – Fill in the blanks

1. Forward propagation is the process by which inputs are passed through a neural network to produce an output, whereas _____________ is the method used to adjust the weights of the network based on the error of the output.
2. To prevent overfitting in a neural network, techniques such as dropout, early stopping, and _____________ are commonly used.
3. The basic computational unit of an artificial neural network is the _____________, which uses activation functions to introduce non-linearity into the network.

Exercise 4 - Fill in the blanks with two options

1. The process of training a neural network involves __________ propagation, where the input data is passed through the network, and __________ propagation, where the network's errors are adjusted backwards to improve performance.
2. Techniques such as __________ and dropout are used to prevent __________ in neural networks, ensuring the model generalizes well to new data.
3. In neural networks, activation functions like ReLU and sigmoid determine the output of a __________, influencing the learning process and helping the network to learn __________ patterns.

Review Questions

1. What is the role of artificial neurons in neural networks, and how do they process information?
2. Explain the purpose of an activation function in a neural network. Why is nonlinearity important in activation functions?
3. Compare and contrast the sigmoid and tanh activation functions in terms of their output ranges and usage.
4. Why is the ReLU activation function widely used in deep learning networks? What is the "dying ReLU" problem?
5. How does the Leaky ReLU activation function address the limitations of the standard ReLU function?

Answers

Exercise 1- 1. b, 2. c, 3. c, 4. c, 5. a, 6. d, 7. c, 8. c, 9. c, 10. c, 11. a.
Exercise 2- 1) True, 2) True, 3) True
Exercise 3- 1) Backpropagation, 2) regularization, 3) Neuron
Exercise 4- 1) forward, back,2) regularization, overfitting, 3) neuron, complex

Online Resources

Online Exam Paper:
Link: https://forms.gle/53KgvhDtCbVXErnm8
QR Code:

Chapter 2 Videos Playlist:
Link: https://www.youtube.com/playlist?list=PLzlh_31VWEFoF2ylm3_gLGZGj89lSDNp6
QR Code:

Chapter 3: Convolutional Neural Networks (CNNs)

3.1 Introduction to Convolutional Neural Networks: Convolutional Neural Networks (CNNs) are a class of deep learning models specifically designed to excel in computer vision tasks. Their architecture is inspired by the visual processing mechanisms in the human brain. In this section, we'll explore the fundamental concepts that underlie CNNs and how they have revolutionized the field of image analysis.

3.1.1 Motivation: Analyzing Visual Data: Traditional neural networks struggle to process images effectively due to their high dimensionality and spatial structure. CNNs address this limitation by leveraging shared weights and local connectivity, making them highly effective in tasks like image classification, object detection, and image segmentation.

3.1.2 Convolutional Layers: Capturing Spatial Hierarchies: The core building block of a CNN is the convolutional layer. This layer employs convolutional operations, where small filters (also known as kernels) slide over the input image, capturing local patterns and features. Each filter detects a specific visual attribute like edges, textures, or shapes. Multiple filters generate multiple feature maps, each highlighting a different aspect of the image.

3.1.3 Pooling Layers: Reducing Spatial Dimensions: Pooling layers follow convolutional layers and serve to reduce the spatial dimensions of feature maps. The most common pooling operation is max pooling, which down samples the feature maps by selecting the maximum value within a certain region. This process retains important features while discarding some spatial information, making the network more computationally efficient and robust to small spatial translations.

3.1.4 Fully Connected Layers: Decision Making: After several convolutional and pooling layers, the feature maps are flattened into a one-dimensional vector and connected to fully connected layers. These layers perform classification or regression tasks, making decisions based on the extracted features. The architecture of CNNs allows them to learn hierarchical representations of visual information, improving their ability to generalize from the data.

3.1.5 Transfer Learning: Leveraging Retrained Models: One of the strengths of CNNs is their ability to learn feature representations that are transferrable across different tasks and datasets. Transfer learning involves using a pretrained CNN as a feature extractor for a new task, fine-tuning only the last few layers to adapt to the specific problem. This approach is particularly useful when labeled data is limited.

3.1.6 Applications of CNNs: CNNs have transformed the field of computer vision and have found applications in various domains:

Image Classification: CNNs excel at classifying images into predefined categories.

Object Detection: By combining localization and classification, CNNs can identify and locate objects within images.

Image Segmentation: CNNs can segment images into distinct regions, assigning each pixel to a specific class.

Face Recognition: CNNs play a key role in facial recognition systems, accurately identifying individuals from images or videos.

3.1.7 Future Directions: CNNs continue to evolve with advancements in architecture, regularization techniques, and optimization algorithms. Research is focused on improving model interpretability, robustness to adversarial attacks, and handling small datasets.

Convolutional Neural Networks have revolutionized the field of computer vision by effectively handling image data through convolutional, pooling, and fully connected layers. They have enabled breakthroughs in image analysis and interpretation, with applications spanning from image classification to object detection. As you delve deeper into this book, you'll explore the intricacies of CNN architectures, training, and their role in reshaping the way we perceive visual data.

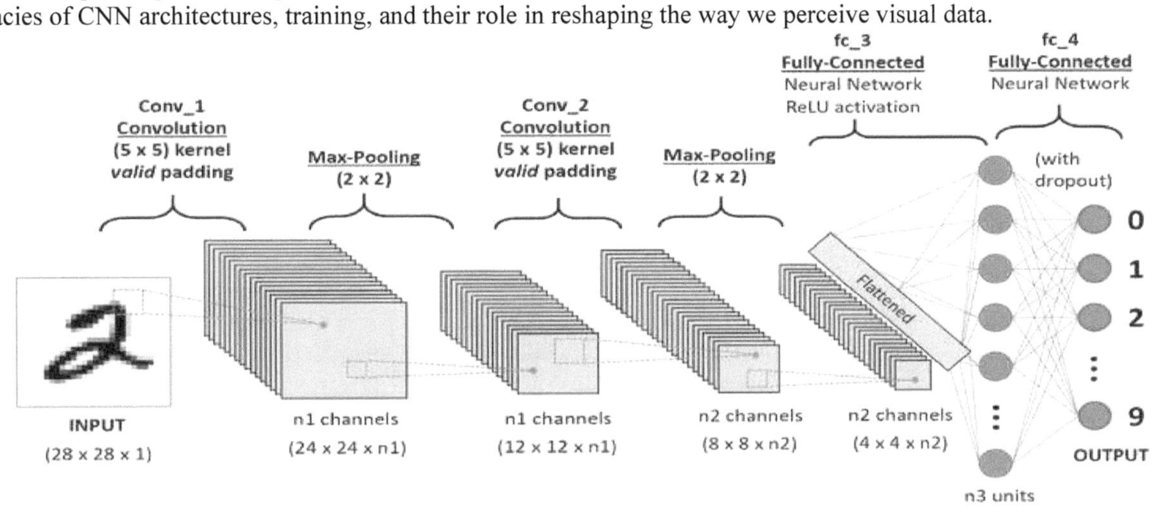

3.2 Convolutional and Pooling Layers: Convolutional Neural Networks (CNNs) derive their power from the unique design of convolutional and pooling layers. These layers are tailored to capture spatial hierarchies in images, enabling CNNs to excel in various computer vision tasks. In this section, we'll delve into the intricacies of convolutional and pooling layers and how they contribute to the success of CNNs.

3.2.1 Convolutional Layers: Capturing Local Patterns: Convolutional layers lie at the heart of CNNs, responsible for extracting local patterns and features from images. The key concept is convolution, where small filters (kernels) slide over the input image. At each position, the filter computes the elementwise product of its weights and the local region of the image. These products are summed to produce a feature map, highlighting specific patterns or attributes.

3.2.2 Filters and Feature Maps: Detecting Visual Attributes: Filters in convolutional layers are designed to detect various visual attributes such as edges, textures, and shapes. They learn to identify simple patterns in early layers and progressively more complex patterns in deeper layers. Each filter's weights are adjusted during training to capture different aspects of the input data.

The resulting feature maps, one for each filter, provide a representation of where and how these visual attributes are present in the input image. Multiple filters capture multiple features, allowing the network to learn intricate details and patterns.

3.2.3 Padding and Stride: Controlling Output Size: Padding and stride are parameters that influence the size of feature maps after convolution. Padding involves adding extra pixels around the input image, allowing filters to slide across the borders without reducing the output size. Stride determines the step size at which filters move during convolution. Properly setting these parameters can help control the spatial dimensions of the feature maps.

3.2.4 Pooling Layers: Down sampling and Invariance: Pooling layers follow convolutional layers and serve to down sample the feature maps, reducing their spatial dimensions. The most common pooling technique is max pooling, where the maximum value within a local region is retained, discarding other values. Pooling achieves spatial invariance, making the network more robust to small variations in the input image.

3.2.5 Spatial Hierarchies and Feature Extraction: The architecture of convolutional and pooling layers allows CNNs to capture spatial hierarchies in images. Early layers focus on basic features like edges and corners, while deeper layers combine these features to recognize more complex patterns. This hierarchical approach enables CNNs to learn progressively abstract and high-level representations of visual data.

3.2.6 Benefits of Convolutional and Pooling Layers:

Feature Sharing: Convolutional layers use shared weights, allowing filters to detect the same features across different spatial locations, reducing the number of parameters and enhancing generalization.

Local Connectivity: By considering only local regions of the input image, convolutional layers capture spatial relationships and patterns relevant to the task.

Translation Invariance: Pooling layers create translation invariant representations, enabling CNNs to recognize patterns regardless of their exact location in the image.

3.2.7 Evolution and Variations: Over the years, various architectural innovations and variations of convolutional and pooling layers have emerged. These include dilated convolutions, separable convolutions, and global average pooling, among others. These adaptations enhance the capabilities of CNNs for specific tasks and computational efficiencies.

Convolutional and pooling layers are the cornerstones of Convolutional Neural Networks. Convolutional layers extract local patterns and features, while pooling layers down sample and create translation invariant representations. Together, these layers enable CNNs to capture spatial hierarchies, learn complex visual patterns, and excel in a wide range of computer vision applications.

3.3 Architectures: LeNet, AlexNet, VGG, ResNet: Convolutional Neural Networks (CNNs) have witnessed remarkable progress due to the development of innovative architectures.

3.3.1 LeNet: Pioneering Convolutional Nets: LeNet, introduced by Yann LeCun in the 1990s, is a pioneering architecture that laid the foundation for CNNs. Designed for handwritten digit recognition, LeNet comprises convolutional and pooling layers, followed by fully connected layers. It introduced concepts like weight sharing and feature hierarchies, demonstrating the power of learned feature extraction.

3.3.2 AlexNet: Sparking the Deep Learning Revolution: AlexNet, presented by Alex Krizhevsky in 2012, marked a breakthrough in the ImageNet Large Scale Visual Recognition Challenge. It consisted of multiple convolutional and pooling layers, followed by fully connected layers. Notably, AlexNet employed Rectified Linear Units (ReLU) as activation functions and used data augmentation and dropout for regularization. Its success catalyzed the deep learning revolution.

3.3.3 VGG: Emphasizing Depth and Simplicity: The VGG architecture, developed by the Visual Geometry Group (VGG) at the University of Oxford, emphasized the role of depth in CNNs. VGG networks consist of small, 3x3 convolutional filters and deep architectures with up to 19 layers. The simplicity of VGG's design and its focus on stacking layers with small receptive fields made it an essential reference architecture for deep CNNs.

3.3.4 ResNet: Resolving Vanishing Gradient: Residual Networks (ResNet), introduced by Kaiming He et al. in 2015, addressed the vanishing gradient problem encountered in very deep networks. ResNet introduced the concept of residual blocks, where shortcut connections allow gradients to flow directly to earlier layers. This enabled the training of extremely deep networks, leading to improved performance.

3.3.5 Architectural Innovations and Impact: These architectures marked critical milestones in CNN development, inspiring further innovations and variations:

Inception Network (GoogLeNet): Introduced the concept of inception modules with multiple filter sizes to capture a range of features.

Xception: An extension of Inception that replaces standard convolutions with depthwise separable convolutions for improved efficiency.

MobileNet: Designed for mobile and embedded devices, MobileNet employs depthwise separable convolutions to achieve lightweight yet accurate models.

EfficientNet: A scalable architecture that balances model size, depth, and width to optimize performance across various resource constraints.

3.3.6 Transfer Learning and Pretrained Models: The impact of these architectures extends to transfer learning, where pretrained models are used as feature extractors for new tasks. Models like VGG, ResNet, and others trained on large datasets serve as valuable starting points for various computer vision tasks, enabling rapid development and finetuning on specific problems.

3.3.7 Future Directions and Beyond: As the field of deep learning continues to evolve, researchers are exploring novel architectures, attention mechanisms, and interpretable networks. Architectures like Transformers, initially designed for natural language processing, are finding applications in computer vision, reshaping the landscape of state of heart models.

In summary, LeNet, AlexNet, VGG, and ResNet are pivotal CNN architectures that have shaped the evolution of computer vision. Their contributions have not only driven progress in image analysis but have also paved the way for new architectural innovations, transfer learning techniques, and interdisciplinary applications. As the field continues to advance, these architectural milestones continue to inspire and guide researchers toward new frontiers in deep learning.

3.4 Transfer Learning and Fine-tuning: Transfer learning and fine-tuning are powerful techniques that leverage pretrained models to boost the performance of Convolutional Neural Networks (CNNs) on new tasks with limited data. In this section, we'll explore the concepts of transfer learning and fine-tuning and how they enable efficient model training and improved generalization.

3.4.1 Transfer Learning: Building on Pretrained Models: Transfer learning involves using a pretrained model as a starting point for a new task. The idea is to leverage the knowledge learned by a model on a source task (typically a large dataset) and apply it to a target task (usually with a smaller dataset). This approach is particularly valuable when the target task lacks sufficient labeled data for training a model from scratch.

3.4.2 Pretrained Models and Feature Extractors: Pretrained models are CNN architectures that have been trained on massive datasets, often for image classification tasks. These models capture rich and generalizable feature representations from the images. When transferring to a new task, the early layers of the pretrained model serve as effective feature extractors that capture basic visual patterns.

3.4.3 FineTuning: Adapting to the Target Task: After using the pretrained layers as feature extractors, finetuning involves training the latter layers of the network on the target task's data. The weights of these layers are initialized with the pretrained model's weights and then updated during training to specialize in the specific characteristics of the target task. Finetuning strikes a balance between utilizing existing knowledge and adapting the model to the nuances of the new data.

3.4.4 Practical Steps for Transfer Learning:

Choose a Pretrained Model: Select a pretrained model that's suitable for your target task and dataset. Common choices include models like VGG, ResNet, and MobileNet.

Remove or Freeze Initial Layers: Remove or freeze the initial layers of the model, preserving their weights as feature extractors.

Add New Layers: Add new layers to the model that are tailored to your target task. These layers are typically responsible for classifying or regressing on your specific data.

FineTuning: Train the model on your target task's data while updating the weights of the newly added layers. Monitor performance on validation data to prevent overfitting.

Hyper parameter Tuning: Adjust hyperparameters like learning rate, batch size, and regularization strength to achieve optimal performance.

3.4.5 Benefits of Transfer Learning and FineTuning:

Efficient Use of Data: Transfer learning allows models to benefit from the extensive data used during pretraining, even when target task data is limited.

Improved Convergence: Pretrained models provide better weight initialization, aiding convergence during finetuning.

Reduced Computational Cost: Finetuning requires fewer epochs compared to training from scratch, saving computational resources.

Generalization: Transfer learning enhances model generalization by leveraging knowledge from diverse datasets.

3.4.6 Considerations and Challenges:

Domain Shift: Pretrained models may be effective when the source and target tasks have similar characteristics, but domain shift can still be a challenge.

Overfitting: Finetuning requires careful monitoring to prevent overfitting, especially when the target dataset is small.

Layer Selection: The choice of layers to finetune depends on the specific task. Earlier layers capture more general features, while later layers capture task specific nuances.

3.4.7 Beyond Images: Transfer Learning in Other Domains: Transfer learning and finetuning are not limited to images. Similar concepts can be applied to other domains like natural language processing, speech recognition, and reinforcement learning, where pretrained models serve as valuable starting points for solving new problems.

3.5 Project

Unsolved Project

Suppose you're developing an image classification application using Convolutional Neural Networks (CNNs). To build a robust model, you need to understand the fundamentals of CNNs, including convolutional and pooling layers, and the architectures of well-known models like LeNet, AlexNet, VGG, and ResNet. Additionally, you'll explore transfer learning and fine-tuning techniques to improve your model's performance. Before starting the development, study the following: the basics of convolutional neural networks, the role of convolutional and pooling layers, the characteristics of different CNN architectures, and how transfer learning and fine-tuning can be applied to your project. This will equip you with the necessary knowledge to create an effective image classification system.

3.6 Lab Activity

Unsolved Lab Activity

Apply transfer learning to fine-tune a pre-trained CNN (e.g., ResNet50) for a specific image classification task (e.g., flower classification).

Exercises

Exercise 1 – Multiple Choice Questions

1. What is the primary motivation for using Convolutional Neural Networks (CNNs) in computer vision tasks?
   A. High dimensionality B. Spatial invariance
   C. Shared weights and local connectivity D. Decision making
2. Which layer in a CNN is responsible for capturing local patterns and features from images?
   A. Convolutional layer C. Fully connected layer
   B. Pooling layer D. Transfer layer
3. What is the purpose of max pooling in a CNN?
   A. Increasing the spatial dimensions of feature maps C. Down sampling feature maps
   B. Reducing computational efficiency D. Capturing global patterns
4. What do fully connected layers in a CNN primarily perform?
   A. Image classification C. Local connectivity
   B. Capturing spatial hierarchies D. Feature extraction
5. How can transfer learning be described in the context of CNNs?
   A. Training a model from scratch C. Applying only fully connected layers to a new task
   B. Using pretrained models as feature extractors D. Training all layers on a new task
6. Which application is NOT mentioned as a use case for CNNs in the provided text?
   A. Image Classification C. Speech Recognition
   B. Object Detection D. Face Recognition
7. What problem did Residual Networks (ResNet) address in deep networks?
   A. Overfitting C. Dimensionality reduction
   B. Vanishing gradient D. Weight initialization
8. Which architectural innovation introduced the concept of inception modules with multiple filter sizes?
   A. LeNet C. VGG
   B. AlexNet D. Inception Network (GoogLeNet)
9. What is the main benefit of using depth wise separable convolutions in models like MobileNet?
   A. Improved efficiency C. Better weight initialization
   B. Increased model complexity D. Enhanced spatial invariance
10. Which of the following is NOT a practical step for transfer learning in CNNs?
    A. Choosing a pretrained model C. Using a completely new model for each task
    B. Removing or freezing initial layers D. Adding new layers tailored to the target task
11. What is the primary advantage of using pretrained models in transfer learning?
    A. Reducing computational cost C. Starting from random weights
    B. Increasing overfitting D. Leveraging knowledge from large datasets
12. What challenge might arise in transfer learning when the source and target tasks have different characteristics?
    A. Efficient weight initialization C. Improved generalization
    B. Domain shift D. Reduced convergence
13. What should be monitored closely during fine-tuning in transfer learning, especially with a small target dataset?

A. Overfitting
B. Computational cost
C. Layer selection
D. Hyperparameter tuning

14. In which domains can transfer learning and finetuning concepts be applied, according to the provided text?
A. Only computer vision
B. Only natural language processing
C. Various domains, including natural language processing and speech recognition
D. None of the above

15. What is the primary purpose of pretrained models in domains beyond computer vision, such as natural language processing?
A. Capturing global patterns
B. Enhancing model generalization
C. Improving weight initialization
D. Solving new problems from scratch

Exercise 2 – True/False

1. Transfer learning involves using a pre-trained model on a new task without any modifications.
2. The pooling layer in CNNs is responsible for reducing the spatial dimensions of the input volume.
3. ResNet introduced the concept of residual learning to address the vanishing gradient problem in deep networks.

Exercise 3 – Fill in the blanks

1. The architecture known for its very deep network and the use of residual connections is called ______________.
2. In Convolutional Neural Networks, the layer responsible for reducing the spatial dimensions of the input through subsampling is called the ______________ layer.
3. ______________ is a technique where a pre-trained model is adapted to a new task by fine-tuning its weights on the new dataset.

Exercise 4 - Fill in the blanks with two options

1. A __________ layer in a Convolutional Neural Network (CNN) is used to reduce the spatial dimensions of the input, commonly used in __________.
2. The __________ architecture introduced the concept of very deep networks by using 16-19 layers and is a significant development in __________.
3. __________ is a technique where a pre-trained model is adapted to a new task by fine-tuning its weights, which is often applied in __________.

Review Questions

1. What is the primary motivation behind the development of Convolutional Neural Networks (CNNs) in the context of computer vision?
2. How do CNNs address the challenges posed by high-dimensional and spatially structured image data?
3. Describe the core building block of a CNN and its role in feature extraction.
4. What are filters (kernels) in convolutional layers, and how do they contribute to feature detection?
5. Explain the purpose of pooling layers in CNNs and the most common pooling operation.
6. What is spatial invariance, and how do pooling layers achieve it in CNNs?
7. How are feature maps generated in convolutional layers, and what do they represent?
8. What is the significance of padding and stride in convolutional layers?
9. How do CNNs learn hierarchical representations of visual information?
10. Discuss the benefits of convolutional layers, including feature sharing and local connectivity.
11. Describe the architectural innovations introduced in CNNs, such as dilated convolutions and separable convolutions.
12. Explain the concept of transfer learning in the context of CNNs and why it is valuable.
13. How do pretrained models serve as feature extractors in transfer learning, and which layers are typically used for this purpose?
14. What is fine-tuning in transfer learning, and which layers are updated during this process?
15. Outline the practical steps for applying transfer learning to a new computer vision task.
16. List the benefits of transfer learning and fine-tuning, including efficiency and generalization.
17. What challenges or considerations should be kept in mind when applying transfer learning, especially concerning domain shift and overfitting?

Answers

Exercise 1- 1. C 2. A 3. C 4. A 5. B 6. C 7. B 8. D 9. A 10. C 11. D 12. B 13. A 14. C 15. B
Exercise 2- 1) False, 2) True, 3) True
Exercise 3- 1) ResNet, 2) Pooling, 3) Transfer Learning
Exercise 4- 1) pooling, down-sampling, 2) VGG, CNNs, 3) Transfer learning, CNNs

Online Resources

Online Exam Paper:
Link: https://forms.gle/Yi6PXhCHGSVgR8kb7
QR Code:

Chapter 3 Videos Playlist:
Link: https://www.youtube.com/playlist?list=PLzlh_31VWEFrMbJxGWnmTNQZQboJfVxNe
QR Code:

Chapter 4: Recurrent Neural Networks (RNNs) and Sequence Models

4.1 Introduction to Recurrent Neural Networks (RNNs) and Their Applications: Recurrence is a fundamental aspect of many real-world phenomena, from language to time series data. Recurrent Neural Networks (RNNs) are a class of neural networks designed to model and understand sequential data.

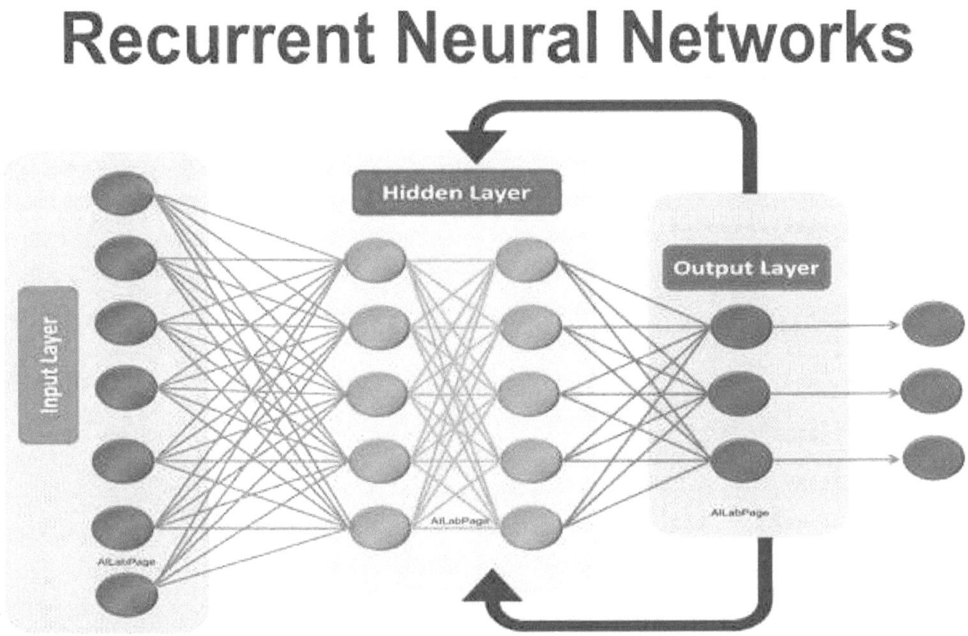

4.1.1 Sequential Data: The Need for Recurrence: In many real-world scenarios, data comes in sequences where the order of elements matters significantly. For instance, sentences in natural language, audio signals in speech, and time-stamped data points in time series analysis are all examples of sequential data. Traditional neural networks, with their fixed structure and lack of memory, struggle to capture the temporal dependencies present in such data.

4.1.2 Architecture of RNNs: Recurrence is the key concept behind Recurrent Neural Networks (RNNs). RNNs are designed to process sequential data by maintaining a hidden state that captures information from previous time steps. This hidden state effectively serves as a form of memory that can store and update relevant context from earlier elements in the sequence. The shared weights across time steps allow RNNs to learn and model sequences of varying lengths.

4.1.3 Hidden State and Temporal Dependencies: The hidden state in an RNN at any given time step encodes the network's understanding of the sequence up to that point. It acts as a memory that combines information from the current input and the hidden state of the previous time step. This mechanism enables RNNs to capture the temporal dependencies and context present in the sequence, making them adept at tasks that involve predicting or generating sequential data.

4.1.4 Vanishing Gradient Problem: While RNNs are powerful for capturing short-term dependencies, they face challenges in capturing long-term dependencies due to the vanishing gradient problem. During training, gradients can become extremely small as they backpropagate through multiple time steps, leading to difficulties in learning and modeling distant dependencies. This issue can hinder the network's ability to maintain information over longer sequences.

4.1.5 Types of RNNs:

Vanilla RNN: The basic RNN architecture suffers from the vanishing gradient problem, limiting its effectiveness in modeling long-range dependencies.

Long Short-Term Memory (LSTM): LSTMs were designed to alleviate the vanishing gradient problem. They incorporate memory cells and various gates (input, output, and forget) that control the flow of information, enabling them to capture both short-term and long-term dependencies.

Gated Recurrent Unit (GRU): GRUs are similar to LSTMs but with fewer parameters. They also tackle the vanishing gradient problem and have been shown to perform comparably on various tasks.

4.1.6 Applications of RNNs: RNNs have found applications across a diverse range of domains:

Natural Language Processing (NLP): RNNs are central to language modeling, machine translation, sentiment analysis, and text generation, where understanding the sequential nature of language is essential.

Speech Recognition: RNNs excel at converting spoken language into written text, enabling accurate and efficient speech recognition systems.

Time Series Analysis: RNNs can predict future values in time series data, making them indispensable for tasks like financial forecasting, weather prediction, and more.

Video Analysis: RNNs process video frames sequentially, making them suitable for action recognition, video captioning, and video generation.

Music Generation: RNNs can learn musical patterns from existing compositions and generate new sequences, contributing to automated music composition.

4.1.7 Challenges and Future Directions: Despite their versatility, RNNs face challenges such as difficulty in modeling very long sequences and the inherent sequential nature that limits parallelization. Researchers are actively investigating hybrid architectures that combine RNNs with other neural network components, as well as exploring attention mechanisms and alternative models to overcome these limitations.

Recurrent Neural Networks are designed to handle sequential data through recurrence and hidden states. Their capacity to capture temporal dependencies makes them a vital tool across various applications. As you delve further into this book, you'll dive deeper into the details of RNN architectures, their training, and their role in understanding and modeling sequential data effectively.

4.2 Long Short-Term Memory (LSTM) Networks: In the realm of Recurrent Neural Networks (RNNs), Long Short-Term Memory (LSTM) networks stand out as a powerful solution to the vanishing gradient problem and the challenge of capturing long-term dependencies.

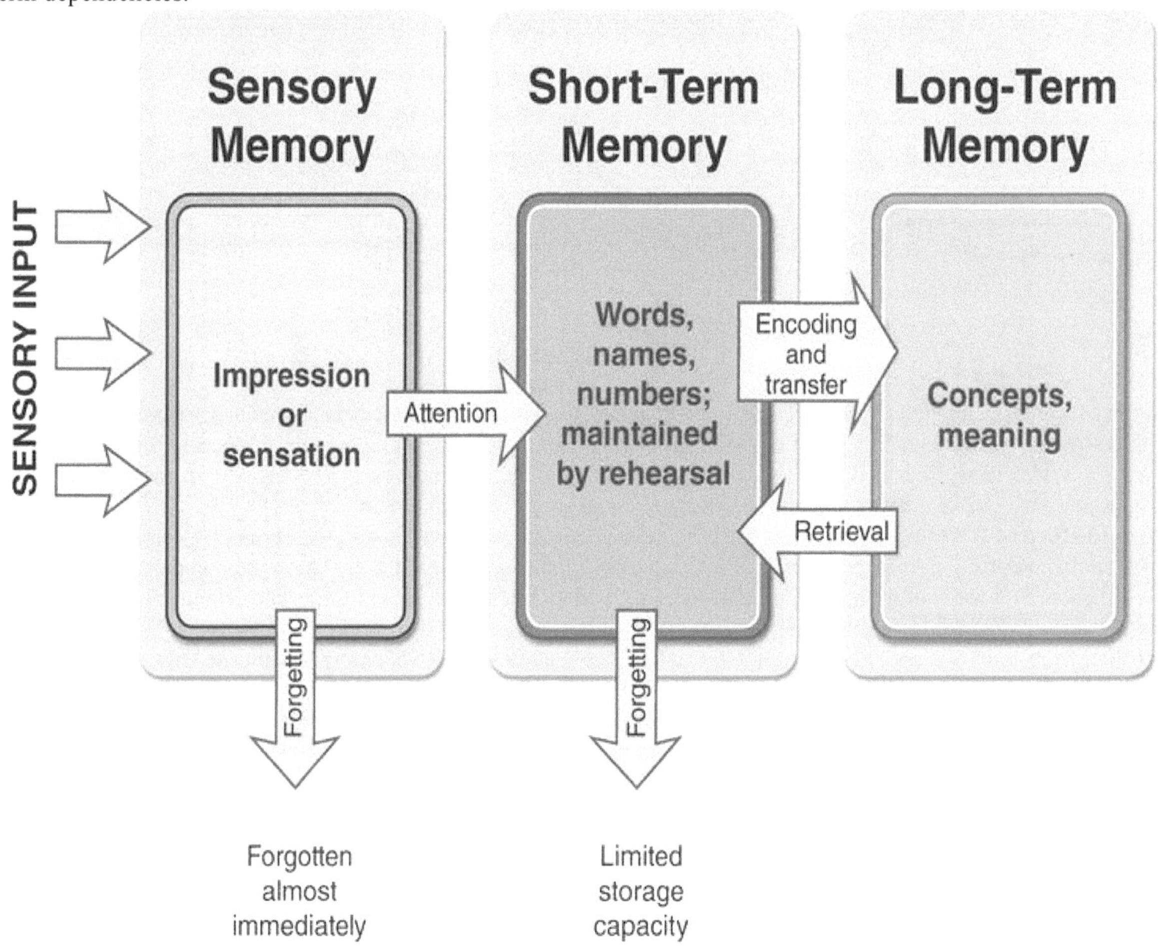

4.2.1 The Need for LSTM Networks: Standard RNNs struggle with learning and maintaining information over long sequences due to the vanishing gradient problem. LSTM networks were designed to overcome this issue by incorporating memory cells and gating mechanisms that allow them to capture both short-term and long-term dependencies.

4.2.2 Architecture of LSTM Networks: At the heart of an LSTM network are memory cells, input, output, and forget gates:

Memory Cells: Memory cells store information over time. They can be read from, written to, and modified by various gates.

Input Gate: The input gate determines which information from the current input should be stored in the memory cells.

Output Gate: The output gate controls what information from the memory cells should be outputted as the hidden state of the LSTM.

Forget Gate: The forget gate decides which information in the memory cells should be discarded or forgotten.

4.2.3 Gating Mechanisms: Managing Information Flow: Gating mechanisms are central to LSTM networks and allow them to regulate the flow of information. These mechanisms enable LSTM networks to selectively store, update, and retrieve information at different time steps, enhancing their ability to model long-range dependencies.

4.2.4 Learning in LSTM Networks: LSTM networks learn the parameters of their gates through backpropagation and gradient descent during training. The gates are updated based on the error signal from the output of the network, allowing the network to adapt and learn to capture complex temporal relationships.

4.2.5 Applications of LSTM Networks: LSTM networks have become indispensable in various domains:

Sequence Modeling: LSTMs excel in sequence-to-sequence tasks such as language translation, where they can handle both short and long sentences effectively.

Time Series Prediction: LSTMs predict future values in time series data, making them ideal for tasks like stock price forecasting and weather prediction.

Speech Recognition: LSTMs process spoken language, enabling highly accurate speech recognition systems.

Natural Language Processing (NLP): LSTMs are crucial for tasks like sentiment analysis, text generation, and named entity recognition.

Video Analysis: LSTMs process video frames, enabling action recognition, video captioning, and more.

4.2.6 Advantages and Challenges:

Advantages: LSTMs can capture long-range dependencies, making them highly effective for tasks requiring memory and context. They excel in scenarios where standard RNNs fail.

Challenges: Despite their strengths, LSTMs can be computationally expensive and require careful hyperparameter tuning. Architectural variations and optimization techniques have emerged to address these challenges.

4.2.7 Future Directions and Innovations: As Long Short-Term Memory (LSTM) networks continue to shape the landscape of Recurrent Neural Networks, researchers are actively exploring future directions and innovative enhancements. These developments aim to further refine the capabilities and applications of LSTMs:

Attention Mechanisms: Integrating attention mechanisms with LSTMs allows the network to focus on specific parts of the input sequence, enhancing their ability to capture important information and context.

Peephole Connections: Extending LSTMs with peephole connections enables the network to have direct access to the memory cell states when updating gates, potentially improving their ability to capture temporal relationships.

Skip Connections: Borrowing from the success of skip connections in other neural architectures, incorporating skip connections in LSTMs could enhance the flow of gradients and information, leading to better convergence and performance.

Hybrid Architectures: Combining LSTMs with other neural network components, such as convolutional layers or attention modules, can create hybrid architectures that leverage the strengths of different network types for improved performance.

Efficiency Improvements: Exploring techniques for reducing the computational complexity of LSTMs can lead to more efficient implementations, enabling them to handle larger datasets and models.

Unsupervised Learning: Investigating unsupervised learning techniques with LSTMs can uncover hidden patterns and structures within data, leading to novel insights and applications.

These future directions and innovations highlight the ongoing commitment of the research community to refine and extend the capabilities of LSTM networks. By addressing challenges and pushing the boundaries of what LSTMs can achieve, these advancements continue to unlock new possibilities for modeling and understanding sequential data.

4.3 Gated Recurrent Unit (GRU) Networks: Gated Recurrent Unit (GRU) networks represent a significant evolution in Recurrent Neural Network (RNN) architectures. With simplified gating mechanisms and improved training efficiency, GRUs offer an effective solution for modeling sequential data. In this section, we'll delve into the architecture of GRU networks, their advantages, and their applications.

4.3.1 Introduction to GRU Networks: GRUs were introduced as a response to some of the challenges posed by Long Short-Term Memory (LSTM) networks. They aim to strike a balance between capturing long-range dependencies and computational efficiency.

4.3.2 Architecture of GRU Networks: GRUs consist of the following key components:

Update Gate: The update gate determines how much information from the previous time step should be retained and combined with the current input.

Reset Gate: The reset gate decides which information from the previous time step should be forgotten, allowing the network to focus on relevant context.

Current Memory Content: This component combines the output of the reset gate and the candidate memory content to create the updated memory content for the current time step.

Hidden State: The hidden state is calculated using the updated memory content and provides the output of the GRU for that time step.

4.3.3 Simplified Gating Mechanism: GRUs simplify the gating mechanism compared to LSTMs, using only two gates instead of three. This simplicity can lead to easier training and faster convergence, making GRUs an attractive choice for various tasks.

4.3.4 Advantages of GRU Networks:

Efficiency: With fewer parameters and simplified gating, GRUs are computationally more efficient than LSTMs, making them well-suited for scenarios with limited resources.

Ease of Training: The simplified architecture can lead to smoother optimization during training, reducing the likelihood of vanishing gradient issues.

Memory Control: GRUs have shown the ability to capture long-range dependencies while effectively controlling the retention of past information.

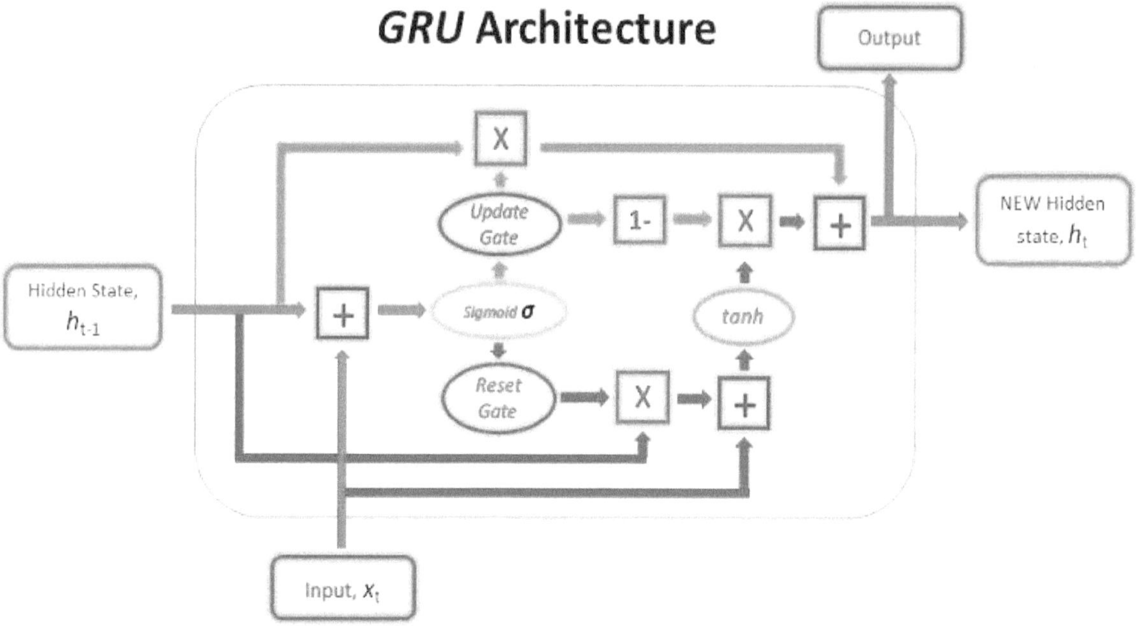

4.3.5 Applications of GRU Networks: Gated Recurrent Unit (GRU) networks have demonstrated their versatility and effectiveness across various domains, contributing to transformative advancements in different fields. Here are the key areas where GRUs have found applications:

Natural Language Processing (NLP):

GRUs play a pivotal role in revolutionizing Natural Language Processing (NLP) tasks:

Language Modeling: GRUs excel at modeling the sequential nature of language. They are used in tasks like autocomplete, where predicting the next word in a sentence enhances user experience.

Sentiment Analysis: Capturing the emotional tone of text is essential in sentiment analysis. GRUs process sequences of words to determine sentiments like positive, negative, or neutral.

Machine Translation: GRUs power sequence-to-sequence models, enabling accurate machine translation between languages. They capture the contextual relationships between words, making translations more coherent.

Time Series Analysis:

GRUs prove valuable in understanding and predicting time-dependent data:

Financial Forecasting: GRUs analyze historical financial data to predict future stock prices and market trends, aiding in investment decisions.

Anomaly Detection: Detecting anomalies in time series data, such as identifying irregular patterns in machinery operation, benefits from GRUs' ability to learn normal behaviors.

Speech Recognition:

GRUs contribute to accurate and efficient speech recognition systems:

Audio-to-Text Conversion: GRUs process audio signals to convert spoken words into text, facilitating applications like transcription services and voice assistants.

Speaker Identification: GRUs assist in identifying speakers by processing speech patterns and extracting unique characteristics from audio inputs.

Video Understanding:

GRUs extend their capabilities to the analysis of video data:

Action Recognition: Analyzing sequences of video frames, GRUs identify actions or activities taking place, enabling applications like surveillance and automated video tagging.

Scene Detection: GRUs help identify changes in scenes within a video, allowing for efficient video indexing and retrieval.

Video Captioning: GRUs contribute to generating descriptive captions for video content, enhancing accessibility and engagement.

4.3.6 Evolving Research and Hybrid Architectures: Continued advancements in Gated Recurrent Unit (GRU) networks are fueled by ongoing research into variations, extensions, and hybrid architectures that aim to enhance their capabilities. These endeavors are expanding the horizons of what GRUs can achieve:

Variations and Extensions: Researchers are exploring modifications to the standard GRU architecture to address specific challenges or tailor the network to certain tasks. These variations might involve adjustments to the gating mechanisms, the incorporation of additional components, or the integration of external information.

Adaptive GRUs: Some variants of GRUs introduce adaptive mechanisms that allow the network to dynamically adjust its architecture or parameters based on the input data or the task requirements. This adaptability can enhance the network's performance on diverse datasets.

Hybrid Architectures: The combination of GRUs with other neural network components, such as convolutional layers or attention modules, has shown promising results. Hybrid models leverage the strengths of both architectures to tackle complex tasks that require both local feature extraction and sequence modeling.

Transfer Learning and Pretraining: Applying transfer learning principles to GRUs involves pretrained models from related tasks serving as initialization points for new tasks. This approach can expedite training and improve performance, especially when labeled data is limited.

Interdisciplinary Applications: As the versatility of GRUs becomes more evident, researchers are exploring applications beyond traditional domains. This includes integrating GRUs into fields like healthcare for patient monitoring, sensor data analysis, and disease prediction.

Efficiency Improvements: Research efforts are aimed at making GRUs more efficient in terms of computation and memory usage. Optimizations can enable GRUs to handle larger datasets and models while still maintaining their efficacy.

Interactions with Attention Mechanisms: Integrating attention mechanisms with GRUs allows the network to focus on specific parts of the input sequence, enhancing its ability to capture relevant information and context.

4.3.7 Anticipating Future Developments: The trajectory of GRU networks is marked by continuous innovation and exploration. Researchers are poised to unravel new possibilities as they delve deeper into the nuances of GRU architectures and their interactions with other neural network components.

the evolving research landscape surrounding Gated Recurrent Unit (GRU) networks showcases a commitment to refining and expanding their capabilities. Variations, extensions, and hybrid architectures are paving the way for enhanced performance across diverse tasks and domains. As you delve further into this subject, you'll gain insights into the forefront of GRU research and the exciting potential it holds for the future.

4.4 Natural Language Processing with RNNs: Recurrence is at the heart of understanding and modeling sequences, making Recurrent Neural Networks (RNNs) a natural fit for Natural Language Processing (NLP) tasks. In this section, we'll explore how RNNs have revolutionized NLP, enabling machines to comprehend and generate human language.

4.4.1 Challenges in Natural Language Processing: Language is inherently sequential, and understanding it requires capturing complex contextual relationships. Traditional methods struggled with long-range dependencies and nuanced language patterns. RNNs address these challenges by leveraging their recurrent architecture.

4.4.2 Language Modeling and Sequence Generation: RNNs excel at language modeling, where they predict the next word in a sequence based on previous words. This ability enables applications like text generation, autocomplete, and predictive typing.

4.4.3 Machine Translation: RNNs have transformed machine translation by modeling the relationship between words in different languages. Sequence-to-sequence architectures, combining an encoder RNN and a decoder RNN, have become the foundation for modern translation systems.

4.4.4 Sentiment Analysis: Analyzing sentiment in text involves capturing emotional nuances. RNNs can learn to distinguish positive, negative, and neutral sentiment by considering the sequence of words and their context.

4.4.5 Named Entity Recognition: Identifying entities like names, locations, and dates in text requires context understanding. RNNs process sequences to recognize patterns that indicate different types of entities.

4.4.6 Text Generation: RNNs have made significant strides in generating human-like text. Whether it's chatbots, story generation, or poetry creation, RNNs can generate coherent and contextually relevant sequences of words.

4.4.7 Challenges and Advances:

Long-range Dependencies: Despite their strengths, RNNs can struggle with very long-range dependencies in language. Techniques like attention mechanisms address this limitation.

Contextual Understanding: Understanding context beyond a fixed window is challenging. Transformers, an evolution of RNNs, have improved contextual modeling.

Ambiguity and Creativity: Dealing with language ambiguity and producing creative responses remain open challenges in NLP.

4.4.8 Evolution: Transformers and BERT: The evolution of NLP architectures extends beyond RNNs:

Transformers: This architecture introduced a novel approach to modeling context using self-attention mechanisms. Transformers excel in capturing relationships across sequences, making them a game-changer in NLP.

BERT (Bidirectional Encoder Representations from Transformers): BERT's pretraining on massive amounts of text followed by fine-tuning on specific tasks achieved remarkable results, pushing the boundaries of NLP performance.

4.4.9 Charting Future Paths: As NLP advances, researchers are actively addressing these challenges and charting future directions:

Interpretable Models: Developing models that offer more interpretability is gaining attention, ensuring that NLP predictions are transparent and explainable.

Multimodal Understanding: NLP is merging with other domains like computer vision and audio analysis, pushing the boundaries of multimodal understanding.

Ethical NLP: Ensuring ethical behavior of NLP models, including fairness and unbiased responses, is an emerging research focus.

4.4.10 NLP's Transformative Journey: The integration of Recurrent Neural Networks into Natural Language Processing has been transformative. From understanding sentiment to enabling multilingual communication, RNNs have paved the way for machines to grasp the intricate nature of human language. As you delve further into this chapter, you'll uncover the intricacies of NLP with RNNs and witness their impact across a multitude of linguistic tasks.

The journey through Natural Language Processing with Recurrent Neural Networks is marked by challenges, innovations, and a continual pursuit of understanding human language. In your exploration, you'll uncover how these challenges have spurred advancements and shaped the trajectory of NLP's transformation.

4.5 Project

Unsolved Project

Suppose you're tasked with developing a language translation application using Recurrent Neural Networks (RNNs) and other sequence models. To create an effective model, you need to understand the basics of RNNs and their applications, as well as more advanced models like Long Short-Term Memory (LSTM) networks and Gated Recurrent Unit (GRU) networks. Additionally, you'll explore how these models can be applied to natural language processing (NLP) tasks. Before starting the development, research the following: the introduction to RNNs and their various applications, the structure and functioning of LSTM and GRU networks, and the implementation of RNNs in NLP tasks. This preparation will help you build a powerful language translation system.

4.6 Lab Activity

Unsolved Lab Activity

Implement an LSTM network for a text generation task using a dataset of your choice (e.g., character-level text generation).

Exercises

Exercise 1 – Multiple Choice Questions

1. What is the primary focus of Recurrent Neural Networks (RNNs)?
   A. Image processing
   B. Sequential data modeling
   C. Audio signal analysis
   D. Spatial data analysis
2. In the context of sequential data, why do traditional neural networks struggle?
   A. They lack memory.
   B. They have too many hidden states.
   C. They have too few parameters.
   D. They are computationally inefficient
3. What is the key concept that allows Recurrent Neural Networks (RNNs) to model sequential data effectively?
   A. Parallel processing
   B. Recurrence
   C. Memory cells
   D. Convolution
4. What problem do Recurrent Neural Networks (RNNs) face when capturing long-term dependencies during training?
   A. Overfitting
   B. Vanishing gradient problem
   C. Exploding gradient problem
   D. Lack of memory capacity
5. Which type of RNN is specifically designed to alleviate the vanishing gradient problem?
   A. Vanilla RNN
   B. Long Short-Term Memory (LSTM)
   C. Gated Recurrent Unit (GRU)
   D. Feedforward neural network
6. What is the primary advantage of Long Short-Term Memory (LSTM) networks over Vanilla RNNs?
   A. Simplicity
   B. Efficiency
   C. Memory capacity
   D. Computational speed
7. Which component of LSTM networks is responsible for deciding which information from the previous time step should be retained?
   A. Input gate
   B. Output gate
   C. Forget gate
   D. Memory cells
8. What is one application of Recurrent Neural Networks (RNNs) in the field of video analysis?
   A. Image classification
   B. 3D modeling
   C. Action recognition
   D. Geospatial analysis
9. What is the main advantage of Gated Recurrent Unit (GRU) networks over Long Short-Term Memory (LSTM) networks?
   A. Greater memory capacity
   B. Simpler architecture
   C. Higher computational efficiency
   D. Improved parallelization
10. Which NLP task involves determining the emotional tone of a text?
    A. Language modeling
    B. Sentiment analysis

C. Named entity recognition
D. Machine translation

11. What architecture introduced self-attention mechanisms and revolutionized NLP?
A. RNN
C. Transformer
B. LSTM
D. GRU

12. What does BERT stand for in the context of NLP?
A. Bidirectional Encoder Representations from Text
C. Basic Extraction and Recognition Technique
B. Biased Entity Recognition Technology
D. Bilingual Entity Representation Test

13. Which area of NLP research focuses on making NLP models more transparent and explainable?
A. Ethical NLP
C. Interpretable models
B. Multimodal understanding
D. Sentiment analysis

14. What is one challenge mentioned in the chapter regarding Recurrent Neural Networks (RNNs)?
A. Lack of memory capacity
C. Inability to process sequential data
B. Difficulty in modeling spatial data
D. Struggle with very long-range dependencies

15. How has the integration of Recurrent Neural Networks (RNNs) impacted the field of Natural Language Processing (NLP)?
A. It has made NLP tasks less computationally intensive.
B. It has enabled machines to understand human language better.
C. It has eliminated the need for pretraining models.
D. It has made NLP tasks less dependent on sequential data.

Exercise 2 – True/False

1. Natural Language Processing (NLP) tasks such as language translation and sentiment analysis can be effectively performed using Recurrent Neural Networks (RNNs).
2. Recurrent Neural Networks (RNNs) are not suitable for applications involving sequential data.
3. Long Short-Term Memory (LSTM) Networks include mechanisms like forget gates and input gates to manage long-term dependencies.

Exercise 3 – Fill in the blanks

1. Long Short-Term Memory (LSTM) Networks are designed to overcome the limitations of traditional RNNs by using special units called _________ to maintain information over long sequences.
2. In the context of Recurrent Neural Networks (RNNs), a popular variant that simplifies the architecture and reduces the number of parameters is known as _________.
3. Recurrent Neural Networks (RNNs) are particularly well-suited for tasks involving _________, such as language modeling and machine translation.

Exercise 4 - Fill in the blanks with two options

1. A __________ network is a type of recurrent neural network designed to handle long-term dependencies by using mechanisms to prevent the vanishing gradient problem, commonly known as __________.
2. __________ units are a simplified version of LSTMs that use fewer gates to achieve similar performance, particularly known as __________.
3. In __________, recurrent neural networks are widely used for tasks such as language modeling, translation, and sentiment analysis, a field known as __________.

Review Questions

1. What is the fundamental role of recurrence in Recurrent Neural Networks (RNNs)?
2. Why do traditional neural networks struggle with sequential data, and how do RNNs address this issue?
3. How does the architecture of RNNs enable them to capture temporal dependencies in sequential data?
4. Explain the concept of the hidden state in an RNN and its significance in modeling sequential data.
5. What is the vanishing gradient problem in RNNs, and how does it impact the network's ability to capture long-term dependencies?
6. What are the three main types of RNNs mentioned in the chapter, and what problems do they aim to solve?
7. Describe the key applications of RNNs in Natural Language Processing (NLP).
8. In which domain do RNNs excel at converting spoken language into written text, and why?
9. How can RNNs be used in time series analysis, and what types of tasks can they perform in this domain?
10. What role do RNNs play in video analysis, and what are some specific applications in this field?
11. How can RNNs contribute to music generation, and what are their applications in automated music composition?
12. What are the primary challenges faced by RNNs, and why do they struggle with very long sequences?
13. What is the key difference between LSTM networks and Vanilla RNNs in terms of addressing the vanishing gradient problem?
14. Describe the components of an LSTM network, including memory cells and gates.

15. How do LSTM networks regulate the flow of information through gating mechanisms?
16. List some of the advantages and challenges associated with using LSTM networks.
17. What future directions and innovations are mentioned for improving LSTM networks and their applications?

Answers

Exercise 1- 1. B 2. A 3. B 4. B 5. B 6. C 7. C 8. C 9. B 10. B 11. C 12. A 13. C 14. D 15. B
Exercise 2- 1) True, 2) False, 3) True
Exercise 3- 1) cells, 2) Gated Recurrent Unit (GRU), 3) sequence data
Exercise 4- 1) Long Short-Term Memory (LSTM); LSTM Networks, 2) Gated Recurrent; GRU Networks, 3) Natural Language Processing; Natural Language Processing with RNNs

Online Resources

Online Exam Paper:
Link: https://forms.gle/C5Z6VTJqkZ1hLMZT6
QR Code:

Chapter 4 Videos Playlist:
Link: https://www.youtube.com/playlist?list=PLzlh_31VWEFqaWmuIt0FaKYOnGfwB-mAe
QR Code:

Chapter 5: Generative Models and Unsupervised Learning

5.1 Introduction to Generative Models: Generative models are a class of machine learning algorithms designed to create new data samples that resemble a given training dataset. These models have applications across a wide range of domains, including image synthesis, text generation, and more. In this section, we'll delve into the fundamental concepts of generative models, their significance, and their various types.

5.1.1 Creating New Data: Generative models are unique in that they focus on the creation of new data rather than making predictions or classifications. They aim to learn the underlying patterns and structures present in the training data so that they can generate novel, realistic samples that exhibit similar characteristics.

5.1.2 Applications of Generative Models: Generative models are versatile tools with applications that span various domains and industries. Their ability to create new data has led to groundbreaking advancements in numerous areas:

Image Generation:

Generative Adversarial Networks (GANs) and Variational Autoencoders (VAEs) have revolutionized image generation. GANs can produce photorealistic images that are nearly indistinguishable from real ones, expanding the possibilities of computer-generated imagery in fields like entertainment, design, and virtual reality.

Text Generation:

Recurrent Neural Networks (RNNs) and Transformers have transformed text generation. They can generate coherent and contextually relevant text, enabling applications such as:

Chatbots: Conversational agents that engage users in natural language dialogue.

Language Translation: Generating translations between languages, contributing to global communication.

Content Creation: Automating the generation of articles, reports, and other written content.

Drug Discovery:

Generative models play a pivotal role in drug discovery:

Molecular Design: Generative models assist researchers in designing new drug molecules with specific properties, accelerating the drug discovery process.

Compound Synthesis: These models propose novel molecular structures that exhibit desired interactions with target proteins.

Anomaly Detection:

Generative models are instrumental in anomaly detection:

Fraud Detection: By learning normal patterns from data, generative models can detect unusual transactions or behaviors indicative of fraud.

Healthcare: Anomalies in medical data can be detected, aiding in early disease diagnosis and treatment.

Data Augmentation:

Generative models contribute to data augmentation:

Enhanced Training Data: Generating new data samples improves the diversity and size of training datasets, enhancing the generalization capability of machine learning models.

Limited Data Scenarios: In cases where collecting extensive labeled data is challenging, generative models can provide additional training samples.

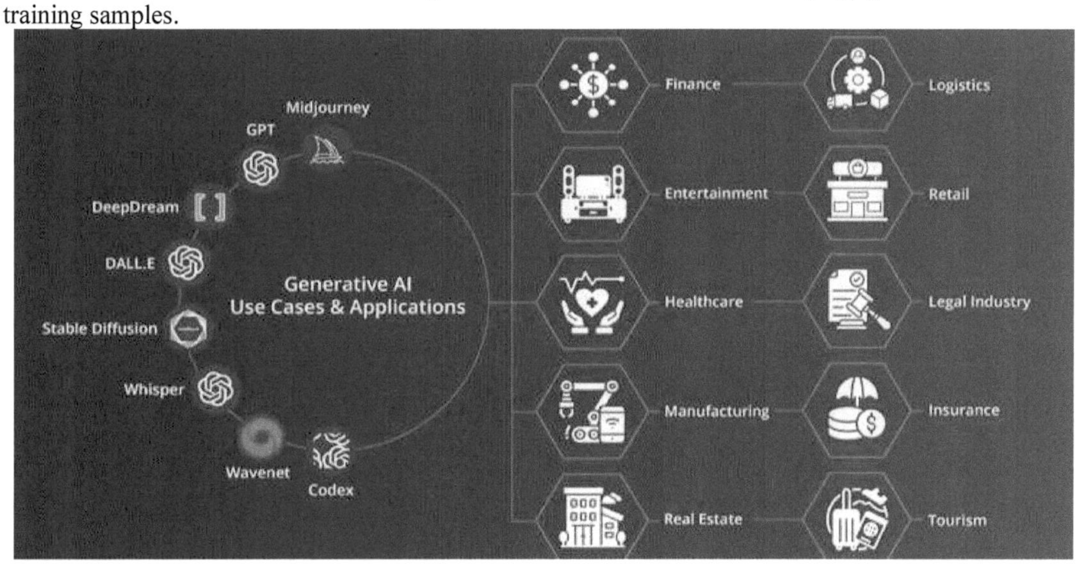

5.1.3 Navigating Diverse Domains: These applications underscore the diverse impact of generative models across domains such as computer vision, natural language processing, pharmaceuticals, and data analytics. As you delve deeper into generative models, you'll gain a comprehensive understanding of their mechanisms, training methods, and the nuances that make them invaluable tools in modern technology.

5.1.4 Future Directions: Generative models are at the forefront of innovation, and their evolution is driven by ongoing research and emerging challenges. As the field continues to expand, several key directions are shaping the future of generative models:

Improving Training Stability:

Challenge: One ongoing challenge in generative modeling is maintaining stable and effective training. Instabilities during training can lead to suboptimal results or even complete failure to converge.

Future Direction: Researchers are actively exploring techniques to enhance training stability. This includes improving optimization algorithms, designing more effective loss functions, and developing regularization strategies that promote balanced learning.

High-Dimensional Data:

Challenge: The current capabilities of generative models are often constrained by the dimensionality of the data they handle. Complex data types like videos, 3D models, and high-resolution images pose challenges due to their high-dimensional nature.

Future Direction: The research community is dedicated to expanding generative models to handle high-dimensional data effectively. Advances in architectures, optimization techniques, and parallel computing are expected to play a crucial role in addressing this challenge.

Ethical Considerations:

Challenge: The rise of generative models has brought attention to ethical concerns, particularly in generating misinformation, deepfakes, and biased content.

Future Direction: Ensuring that generative models produce responsible and unbiased content is of paramount importance. Researchers are working on methods to detect and mitigate harmful content generated by these models, as well as on techniques for enhancing transparency and interpretability.

Cross-Domain Applications:

Challenge: Adapting generative models to work seamlessly across different domains and modalities, such as images and text, remains an active research area.

Future Direction: Developing versatile generative models that can handle multiple types of data and generate coherent outputs across domains is a key focus. This involves exploring novel architectures and training strategies that facilitate cross-domain learning.

Hybrid Models:

Challenge: Combining the strengths of different generative models and architectures to create more powerful and efficient models is a complex challenge.

Future Direction: The future of generative modeling might involve the development of hybrid models that integrate the advantages of various architectures, such as combining GANs with VAEs or leveraging transformers with autoregressive models.

In summary, the landscape of generative models is dynamic and evolving. As you delve further into this topic, you'll gain insights into the cutting-edge research that's shaping the future of generative modeling and the innovative ways these models are being applied across diverse domains.

5.1.5 Future Directions: Generative models continue to evolve:

Improving Training Stability: Developing techniques to stabilize training and prevent mode collapse (when a generative model produces only a few types of samples) is an ongoing challenge.

High-Dimensional Data: Expanding generative models to handle high-dimensional data like video and 3D models remains a research focus.

Ethical Considerations: Ensuring generative models produce responsible and unbiased content is gaining attention in the context of misinformation and deep fakes.

In summary, generative models hold immense potential for creating new data in various domains. As you delve further into this chapter, you'll uncover the intricacies of different generative models, their training procedures, and the creative possibilities they offer.

5.2 Autoencoders and Variational Autoencoders: Autoencoders and Variational Autoencoders (VAEs) are fundamental architectures in the realm of unsupervised learning. These models enable data compression, denoising, and even generative capabilities. In this section, we'll explore the principles, applications, and innovations surrounding autoencoders and VAEs.

5.2.1 Autoencoders: Fundamentals and Architecture: Autoencoders are neural networks designed for unsupervised feature learning and data reconstruction. They consist of two main components:

Encoder: This component compresses the input data into a lower-dimensional representation, often referred to as a "latent space."

Decoder: The decoder reconstructs the original input data from the latent space representation.

Autoencoders learn to capture essential features from the data while discarding noise and irrelevant details. They find applications in data compression, dimensionality reduction, and denoising.

5.2.2 Variational Autoencoders (VAEs): Probability and Generative Capability: Variational Autoencoders (VAEs) build upon the foundation of autoencoders by introducing probabilistic elements. VAEs address the limitation of autoencoders' deterministic latent space by incorporating stochasticity.

Encoding Distribution: VAEs map input data to a distribution in the latent space rather than a fixed point. This distribution is often chosen to be Gaussian.

Reparameterization Trick: To facilitate gradient-based optimization, VAEs use the reparameterization trick, enabling the model to sample from the encoding distribution while remaining differentiable.

Generative Property: VAEs' probabilistic nature allows them to generate new data samples by sampling from the latent space distribution and decoding them.

5.2.3 Applications of Autoencoders and VAEs: Autoencoders and VAEs find applications across various domains:

Image Denoising: Autoencoders remove noise from images by learning a representation that captures essential features.

Anomaly Detection: Autoencoders can identify anomalies by reconstructing data and detecting significant reconstruction errors.

Dimensionality Reduction: Autoencoders compress high-dimensional data while retaining essential information.

Generative Models: VAEs' generative ability enables the creation of new data samples, contributing to image generation, data augmentation, and more.

5.2.4 Enhancements and Future Directions: Sparse Autoencoders: Encouraging sparsity in the latent representations improves interpretability and feature learning.

Variational Regularization: Enhancing VAEs' latent space regularization techniques can lead to more robust generative models.

Conditional Autoencoders: Extending autoencoders to handle conditional data and generate samples based on specific conditions.

Semi-Supervised Learning: Combining labeled and unlabeled data to enhance the learning process.

5.2.5 Your Journey with Autoencoders and VAEs: Autoencoders and Variational Autoencoders represent powerful tools in unsupervised learning, data compression, and generative modeling. As you delve deeper into this chapter, you'll uncover the intricacies of these architectures, their applications, and the ongoing research that continues to shape their capabilities.

5.3 Generative Adversarial Networks (GANs): Generative Adversarial Networks (GANs) have emerged as a revolutionary framework for generating realistic and high-quality data. This groundbreaking concept introduced by Ian Goodfellow in 2014 has transformed the landscape of generative modeling, enabling the creation of diverse content ranging from images to text. In this section, we'll delve deep into the principles, components, training process, applications, and advancements of Generative Adversarial Networks.

5.3.1 GANs at a Glance: At the heart of GANs is a two-player game between two neural networks: the Generator and the Discriminator.

Generator: The generator's task is to create data samples that resemble real data from a given training distribution. It transforms random noise into data-like samples.

Discriminator: The discriminator, also known as the critic in some formulations, evaluates whether a given data sample is real (from the training data) or fake (generated by the generator).

The key idea is that the generator and the discriminator are in a continuous competition, improving each other's performance in an adversarial manner.

5.3.2 GAN Training Process: GANs are trained iteratively through a process that involves alternating updates to the generator and discriminator:

Initialization: The generator starts with random noise as input and generates samples that are passed to the discriminator.

Discriminator Training: The discriminator is trained on both real data samples and generated samples. It learns to distinguish real from fake samples.

Generator Training: The generator takes random noise as input and generates samples. These generated samples are presented to the discriminator, and the generator learns to produce samples that fool the discriminator.

Adversarial Iterations: Steps 2 and 3 are repeated in an adversarial loop. The discriminator gets better at distinguishing real from fake, and the generator gets better at generating more convincing samples.

5.3.3 Loss Functions and Training Dynamics:

Generator Loss: The generator aims to minimize the discriminator's ability to distinguish between real and fake samples. Its loss is based on the discriminator's assessment of the generated samples.

Discriminator Loss: The discriminator's goal is to accurately classify real and fake samples. Its loss is computed based on the accuracy of these classifications.

As the training progresses, the generator becomes proficient at creating samples that resemble real data, while the discriminator becomes more discerning.

5.3.4 Applications of GANs: Generative Adversarial Networks have catalyzed advancements across multiple domains:

Image Generation: GANs produce photorealistic images that are nearly indistinguishable from real ones. This capability has applications in art, entertainment, and design.

Style Transfer: GANs can transform the style of an image, allowing for creative applications like artistic rendering.

Data Augmentation: GANs enhance training datasets by generating new samples, improving the generalization of machine learning models.

Image-to-Image Translation: GANs can convert images from one domain to another, such as turning satellite images into maps or sketches into realistic images.

5.3.5 Advancements and Future Directions:

Conditional GANs: Extending GANs to generate data based on specific conditions, contributing to tasks like text-to-image synthesis.
Progressive GANs: Gradually increasing the complexity of generated samples during training, resulting in higher-quality outputs.
Attention and Feedback Mechanisms: Incorporating attention mechanisms and feedback loops for more fine-grained control over generated content.
Interdisciplinary Applications: GANs are expanding into fields like healthcare for generating medical images, drug discovery, and simulations.
5.3.6 GANs' Impact on the Future: Generative Adversarial Networks have reshaped the landscape of generative modeling by introducing a competitive and adversarial learning paradigm. Their ability to create highly realistic data samples has profound implications across industries, art, and scientific research. As you explore further into this chapter, you'll uncover the intricacies of GAN architectures, their training dynamics, and the innovative applications that continue to emerge from this powerful framework.
5.4 GAN Applications: Image Generation and Beyond: Generative Adversarial Networks (GANs) have made a profound impact on various applications, particularly in the domain of image generation. However, their influence extends far beyond creating lifelike images. In this section, we will deeply explore the applications of GANs, their significance in image synthesis, and their diverse roles in other fields.
5.4.1 GANs in Image Generation: GANs have revolutionized image generation by producing highly realistic and visually appealing images. This application is often referred to as unconditional image synthesis, where GANs create images from random noise. The generator network transforms this noise into images that are remarkably similar to real-world photographs.
5.4.2 Style Transfer: GANs excel in style transfer, a process that involves transforming the style of an image while retaining its content. Style transfer involves using a pretrained network, often a Convolutional Neural Network (CNN), to extract content and style features from two different images. The generator then synthesizes an image that combines the content of one image with the artistic style of another.
5.4.3 Super-Resolution: GANs contribute to enhancing image resolution. Super-resolution GANs take low-resolution images and generate high-resolution counterparts that are rich in detail. This technology has applications in improving the quality of images captured in various scenarios, including medical imaging and surveillance.
5.4.4 Image-to-Image Translation: Image-to-image translation involves converting images from one domain to another while preserving essential content. CycleGANs, a variant of GANs, excel at this task. They can transform photos into artworks, convert maps to satellite images, or turn sketches into photorealistic images.
5.4.5 Text-to-Image Synthesis: Conditional GANs bridge the gap between text and images. Given textual descriptions, these models can generate corresponding images, opening doors to applications like generating images from written prompts and aiding in creating visual content for stories.
5.4.6 GANs beyond Image Generation: While GANs have gained prominence in image synthesis, their influence extends to diverse domains:
Data Augmentation: GANs contribute to data augmentation by generating additional training samples, enhancing model generalization and performance.
Anomaly Detection: GANs learn the distribution of normal data and can identify anomalies by detecting deviations from this distribution.
Image Inpainting: GANs can fill in missing parts of images, a technique known as inpainting. This has applications in restoring damaged images or removing unwanted objects.
Medical Imaging: GANs generate medical images for training and research purposes, aiding in diagnostics, surgical planning, and treatment evaluation.
5.4.7 Ethical Considerations: The impressive capabilities of GANs also raise ethical concerns, particularly in relation to deepfakes—synthetic media that can convincingly mimic real content. Ensuring responsible use of GAN technology and addressing its implications on privacy, misinformation, and trust are crucial considerations.
5.4.8 Future Directions:
The future of GAN applications is exciting:
Interactive Content Generation: Creating tools that allow users to interactively influence the generated content, enabling customization and creative exploration.
Cross-Domain Innovation: Applying GANs to more diverse data types like audio and video, expanding their applications to new domains.
Synthetic Data Generation: GANs can generate synthetic data that helps train machine learning models when real data is scarce or sensitive.
In summary, the applications of GANs are transformative, spanning from producing photorealistic images to enhancing data quality and enabling cross-domain transformations. As you delve further into this chapter, you'll discover the intricate details of how GANs have shaped the creative and practical aspects of multiple fields and continue to drive innovation in technology and art.

5.5 Project

Unsolved Project

Suppose you're embarking on a project to create realistic synthetic images using generative models and unsupervised learning techniques. To successfully develop this project, you need to understand the basics of generative models, including autoencoders, variational autoencoders, and generative adversarial networks (GANs). Additionally, you'll explore various applications of GANs, such as image generation and other creative tasks. Before starting, study the following: the fundamentals of generative models, the principles and functioning of autoencoders and variational autoencoders, the architecture and training process of GANs, and the different applications of GANs in image generation and beyond. This foundational knowledge will enable you to design and implement a high-quality synthetic image generation system.

5.6 Lab Activity

Unsolved Lab Activity

Implement a variational autoencoder for generating new samples from a dataset (e.g., generating new handwritten digits from the MNIST dataset).

Exercises

Exercise 1 – Multiple Choice Questions

1. What is the primary focus of generative models?
   a. Making predictions
   b. Data classification
   c. Creating new data
   d. Feature extraction
2. Which of the following is NOT an application of generative models?
   a. Image synthesis
   b. Text generation
   c. Data classification
   d. Drug discovery
3. What is the main objective of Generative Adversarial Networks (GANs)?
   a. Making accurate predictions
   b. Creating realistic data samples
   c. Classifying data
   d. Reducing data dimensionality
4. Which type of generative model directly learns the mapping from data space to a latent space?
   a. Variational Autoencoders (VAEs)
   b. Autoregressive Models
   c. Generative Adversarial Networks (GANs)
   d. Flow-Based Models
5. What is mode collapse in generative modeling?
   a. Generating a wide variety of data samples
   b. Producing only a few types of data samples
   c. Generating random data
   d. None of the above
6. Which metric is commonly used to evaluate the quality of generated samples?
   a. Accuracy
   b. F1-score
   c. Inception Score
   d. Mean Absolute Error
7. What is the reparameterization trick used for in Variational Autoencoders (VAEs)?
   a. To make training more challenging
   b. To increase the size of the latent space
   c. To make sampling from the encoding distribution differentiable
   d. To add more layers to the neural network
8. In GANs, what is the role of the discriminator?
   a. Generate data samples
   b. Evaluate whether a data sample is real or fake
   c. Enhance the quality of generated data
   d. Transform random noise into data samples
9. How are Generative Adversarial Networks (GANs) trained iteratively?
   a. Only the generator is updated
   b. Only the discriminator is updated
   c. Both the generator and discriminator are updated in an adversarial loop
   d. Training is done in a single pass
10. What is the primary goal of the generator in GANs during training?
   a. To create random data samples
   b. To minimize the discriminator's ability to distinguish between real and fake samples
   c. To maximize the discriminator's accuracy
   d. To increase the complexity of generated samples
11. What is the primary application of Style Transfer using GANs?
   a. Image denoising
   b. Image resolution enhancement
   c. Transforming the style of an image while retaining content

d. Anomaly detection

12. What role do Conditional GANs play in text-to-image synthesis?
   a. They generate random images from noise.
   b. They bridge the gap between text and images, generating images based on textual descriptions.
   c. They classify text data.
   d. They convert images into text.

13. In which domain do GANs find applications related to medical imaging?
   a. Image resolution enhancement
   b. Data augmentation
   c. Image inpainting
   d. Image generation for diagnostics and surgical planning

Exercise 2 – True/False

1. Variational Autoencoders (VAEs) are a type of generative model that can be used for unsupervised learning.
2. Generative Adversarial Networks (GANs) are primarily used for supervised learning tasks.
3. Autoencoders and Variational Autoencoders are both used for dimensionality reduction and feature learning.

Review Questions

1. What is the primary focus of generative models in machine learning?
2. How do generative models differ from models used for predictions and classifications?
3. Name some of the diverse applications of generative models.
4. How do Generative Adversarial Networks (GANs) contribute to image generation?
5. Which types of generative models are commonly used for text generation?

Answers

Exercise 1- 1. c 2. c 3. b 4. d 5. b 6. c 7. c 8. b 9. c 10. b 11. c 12. b 13. d
Exercise 2- 1) True, 2) False, 3) True

Online Resources

Online Exam Paper:
Link: https://forms.gle/LYgbrdNs5tat2UuWA
QR Code:

Chapter 5 Videos Playlist:
Link: https://www.youtube.com/playlist?list=PLzlh_31VWEFpu7ARqlhxr1j4igFbu-wv1
QR Code:

Chapter 6: Reinforcement Learning and Deep Learning

6.1 Basics of Reinforcement Learning: Reinforcement Learning (RL) is a dynamic field of machine learning that deals with how agents learn to make sequential decisions in an environment to maximize a reward signal. This learning paradigm draws inspiration from how humans and animals learn from trial and error to achieve desired goals. In this section, we will delve deeply into the foundational concepts of reinforcement learning, including agents, environments, actions, rewards, and exploration-exploitation trade-offs.

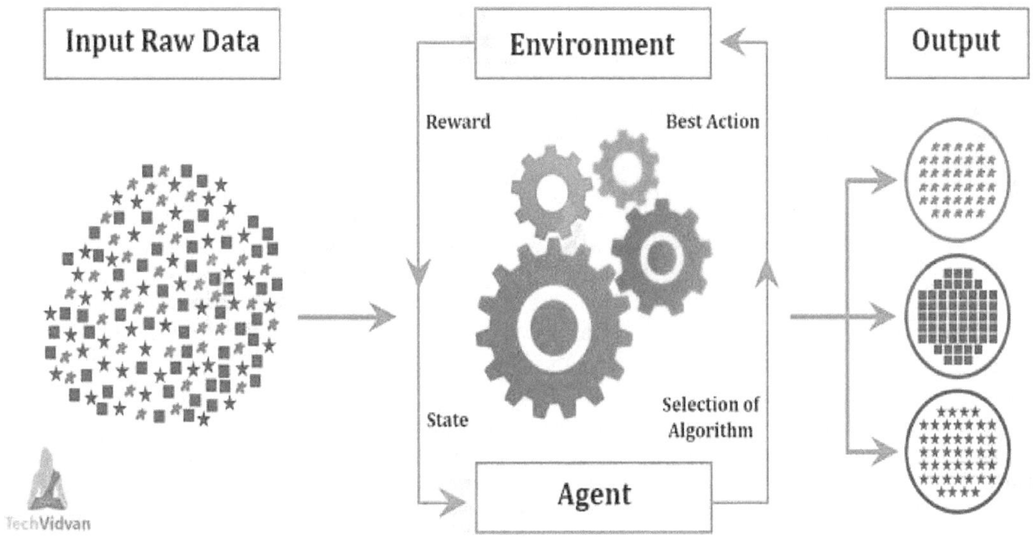

6.1.1 Key Components of Reinforcement Learning: At the core of reinforcement learning are three fundamental components:
Agent: The agent is the learner or decision-maker that interacts with the environment. It takes actions based on its observations and aims to learn a strategy that leads to the maximum cumulative reward over time.
Environment: The environment encompasses the external system with which the agent interacts. It responds to the agent's actions and provides feedback in the form of rewards and new observations.
Policy: The policy represents the strategy that the agent uses to decide on actions given its current state. It defines the mapping from states to actions and encapsulates the agent's decision-making process.
6.1.2 Reinforcement Learning Process: The RL process unfolds through a sequence of steps:
Observation: The agent observes the current state of the environment. The state contains all the relevant information needed to make decisions.
Action: Based on the observed state, the agent selects an action from its available set of actions according to its policy.
Environment Response: The environment reacts to the agent's action by transitioning to a new state and providing a numerical reward that indicates how good or bad the action was in the given state.
Learning: The agent updates its policy based on the observed state, taken action, received reward, and resulting state. This learning process aims to improve the agent's future decision-making.
6.1.3 Reward Signal and Goal: The ultimate objective of reinforcement learning is to learn a policy that maximizes the cumulative reward over time. The reward signal is a numerical value that quantifies the goodness or utility of an agent's action in a particular state. The agent's goal is to find the policy that leads to the highest expected cumulative reward, often referred to as the "return."
6.1.4 Exploration and Exploitation: In the pursuit of maximizing cumulative rewards, the agent faces a crucial trade-off between exploration and exploitation:
Exploration: The agent needs to explore different actions and states to discover the best strategies. Exploration helps the agent gain information about the environment and update its policy effectively.
Exploitation: The agent's learned policy should be exploited to take actions that are expected to yield high rewards based on its current knowledge.
Balancing exploration and exploitation is a central challenge in RL, as too much exploration may delay optimal decisions, while too much exploitation can lead to suboptimal solutions.
6.1.5 Reinforcement Learning Taxonomy: Reinforcement learning approaches can be categorized into model-free and model-based methods:
Model-Free Methods: These methods directly learn the optimal policy from experience without explicitly modeling the environment's dynamics.
Model-Based Methods: These methods involve learning a model of the environment's dynamics, which can be used to simulate different scenarios and plan actions.

6.1.6 Applications and Real-World Impact: Reinforcement learning has gained prominence in a variety of applications:
Game Playing: RL agents have mastered complex games like Go, chess, and video games, demonstrating their capability to learn strategic decision-making.
Robotics: RL guides robots in tasks such as autonomous navigation, manipulation, and even learning from human demonstrations.
Autonomous Vehicles: RL contributes to training self-driving cars to make safe and efficient decisions on the road.
Healthcare: RL is used in personalized treatment recommendations and optimizing treatment plans for chronic diseases.
6.1.7 Challenges and Future Directions: Reinforcement learning presents challenges like exploration strategies, dealing with high-dimensional state spaces, and sample efficiency. Future directions include improving algorithms for handling continuous actions and incorporating safety considerations in decision-making.
6.1.8 Unveiling the Power of Reinforcement Learning: Reinforcement learning's ability to enable agents to learn from interactions and make intelligent decisions has transformed various industries. As you explore further into this chapter, you'll uncover the intricacies of RL algorithms, advanced techniques, and the innovations that continue to shape its impact on real-world scenarios.
6.2 Deep Q-Networks (DQN) and Q-Learning: Reinforcement learning (RL) has taken a significant leap forward with the emergence of Deep Q-Networks (DQN), a groundbreaking framework that combines reinforcement learning with deep neural networks. At the core of DQN lies Q-learning, a foundational algorithm that has been enhanced and extended to handle complex, high-dimensional environments. In this section, we will embark on a comprehensive journey through the world of DQN and Q-learning, uncovering their mechanisms, challenges, and transformative impact on the field of artificial intelligence.
6.2.1 Foundations of Q-Learning: Q-learning is a model-free reinforcement learning algorithm designed to find an optimal policy for an agent to maximize cumulative rewards. Central to Q-learning is the Q-function, denoted as Q(s, a), which represents the expected cumulative reward an agent can achieve by taking action "a" in state "s" and then following the optimal policy thereafter. The Q-values are updated iteratively through the Bellman equation:
Q(s, a) = R(s, a) +? max [Q(s', a')]
Here, R(s, a) is the immediate reward for taking action "a" in state "s," ? is the discount factor that balances short-term and long-term rewards, and max[Q(s', a')] represents the maximum Q-value achievable in the next state "s'" by selecting the optimal action "a'."
6.2.2 Enter Deep Q-Networks (DQN): Traditional Q-learning faces limitations in handling high-dimensional state spaces, often found in complex real-world environments. DQN addresses this challenge by leveraging deep neural networks to approximate the Q-values. Instead of explicitly tabulating Q-values, a deep neural network, known as the Q-network, takes the state as input and outputs Q-values for each possible action.
6.2.3 Experience Replay: DQN introduces a novel concept called "experience replay," which enhances learning efficiency and stability. During experience replay, the agent stores experiences—tuples of (state, action, reward, next state)—in a replay memory. Instead of updating the Q-network using only the most recent experience, DQN randomly samples experiences from the replay memory. This mitigates issues like data correlation and helps the agent learn from diverse experiences.
6.2.4 Target Networks: To prevent instability during training, DQN employs two Q-networks: the online network and the target network. The online network is updated frequently during training, while the target network is updated less frequently and serves as a stable target for Q-value approximation. This approach reduces the risk of oscillations and divergence during learning.
6.2.5 Exploration Strategies: Exploration remains a fundamental challenge in reinforcement learning. DQN tackles this challenge using e-greedy exploration, where the agent selects the action with the highest Q-value with probability (1 e) and a random action with probability e. This strategy balances exploration and exploitation, ensuring that the agent both learns from its past experiences and explores new actions.
6.2.6 Challenges and Advances: Despite its revolutionary impact, DQN and Q-learning face challenges:
Overestimation of Q-values: Traditional Q-learning can overestimate Q-values, leading to suboptimal policies. Techniques like Double Q-learning and Dueling Networks mitigate this issue.
Sparse Rewards: Learning in environments with sparse rewards can be challenging. Prioritized Experience Replay and reward shaping help address this challenge.
6.2.7 DQN Applications and Impact: The power of DQN and Q-learning is evident across various domains:
Game Playing: DQN has conquered classic video games and complex board games like Go, demonstrating its adaptability and capability to learn optimal strategies.
Robotics: DQN guides robots in decision-making, enabling autonomous navigation, object manipulation, and task completion.
Finance: DQN models have been applied to algorithmic trading, optimizing trading strategies based on market data.
6.2.8 Future Directions: The journey of DQN and Q-learning continues:
Deep Reinforcement Learning Algorithms: Advancements like Double DQN, Rainbow DQN, and A3C (Asynchronous Advantage Actor-Critic) are shaping the future of deep reinforcement learning.
Hierarchical Reinforcement Learning: Developing methods that learn policies at multiple levels of abstraction, enhancing efficiency and adaptability.
Safe Exploration and Transfer Learning: Ensuring safe exploration in complex environments and transferring learned policies to new tasks.

6.2.9 Unleashing AI Potential with DQN and Q-Learning: Deep Q-Networks and Q-learning have reshaped the landscape of reinforcement learning, opening doors to solving intricate challenges across diverse domains. As you delve deeper into this chapter, you'll uncover the intricate details of DQN architectures, training techniques, and the profound impact they've had on advancing AI systems and decision-making agents.

6.3 Policy Gradient Methods: Mastering Reinforcement Learning through Gradient Ascent: Policy Gradient Methods represent a powerful class of algorithms within the realm of reinforcement learning (RL). These methods directly optimize the policy of an agent to maximize cumulative rewards, making them particularly well-suited for tasks involving continuous action spaces and stochastic policies. In this section, we'll embark on a comprehensive journey through the world of Policy Gradient Methods, exploring their foundations, training process, applications, challenges, and the impact they have on creating intelligent decision-making agents.

6.3.1 Reinforcement Learning Recap: Reinforcement learning revolves around the interaction between an agent and an environment. The agent learns by taking actions in the environment, receiving rewards, and adjusting its behavior to maximize cumulative rewards over time. One approach to RL involves learning a policy—a mapping from states to actions—that guides the agent's decision-making process.

6.3.2 Introducing Policy Gradient Methods: Policy Gradient Methods focus on optimizing the policy directly to improve an agent's decision-making capabilities. Rather than estimating the value of different state-action pairs, these methods adjust the policy parameters to find the optimal policy that leads to the highest expected cumulative reward.

6.3.3 Policy Gradient Theorem: The Policy Gradient Theorem is a cornerstone of Policy Gradient Methods. It states that the gradient of the expected cumulative reward with respect to policy parameters is proportional to the gradient of the expected reward with respect to the policy's log-probabilities. Mathematically, this relationship allows us to perform gradient ascent to find policy parameters that increase the expected reward.

6.3.4 Training Process: The training process of Policy Gradient Methods involves two key steps:

Collecting Trajectories: The agent interacts with the environment by following its current policy. This generates a trajectory—a sequence of states, actions, and rewards—over a certain number of time steps.

Updating Policy Parameters: Using the policy gradient theorem, the policy's parameters are updated by performing gradient ascent on the expected reward with respect to the policy's log-probabilities. This encourages the policy to select actions that lead to higher rewards.

6.3.5 Exploration and Exploitation: As with other RL methods, the exploration-exploitation trade-off is crucial in Policy Gradient Methods. Strategies like stochastic policies, which add randomness to action selection, allow the agent to explore different actions and learn about the environment's dynamics.

6.3.6 Variance Reduction Techniques: A challenge in policy gradient methods is the high variance of gradient estimates, which can lead to slow convergence. Techniques like baseline subtraction and advantage estimation help reduce variance by providing a reference point for rewards and focusing on the difference between actual rewards and expected rewards.

6.3.7 Applications: Policy Gradient Methods find applications in various domains:

Continuous Control: These methods are well-suited for tasks with continuous action spaces, such as robotic control and autonomous navigation.

Game Playing: Policy Gradient Methods have achieved impressive results in training agents to play games, from classic board games to complex video games.

Natural Language Processing: They've been applied to tasks like text generation, where the policy is used to generate coherent and contextually relevant text.

6.3.8 Challenges and Advances:

Sample Efficiency: Policy Gradient Methods often require a large number of samples to achieve good performance, leading to slow learning.

Exploration in High-Dimensional Spaces: Designing effective exploration strategies in high-dimensional action spaces remains challenging.

6.3.9 Future Directions: Policy Gradient Methods continue to evolve:

Proximal Policy Optimization (PPO): PPO aims to strike a balance between stability and sample efficiency, making it suitable for both on-policy and off-policy settings.

Actor-Critic Methods: Combining policy gradient methods with value-based methods to create more stable and efficient algorithms.

Hierarchical Policies: Developing policies that operate at multiple levels of abstraction to handle complex tasks.

6.3.10 Transforming Decision-Making with Policy Gradient Methods: Policy Gradient Methods offer a compelling framework for training agents to make intelligent decisions in a wide range of environments. As you delve deeper into this chapter, you'll uncover the intricacies of policy gradient algorithms, explore advanced techniques, and witness firsthand how these methods have enabled the creation of agents that excel in various real-world scenarios.

6.4 Combining Deep Learning and Reinforcement Learning: The fusion of deep learning and reinforcement learning has brought forth a paradigm shift in the field of artificial intelligence. This combination, often referred to as Deep Reinforcement Learning (DRL), marries the capabilities of deep neural networks with the sequential decision-making process of reinforcement learning. In this section, we embark on an in-depth exploration of the symbiotic relationship between deep learning and reinforcement learning, uncovering the foundations, applications, challenges, and transformative potential of this interdisciplinary approach.

6.4.1 Deep Learning Primer: Deep learning revolves around neural networks with multiple layers (deep architectures) that can learn hierarchical representations from data. These networks, inspired by the human brain's structure, are particularly adept at extracting intricate patterns and features from raw data.

6.4.2 Reinforcement Learning Primer: Reinforcement learning revolves around an agent interacting with an environment to learn optimal decision-making strategies. The agent's goal is to find a policy that maximizes cumulative rewards by taking actions in different states of the environment.

6.4.3 Emergence of Deep Reinforcement Learning: Deep Reinforcement Learning (DRL) emerged with the integration of deep neural networks into the reinforcement learning framework. By using deep networks to approximate value functions, Q-values, and policies, DRL enables agents to handle high-dimensional input spaces and learn complex mappings from states to actions.

6.4.4 Applications of Deep Reinforcement Learning: Deep Reinforcement Learning has revolutionized a wide array of domains:

Game Playing: DRL algorithms have mastered classic games like Chess, Go, and Poker, demonstrating their capacity to learn optimal strategies through self-play and exploration.

Robotics: DRL guides robots in tasks such as manipulation, locomotion, and navigation in dynamic environments, enabling more versatile and adaptable robotic systems.

Autonomous Vehicles: DRL has contributed to training self-driving cars to make safe and efficient decisions on the road, improving road safety and traffic efficiency.

Natural Language Processing: DRL has been applied to conversational AI, dialogue systems, and text generation, where agents learn to produce contextually relevant and coherent responses.

6.4.5 Challenges in Deep Reinforcement Learning: The integration of deep learning and reinforcement learning introduces challenges:

Sample Efficiency: One of the prominent challenges in Deep Reinforcement Learning (DRL) is sample efficiency. DRL methods often require a large number of interactions with the environment to learn optimal policies. This can be particularly problematic in scenarios where obtaining real-world samples is expensive or time-consuming. For instance, training robots or autonomous vehicles in the real world may entail risks and resource-intensive efforts.

Stability and Convergence: Training deep neural networks with RL can lead to instability and convergence issues. The non-linearity and complexity of deep networks can result in volatile learning dynamics, where updates may oscillate or diverge. This challenge is exacerbated by the fact that RL involves learning from sequential interactions, which can introduce instability during the learning process. Ensuring that the learning process converges to meaningful policies requires careful design of training strategies, such as adjusting learning rates, employing proper weight initialization, and implementing gradient clipping techniques.

Exploration vs. Exploitation: The exploration-exploitation trade-off remains a fundamental dilemma in reinforcement learning, amplified when combined with deep learning. DRL methods need to strike a balance between exploring new actions to discover their effects and exploiting learned policies that are known to yield rewards. Ensuring effective exploration is particularly challenging when dealing with high-dimensional action spaces or when the environment is stochastic. Selecting actions that are neither too conservative nor too risky requires innovative exploration strategies that enable agents to gather informative samples efficiently.

Generalization: Generalization is a critical challenge in DRL, especially when transitioning from learning in simulation to real-world deployment. While agents might perform well in training environments, ensuring that they generalize to new, unseen environments is vital for practical applications. Real-world scenarios often exhibit variations and complexities that training environments might not fully capture. Developing techniques that facilitate seamless adaptation from simulated environments to real-world situations is an ongoing research area. Methods like domain adaptation and transfer learning play a pivotal role in addressing this challenge by enabling agents to leverage knowledge gained in one domain to improve performance in another.

In summary, while the integration of deep learning and reinforcement learning opens doors to remarkable advancements, these challenges remind us of the intricacies of real-world applications. Addressing these challenges not only contributes to the effectiveness of DRL methods but also propels the field towards more robust, adaptable, and intelligent decision-making agents.

The landscape of Deep Reinforcement Learning (DRL) is enriched by a plethora of techniques designed to overcome challenges and enhance the performance of agents. These techniques, each offering unique advantages, play a vital role in shaping the efficacy and efficiency of DRL algorithms.

6.4.6 Addressing Challenges with DRL Techniques: Several techniques address these challenges:

Experience Replay: Experience Replay is a technique that addresses the challenge of sample efficiency. It involves storing experiences—tuples of (state, action, reward, next state)—in a replay memory during an agent's interactions with the environment. Instead of updating the model with the most recent experience, DRL algorithms sample batches of experiences from the replay memory for training. This strategy mitigates issues of sample correlation and temporal dependencies by breaking the sequential nature of data and improving learning stability. By enabling the agent to learn from a diverse range of experiences, Experience Replay contributes to more efficient and effective learning.

Target Networks: Target Networks are a pivotal innovation to stabilize training in DRL. In value-based algorithms like Deep Q-Networks (DQN), target networks are employed to address convergence issues arising from using the same set of parameters for both value approximation and target estimation. Separate target networks, with periodically updated parameters, provide a fixed and consistent reference for target Q-value calculation. This decoupling of target estimation from value approximation reduces the risk of oscillations during training and contributes to smoother convergence. Target Networks play a crucial role in maintaining stability while training deep Q-learning algorithms.

Advantage Actor-Critic (A2C): Advantage Actor-Critic (A2C) is a hybrid approach that combines the strengths of both value-based and policy-based methods. In A2C, the agent maintains two components: the actor and the critic. The actor updates the policy by maximizing the expected cumulative rewards, while the critic evaluates the value of states or state-action pairs. The "advantage" in A2C refers to the difference between the estimated value of a state and the expected value under the current policy. By utilizing both value-based and policy-based approaches, A2C achieves stability and convergence in learning while offering faster convergence compared to some traditional policy gradient methods.

Proximal Policy Optimization (PPO): Proximal Policy Optimization (PPO) is a policy optimization technique that prioritizes stable and incremental policy updates. PPO aims to strike a balance between policy improvement and preventing large policy changes that could lead to instability. It constrains policy updates using a surrogate objective function that measures how much the new policy deviates from the old policy. By iteratively adapting the policy while maintaining a proximity to the previous policy, PPO achieves more gradual updates and helps agents learn optimal strategies efficiently. PPO's design promotes safety in policy updates, preventing drastic changes that might hinder learning.

Advancing Deep Reinforcement Learning: These techniques collectively exemplify the innovative strides made in DRL to tackle challenges and optimize learning. Experience Replay enhances learning efficiency by diversifying the training data, while Target Networks contribute to stability during training. Advantage Actor-Critic combines the best of both value and policy-based approaches for faster convergence, and Proximal Policy Optimization ensures controlled policy updates for enhanced learning safety. As DRL continues to evolve, these techniques provide a foundation for creating more robust, efficient, and adaptable intelligent agents capable of mastering intricate real-world tasks.

6.4.7 Transfer Learning in DRL: Transfer learning, where knowledge gained in one task is applied to another, has been successfully integrated into DRL:

Pretrained Networks: Pretraining neural networks on related tasks allows agents to leverage learned features when tackling new tasks.

Domain Adaptation: Techniques like domain adaptation enable agents to generalize across different environments by transferring knowledge.

6.4.8 Future Directions: The future of DRL holds exciting possibilities:

Meta-Learning: Developing agents that can learn to learn, adapting quickly to new tasks with minimal samples.

Hierarchical Learning: Expanding DRL to handle tasks at different levels of abstraction, enhancing decision-making in complex environments.

Multi-Agent DRL: Extending DRL to scenarios with multiple interacting agents, such as collaborative robotics and autonomous traffic management.

6.4.9 Transforming AI Landscape with Deep Reinforcement Learning: Deep Reinforcement Learning represents a convergence of cutting-edge technologies that enables agents to make intelligent decisions in complex and dynamic environments. As you delve deeper into this chapter, you'll uncover the intricate details of DRL algorithms, the synergy between deep learning and reinforcement learning, and the transformative impact this interdisciplinary approach has on shaping the future of AI systems and intelligent agents. The integration of deep learning and reinforcement learning indeed brings forth a powerful approach, but it also presents several challenges that need to be carefully addressed for successful application. These challenges, while demanding, offer opportunities for innovation and advancement in the field of artificial intelligence.

6.5 Project

Unsolved Project

Suppose you're tasked with developing a self-learning game-playing agent using reinforcement learning and deep learning techniques. To create an effective agent, you need to understand the basics of reinforcement learning, including Q-Learning and Deep Q-Networks (DQN), as well as policy gradient methods. Additionally, you'll explore how to combine deep learning with reinforcement learning to enhance the agent's performance. Before starting the development, research the following: the fundamentals of reinforcement learning, the concepts of Q-Learning and DQN, the principles behind policy gradient methods, and the ways deep learning can be integrated with reinforcement learning. This preparation will equip you with the knowledge needed to design and train a robust self-learning game-playing agent.

6.6 Lab Activity

Unsolved Lab Activity

Implement a simple reinforcement learning algorithm (e.g., Q-Learning) to solve a grid-world problem.

Task: Use a programming language (e.g., Python) to implement a Q-Learning algorithm for a grid-world problem. Document each step of the implementation and report the agent's performance in solving the problem.

Exercises

Exercise 1 – Multiple Choice Questions

1. What is the primary objective of reinforcement learning?
   a. Image recognition
   b. Sequence generation
   c. Maximizing cumulative rewards
   d. Data clustering
2. Which of the following is NOT one of the fundamental components of reinforcement learning?
   a. Agent
   b. Environment
   c. Policy
   d. Database
3. In reinforcement learning, what is the role of the "policy"?
   a. It defines the agent's strategy for decision-making.
   b. It represents the external environment.
   c. It stores past experiences for learning.
   d. It calculates the immediate rewards.
4. What does the Bellman equation define in Q-learning?
   a. The Q-value for a given state-action pair.
   b. The probability of taking an action.
   c. The discounted cumulative reward.
   d. The optimal policy.
5. How does Deep Q-Network (DQN) address the challenge of high-dimensional state spaces?
   a. By using Q-learning with larger tables
   b. By leveraging deep neural networks
   c. By reducing the dimensionality of states
   d. By increasing the number of actions

Exercise 2 – True/False

1. Deep Q-Networks (DQN) are a type of reinforcement learning algorithm that combines Q-Learning with deep neural networks.
2. Policy Gradient Methods are primarily used for supervised learning tasks.
3. Combining deep learning with reinforcement learning can enhance the ability to handle high-dimensional state spaces.

Review Questions

1. What are the three fundamental components of reinforcement learning?
2. How does the agent interact with the environment in reinforcement learning?
3. Define "policy" in the context of reinforcement learning.
4. Describe the key steps in the reinforcement learning process.
5. What is the ultimate goal of reinforcement learning, and how is it quantified?
6. What is the Q-function, and how does it relate to Q-learning?
7. How does DQN address the challenge of handling high-dimensional state spaces?
8. Explain the concept of experience replay and its significance in DQN.
9. What are target networks, and why are they used in DQN?
10. How does DQN handle the exploration-exploitation trade-off?
11. What is the fundamental focus of Policy Gradient Methods in reinforcement learning?
12. What does the Policy Gradient Theorem state, and how does it relate to policy optimization?
13. Describe the training process of Policy Gradient Methods.
14. Why is exploration important in Policy Gradient Methods, and how is it achieved?
15. What challenges do Policy Gradient Methods face in terms of sample efficiency?
16. How does Deep Reinforcement Learning (DRL) integrate deep learning and reinforcement learning?
17. What are some of the applications of Deep Reinforcement Learning mentioned in the chapter?
18. Identify and explain some of the challenges in Deep Reinforcement Learning.
19. Describe the role of techniques like Experience Replay and Target Networks in addressing DRL challenges.
20. How does transfer learning, specifically domain adaptation, benefit DRL?

Answers

Exercise 1- 1. c. 2. d. 3. a. 4. a. 5. b
Exercise 2- 1) True, 2) False, 3) True

Online Resources

Online Exam Paper:
Link: https://forms.gle/q15HXYnKbezGZniJ9
QR Code:

Chapter 6 Videos Playlist:
Link: https://www.youtube.com/playlist?list=PLzlh_31VWEFqq1Xj4kI4wPe0Z6oHEe--J
QR Code:

Chapter 7: Advanced Topics in Deep Learning

7.1 Attention Mechanisms in Deep Learning: Unleashing Contextual Focus for Enhanced Representations: Attention mechanisms, a breakthrough innovation in the realm of deep learning, have revolutionized the way models process and understand sequential and contextual information. Derived from their human cognitive counterpart, attention mechanisms provide the capability to selectively focus on specific parts of input data while performing tasks like language translation, image captioning, and more. In this section, we embark on a comprehensive journey through the world of attention mechanisms, unraveling their foundations, mechanisms, applications, and transformative impact on the efficacy of deep learning models.

7.1.1 Foundations of Attention: At the heart of human perception lies the ability to concentrate on relevant details while processing complex information. Attention mechanisms in deep learning mimic this cognitive process, enabling models to emphasize certain parts of the input data for improved understanding and performance. This is particularly powerful in scenarios where context and relevance play crucial roles, such as natural language understanding and computer vision.

7.1.2 Mechanisms of Attention: Attention mechanisms enable models to assign different importance weights to different parts of input data. These mechanisms work in concert with deep neural networks to dynamically adjust the contribution of each element based on its relevance to the task at hand. The attention process involves three key components:

Query: The query represents the current element under consideration, which seeks to understand the relationship with other elements.

Key: The keys are the elements in the input sequence that the query interacts with to establish relevance.

Value: The values correspond to the information associated with each key, determining the weight and contribution of the corresponding key to the final output.

7.1.3 Self-Attention and Transformer Architecture: One of the most notable applications of attention mechanisms is the Transformer architecture, which has revolutionized natural language processing and beyond. Self-attention, a variant of attention, allows a model to weigh the importance of different words in a sentence while generating contextualized representations. The Transformer architecture leverages multi-head self-attention to capture different types of relationships in the data and enable efficient parallel processing.

7.1.4 Applications of Attention Mechanisms:

Attention mechanisms have found applications across various domains: Attention mechanisms, a cornerstone of deep learning, have transcended disciplinary boundaries to enhance the capabilities of artificial intelligence systems across various domains. These mechanisms, initially inspired by human cognitive processes, offer a remarkable way to allocate focus and relevance in AI models. Here, we delve into the tangible applications of attention mechanisms across distinct domains, showcasing their transformative impact on machine translation, image captioning, question answering, and speech recognition.

Machine Translation: Attention mechanisms have ushered in a new era of machine translation, enabling models to grasp the nuanced relationships between words in different languages. In the realm of language translation, these mechanisms empower models to selectively focus on specific words or phrases in the source sentence while generating the corresponding translation. This contextual focus allows models to accurately capture idiomatic expressions, syntactic structures, and cultural nuances, thus improving the quality and fluency of translated text. As a result, attention-equipped models have become the bedrock of state-of-the-art translation systems, breaking down language barriers and fostering cross-cultural communication.

Image Captioning: In the realm of computer vision, attention mechanisms have revolutionized image captioning, bridging the gap between visual perception and natural language understanding. These mechanisms empower models to zoom in on specific regions of an image that are most relevant to generating accurate and contextually coherent captions. By aligning the attention of the model with salient visual features, attention-equipped models create captions that are not only descriptive but also semantically enriched, providing a more comprehensive understanding of the visual content. This fusion of vision and language has propelled image captioning systems to convey intricate details and nuances that were previously beyond the reach of traditional methods.

Question Answering: Attention mechanisms have proven invaluable in the domain of question answering, where models strive to comprehend complex textual inputs and provide accurate responses. These mechanisms enable models to dynamically focus on segments of the input passage that are most pertinent to answering the given question. By directing attention to relevant context, attention-equipped models extract and integrate information effectively, enhancing the accuracy and depth of their responses. This capability finds applications in a range of scenarios, from information retrieval to complex reading comprehension tasks, enriching the quality and efficiency of AI-driven question answering systems.

Speech Recognition: The domain of speech recognition has also witnessed the transformative power of attention mechanisms. In the intricate realm of audio signals, these mechanisms aid models in pinpointing critical acoustic features that carry phonetic and linguistic information. By directing attention to segments of the audio waveform that hold key characteristics, attention-equipped models enhance their ability to discern spoken words accurately, even in the presence of background noise and variations. As a result, attention mechanisms have elevated the performance of speech recognition systems, making them more robust and versatile across diverse acoustic environments.

Expanding the Horizon: The versatility of attention mechanisms is evident in their wide-ranging applications, from bridging language gaps to fusing vision and language, and enhancing information extraction in text and audio data. As attention mechanisms continue to evolve, their adaptability and effectiveness are likely to extend further into uncharted territories, powering innovations in domains yet to be fully explored. As you delve into the landscape of attention mechanisms, you'll uncover not only their applications but also their intricate workings, enriching your understanding of how they drive the advancement of AI in a variety of real-world contexts.

7.1.5 Transformer's Impact on NLP: The advent of the Transformer architecture heralded a groundbreaking shift in the landscape of natural language processing (NLP). With its revolutionary design, the Transformer architecture brought about a departure from conventional recurrent and convolutional networks, introducing self-attention mechanisms that have catalyzed the creation of transformative language models. This section delves into the profound impact of the Transformer architecture on NLP, its pivotal role in the emergence of models like BERT, GPT, and T5, and how it has redefined the boundaries of language understanding.

The Rise of the Transformer: The Transformer architecture emerged as a solution to address the limitations of recurrent neural networks (RNNs) and convolutional neural networks (CNNs) in capturing long-range dependencies and contextual relationships in language sequences. The inherent sequential nature of RNNs led to slow training times, while CNNs struggled with capturing contextual nuances across variable-length sentences.

Unveiling Self-Attention: The Transformer architecture harnessed the power of self-attention mechanisms to fundamentally reshape the way models understand language. Self-attention allows a model to weigh the importance of different words in a sentence while generating contextualized representations. This mechanism enables the model to dynamically adjust its focus on specific words, capturing intricate relationships and dependencies across the entire sequence. As a result, the Transformer architecture excels in processing sentences with varying lengths, capturing context, and understanding nuances in text.

Transformer Models: BERT, GPT, T5, and Beyond: The Transformer architecture paved the way for a lineage of groundbreaking models:

BERT (Bidirectional Encoder Representations from Transformers): BERT introduced bidirectional context by training on both left and right contexts of each word, allowing it to grasp the full contextual nuances of language. This enabled BERT to achieve exceptional performance in various NLP tasks, including question answering, sentiment analysis, and named entity recognition.

GPT (Generative Pretrained Transformer): GPT leveraged the power of self-attention in a generative model. By conditioning the model on previous words in a text, GPT generated coherent and contextually relevant text. This marked a significant leap in language generation tasks, from text completion to story writing.

T5 (Text-To-Text Transfer Transformer): T5 extended the versatility of the Transformer architecture by framing various NLP tasks as text-to-text problems. This unified approach simplified the training pipeline and achieved remarkable results across tasks like translation, summarization, and question answering.

Contextual Understanding and Nuances: The Transformer's impact is most palpable in its ability to capture contextual relationships between words in a sentence. Traditional models struggled with long-range dependencies and understanding context beyond a fixed window. The self-attention mechanism equips Transformer models with the ability to consider every word in the context of the entire sentence, enabling them to grasp complex sentence structures, idiomatic expressions, and context-dependent semantics.

Beyond Traditional Tasks: The Transformer's prowess extends beyond traditional NLP tasks. It has revolutionized language understanding in sentiment analysis, language translation, summarization, and even creative writing. Its capacity to comprehend context-rich text contributes to more accurate and contextually coherent outputs.

Paving the Way Forward: The Transformer architecture, with its self-attention mechanisms, has irrevocably transformed the landscape of NLP. As researchers and practitioners delve deeper into this architectural paradigm, we can anticipate further innovations that will amplify the capabilities of language models. With each new iteration, the Transformer family of models continues to redefine the boundaries of what is possible in language understanding, carving a path towards more human-like, context-aware, and nuanced AI systems.

7.1.6 Challenges and Advances:

Computational Complexity: Attention mechanisms, especially in large-scale models, can be computationally expensive.

Interpretability: As models grow in complexity, understanding the inner workings of attention mechanisms becomes more challenging.

Advancements include techniques to reduce computational complexity, such as sparse attention patterns and efficient approximations. Researchers are also exploring interpretability methods to shed light on how attention mechanisms make decisions.

7.1.7 Future Directions: Attention mechanisms continue to evolve:

Sparse Attention: Exploring ways to use attention more efficiently by focusing only on relevant parts of the input.

Cross-Modal Attention: Extending attention mechanisms to process multiple modalities like text and images together.

Explainable Attention: Developing techniques to make attention mechanisms more interpretable for understanding model decisions.

7.1.8 Unveiling Deeper Context with Attention Mechanisms: Attention mechanisms have breathed new life into deep learning by enabling models to capture contextual relationships effectively. As you delve deeper into this chapter, you'll uncover the intricate details of attention mechanisms, their integration into cutting-edge architectures, and the transformative potential they hold for reshaping the landscape of AI and intelligent systems.

7.2 Transformers and Their Applications: Redefining Language Understanding and Beyond: The emergence of Transformers has redefined the landscape of natural language processing (NLP) and extended its impact far beyond linguistic tasks. These architectures, characterized by self-attention mechanisms and parallel processing, have propelled language models to unprecedented heights of performance, transforming the way we approach various AI applications. In this section, we delve into the intricacies of Transformers, their innovative mechanisms, and their versatile applications across different domains.

7.2.1 The Transformer Architecture: The Transformer architecture is a revolutionary paradigm shift from traditional sequential models. Its core strength lies in self-attention mechanisms, enabling models to capture dependencies between words in a sequence regardless of their distance. This liberates Transformers from the constraints of sequential processing, accelerating both training and inference.

7.2.2 Self-Attention Mechanisms: Self-attention mechanisms allow each word in a sequence to dynamically weigh its significance against every other word. This contextual focus forms the basis for capturing long-range dependencies, contextual nuances, and relationships that were previously challenging to grasp. By aligning self-attention with salient information, Transformers excel in understanding context-rich data.

7.2.3 Applications in NLP:

BERT (Bidirectional Encoder Representations from Transformers): BERT, a prominent Transformer-based model, revolutionized NLP by introducing bidirectional context. This means BERT processes both left and right contexts of each word during training, enabling it to understand the full context and nuances of language. BERT's contextual embeddings serve as pre-trained representations for various downstream NLP tasks, resulting in impressive performance improvements across domains.

GPT (Generative Pretrained Transformer): GPT leverages Transformers for generative tasks. By conditioning on previous words, GPT generates coherent and contextually relevant text. This innovation has pushed the boundaries of text generation, enabling applications like creative writing, automatic summarization, and dialogue generation.

T5 (Text-To-Text Transfer Transformer): T5 presents a transformative perspective on NLP by framing all tasks as text-to-text problems. This unified approach simplifies the training pipeline and showcases the versatility of Transformers. T5's efficacy in translation, summarization, question answering, and more underscores the adaptability of the architecture.

7.2.4 Beyond NLP: The impact of Transformers transcends NLP, extending into domains like:

Computer Vision: Vision Transformers (ViTs) apply the Transformer architecture to image data by segmenting images into patches and treating them as "words." This innovation challenges traditional convolutional architectures and is already demonstrating competitive performance on image classification tasks.

Graph Representation Learning: Transformers have found applications in graph-based data like social networks and molecular structures. By considering the interconnections between nodes, Transformers can learn representations that capture complex relationships and patterns within graphs.

Reinforcement Learning: Transformers are making headway in reinforcement learning as well. They enable agents to capture sequential dependencies in tasks where understanding context is critical, such as video game playing and robotic control.

7.2.5 Continual Advancements: The versatility and impact of Transformers continue to expand:

Efficiency Enhancements: Efficiency is a cornerstone in the evolution of Transformers. Researchers are dedicated to making these models more computationally efficient, enabling broader deployment. Sparse attention patterns represent a compelling approach, where only a subset of elements attends to others, significantly reducing computational complexity without sacrificing performance. Moreover, model compression techniques, such as pruning and quantization, are under exploration, aiming to create smaller and faster Transformers that retain their powerful capabilities.

Multimodal Fusion: The journey of Transformers extends beyond language and images. Researchers are boldly venturing into the realm of multimodal understanding, where Transformers process multiple data modalities—text, images, audio—simultaneously. This innovation enables more holistic comprehension by leveraging cross-modal interactions. By fusing information from diverse sources, these multimodal Transformers enrich their understanding of complex contexts, thus driving advancements in tasks that require comprehensive insight across different data types.

Interpretable Transformers: The black-box nature of deep learning models has spurred the pursuit of interpretability, a goal that holds immense importance for real-world applications. Researchers are pioneering methods to peel back the layers of Transformers, revealing their decision-making processes. This involves techniques to visualize attention patterns, attribute model decisions to specific input features, and generate explanations for model outputs. By rendering Transformers interpretable and explainable, we bridge the gap between AI and human understanding, fostering trust and insight into the models' inner workings.

7.2.6 Unleashing the Potential of Transformers: Transformers stand as a testament to the transformative power of architecture design. By embracing self-attention mechanisms, Transformers have not only revolutionized NLP but have also influenced diverse domains. Their ability to capture intricate dependencies and context-rich information makes them an invaluable tool for AI innovation, shaping the evolution of intelligent systems across applications.

As Transformers continue to evolve, their impact reverberates across domains:

Customized Architectures: Researchers are crafting specialized Transformers for domain-specific challenges, further tailoring the architecture to unique requirements.

Pretrained Models: The advancements in pretrained models continue, with larger and more capable models being developed to capture even finer nuances in data.

Transfer Learning: Transformers' transfer learning capabilities persist in revolutionizing how we approach various tasks, enabling models to generalize knowledge across different contexts.

7.2.7 Shaping the Future with Transformers: The story of Transformers is an ever-evolving narrative, marked by continuous innovation and transformation. As each enhancement is introduced, the scope of possibilities widens, offering avenues for more efficient, adaptable, and interpretable AI systems. The impact of Transformers, spanning NLP, computer vision, and beyond, demonstrates that this architecture has transcended being a mere technological advancement—it's a catalyst for reshaping the very landscape of artificial intelligence. The journey of innovation continues, propelling us towards a future where Transformers continue to redefine our understanding of intelligent systems and their profound potential.

7.3 Interpretable and Explainable AI: Interpretable and explainable AI (XAI) stands at the crossroads of technological innovation and human comprehension, seeking to demystify the enigmatic workings of complex artificial intelligence systems. As AI models become more sophisticated, their decision-making processes often remain obscured by layers of intricate computations. Interpretable and explainable AI aims to bridge this gap by providing insights into why AI systems make specific predictions or decisions. In this section, we delve into the profound realm of interpretable and explainable AI, exploring its significance, methods, applications, and its pivotal role in fostering trust and accountability in AI.

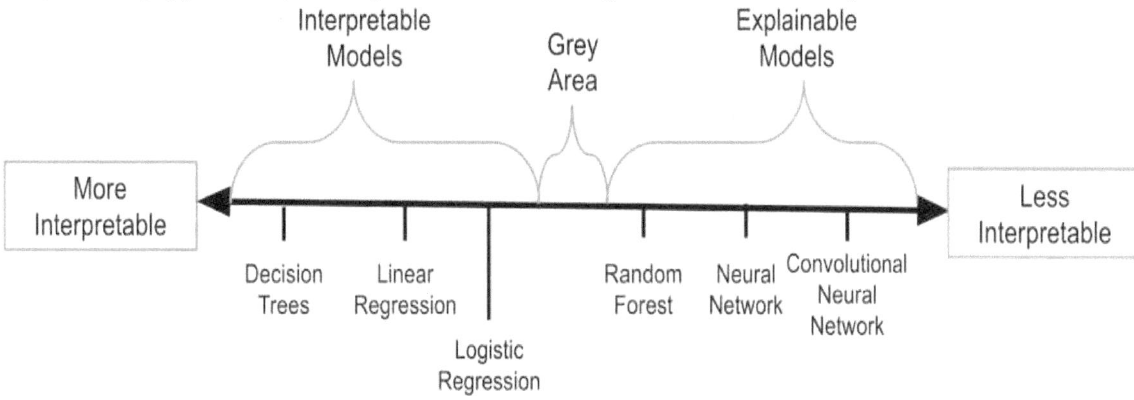

7.3.1 The Significance of Interpretable AI: In an era where AI-driven systems impact critical decisions in various domains, the ability to understand, trust, and validate AI outcomes is paramount. Interpretable AI addresses the "black box" nature of complex models, making their decisions transparent and comprehensible to both technical experts and non-experts alike. This transparency holds the key to building trust, complying with regulations, and ensuring accountability in AI applications.

7.3.2 Approaches to Interpretability: Several approaches are employed to achieve interpretable AI:

Interpretable AI is a pivotal step toward bridging the gap between complex AI models and human comprehension. A multitude of approaches have been devised to achieve this, shedding light on the decision-making processes of AI systems. Each method offers a unique perspective, illuminating the intricate pathways AI traverses to arrive at its predictions. Here, we delve into these approaches, showcasing their significance and implications.

Feature Importance: This approach delves into understanding which features or inputs wield the most influence over a model's decisions. In linear models, this is often achieved by analyzing the magnitude of feature weights, with larger magnitudes indicating greater importance. In tree-based models, feature relevance scores can be calculated, revealing the contribution of each feature to the final outcome. This approach offers insights into which aspects of input data guide the model's reasoning, contributing to interpretable decision-making.

Visualizations: Visualizations serve as a powerful tool to demystify AI model behavior. Through graphical representations, complex processes are distilled into comprehensible images. For instance, in image analysis, heatmaps can be generated to highlight regions of images that significantly influenced predictions. Decision boundaries can also be visualized in data to showcase how a model separates different classes. These visual aids empower users to discern patterns, relationships, and decision factors, transforming intricate model behavior into intuitive insights.

Surrogate Models: Surrogate models emerge as interpretable approximations of complex AI models. They encapsulate the essence of intricate decision-making, offering a simplified view that mirrors the behavior of the original model. By training a more transparent surrogate model on the same data, users can gain insights into how the complex model arrives at its decisions. Surrogate models bridge the gap between complexity and interpretability, enabling experts and non-experts alike to grasp the driving factors behind AI predictions.

Attention Mechanisms: Attention mechanisms, popularized by Transformers, offer a remarkable avenue for unveiling AI decision processes. These mechanisms spotlight specific input elements that garnered the model's attention during prediction. In language models, for instance, attention mechanisms can highlight words or phrases that significantly contributed to a generated text. This approach provides a dynamic perspective on how AI assigns importance to different parts of input data, enhancing transparency and insight.

Local Explanations: Local explanations focus on individual predictions, explaining why a particular outcome was reached. Pertinent inputs are identified, and their impact on the model's decision is elucidated. This method is particularly useful for understanding outlier predictions or instances where the model's behavior deviates from expectations. By dissecting specific predictions, local explanations offer a micro-level understanding of model reasoning, enabling users to validate and comprehend model outputs.

Synthesizing Clarity from Complexity: Interpretable AI approaches unravel the complexity embedded within AI systems, providing an array of tools for comprehending and validating model behavior. These approaches not only empower experts to refine and optimize models but also extend AI's reach to non-experts who seek to engage confidently with AI-generated insights. As the field of interpretable AI continues to evolve, each approach contributes to fostering transparency, trust, and accountability in the deployment of AI technologies across various domains.

7.3.3 Applications of Explainable AI: Explainable AI extends its influence across diverse domains:

Explainable AI transcends technical nuances, weaving its impact across diverse sectors and domains. By offering insights into AI decision-making, it brings clarity to complex processes and enables stakeholders to understand, validate, and trust the outcomes. Let's explore how explainable AI finds practical application in various fields, revolutionizing decision-making and enhancing accountability.

Healthcare: In the realm of healthcare, where AI assists in critical medical diagnoses, explainable AI takes center stage. Medical professionals can't solely rely on AI's recommendations: they need to comprehend the reasoning behind each decision. Interpretable AI bridges the gap, explaining why a certain diagnosis or treatment recommendation was made. This enables doctors to validate AI-driven suggestions, fostering collaboration between human expertise and machine insights. Additionally, transparent AI aids in complying with medical ethics and standards, ensuring that decisions align with patient well-being.

Finance: Explainable AI finds its place in the financial sector, especially in credit scoring. When an AI model determines creditworthiness, it's imperative to understand the factors that led to a particular credit decision. By unraveling the model's rationale, financial institutions can enhance transparency, ensuring that creditworthiness determinations are fair and accountable. Borrowers benefit from comprehensible insights into why their credit application was approved or denied, fostering trust in the lending process.

Autonomous Vehicles: The intersection of AI and autonomous vehicles relies heavily on trust and safety. When an autonomous vehicle makes a split-second decision, passengers and pedestrians need to understand the logic behind that choice. Explainable AI provides transparency, offering clear explanations for why a vehicle took a specific action—whether it accelerated, braked, or changed lanes. This transparency not only enhances public acceptance of autonomous vehicles but also aids regulatory bodies in evaluating the safety of these advanced systems.

Legal and Compliance: In legal contexts, AI decisions hold ethical, legal, and regulatory significance. For instance, when AI is involved in legal research or contract analysis, understanding the reasoning behind decisions becomes crucial. Explainable AI ensures that legal professionals comprehend why a certain judgment or recommendation was made. It aids in complying with regulations that demand accountability and transparency in decision-making processes, reinforcing ethical standards in the legal domain.

Shaping Trust and Collaboration: Explainable AI isn't confined to a single domain: it acts as a bridge between AI's capabilities and human comprehension across industries. By fostering transparency, it facilitates collaboration between AI systems and human experts, enriching decision-making with diverse perspectives. Moreover, explainable AI underscores the ethical underpinnings of technology, ensuring that AI-driven decisions align with human values, ethics, and regulatory standards. As the landscape of AI applications expands, the demand for explainable AI continues to grow, carving a path toward responsible, trustworthy, and accountable AI integration.

7.3.4 Striking a Balance: While interpretability is crucial, it's often a trade-off with model performance. Highly interpretable models might not achieve the same level of accuracy as complex black-box models. Thus, finding the right balance between interpretability and performance becomes a crucial consideration, especially in high-stakes applications.

7.3.5 Building Trust and Accountability: Explainable AI addresses the "AI trust gap" by allowing users to understand and validate the decisions made by AI models. This transparency fosters accountability, enabling users to question and refine models when necessary. Moreover, XAI supports compliance with regulations like the General Data Protection Regulation (GDPR), which mandates that individuals have the right to an explanation for automated decisions.

7.3.6 Challenges and the Path Ahead: The journey to achieving true interpretability and explainability faces challenges:

Trade-offs: Balancing interpretability with model complexity and performance remains a challenge.

Context Sensitivity: Providing explanations that are relevant and comprehensible to non-experts is complex.

Black-Box Components: Even in interpretable models, certain components might remain black boxes due to their inherent complexity.

Human-Centric Design: Developing interfaces and visualization techniques that effectively convey explanations to users is an ongoing challenge.

7.3.7 Illuminating the Future of AI: Interpretable and explainable AI transcends technical nuances, driving a paradigm shift towards AI systems that are transparent, accountable, and understandable to humans. As AI plays an increasingly pivotal role in our lives, the ability to comprehend and trust AI's decisions is crucial. Interpretable AI holds the promise of not only empowering experts but also enabling every individual to engage confidently with AI-driven insights, bridging the gap between technology and humanity.

7.4 Adversarial Attacks and Defenses: In the intricate world of artificial intelligence, vulnerabilities can hide beneath the surface, waiting to be exploited. Adversarial attacks and their corresponding defenses illuminate a realm where AI systems can be deceived by meticulously crafted inputs. This section delves into the fascinating realm of adversarial attacks, where the art of manipulation intersects with technology, and explores the strategies employed to thwart these attacks, safeguarding AI systems against malicious exploitation.

7.4.1 Adversarial Attacks: Unveiling the Intricacies: Adversarial attacks are orchestrated attempts to mislead AI models by introducing carefully crafted perturbations into input data. These perturbations might be imperceptible to the human eye, yet they are potent enough to deceive AI systems, causing them to make erroneous predictions or classifications. Adversarial attacks take advantage of AI models' susceptibility to slight alterations in data, highlighting the brittleness of these models in the face of novel inputs.

7.4.2 Types of Adversarial Attacks:

White-Box Attacks: Attackers have complete knowledge of the target model's architecture and parameters, allowing them to devise precise perturbations to exploit vulnerabilities.

Black-Box Attacks: Attackers have limited knowledge about the target model and craft adversarial examples using only input-output pairs, making these attacks more challenging to execute.

Transfer Attacks: Adversarial examples generated for one model are applied to a different model, exploiting shared vulnerabilities across different systems.

Physical Attacks: Adversarial perturbations are introduced into the real world, impacting AI systems operating in physical environments, like autonomous vehicles or drones.

7.4.3 Defenses Against Adversarial Attacks: In the ever-evolving landscape of AI security, the pursuit of defenses against adversarial attacks takes center stage. These defenses aim to fortify AI systems against meticulously crafted manipulations, mitigating the vulnerabilities that adversaries exploit. Here, we explore the array of strategies that researchers and practitioners employ to arm AI against adversarial onslaughts.

Adversarial Training: At the forefront of defense, adversarial training transforms adversity into strength. Models are exposed to adversarial examples during training, effectively teaching them to recognize and withstand such inputs. Through this exposure, models learn to generalize their understanding beyond pristine data, gaining resilience against adversarial perturbations. Adversarial training equips AI with the ability to identify manipulation attempts and respond with accurate predictions.

Defensive Distillation: Defensive distillation leverages the collective wisdom of multiple models to elevate resilience. A model is trained on "soft" probabilities produced by another model. These probabilities encapsulate nuanced insights into the target model's decision-making process. By imbibing this distilled knowledge, the model becomes adept at navigating adversarial attacks. Defensive distillation acts as a bridge between models, enhancing their ability to handle adversarial examples.

Feature Squeezing: Feature squeezing orchestrates a transformation of input data, making it less prone to adversarial alterations. By reducing high-frequency noise in the input, the space available for adversarial perturbations shrinks. This strategy minimizes the effectiveness of subtle manipulations, impeding adversaries' attempts to deceive the model. Feature squeezing is a proactive defense mechanism that narrows the window of vulnerability in AI systems.

Ensemble Methods: Ensemble methods draw strength from unity, combining predictions from multiple models to form a robust collective decision. Different models possess varying vulnerabilities, and adversaries exploiting one model might falter against another. By blending predictions, ensemble methods bolster AI resilience, reducing the impact of adversarial inputs. This approach taps into the diversity of models to create a more robust defense against manipulation attempts.

Certified Defenses: Certified defenses offer a mathematical safeguard against adversarial attacks. These methods provide rigorous guarantees of a model's robustness by employing formal verification techniques. By bounding the model's sensitivity to perturbations, certified defenses ensure that even under adversarial inputs, the model remains steadfast in its predictions. This approach hinges on rigorous mathematical proofs, assuring AI's integrity in the face of manipulation.

The Resilient Shield: The defenses against adversarial attacks are a testament to the proactive and multifaceted approach to AI security. By adapting adversarial examples as a training tool, combining insights from multiple models, and applying mathematical rigor, AI systems are equipped to withstand the onslaught of manipulation. These defenses underscore the significance of proactive security measures, urging us to embrace robustness in AI development to safeguard its integrity and reliability against a world brimming with adversarial intent.

7.4.4 Adversarial Attacks in Different Domains: Adversarial attacks, with their potential to manipulate AI systems, transcend the boundaries of domains, infiltrating various sectors where AI's impact is profound. These attacks target the vulnerabilities of AI models, demonstrating their potency to disrupt and deceive across distinct realms. Here, we explore the adverse impact of adversarial attacks in different domains, underscoring the pervasive nature of this multifaceted threat.

Computer Vision: In the realm of computer vision, where AI interprets and analyzes visual data, adversarial attacks take on a visual disguise. These attacks alter images subtly, introducing perturbations that evade human perception but mislead image classifiers. As a result, AI systems can misclassify objects or scenes, impacting security systems, autonomous vehicles, or even medical image analysis. A manipulated stop sign might be misinterpreted by an autonomous vehicle, posing risks to safety. The delicate balance between image authenticity and manipulation showcases the complexity of safeguarding AI's visual perception.

NLP: Text generation, a domain dominated by natural language processing (NLP), is not immune to adversarial attacks. Attackers exploit linguistic nuances, introducing slight modifications to generate misleading or harmful content. Such alterations can lead to the creation of inappropriate messages, misinformation, or even toxic language. In the age of social media and online communication, adversarial attacks on NLP models can amplify the spread of false information and harmful discourse, underscoring the urgency of securing AI-driven language generation.

Speech Recognition: Speech recognition systems, which enable machines to interpret spoken language, fall prey to adversarial attacks that manipulate audio inputs. Attackers can subtly alter spoken words or introduce noise that misleads these systems into incorrect transcriptions. Such attacks have ramifications for applications like automated transcription services or voice-controlled devices. The vulnerability of speech recognition models to adversarial perturbations highlights the challenges in ensuring accurate and reliable voice-based interactions.

A Unified Vigilance: The phenomenon of adversarial attacks reaches across domains, rendering the need for security and resilience an urgent imperative. As AI's influence permeates various sectors, from autonomous vehicles to online communication, the potential impact of manipulative attacks grows in magnitude. The unifying thread is the relentless need to bolster AI defenses, developing strategies that can thwart adversarial attempts irrespective of the domain. By embracing a multidimensional vigilance, we empower AI systems to navigate the complexities of their environment, ensuring that their decisions remain steadfast against the subtle tactics of manipulation.

7.4.5 The Ongoing Battle: The cat-and-mouse game between adversaries and defenders continues to evolve:

Black-Box Attacks: Attackers devise strategies to breach defenses even with limited information about the target model.

Transferability: Adversarial examples generated for one model might still fool another model, showcasing the need for robust defenses.

Real-World Attacks: As AI systems become integrated into physical environments, adversaries explore methods to impact real-world AI systems.

7.4.6 Fortifying AI against Deception: The landscape of adversarial attacks and defenses underscores the complexity of AI security. As AI systems play an increasingly pivotal role in critical applications, the need to shield them from manipulation becomes paramount. While defenses have made significant strides, the elusive nature of adversarial attacks demands continuous research, innovative strategies, and cross-disciplinary collaboration. This battle for AI security prompts us to acknowledge that as AI systems advance, so do the challenges in safeguarding their integrity against cunning adversaries.

7.5 Project

Unsolved Project

Suppose you're working on a project to enhance the security and interpretability of deep learning models in a real-world application. To achieve this, you need to understand advanced topics such as attention mechanisms, transformers, interpretable and explainable AI, and adversarial attacks and defenses. Before starting your project, study the following: the role and functioning of attention mechanisms in deep learning, the architecture and applications of transformers, techniques for making AI models interpretable and explainable, and methods for defending against adversarial attacks. This comprehensive understanding will enable you to develop a secure and interpretable deep learning model for your application.

7.6 Lab Activity

Unsolved Lab Activity

Implement an adversarial attack on a pre-trained image classification model and evaluate its robustness.

Task: Use a deep learning framework to implement an adversarial attack (e.g., FGSM) on a pre-trained image classification model. Document the attack process and evaluate the model's robustness by measuring the performance before and after the attack.

Exercises

Exercise 1 – Multiple Choice Questions

1. What are attention mechanisms in deep learning inspired by?
   A. Human cognition
   B. Computer vision
   C. Natural language understanding
   D. Transformer architecture
2. What is the primary purpose of attention mechanisms in deep learning?
   A. Capturing complex data
   B. Enhancing model training speed
   C. Selectively focusing on input data
   D. Generating text sequences
3. Which components are involved in the attention process?
   A. Query, key, and value
   B. Input, output, and context
   C. Encoder, decoder, and token
   D. Attention, focus, and relevance
4. How has the Transformer architecture impacted natural language processing (NLP)?
   A. It has introduced convolutional networks.
   B. It has improved training times for RNNs.
   C. It has revolutionized the understanding of language.
   D. It has simplified language translation tasks.

5. What is the primary advantage of self-attention in the Transformer architecture?
A. It reduces model complexity.
B. It allows for parallel processing.
C. It captures long-range dependencies.
D. It improves speech recognition.

Exercise 2 – True/False

1. Attention mechanisms in deep learning are used to improve the performance of neural networks by focusing on important parts of the input data.
2. Transformers are primarily used for image recognition tasks and are not applicable to natural language processing.
Explainable AI aims to make the outcomes of AI models more understandable and transparent to humans.

Review Questions

1. What are attention mechanisms in deep learning, and how do they revolutionize model processing?
2. How do attention mechanisms mimic human cognitive processes, and why is this important in deep learning?
3. Explain the three key components of the attention process: Query, Key, and Value.
4. How does self-attention differ from traditional attention mechanisms, and what is its significance in the Transformer architecture?
5. What are some applications of attention mechanisms in deep learning, and how do they improve model performance?

Answers

Exercise 1- 1. A 2. C 3. A 4. C 5. C
Exercise 2- 1) True, 2) False, 3) True

Online Resources

Online Exam Paper:
Link: https://forms.gle/3NZvEkSTivs2pGfY9
QR Code:

Chapter 7 Videos Playlist:
Link: https://www.youtube.com/playlist?list=PLzlh_31VWEFqDcuCq347CJOJ53pSdv8H0
QR Code:

Chapter 8: Practical Implementation and Tools

8.1 TensorFlow vs. PyTorch: Deciphering the Framework Dilemma: In the ever-expanding landscape of deep learning, the choice of framework serves as a crucial decision, influencing the development, deployment, and performance of AI models. TensorFlow and PyTorch, two of the most prominent deep learning frameworks, vie for dominance, each with its own set of strengths and characteristics. This section navigates the intricacies of the TensorFlow vs. PyTorch dilemma, unraveling the distinctions, capabilities, and considerations that guide the choice between these two powerhouse frameworks.

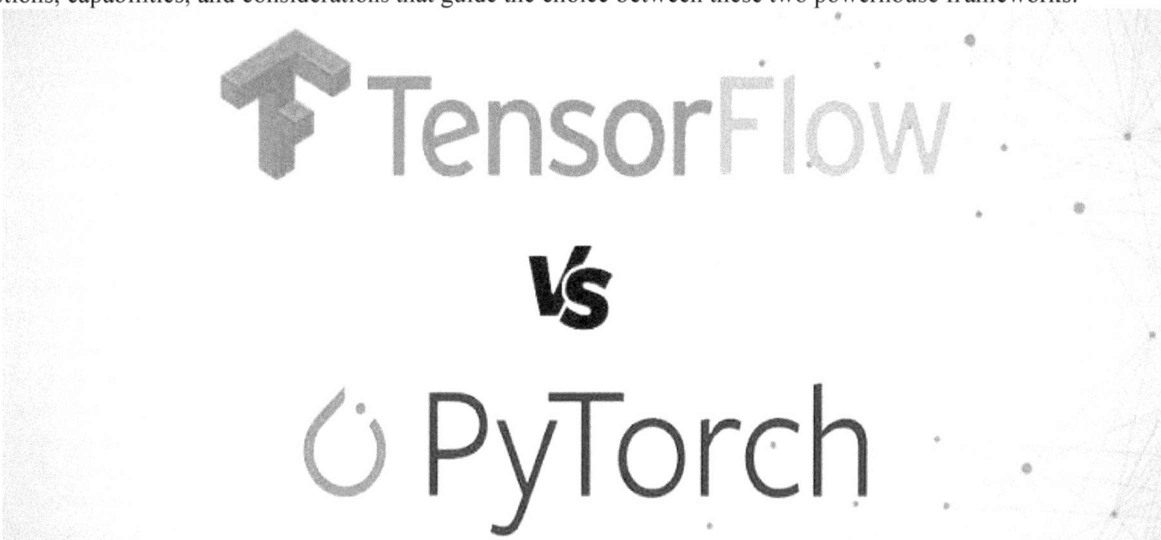

8.1.1 TensorFlow: Engineering Precision: TensorFlow, developed by Google, stands as a cornerstone in the deep learning ecosystem. Renowned for its scalability and robustness, TensorFlow offers a high-level abstraction that facilitates the development of complex neural networks. Its dataflow and computation graph model enable efficient execution on a range of hardware, from CPUs to GPUs and even specialized accelerators.

Strengths of TensorFlow:

Production-Ready: TensorFlow's focus on scalability and deployment readiness makes it an ideal choice for production environments. It offers tools like TensorFlow Serving and TensorFlow Lite for serving models in various contexts.

Wide Adoption: TensorFlow's strong presence in academia and industry results in a plethora of resources, tutorials, and pre-trained models. This ecosystem supports rapid development and experimentation.

TensorBoard: An integrated visualization tool, TensorBoard, aids in model debugging, visualization, and monitoring, enhancing the development process.

8.1.2 PyTorch: Researcher's Playground: PyTorch, backed by Facebook's AI Research group, has gained rapid popularity, especially in the research community. It offers dynamic computation graphs, allowing developers to define and modify models on the fly. PyTorch's "define-by-run" philosophy aligns well with experimentation and research-driven development.

Strengths of PyTorch:

Elegant and Intuitive: PyTorch's dynamic computational graph and Pythonic design make it intuitive and easy to learn, ideal for researchers who want to iterate quickly.

Debugging and Profiling: PyTorch's dynamic nature simplifies model debugging and profiling, facilitating faster identification and resolution of issues.

Tight Integration: The PyTorch ecosystem offers seamless integration with libraries like NumPy, SciPy, and scikit-learn, enhancing flexibility and compatibility.

8.1.3 Choosing between TensorFlow and PyTorch: Considerations: The choice between TensorFlow and PyTorch depends on various factors:

Use Case: TensorFlow's production-oriented capabilities make it a solid choice for deploying models at scale. PyTorch's research-friendly design caters to iterative experimentation and prototyping.

Learning Curve: TensorFlow's abstraction may feel more familiar to software engineers, while PyTorch's dynamic nature appeals to those who prefer a more hands-on approach.

Community and Resources: TensorFlow's extensive community and resources provide comprehensive support, while PyTorch's growing popularity is rapidly expanding its resource pool.

Hardware and Deployment: TensorFlow's support for a wide range of hardware makes it an excellent choice for edge devices and cloud deployments. PyTorch, although catching up, might have slightly fewer deployment options.

8.1.4 The Framework Evolution: Navigating TensorFlow and PyTorch's Progress: In the ever-evolving landscape of deep learning frameworks, TensorFlow and PyTorch stand as beacons of innovation. Both frameworks continually push boundaries, introducing new features and enhancements that cater to diverse needs, from research-driven experimentation to production-grade deployments.

TensorFlow: TensorFlow, as a stalwart in the deep learning realm, has undergone significant changes in its evolution. The transition to TensorFlow 2.x marked a pivotal shift, introducing eager execution and an enhanced API design. Eager execution allows developers to execute operations immediately, resulting in more intuitive and dynamic development experiences. This departure from the traditional static computation graph model has bridged the gap between imperative programming and TensorFlow's inherent computational power. As a result, TensorFlow 2.x offers a smoother learning curve and facilitates rapid prototyping, enabling developers to iterate swiftly.

PyTorch: PyTorch, renowned for its researcher-friendly design, continues to evolve with a dual focus on research and deployment. The introduction of TorchScript exemplifies this evolution, enabling the conversion of PyTorch models into a serialized representation that can be executed independently. This enhancement propels PyTorch into the realm of production, making it easier to deploy models to environments beyond research and experimentation. TorchScript's integration with PyTorch seamlessly marries research agility with production readiness.

Furthermore, the emergence of PyTorch Lightning further streamlines model development and training. PyTorch Lightning abstracts away boilerplate code, simplifying complex training loops and enabling researchers to focus on model architecture and experimentation. This abstraction enhances code readability, maintainability, and collaboration, amplifying PyTorch's appeal as a research-oriented framework.

Paving the Path Ahead: The framework evolution of both TensorFlow and PyTorch underscores their adaptability and commitment to meeting the evolving needs of the AI community. TensorFlow's embrace of eager execution and a more intuitive API amplifies its appeal to developers seeking seamless prototyping and experimentation. PyTorch, on the other hand, responds to the demands of both researchers and deployers, augmenting its capabilities with TorchScript and PyTorch Lightning.

8.1.5 Embracing Versatility: Navigating the Dynamic AI Landscape: The perpetual debate between TensorFlow and PyTorch stands as a testament to the rich diversity that defines the AI landscape. This dilemma mirrors the intricate tapestry of possibilities, needs, and aspirations that shape the realm of deep learning. The choice between these two powerhouse frameworks is not merely a technical decision: it's an exploration of the spectrum of capabilities they offer, each catering to distinct facets of AI development. In this realm of choice, myriad factors intertwine to guide your selection, and the framework you choose becomes a compass steering your path through the multifaceted world of deep learning.

A Multidimensional Choice: The decision between TensorFlow and PyTorch transcends a one-size-fits-all solution. It's a nuanced deliberation where project requirements, developer preferences, and the intended application converge. The nature of your endeavor wields considerable influence. If you're venturing into the domain of production systems, TensorFlow's prowess in scalability and deployment readiness beckons. Its tools for serving models and established presence in the industry offer a stable foundation for real-world implementations.

The Confluence of Factors:

The TensorFlow vs. PyTorch dilemma embraces a constellation of factors that intertwine and influence your decision:

Learning Curve: TensorFlow's structured abstraction and PyTorch's dynamic nature cater to different learning preferences. Your comfort with these paradigms plays a role in determining which framework aligns with your style.

Community and Resources: TensorFlow's extensive community and PyTorch's burgeoning popularity endow you with a plethora of resources, tutorials, and pre-trained models. The ecosystem you wish to immerse yourself in affects your ability to tap into a wealth of knowledge.

Use Case and Domain: The nature of your project—be it production deployment, research experimentation, computer vision, NLP, or any other domain—shapes the framework that aligns with your needs.

Deployment and Hardware: TensorFlow's versatile deployment options and compatibility with various hardware platforms offer stability for diverse scenarios. PyTorch's deployment capabilities, although expanding, might have slight limitations in certain contexts.

An Evolutionary Journey: As you embark on your deep learning journey, the choice between TensorFlow and PyTorch is more than a selection—it's a testament to your adaptability and flexibility. Just as AI models evolve, so does your decision-making. The framework you choose molds your experience, guiding how you develop, experiment, and deploy AI solutions. Embracing this versatility, you acknowledge that the AI landscape is a tapestry woven from diverse threads, and your choice of framework adds a unique hue to this vibrant canvas.

8.2 Data Preprocessing and Augmentation Techniques: Crafting Robust Training Data

In the intricate dance of deep learning, the quality of training data plays a pivotal role in shaping the performance and generalization of AI models. Data preprocessing and augmentation techniques emerge as powerful allies, equipping developers with tools to enhance the quality, diversity, and resilience of their training datasets. This section delves into the art of data preparation, exploring how preprocessing and augmentation empower AI models to navigate real-world complexities and deliver remarkable results.

8.2.1 Data Preprocessing: Laying the Foundation: Data preprocessing serves as the cornerstone of effective deep learning. It involves transforming raw data into a format that AI models can comprehend and process. The goals of preprocessing include normalizing data, handling missing values, and ensuring data consistency. Techniques such as feature scaling, one-hot encoding, and data imputation contribute to a cleaner, standardized dataset, setting the stage for meaningful learning.

8.2.2 Data Augmentation: Cultivating Diversity for Robust Learning: In the realm of deep learning, data augmentation stands as a transformative technique that infuses datasets with vitality and adaptability. This artful approach addresses the conundrum of overfitting while elevating models' capacity to generalize beyond the confines of their training samples. With a palette of controlled transformations, data augmentation enhances the richness of training examples, unveiling a tapestry of possibilities that embolden AI models to thrive in the real world.

Augmentation's Mission: Overfitting, the arch-nemesis of model performance, occurs when a model becomes too attuned to the peculiarities of the training data. Subpar generalization and compromised performance on unseen data. Data augmentation offers a strategic countermeasure, introducing controlled variations that simulate real-world scenarios. This empowers models to adapt and make accurate predictions across diverse inputs.

Transformation Palette: Data augmentation's creative palette is brimming with transformations that rejuvenate existing images:

Rotation: Rotating images by specified degrees introduces angular diversity, mimicking different orientations commonly encountered in real-world scenarios.

Cropping: Cropping focuses attention on specific regions, enhancing models' robustness against varied framing and object positioning.

Flipping: Horizontal or vertical flipping introduces mirror images, equipping models to recognize objects regardless of their orientation.

Color Adjustments: Tinkering with brightness, contrast, and saturation imbues images with variations in lighting and tonality.

Diverse Impacts: The diversity bestowed by data augmentation extends beyond numerical metrics—it equips models to tackle intricacies in real-world settings. When a self-driving car navigates through shifting lighting conditions or an image classifier identifies objects from multiple angles, the robustness forged through augmentation becomes evident. Augmentation ensures that AI models are well-equipped to traverse the diverse landscapes they'll inevitably encounter.

Enrichment through Diversity: Data augmentation amplifies the richness of the training dataset. By generating multiple variations of each original image, augmentation augments the dataset's size, facilitating more comprehensive learning. The enhanced dataset includes a myriad of plausible scenarios, allowing models to grasp a more nuanced understanding of the underlying patterns.

Nurturing Generalization: Data augmentation's role transcends mere augmentation—it's about nurturing generalization. The controlled variations infused into the training data elevate models from memorizers to adaptable learners. Models trained with augmented data learn to perceive objects, features, and patterns in a manner that embraces variations. As AI models venture beyond their training cocoon, their ability to recognize, adapt, and predict across diverse inputs becomes their hallmark of excellence.

8.2.3 Text Data Preprocessing: Beyond Words: Text data preprocessing brings order to the world of language. Tokenization splits text into meaningful units, such as words or subwords. Stemming and lemmatization reduce words to their root forms, enhancing the model's ability to grasp context. Stop-word removal eliminates insignificant words, streamlining text representation. Text vectorization techniques, like TF-IDF and word embeddings, transform text into numerical representations compatible with AI models.

8.2.4 Image Data Augmentation: Visual Diversity: Image data augmentation adds a visual spin to data enrichment. Techniques like random cropping, flipping, rotation, and zooming expand the diversity of training images, making models robust to variations in lighting, orientation, and perspective. By applying these transformations randomly, during training, models learn to recognize objects irrespective of their presentation in the training set.

8.2.5 Audio Data Preprocessing: Sound Engineering: In the realm of deep learning, the resonance of audio data poses unique challenges and opportunities. Audio data preprocessing emerges as the conductor of this sonic symphony, orchestrating the harmonization and transformation of auditory signals into a format comprehensible to AI models. This melodic journey involves techniques that span from visual representation to quality enhancement, forging a path for AI models to decipher spoken language, identify sounds, and even create music.

The Harmony of Spectrogram Conversion: Audio data, a cascade of sound waves, finds an unconventional translation through spectrogram conversion. This transformative technique breaks down audio into its constituent frequencies and time intervals, yielding a visual representation. Spectrograms enable AI models to process audio like images, discerning patterns across time and frequency. This fusion of sight and sound equips models to recognize phonemes, distinguish musical notes, and even unravel the rhythms of spoken language.

Fine-Tuning with Normalization and Resampling: The sonorous tapestry of audio data often carries fluctuations in volume and frequency. Normalization sweeps through this auditory landscape, adjusting the amplitude to ensure consistent loudness across different samples. Resampling enters the scene, altering the sampling rate to harmonize the data, facilitating easier analysis and comparison. By fine-tuning the quality of audio data, normalization and resampling pave the way for more robust model training and accurate results.

Reducing Noise, Amplifying Signal: In the auditory realm, noise is a pervasive companion that obscures the clarity of signals. Noise reduction techniques arise as saviors, aiming to isolate and extract the desired signal from the noise-laden backdrop. Filtering methods, like spectral subtraction, and machine learning approaches, such as denoising autoencoders, dive into the realm of sound to differentiate signal from noise. This careful extraction restores the fidelity of audio data, enhancing the model's capacity to perceive and understand.

Crafting Sound for AI's Ears: The orchestra of audio preprocessing lays the foundation for AI models to excel in an array of auditory tasks:

Speech Recognition: By deciphering spoken language, AI models transform audio into text, enhancing accessibility and communication.

Sound Identification: From recognizing bird calls to identifying musical instruments, AI models trained on preprocessed audio unveil a world of soundscapes.

Music Generation: Audio preprocessing fuels AI models that compose music, harnessing patterns and harmonies from preprocessed data.

The Sonata of Preprocessing: Audio data preprocessing transcends traditional analysis—it's a multisensory journey that bridges the realms of sound and sight. Through spectrogram conversion, normalization, resampling, and noise reduction, audio data is harmonized, refined, and empowered for the AI realm. Just as an audio engineer sculpts soundscapes, data preprocessing crafts a symphony of data ready for AI models to learn, interpret, and ultimately transform the auditory world into a domain of insight and creativity.

8.2.6 The Art of Balancing: Class Imbalance: Data preprocessing extends its influence to addressing class imbalance—a scenario where certain classes are underrepresented. Techniques like oversampling, undersampling, and generating synthetic samples restore balance, ensuring that AI models don't disproportionately favor dominant classes and can generalize effectively across all classes.

8.2.7 Data Preprocessing and Augmentation Tools: Framework Integration: Deep learning frameworks often incorporate data preprocessing and augmentation tools. TensorFlow's `tf.data` API and Keras's image data generators streamline these processes. Similarly, PyTorch's `torchvision. Transforms` offers image augmentation, and text preprocessing libraries like NLTK and spaCy enrich text data.

8.2.8 The Path to Resilient Models: Data preprocessing and augmentation techniques act as sculptors, refining raw data into the clay from which AI models are molded. The transformation and diversification they provide enable models to thrive in complex, real-world environments. Just as a craftsman shapes a masterpiece, developers wield preprocessing and augmentation to craft resilient AI models that adapt, generalize, and perform with finesse across diverse scenarios.

8.3 Model Deployment: Navigating Challenges and Embracing Best Practices: The journey of a deep learning model doesn't culminate in training: it extends to deployment—a critical phase where AI ventures into the real world to make an impact. However, the path to successful model deployment is laden with challenges, from compatibility issues to performance bottlenecks. This section delves into the intricacies of model deployment, highlighting the challenges that await and unveiling best practices to ensure a seamless transition from training to real-world application.

8.3.1 Challenges on the Deployment Horizon: Model deployment isn't without its share of obstacles, each demanding thoughtful consideration:

Platform Compatibility: Models trained on specific frameworks might encounter compatibility issues when deployed on different platforms or devices. Ensuring the model's compatibility across different environments is paramount.

Latency and Speed: Real-world applications demand speedy predictions. Balancing model complexity and computational demands with low latency is a perpetual challenge.

Resource Constraints: Deploying on edge devices or in resource-constrained environments requires optimizing models for efficient memory and processing utilization.

Scalability: When models need to serve numerous users concurrently, scalability becomes a key concern, necessitating deployment solutions that can handle increased demand.

Data Privacy and Security: Deployed models must adhere to stringent privacy regulations and protect sensitive user data, necessitating robust security measures.

Versioning and Updates: Models evolve with time, demanding mechanisms for version control and seamless updates to ensure that deployed models remain current and effective.

8.3.2 Best Practices for Seamless Model Deployment: The art of model deployment requires finesse and meticulous planning to ensure that the journey from the AI laboratory to the real world is smooth and impactful. To overcome the challenges that await and unlock the potential of your models, consider these best practices:

Containerization: Containerization, led by tools like Docker, encapsulates your model, its dependencies, and configurations into a single package. This package, or container, ensures that your model behaves consistently across different environments, eliminating the notorious "it works on my machine" phenomenon.

Microservices Architecture: Breaking your application into Microservices facilitates modular deployment. Each microservice handles a specific component, allowing for independent updates and scalability. This architecture streamlines development, testing, and deployment of individual services without affecting the entire system.

Model Optimization: Optimizing your model is crucial for deployment efficiency. Techniques like quantization, pruning, and compression reduce the model's size and resource demands while maintaining performance. This optimization enhances both deployment speed and resource utilization.

Load Testing: Rigorous load testing replicates real-world usage patterns, unveiling performance bottlenecks and areas that require optimization. By subjecting your deployed model to simulated high-demand scenarios, you gain insights into its behavior under stress and can fine-tune its performance.

Continuous Monitoring: Ongoing monitoring and logging are essential to track your model's performance in the wild. They help you identify anomalies, unusual behaviors, and potential issues that might arise as your model interacts with real-world data. This vigilance allows for timely interventions and improvements.

A/B Testing: Deploying different versions of your model concurrently—known as A/B testing—enables performance comparison and gradual rollout of updates. This iterative approach allows you to evaluate the impact of changes in a controlled manner before deploying them to a broader audience.

Security Measures: Implement robust security measures to protect your model and user data. Encryption, access controls, and regular security audits ensure that your deployed model adheres to privacy regulations and safeguards sensitive information from potential threats.

Orchestrating Excellence: Each best practice in model deployment orchestrates a symphony of preparation, execution, and optimization. Just as a conductor guides musicians to create harmonious melodies, these practices guide your model from its creation to a crescendo of real-world impact. As you navigate the intricacies of deployment, remember that excellence lies in the intersection of technical prowess, thoughtful planning, and unwavering dedication to ensuring that your AI model's journey delivers exceptional results.

8.3.3 Ethical Considerations and Transparency: Beyond technical challenges, ethical concerns loom large in model deployment. Ensuring models are unbiased, transparent, and accountable is paramount. Models that impact human lives—be it in healthcare, finance, or criminal justice—must undergo rigorous testing for fairness and unintended biases.

8.3.4 The Deployment Dance: A Continuous Iteration of Excellence: Model deployment marks the transition of AI from theory to action, but it's not a grand finale—it's the opening act of an ongoing performance. Like a dance that evolves with each step, model deployment is an iterative process that demands constant adaptation, refinement, and engagement. This section unveils the intricacies of this deployment dance, where models interact with real-world scenarios and user feedback to evolve and thrive.

The Dance Begins: Initial Deployment: The deployment dance commences with the release of your AI model into the wild. As it interacts with real-world data, it faces the trials and triumphs that are impossible to foresee in controlled environments. The insights gained from this initial deployment serve as the foundation for the ongoing refinement process.

Embracing User Feedback: A Dynamic Choreography: Users' experiences and feedback fuel the iterative nature of model deployment. Their interactions reveal nuances, uncover shortcomings, and inspire improvements. Whether it's a recommendation system that learns from user preferences or a healthcare AI that adapts based on medical professional feedback, user engagement is integral to the dance's evolution.

Refinement through Regular Updates: A Dance of Progress: Just as dancers rehearse to enhance their performance, models require regular updates to refine their capabilities. As your model encounters new scenarios, unexpected challenges, and novel data distributions, these updates enable it to adapt and improve its performance. These updates ensure that your model remains current and effective in the face of changing dynamics.

Continuous Monitoring: The Dance's Rhythm: Monitoring becomes the rhythm of the deployment dance. Real-world scenarios are unpredictable, and as your model navigates them, monitoring reveals performance insights, detects anomalies, and prompts timely interventions. Like the beat that guides a dancer's steps, monitoring guides the model's path to success.

Adapting to Evolving Needs: Dance of Relevance: The world evolves, and so do the needs of users. The deployment dance demands that your model remains relevant by understanding shifting preferences and requirements. Whether it's adjusting an AI-driven e-commerce recommendation system to align with changing consumer trends or fine-tuning a chatbot's responses based on evolving user interactions, relevance is key.

Scaling and Expansion: A Dance Ensemble: The dance doesn't end with one model—it's a synchronized ensemble. As your model proves its mettle in one context, it may be time to expand its reach. Scaling to serve more users, accommodating different languages, or adapting to diverse regions all require the model to perform flawlessly in new stages of the deployment dance.

The Ongoing Overture of Impact: The deployment dance isn't a static performance: it's an ongoing overture of impact. Each iteration, user interaction, and update propel the model towards excellence. Like a dance that resonates with the audience, your model's continuous evolution ensures it remains attuned to real-world needs, dances through challenges, and evolves into a powerful force that transforms industries and experiences.

8.3.5 The Realization of Impact: Model deployment is the conduit through which deep learning transforms from theory to reality. It's where models cease to be experiments and start affecting the lives of individuals and industries. While challenges abound, they're surmountable with a strategic approach and dedication to best practices. By navigating compatibility, performance, and ethical considerations, you're poised to embark on a journey where the impact of AI unfolds in tangible, transformative ways.

8.4 Tools for Navigating the Depths: Monitoring and Debugging Deep Learning Models: As deep learning models embark on their journeys, traversing intricate landscapes of data and computation, the need for effective monitoring and debugging becomes paramount. This section delves into the tools that illuminate the path, revealing insights, diagnosing issues, and ensuring that models sail smoothly through their development and deployment phases.

8.4.1 Insights from Model Visualization: Visualization tools cast light into the dark corners of model behavior:

TensorBoard (TensorFlow): This visualization suite offers a graphical representation of model metrics, learning curves, and even interactive visualizations of network architectures.

Weights & Biases: With a focus on experiment tracking and visualization, this tool helps you visualize model performance, hyperparameters, and even individual predictions.

8.4.2 Probing with Debugging Tools: Debugging tools pierce through the veil of complexity to uncover issues:

The intricate world of deep learning models can often conceal issues that impact performance and reliability. Debugging tools emerge as powerful instruments to pierce through this veil of complexity, uncovering hidden anomalies and hitches that might otherwise go unnoticed. This section shines a spotlight on the tools that serve as your virtual magnifying glasses, allowing you to identify and address issues in your models with precision.

tf.debugging (TensorFlow): Unveiling Hidden Anomalies:

TensorFlow's debugging module, tf.debugging, acts as a virtual detective, equipped to uncover issues in different facets of your model:

Model Inputs and Outputs: tf.debugging tools let you inspect and validate your model's inputs and outputs, ensuring that they align with your expectations. This scrutiny is particularly useful for catching data-related issues that could impact training and inference.

Intermediate Values: Debugging intermediate values during training is crucial for identifying anomalies that arise during computation. tf.debugging empowers you to peek into these values, revealing unexpected patterns or irregularities.

torch.autograd.detect_anomaly (PyTorch): Spotting the Unusual:

In the realm of PyTorch, the torch.autograd.detect_anomaly function takes on the role of a vigilant anomaly detector:

Autograd Computations: This function acts as a sentinel during Autograd computations, flagging any anomalies it encounters. It's particularly valuable during backpropagation, as it can help you pinpoint where numerical issues or irregularities might be creeping in.

Anomaly Origins: Not only does detect_anomaly flag anomalies, but it also traces their origins. This provides critical insights into which part of your model's computation chain might be giving rise to unexpected behaviors.

Precision Diagnosis for Swift Resolution: Debugging tools are the scalpel in your toolkit, allowing you to perform precision diagnosis on your deep learning models. Whether it's TensorFlow's tf.debugging suite, which exposes anomalies in inputs, outputs, and intermediate values, or PyTorch's torch.autograd.detect_anomaly function, which spots issues during Autograd computations, these tools empower you to identify problems and their origins. Armed with these tools, you're ready to execute swift resolutions, ensuring that your models navigate the complex landscape of deep learning with grace and precision.

8.4.3 Monitoring Performance and Behavior: Monitoring tools keep a watchful eye on model performance and dynamics:

Prometheus and Grafana: This dynamic duo allows you to collect, store, and visualize metrics, offering insights into system performance, resource usage, and more.

Weights & Biases (Again!): Beyond visualization, it excels in monitoring, tracking metrics in real time during training and deployment.

8.4.4 Alerts and Notifications: Tools that notify you when the unexpected occurs:

In the intricate dance of deep learning models, where every step holds the potential for both success and stumbling, staying informed is paramount. Alerts and notifications emerge as the vigilant partners that keep you apprised of the unexpected, ensuring that you're always poised to respond swiftly and effectively. This section delves into the tools that act as your guardians, alerting you when errors or anomalies arise, and custom integrations that ensure critical updates and insights reach you promptly.

Sentry: The Guardian of Codebase:

Integrating seamlessly with your codebase, Sentry steps into the role of a vigilant guardian, equipped to alert you when errors or anomalies rear their heads:

Error Monitoring: Sentry detects errors in your application, from minor hiccups to critical failures. It captures error context, stack traces, and related information for thorough diagnosis.

Alerts and Notifications: When an error occurs, Sentry sends alerts to notify you. These alerts can be tailored to your preferences, ensuring that you're informed in the manner that best suits your workflow.

Slack and Email Notifications: Custom Signals of Vigilance: Custom integrations with platforms like Slack and email become your tailored signals of vigilance, pinging you with the critical updates and insights you need:
Slack: With Slack integrations, alerts can be channeled directly to dedicated channels or your preferred teams. This ensures that the right individuals are notified, fostering swift collaboration and response.
Email Notifications: Email notifications act as a traditional yet reliable means of conveying critical updates. Customizable email alerts keep you informed even when you're away from your immediate work environment.
Swift Response and Continuous Vigilance: In the realm of deep learning, where models navigate complex terrain and unforeseen challenges, a swift response can make all the difference. Alerts and notifications tools are your watchful sentinels, standing ready to alert you when errors, anomalies, or critical updates arise. Whether it's Sentry that keeps a watchful eye on your codebase or custom integrations that ensure updates reach you in real time, these tools ensure that you're always poised to respond with agility, safeguarding the integrity and performance of your deep learning endeavors.
8.4.5 Profiling and Optimization: In the intricate realm of deep learning, achieving optimal performance requires more than just elegant architectures and sophisticated algorithms. Profiling and optimization tools emerge as the magnifying glasses that uncover the hidden layers of efficiency bottlenecks, allowing you to fine-tune your models for peak performance. This section delves into the tools that dissect performance bottlenecks and enable you to optimize the efficiency of your deep learning endeavors.
TensorFlow Profiler and PyTorch Profiler: Navigating the Labyrinth: These profiling tools—TensorFlow Profiler and PyTorch Profiler—are like expert navigators that guide you through the labyrinth of model performance:
TensorFlow Profiler: With TensorFlow Profiler, you're equipped to dissect intricate layers of performance metrics during model training and inference. It unveils where time and resources are being consumed, allowing you to pinpoint bottlenecks that might be impeding efficiency.
PyTorch Profiler: Just like a skilled investigator, PyTorch Profiler delves deep into the operations of your PyTorch model. It aids in uncovering areas that demand optimization, revealing how time is allocated across different parts of your model.
NVIDIA Nsight Systems and Intel VTune Profiler: Delving into the Hardware Abyss: For those diving into the depths of hardware-level performance analysis, NVIDIA Nsight Systems and Intel VTune Profiler shine as luminous beacons:
NVIDIA Nsight Systems: When your model harnesses the power of GPUs, NVIDIA Nsight Systems takes you to the core of GPU performance. It offers insights into GPU utilization, memory access patterns, and more, ensuring your model effectively leverages the GPU's computational prowess.
Intel VTune Profiler: For CPU profiling, Intel VTune Profiler reveals the intricacies of how your model interacts with the CPU. It offers insights into threading, memory usage, and other hardware-related aspects that influence overall performance.
Optimization: Sculpting Efficiency: Once you've identified performance bottlenecks through profiling, optimization becomes your chisel to sculpt efficiency:
Parallelism and Concurrency: Profiling might reveal opportunities to exploit parallelism and concurrency in your model's operations, optimizing resource utilization.
Memory Management: Efficient memory allocation and usage can significantly impact performance. Optimization involves minimizing memory overhead and avoiding unnecessary allocations.
Algorithmic Tweaks: Profiling might expose algorithmic inefficiencies. Fine-tuning algorithms can lead to significant performance improvements.
Hardware-Specific Optimization: With insights from profiling tools, you can tailor optimizations to specific hardware architectures, ensuring that your model takes full advantage of available resources.
The Quest for Efficiency: In the realm of deep learning, efficiency is a treasure worth pursuing. Profiling and optimization tools are the compasses that guide you through this quest. Armed with insights from TensorFlow Profiler, PyTorch Profiler, NVIDIA Nsight Systems, and Intel VTune Profiler, you're empowered to unearth bottlenecks, optimize performance, and sculpt models that achieve peak efficiency. Just as master artisans shape raw materials into exquisite creations, these tools empower you to shape your deep learning models into efficient and impactful solutions.
8.4.6 Ethical Auditing: Tools that ensure your models adhere to ethical standards:
IBM AI Fairness 360: This toolkit helps detect and mitigate bias in machine learning models, ensuring ethical and unbiased outcomes.
Google's What-If Tool: It empowers you to probe and visualize the impact of various inputs on model predictions, aiding in ethical decision-making.
8.4.7 Navigating Unseen Depths: Monitoring and debugging tools are the compasses that guide you through the intricate depths of deep learning. Armed with visualization, debugging, monitoring, and optimization tools, you're equipped to illuminate model behavior, diagnose issues, optimize performance, and ensure ethical integrity. As you traverse the journey from inception to deployment, these tools stand as your trusted companions, ensuring that your models perform with the precision and impact they were designed for.

8.5 Project

Unsolved Project

Suppose you're preparing to deploy a deep learning model for a real-world application. To ensure a smooth and effective deployment, you need to choose the right framework, preprocess and augment your data, understand the challenges and best practices of model deployment, and be familiar with tools for monitoring and debugging deep learning models. Before starting, study the following: the differences between TensorFlow and PyTorch and how to choose the right framework for your project, various data preprocessing and augmentation techniques, the challenges you might face during model deployment and best practices to overcome them, and the tools available for monitoring and debugging deep learning models. This foundational knowledge will help you deploy a robust and reliable deep learning model.

8.6 Lab Activity

Unsolved Lab Activity

Implement data preprocessing and augmentation techniques on an image dataset using a deep learning framework.

Task: Use a deep learning framework to apply preprocessing and augmentation techniques to an image dataset (e.g., CIFAR-10). Document the implementation process and provide visualizations of the augmented images.

Exercises

Exercise 1 – Multiple Choice Questions

1. What is the main focus of the chapter titled "TensorFlow vs. PyTorch"?
   a. Comparing TensorFlow and PyTorch in terms of popularity
   b. Exploring the evolution of deep learning frameworks
   c. Discussing the importance of data preprocessing
   d. Deciphering the differences between TensorFlow and PyTorch
2. Which organization developed TensorFlow?
   a. Facebook
   b. Google
   c. Amazon
   d. Microsoft
3. What is one of the strengths of TensorFlow mentioned in the text?
   a. Its dynamic computation graph
   b. Its "define-by-run" philosophy
   c. Wide adoption and available resources
   d. Integration with libraries like NumPy
4. Which visualization tool is integrated with TensorFlow to aid in model debugging and monitoring?
   a. TensorBoard
   b. Matplotlib
   c. PyPlot
   d. Chart.js
5. What is PyTorch known for in the deep learning community?
   a. Scalability
   b. Robustness
   c. "Define-by-run" philosophy
   d. Hardware compatibility

Exercise 2 – True/False

1. PyTorch is known for its dynamic computation graph, which makes it more flexible and easier to debug compared to TensorFlow.
2. Data preprocessing and augmentation techniques are only necessary for small datasets.
3. One of the main challenges in model deployment is ensuring that the deployed model performs consistently in different environments.

Review Questions

1. What are the key strengths of TensorFlow, and how does it excel in production environments?
2. Describe the "define-by-run" philosophy of PyTorch and why it is favored by researchers.
3. How does TensorBoard aid in model development and debugging in TensorFlow?
4. What are some considerations when choosing between TensorFlow and PyTorch for a deep learning project?
5. What is the purpose of data preprocessing in deep learning, and what are some common techniques used in this phase?
6. How does data augmentation contribute to model robustness, and what are some common image data augmentation techniques?
7. Why is class imbalance an issue in deep learning, and what methods can be employed to address it?
8. What are some challenges faced during model deployment, and why is platform compatibility important?
9. How can model optimization help in achieving efficient deployment?

Answers

Exercise 1- 1. d 2. b 3. c 4. a 5. c

Exercise 2- 1) True, 2) False, 3) True

Online Resources

Online Exam Paper:
Link: **https://forms.gle/yRFfmbcbaKpyKep99**
QR Code:

Chapter 8 Videos Playlist:
Link: **https://www.youtube.com/playlist?list=PLzlh_31VWEFrrjDjyLWypIIpkkt9kRkKC**
QR Code:

Chapter 9: Ethical Considerations and Future Directions

9.1 Navigating Bias and Fairness in Deep Learning: As deep learning models increasingly shape our world, the need to address bias and ensure fairness becomes a moral and ethical imperative. This chapter takes you on a profound exploration of the challenges and strategies involved in addressing bias and promoting fairness within the realm of deep learning.

9.1.1 Understanding Bias in AI: Bias in AI isn't a mere technical glitch: it's a reflection of real-world inequalities that can perpetuate discrimination and reinforce societal disparities. This section delves into the nuances of bias in AI, highlighting its origins, manifestations, and impact on decision-making processes.

9.1.2 The Fairness Conundrum: Ensuring fairness isn't a one-size-fits-all solution: it's a multifaceted challenge that requires delicate handling. This section uncovers the complexity of fairness considerations, illuminating how different notions of fairness can clash and how ethical trade-offs come into play.

9.1.3 Quantifying Bias and Fairness: Unveiling Hidden Biases: In the realm of AI, where models wield influence and shape decisions, the need to quantify bias and assess fairness is paramount. This section unfurls the toolkit of robust metrics and methodologies that empower you to dissect bias in AI models and gauge their fairness. It offers a glimpse into how to unravel potential sources of discrimination that might otherwise remain concealed.

Bias Metrics: Illuminating Disparities: Bias metrics are the magnifying glasses that expose disparities within AI models:

Disparate Impact: This metric gauges whether different groups are treated differently by a model's predictions, focusing on the ratio of favorable outcomes across groups.

Statistical Parity: Statistical parity examines whether groups receive favorable outcomes at similar rates, irrespective of their demographic characteristics.

Fairness Metrics: Balancing Equitability: Fairness metrics strive to balance the scales of equitability within AI models:

Equal Opportunity Difference: This metric quantifies the disparity in true positive rates between different groups, focusing on the equality of opportunity for positive outcomes.

Average Odds Difference: Average odds difference probes into both false positive and true positive disparities, encompassing a broader assessment of fairness.

Methodologies for Fairness Assessment: Peeling Back Layers: Fairness assessment methodologies act as detectives, peeling back layers to uncover hidden biases:

Group-Based Metrics: These assess bias across different demographic groups, unearthing disparities that might arise based on race, gender, or other protected attributes.

Individual Fairness: Going beyond groups, individual fairness assesses whether similar individuals receive similar predictions, mitigating bias at a granular level.

Identifying Discrimination Sources: Shining a Light: Quantifying bias and assessing fairness isn't just about numbers: it's about identifying the sources of discrimination:

Causal Analysis: This methodology delves into causality, uncovering whether bias arises due to unjustifiable factors or legitimate ones.

Feature Importance Analysis: By assessing which features carry more weight in predictions, this analysis helps unveil whether bias emanates from specific input attributes.

The Pursuit of Unveiling: In the journey toward addressing bias and promoting fairness, quantifying and assessing are the torches that light the way. With bias metrics and fairness metrics, you shine a light on disparities and disparities, gauging whether equitability prevails. Methodologies like group-based metrics and individual fairness methodologies act as your guides, leading you through the labyrinth of potential discrimination. Armed with these tools, you're equipped to scrutinize AI models, reveal hidden biases, and champion fairness that resonates with the core values of equity and justice.

9.1.4 Unveiling Sources of Bias: Bias often emerges from the data itself, reflecting historical inequities and societal prejudices. This section guides you through techniques that unveil the sources of bias, from data collection and preprocessing to model architecture, offering strategies to mitigate its influence.

9.1.5 Fairness-Aware Machine Learning: Redesigning the Blueprint: In the quest to promote fairness, machine learning must undergo a transformation. This section unveils the burgeoning landscape of fairness-aware machine learning, a realm dedicated to infusing models with a heightened sensitivity to bias and fairness considerations. It explores how this novel approach shapes the very essence of models, from their training to their deployment, to ensure that equity and justice permeate every facet of their existence.

Sensitizing Training Data: Nurturing Fairness: Fairness-aware machine learning commences at the heart of models—the training data:

Fair Data Sampling: This approach involves re-sampling training data to ensure balanced representation across different demographic groups. It mitigates the influence of skewed data distributions that might lead to biased models.

Reweighting Loss Functions: By assigning different weights to different groups, models can be trained to pay equal attention to all demographic categories, mitigating favoritism.

Fairness Constraints: Guiding Model Behavior: Integrating fairness constraints into model training constrains models to behave in a manner that upholds fairness:

Equalized Odds Constraint: This constraint ensures that different groups experience equal false positive and false negative rates, neutralizing disparate impact.
Demographic Parity Constraint: By enforcing that groups receive similar treatment, models avoid perpetuating biases based on protected attributes.
Adversarial Debiasing: Pitting Against Bias: Adversarial debiasing injects a counteracting force against bias during model training:
Adversarial Networks: These networks compete against each other—one strives to predict the protected attribute, while the other aims to make predictions. This adversarial dynamic reduces the model's reliance on protected attributes.
In the Crucible of Deployment: Fairness-aware machine learning doesn't merely shape models during training: it molds their very essence. By sensitizing training data, imposing fairness constraints, and leveraging adversarial debiasing, models emerge as beacons of equity. These models, imbued with a consciousness of fairness, are poised to navigate the real world with sensitivity to bias, promoting fairness in every decision they influence. The emerging field of fairness-aware machine learning reshapes the blueprint of machine learning, ensuring that its creations mirror the values of a just and inclusive society.
9.1.6 Mitigation Strategies: Unveiling the Arsenal: The pursuit of addressing bias and promoting fairness requires a robust toolkit of mitigation strategies. This section unfurls a collection of techniques that span the spectrum, each designed to mitigate bias and foster fairness in the realm of deep learning models.
Pre-Training and Transfer Learning: Anchoring Fairness: Pre-training methods anchor fairness by starting with models that have already learned from diverse data sources:
Domain Adaptation: This technique adapts models from a source domain to a target domain, reducing the impact of distribution shifts that might lead to biased predictions.
Representation Learning: Pre-training models to learn unbiased representations of data, ensuring that sensitive attributes don't dominate predictive outcomes.
Adversarial Training: Pitting Against Bias: Adversarial training introduces a counterbalance to bias by pitting models against themselves:
Adversarial Debiasing: Adversarial networks compete to predict sensitive attributes and predictions. This adversarial dynamic minimizes the influence of these attributes on the model's decisions.
Post-Processing Techniques: Correcting Bias: Post-processing techniques correct models' predictions after they've been made:
Calibration: Calibrating predicted probabilities to align with observed outcomes, reducing the disparities in predicted and actual outcomes.
Re-ranking: Adjusting the ranking of predictions to achieve fairness in the distribution of outcomes.
9.1.7 Beyond Technical Solutions: The Ethical Nexus: While technical solutions form the backbone of addressing bias and promoting fairness, the quest goes beyond algorithms.
Accountability: Fairness isn't just a metric: it's a commitment to accountability. Developers must take responsibility for their models' impact on society, ensuring that biases are proactively addressed.
Transparency: Models' behavior should be transparent, with clear explanations of how decisions are made, enabling stakeholders to scrutinize and understand their workings.
Ethical Considerations: The quest for fairness must be guided by ethical considerations that reflect societal values and principles. Ethical guidelines shape the choices made throughout the development lifecycle.
A Balanced Pursuit: The pursuit of bias mitigation and fairness isn't confined to technical corridors: it's a balanced journey that weds technical excellence with ethical considerations. Through a toolkit of mitigation strategies—pre-training, adversarial training, and post-processing—models are transformed into instruments of equity. Beyond the technical realm, ethical considerations pave the path forward, ensuring that fairness isn't just a metric but a commitment to accountability, transparency, and alignment with societal values. In this holistic approach, AI models cease to be mere algorithms: they emerge as embodiments of ethical and equitable AI.
9.1.8 A Collaborative Pursuit: Building Inclusive AI: Addressing bias and promoting fairness in deep learning is a collaborative endeavor that spans industries, disciplines, and communities. This section emphasizes the importance of multidisciplinary approaches, collaboration, and inclusive design in crafting AI systems that reflect our shared values and aspirations.
9.1.9 Navigating the Moral Compass: In the voyage through the intricate landscape of deep learning, addressing bias and promoting fairness is the moral compass that guides us. From understanding the roots of bias to quantifying and mitigating its impact, this chapter equips you with the tools, strategies, and ethical insights to navigate the complexities of bias and fairness in AI. Armed with this knowledge, you'll be poised to foster a more equitable and just AI future—one that respects the dignity and diversity of all.
9.2 Privacy Concerns and Data Security: Safeguarding the Digital Sanctum: In the age of data-driven technology, privacy concerns and data security have risen to the forefront of the AI landscape. This chapter delves deep into the intricate web of challenges and strategies that revolve around preserving privacy, fortifying data security, and striking a delicate balance between technological advancements and individual rights.
9.2.1 The Spectrum of Privacy Concerns: Balancing Data Utilization and Individual Rights: The realm of privacy concerns is a complex landscape forged by the interplay of data's potential and the preservation of individual rights. This section

embarks on a journey through the intricate nuances of privacy concerns, tracing the contours of the tension between the utilization of data and the protection of individual autonomy.

Data Collection and Usage: At the heart of privacy concerns lies the manner in which data is collected and harnessed. From the vast expanse of personal data collected by organizations to the utilization of user-generated content, this section unravels the multifaceted dimensions of data collection and usage that give rise to privacy considerations.

Potential Misuse of Personal Information: The specter of personal information being exploited for nefarious purposes casts a long shadow over privacy. This section delves into the risks associated with the misuse of sensitive data, ranging from identity theft and financial fraud to the manipulation of user behavior, highlighting the pressing need for safeguards.

Ethical Imperative of Privacy: Privacy isn't just a legal construct: it's an ethical imperative. This section underscores the moral obligation to respect individuals' right to privacy, emphasizing that the quest for data-driven insights must be conducted within the boundaries of ethical considerations that honor personal autonomy and dignity.

9.2.2 Data Privacy Regulations: Guardrails in the Data-Driven Era: In the era of unprecedented data generation and utilization, data privacy regulations have emerged as essential guardrails that shape the landscape. This section delves into the pivotal role played by regulatory frameworks such as GDPR and CCPA in preserving individuals' data rights and redefining the obligations of data handlers.

GDPR (General Data Protection Regulation): This monumental European regulation serves as a cornerstone in the realm of data privacy.

CCPA (California Consumer Privacy Act): Hailing from the tech epicenter of the world, CCPA has set new standards for data privacy in the United States. This section navigates the landscape of CCPA, highlighting its influence on data handling practices and its implications for businesses operating within California's jurisdiction.

Legal Obligations and Accountability: Data processors and controllers bear legal responsibilities to ensure the protection of individuals' data. This section illuminates the legal obligations imposed by these regulations, emphasizing the need for transparency, consent, and mechanisms for individuals to exercise their data rights.

9.2.3 A Tapestry of Safeguards: In the intricate tapestry of privacy concerns and data privacy regulations, the tension between data utilization and individual rights finds a delicate equilibrium. As data becomes a currency of the digital age, privacy concerns become paramount, underpinned by the ethical mandate to protect individuals' autonomy. The emergence of data privacy regulations like GDPR and CCPA brings legal and regulatory dimensions to this discourse, shaping the contours of data utilization within the bounds of individual rights.

9.2.3 Techniques for Privacy-Preserving AI: Nurturing Insight Amidst Privacy: The preservation of privacy need not come at the cost of relinquishing the power of artificial intelligence. This section embarks on an exploration of a diverse array of techniques, each meticulously crafted to enable AI models to glean insights from data without infringing upon the sanctity of privacy.

Differential Privacy: Veiling Individuality in Noise: Differential privacy emerges as a sentinel at the intersection of data utility and privacy preservation. This technique, akin to adding controlled noise, enables data contributors to remain indistinguishable while still yielding valuable insights. By blurring the fine lines between individuals' contributions and ensuring that personal details remain obfuscated, differential privacy safeguards sensitive information without compromising the overarching goal of AI-enabled insights.

Homomorphic Encryption: A Shroud of Encryption Amidst Computation: Homomorphic encryption transcends the boundaries of traditional encryption by allowing computations to be performed directly on encrypted data. This innovation ensures that data remains encrypted throughout the entire processing pipeline, shielding it from prying eyes even during analytical operations. Homomorphic encryption presents a powerful paradigm where AI models can delve into encrypted data, making strides in data analytics while preserving privacy.

Federated Learning: The Collaborative Tapestry of Privacy and Learning: Federated learning paints a vivid picture of privacy preservation achieved through collaborative learning. In this paradigm, models are trained across a network of distributed devices, each harboring its own data. By decentralizing data while centralizing knowledge, federated learning imbues models with insights without ever centralizing sensitive information. This harmonious marriage of distributed data and collective learning not only preserves privacy but also enhances the model's performance.

A Symphony of Techniques: In the symphony of techniques for privacy-preserving AI, the crescendo of innovation is a testament to the human capacity to harmonize technological advancement with ethical considerations. Differential privacy, homomorphic encryption, and federated learning form the cornerstone of this symphony, each note resonating with the desire to unlock the potential of AI while safeguarding individual privacy. As AI ventures further into the realm of data-driven insights, these techniques stand as guardians of personal autonomy, embodying the aspiration to nurture knowledge without sacrificing privacy.

9.2.4 Ethical Considerations: Balancing Innovation and Privacy: The ethical dimensions of privacy and data security are a pivotal anchor. This section emphasizes the need for ethical considerations in technology development, urging practitioners to weigh the potential benefits of AI against the risks of privacy invasion and data breaches.

9.2.5 Evolving Threats and Robust Defense Strategies: In the landscape of data security, threats are dynamic and ever-evolving. This section unveils the array of threats that can compromise data security—ranging from data breaches to adversarial attacks—and sheds light on the defense strategies that safeguard AI systems from potential breaches.

9.2.6 A Harmonious Coexistence: The convergence of technological advancement and individual rights defines the landscape of privacy concerns and data security. With a profound understanding of privacy regulations, privacy-preserving techniques, and the ethical considerations that underpin them, AI practitioners navigate this landscape with the utmost responsibility. In the interplay between innovation and protection, the quest for privacy and data security mirrors the balance between progress and human dignity—an equilibrium that we must steadfastly uphold as we shape the AI-driven future.

9.3 The Future of Deep Learning: Unfolding Emerging Trends: The evolution of deep learning is an ongoing journey, marked by perpetual innovation and transformative shifts. This section peers into the horizon of possibilities, unraveling the emerging trends that promise to redefine the landscape of deep learning in the years to come.

9.3.1 Interdisciplinary Synergy: Unveiling the Confluence of AI and Other Disciplines: The future trajectory of deep learning is marked by a captivating convergence with a myriad of diverse domains. This section serves as a compass, guiding us through the profound intersections that hold the promise of reshaping industries, enhancing understanding, and propelling innovation.

AI and Healthcare: Illuminating Medical Frontiers: Deep learning's foray into healthcare is poised to be transformative. With its remarkable ability to decipher intricate patterns within medical images, deep learning is poised to revolutionize diagnostics. From identifying anomalies in radiological scans to detecting early signs of diseases, such as cancer, the fusion of AI and healthcare is expected to elevate precision medicine to unprecedented levels. Furthermore, deep learning's predictive prowess is set to reshape patient care by forecasting outcomes, enabling timely interventions, and personalizing treatment plans.

AI and Climate Science: Accelerating Environmental Insights: Deep learning is emerging as a stalwart ally in the realm of climate science. The complexities of climate data call for innovative approaches, and AI rises to the challenge. By deciphering intricate data patterns, deep learning holds the potential to forecast climate changes, predict extreme weather events, and model environmental trends. This confluence promises to accelerate climate research, offering insights that can inform policy decisions, guide sustainable practices, and amplify our understanding of the delicate balance of our planet's ecosystems.

AI and Natural Language Processing: Amplifying Linguistic Frontiers: The harmonious fusion of deep learning and natural language processing (NLP) is set to breathe new life into language-driven interactions. Conversational AI, empowered by deep learning, is poised to transcend conventional boundaries, enabling more fluent and contextually relevant interactions between humans and machines. Language translation, content generation, and sentiment analysis are poised to attain unprecedented accuracy and fluidity. As AI becomes more adept at understanding nuances, context, and even emotions embedded in language, it opens doors to a realm of communication that is more natural, intuitive, and human-centric. .

A Symphony of Convergence: The future heralds a symphony of convergence, where the orchestration of AI and various disciplines creates harmonious resonance. The alliance of AI with healthcare, climate science, and natural language processing is not only a testament to the boundless potential of AI but also a testament to the capacity of human ingenuity. As these domains meld and merge, they pave the way for a future where technology and human endeavors coalesce, leading to a reimagined landscape that pushes the boundaries of what is achievable and profoundly impacting the course of humanity.

9.3.2 Federated Learning: The Dawn of Decentralized Intelligence: The trajectory of federated learning is destined to ascend beyond its current status, evolving into a paramount paradigm for nurturing privacy-preserving AI. This section unveils the transformative potential that federated learning holds, ushering in a new era of decentralized intelligence and reshaping the landscape of AI innovation.

Decentralized AI: Nurturing Privacy Through Collaboration: Federated learning emerges as a beacon of privacy preservation by reimagining the way AI models are trained. This collaborative paradigm orchestrates model training across a network of disparate devices, each housing its own treasure trove of data. This decentralized approach is rooted in the philosophy of individual data privacy, allowing AI models to be trained without the need to centralize sensitive information. With federated learning, the power to unlock insights coexists harmoniously with the imperative to respect the privacy and autonomy of each data contributor.

Edge AI: Empowering Intelligence at the Edge: Federated learning's transformative influence extends to the very edge of technology. Edge devices, ranging from smartphones to IoT sensors, become hubs of intelligent decision-making through the potency of federated learning. These devices, equipped with localized models trained through federated learning, transcend mere data collectors and become intelligent actors. This paradigm shift reduces the dependency on centralized processing, expediting decision-making and enhancing responsiveness. The fusion of federated learning and edge AI paints a portrait of a future where intelligence is disseminated, empowering devices to make informed choices locally, without relinquishing data privacy.

The Decentralized Utopia Unveiled: As federated learning matures and extends its influence, the decentralized utopia it paints is one where AI and privacy coexist symbiotically. The collaborative training of models across devices converges with the empowerment of edge devices, birthing a landscape where intelligence isn't confined to centralized systems. The future it envisions is one where AI's prowess is augmented by its alignment with individual autonomy and the intelligent fabric of our connected world.

9.3.3 Explainable and Trustworthy AI: Navigating the Terrain of Accountability: As artificial intelligence finds its way into the very core of critical systems, the clarion call for explainable and trustworthy AI resonates with heightened urgency. This section ventures into the realm where accountability, transparency, and reliability converge, illuminating the pathways towards an AI landscape that is both comprehensible and dependable.

Ethical Considerations: Unveiling the Veil of Decisions: The evolution of AI comes hand in hand with a moral imperative – the demand for AI systems to be accountable for their decisions. Explainability emerges as a guiding light, illuminating the decision-making process within the depths of AI models. Models are no longer enigmatic black boxes: they are required to provide understandable explanations for their choices. This transparency fosters accountability and paves the way for humans to comprehend the rationale behind AI decisions. From medical diagnoses to loan approvals, the ethical underpinning of AI's choices becomes a pillar of trust, enabling users to assess fairness, assess potential biases, and ensure that AI remains a tool for positive impact.

Trustworthy AI: Ensuring the Pillars of Reliability: In an AI-driven world, trustworthiness assumes a position of paramount importance. As AI systems permeate sectors from healthcare to finance, their reliability, robustness, and resilience come to the fore. Ensuring that AI performs optimally in real-world scenarios, despite adversarial challenges or unexpected conditions, becomes a linchpin for its deployment. Models need to withstand the test of real-world complexity, retaining their efficacy and precision. This entails fortifying AI systems against vulnerabilities, addressing potential biases, and enhancing their generalizability. Trustworthy AI upholds its promises even amidst the most intricate landscapes, securing its position as a transformative force that can be entrusted with critical decisions.

Forging the Path of Trust: The journey towards explainable and trustworthy AI isn't just a technological trajectory: it's a covenant that shapes the symbiotic relationship between humans and machines. Ethical considerations, transparency, and the fortification of AI systems lay the foundation for an AI realm where accountability isn't just an aspiration but a reality. As AI transcends its potential and integrates deeper into our lives, the demand for AI to be comprehensible and dependable becomes a resounding chorus – a harmonious blend of technological prowess and ethical stewardship.

9.3.4 Quantum Computing and AI: Unleashing a Nexus of Possibilities: The convergence of quantum computing and artificial intelligence heralds an era of untapped potential. This section delves into the synergy between these two transformative realms, unveiling how quantum computing's capabilities stand poised to propel deep learning into uncharted territories.

Enhanced Optimization: The Quantum Leap: Quantum computing offers a quantum leap in optimization capabilities. Complex functions that form the crux of deep learning, from loss functions to parameter tuning, are poised to experience a revolutionary transformation. Quantum algorithms excel at traversing intricate landscapes of possibilities, accelerating optimization processes that would otherwise be computationally daunting. This newfound optimization prowess augments the training of deep learning models, expediting convergence, enabling the training of deeper architectures, and fostering the exploration of a broader design space.

Solving Complex Problems: Quantum AI's Grand Voyage: Quantum AI embarks on a grand voyage to navigate the depths of complexity. While quantum computing's initial focus may extend to fields like chemistry, physics, and material science, its ramifications echo across the landscape of artificial intelligence. Quantum AI holds the promise of unraveling intricate data patterns, facilitating pattern recognition at an unprecedented scale, and accelerating the processing of massive datasets. The melding of quantum computing's parallel processing and deep learning's pattern extraction capabilities hints at solutions to previously insurmountable challenges, propelling both fields to greater heights.

The Quantum Nexus Unveiled: The nexus of quantum computing and AI isn't just a fusion of technologies: it's a symphony of possibilities. As quantum computing's potential intertwines with deep learning's capabilities, the realm of optimization is redefined, and the frontiers of complexity are redrawn. The partnership between these two transformative fields promises a future where AI's prowess is magnified by the enigmatic power of quantum mechanics, propelling humanity into a realm of innovation and discovery that defies conventional boundaries.

9.3.5 A Glimpse into Human-Centric AI: Navigating the Terrain of Empathy: The horizon of AI's evolution paints a vivid picture of human-centricity, where AI models become attuned to human emotions, contexts, and intricacies. This section unveils the panorama of this transformative shift, offering a glimpse into a future where AI transcends its role as a tool to become a companion that understands, resonates, and enriches human experiences.

Emotion Recognition: Bridging the Emotional Chasm: The future of AI is one where it bridges the emotional chasm that separates humans and machines. AI systems endowed with emotion recognition capabilities not only decipher human emotions but also respond to them with empathy and sensitivity. From chatbots that offer words of encouragement to AI companions that understand and soothe, the narrative of AI transforms from transactional to empathetic. This evolution ushers in a realm where interactions with AI carry a touch of humanity, fostering connections that resonate beyond mere algorithms.

Personalized AI: Tailoring Experiences to Individual Uniqueness: The symphony of AI's future harmonizes with the melodies of individual uniqueness. Personalized AI becomes the anthem, adapting to individual preferences, behaviors, and aspirations. The AI of tomorrow isn't a one-size-fits-all entity: it's a dynamic companion that tailors experiences across a spectrum of applications. From content recommendations that align with personal tastes to AI assistants that understand communication nuances, the personalized AI revolution caters to the intricate tapestry of human individuality.

The Symphony of Humanity and AI: The tapestry of human-centric AI is woven from threads of empathy, personalization, and understanding. The vision that unfolds isn't just about enhancing technology: it's about enriching the human experience. As AI becomes an entity that not only understands but resonates with emotions, and as it tailors experiences to individual uniqueness, it emerges as a confidante that complements the human journey. The future it paints is one where AI stands not as an artificial entity but as an extension of our own humanity, augmenting our lives with companionship, understanding, and enrichment.

9.3.6 The Canvas of Imagination: The future of deep learning is a canvas upon which technological innovations and human aspirations are woven. As AI converges with diverse disciplines, forges decentralized paths with federated learning, and evolves with ethics, trustworthiness, and quantum computing, the tapestry of possibilities unfurls. With each stroke of innovation, the future beckons AI practitioners to explore, innovate, and co-create a landscape where AI's potential transforms into a powerful force for positive change.

9.4 Project

Unsolved Project

Suppose you're tasked with developing a comprehensive report on the ethical considerations and future directions of deep learning. To create a well-rounded report, you need to understand how to address bias and fairness in deep learning models, tackle privacy concerns and ensure data security, and explore emerging trends that may shape the future of deep learning. Before starting, research the following: methods for identifying and mitigating bias in deep learning, strategies for maintaining privacy and data security in AI applications, and current trends and potential future advancements in the field of deep learning. This preparation will enable you to produce an insightful and forward-thinking report.

9.5 Lab Activity

Unsolved Lab Activity

Implement a privacy-preserving technique (e.g., federated learning) to train a deep learning model on a sensitive dataset.

Task: Use a deep learning framework to implement federated learning on a sensitive dataset (e.g., medical records). Document the implementation process, including data distribution, model training, and evaluation of model performance while preserving data privacy.

Exercises

Exercise 1 – Multiple Choice Questions

1. What does the chapter emphasize as a moral and ethical imperative?
   a. Data collection
   b. Addressing bias and ensuring fairness
   c. Privacy concerns
   d. Quantum computing
2. What is emphasized as an ethical imperative in the context of privacy concerns and data security?
   a. Data collection
   b. Data sharing
   c. Transparency
   d. Data deletion
3. Which metric examines whether different groups are treated differently by a model's predictions?
   a. Equal Opportunity Difference
   b. Statistical Parity
   c. Disparate Impact
   d. Average Odds Difference
4. what is the purpose of post-processing techniques in privacy-preserving AI?
   a. To collect more data
   b. To correct models' predictions after they've been made
   c. To enhance model training
   d. To prevent data breaches
5. Which regulatory framework is highlighted as playing a pivotal role in data privacy?
   a. CCPA
   b. GDPR
   c. AI Ethics Guidelines
   d. HIPAA

Exercise 2 – True/False

1. Addressing bias and fairness in deep learning is not crucial since algorithms are inherently neutral.
2. Privacy concerns and data security are significant issues in the deployment of deep learning models.
3. Ensuring fairness in deep learning algorithms helps in mitigating bias and promoting equality.

Review Questions

1. What is the significance of addressing bias and promoting fairness in deep learning models?
2. How does bias in AI reflect real-world inequalities, and why is it a concern?
3. Explain the concept of the fairness conundrum in the context of AI.
4. What are bias metrics, and how do they help in quantifying disparities in AI models?
5. Describe the difference between Disparate Impact and Statistical Parity as bias metrics.

6. What is the role of fairness metrics, and how do they aim to balance equitability in AI models?
7. Explain the Equal Opportunity Difference and its significance in assessing fairness.
8. How does Average Odds Difference differ from Equal Opportunity Difference in fairness assessment?
9. What are some methodologies for assessing fairness in AI models, and why are they important?
10. How does causal analysis help identify the sources of bias in AI models?
11. What is feature importance analysis, and how can it unveil bias sources in AI models?
12. How does fairness-aware machine learning differ from traditional machine learning approaches?
13. What are some techniques for mitigating bias in data collection and preprocessing?
14. How can fairness constraints be integrated into model training to ensure equitable outcomes?
15. Describe the concept of adversarial debiasing and how it works in mitigating bias.
16. What are some post-processing techniques for correcting bias in AI models' predictions?
17. Beyond technical solutions, what are the ethical considerations in addressing bias and promoting fairness in AI?

Answers

Exercise 1- 1. b 2. c 3. c 7. b 5
Exercise 2- 1) False, 2) True, 3) True

Online Resources

Online Exam Paper:
Link: https://forms.gle/GTFD5fz1Ht26V2KMA
QR Code:

Chapter 9 Videos Playlist:
Link: https://www.youtube.com/playlist?list=PLzlh_31VWEFrGGGXpOi1SIMeFRo2pMg-C
QR Code:

Chapter 10: Case Studies and Projects

10.1 Image Classification Project: Navigating the Journey from Data to Model:

Data Collection and Preprocessing: The Foundation of Insight: The journey commences with the acquisition and preprocessing of data. Images, the raw materials of this endeavor, are collected, organized, and subjected to a meticulous preprocessing regime. This regime encompasses resizing, normalization, and augmentation, breathing life into the dataset while ensuring its quality and diversity. Data augmentation techniques introduce controlled variations, enriching the dataset and mitigating overfitting. The foundation is laid for the subsequent steps that lead to model creation.

Model Architecture Selection: Crafting the Blueprint of Intelligence: The selection of an appropriate model architecture is a pivotal juncture in the project's trajectory. This decision is informed by the complexity of the problem, the dataset's scale, and the desired performance metrics. From the classical Convolutional Neural Networks (CNNs) to more advanced architectures like ResNet and VGG, each choice brings its own set of strengths and trade-offs. The chosen architecture defines the blueprint that will unravel the intricacies within the images.

Training and Validation: Nurturing Intelligence through Iteration: The training and validation phase marks the convergence of data, architecture, and intelligence. The dataset is split into training and validation sets, each facilitating a distinct aspect of the model's development. The model learns to discern patterns and features within the images, iteratively refining its ability to classify and differentiate. The training process involves loss optimization, where the model fine-tunes its internal parameters to minimize error. Validation ensures that the model doesn't overfit but generalizes well to unseen data.

Evaluation and Fine-Tuning: A Quest for Precision: The evaluation phase gauges the model's performance on a separate test dataset, offering insights into its real-world efficacy. Metrics like accuracy, precision, recall, and F1 score provide a nuanced understanding of the model's strengths and limitations. Fine-tuning involves tweaking hyperparameters, adjusting architectures, or introducing regularization techniques to enhance the model's performance further.

Deployment and Real-World Impact: From Digital Realm to Tangible Utility: The culmination of this journey isn't just a digital entity: it's a tool that has the potential to shape the tangible world. The deployment phase transforms the model from a construct of code into a practical solution. The model's integration into applications, devices, or systems brings its insights to the forefront, impacting sectors from healthcare to commerce, security to entertainment.

10.1.1 A Tapestry of Intelligence Woven: The image classification project transcends its role as a technological pursuit: it's a tapestry woven from the threads of data, architecture, training, and deployment. As each step converges, the fabric of intelligence takes form, reshaping how we perceive, understand, and interact with the visual world. The journey isn't merely a series of technical tasks: it's a narrative of human ingenuity that transforms raw data into tools that empower and enrich the human experience.

10.2 Natural Language Processing Project: Illuminating Sentiments through Text: This section embarks on an illuminating journey through a natural language processing (NLP) project centered around sentiment analysis. From the foundation of data collection to the creation of a sentiment-aware model, every facet of this transformative journey is intricately detailed, providing insights into the methodologies, challenges, and triumphs that pave the path from unstructured text to AI-driven sentiment understanding.

Data Collection and Preprocessing: Harvesting Textual Insights: The journey commences with the collection and preprocessing of textual data. Textual sources, ranging from social media posts to customer reviews, are harvested and subjected to rigorous preprocessing. Tokenization segments text into units, removing punctuation and transforming words into standardized forms. Stop words are discarded, and stemming or lemmatization techniques are applied to ensure uniformity. The text is transformed into a structured format, laying the groundwork for subsequent analysis.

Feature Extraction and Representation: Transforming Text into Insights: Textual data doesn't directly fit into machine learning models: it requires transformation into numerical representations. Techniques like TF-IDF (Term Frequency-Inverse Document Frequency) and word embeddings convert text into vectors, capturing semantic relationships between words. These vectors become the foundation for machine learning models to analyze and comprehend text.

Model Selection and Training: Crafting a Sentiment-Reading AI: The selection of an appropriate model architecture is paramount to understanding sentiments from text. Classification models, such as recurrent neural networks (RNNs) or transformer-based architectures, are fine-tuned for sentiment analysis. Training data is labeled with sentiments, teaching the model to recognize the emotional tones encoded within the text. The model learns to associate words, phrases, and context with positive, negative, or neutral sentiments.

Evaluation and Fine-Tuning: The Quest for Sentiment Precision: Evaluation metrics like accuracy, precision, recall, and F1 score are deployed to measure the model's sentiment analysis accuracy. Fine-tuning involves tweaking hyperparameters, experimenting with different architectures, or employing regularization techniques to enhance the model's sentiment prediction prowess.

Deployment and Real-World Impact: Empowering Sentiment Insights: The crescendo of this journey is the deployment of the sentiment analysis model into real-world applications. Social media platforms, customer service chatbots, or market research tools become the stage where the model's insights shine. The model interprets the sentiments hidden within text, unveiling emotional undercurrents and opinions that empower decision-making processes and offer insights into human sentiments at scale.

10.2.1 A Symphony of Textual Understanding: The sentiment analysis NLP project transcends its role as a technological endeavor: it's a symphony that harmonizes linguistic nuances, machine learning capabilities, and human emotions. From data preprocessing to model training, the journey fuses data science and linguistics, unraveling sentiments within text and presenting them as actionable insights. Each step isn't merely a technical task: it's a thread woven into the fabric of understanding human expression, enriching the interaction between AI and language with emotional depth and insightful precision.

10.3 Reinforcement Learning Project: Game Playing Agent Navigating the Virtual Battleground: In the realm of artificial intelligence, where games become the battleground for intelligence, the Reinforcement Learning Project introduces us to the exhilarating world of training an AI game-playing agent. This chapter takes us on a captivating journey through the mechanics of reinforcement learning, revealing how an agent learns from its actions and interactions to become a formidable player in the digital arena.

10.3.1 The Symphony of Reinforcement Learning: At the heart of this project lies the symphony of reinforcement learning—an AI paradigm inspired by the way humans learn from trial and error. We embark on a deep dive into the fundamental components of reinforcement learning: agents, environments, actions, and rewards. This ecosystem is the crucible where our game-playing agent evolves its strategy to master a virtual domain.

The Agent: Forging Intelligence Through Interaction: Meet our protagonist—the agent—a virtual entity navigating the game. We uncover how the agent perceives its surroundings, makes decisions, and undertakes actions within the digital realm. Armed with a policy, the agent's blueprint for decision-making, it sets out on an adventure where its goal is not just victory but mastery through continuous learning.

The Environment: A Dynamic Playground for Learning: Every game requires a stage, and in reinforcement learning, that's the environment—an intricate world where the agent navigates and interacts. We decipher the environment's role in shaping the agent's learning process. From game rules to states and rewards, we explore how the environment crafts challenges and opportunities that propel the agent's journey.

Actions and Rewards: The Language of Learning: In the lexicon of reinforcement learning, actions and rewards forge a dialogue between the agent and the environment. We unravel how actions—decisions made by the agent—have consequences that ripple through the environment, influencing rewards that signify success or failure. The agent learns to optimize its actions to accumulate maximum rewards, becoming a strategic player.

10.3.2 The Learning Loop: Markov Decision Process: The journey of our game-playing agent unfurls within the framework of a Markov Decision Process (MDP). This intricate loop of interactions and adaptations governs how the agent navigates through decisions, actions, and outcomes, evolving its strategies through observation and reflection.

State Transitions: The Dynamic Dance: In the world of MDPs, states orchestrate the game. We delve into state transitions—the dynamic progression from one state to another based on the agent's actions and environmental responses. This dance of states defines the agent's path and forms the basis for its learning process.

Reward Signal: The North Star: Rewards act as the agent's North Star, guiding its decisions towards victory. We demystify the role of rewards in shaping the agent's behavior. From positive reinforcements to penalties, rewards sculpt the agent's strategy, training it to discern the optimal actions that lead to the greatest bounty of rewards.

The Bellman Equation: Mapping Future Rewards: A cornerstone of reinforcement learning, the Bellman equation, maps future rewards to guide the agent's decision-making. We unravel its mathematical essence, showcasing how it balances immediate gratification with long-term goals, enabling the agent to weigh actions based on the potential harvest of rewards down the line.

10.3.3 Learning Strategies: From Exploration to Exploitation: The agent's journey isn't a linear path: it's a delicate balance between exploration and exploitation. We delve into learning strategies that shape how the agent traverses the learning curve. From the exhilaration of exploration—where the agent uncovers new paths—to the sophistication of exploitation—where it leverages learned insights—we reveal how these strategies sculpt the agent's growth.

Exploration: Navigating Uncharted Territory: Exploration forms the heart of learning. We explore techniques like e-greedy, where the agent occasionally takes random actions, allowing it to venture into uncharted territory. We also encounter Thompson sampling—a probabilistic approach that balances known and unknown paths, facilitating discovery in the learning process.

Exploitation: Leveraging Learned Insights: Exploitation marks the phase where the agent capitalizes on its accrued wisdom. We investigate techniques like Q-learning, where the agent refines its policy based on past experiences, and policy gradient methods that optimize its strategy through gradient descent. These techniques embody the agent's transformation from a curious explorer to a shrewd strategist.

10.3.4 The Marvel of Deep Q-Networks: Melding Deep Learning with Reinforcement Learning: In this section, we don't just witness the evolution of a game-playing agent: we witness the intersection of deep learning and reinforcement learning through Deep Q-Networks (DQNs). We unravel the synergy between these realms, understanding how DQNs empower our agent to comprehend complex game dynamics and craft strategies beyond human intuition.

The Fusion of Deep Learning and Reinforcement Learning: Deep Q-Networks fuse the power of deep learning with the strategic prowess of reinforcement learning. We embark on a journey through the architecture of DQNs, from input layers that interpret game states to hidden layers that capture the nuances of strategy, culminating in output layers that dictate the agent's actions.

Target Networks: Stabilizing the Learning Odyssey: Deep Q-Networks harness a strategic technique—target networks—to stabilize the learning process. We delve into how target networks act as guideposts, providing stable reference points for the agent's learning trajectory. This technique curtails the turbulence of learning and bestows the agent with a reliable compass on its journey towards mastery.

Experience Replay: Reliving and Learning: Experience replay breathes life into learning. We unveil how this technique enables the agent to recycle past experiences—stored in a replay memory—to reinforce its learning. By reencountering scenarios, the agent hones its strategies and evolves as a seasoned player capable of tackling an array of challenges.

10.3.5 Challenges on the Path to Mastery: The journey of our game-playing agent is not without challenges. We traverse the landscape of obstacles—like the exploration-exploitation dilemma, reward engineering, and the notorious issue of overfitting—to understand the hurdles that AI navigators must overcome to thrive in the virtual arena.

The Exploration-Exploitation Conundrum: Balancing exploration and exploitation poses a conundrum. We delve into the challenges of making decisions that oscillate between these two phases. The agent must discern when to explore novel paths and when to exploit learned strategies—a delicate dance that can shape the agent's learning trajectory.

Crafting Rewards: The Art of Game Balancing: Rewards wield immense influence in the learning process, yet crafting them isn't an arbitrary task. We uncover the art of reward engineering, exploring how designing reward structures that align with desired outcomes can accelerate the agent's learning and lead to more adept strategies.

Overfitting: Navigating the Abyss of Extremes:

Overfitting—the bane of learning systems—plagues AI agents too. We examine how overfitting arises when the agent memorizes

past experiences, failing to generalize beyond them. Strategies like regularization and experience replay emerge as the agent's guardians, shielding it from the abyss of overfitting.

10.3.6 Beyond the Game: Real-World Applications: The realm of game-playing agents extends beyond entertainment. We explore how the strategic acumen cultivated by these agents manifests in real-world applications—from finance and robotics to healthcare and optimization. The chapter concludes by transcending the virtual battleground and embracing the transformative potential of game-playing agents in diverse domains.

10.3.7 Unleashing the Player: From Learning to Mastery: The tale of our game-playing agent transcends mere training—it's a transformative journey from a novice to a virtuoso. As we conclude this chapter, we acknowledge that the journey doesn't end here: instead, it marks the beginning of an unending exploration of AI's potential to master challenges through learning and interaction. The world beckons, and the agent's strategic prowess is its compass.

10.4 Creative Applications: Art Generation with Deep Learning Painting with Algorithms: The intersection of deep learning and artistry unveils a realm of boundless creativity—where algorithms become brushes and pixels become canvases. In this section, we embark on a captivating exploration of the synergy between machine learning and art, unveiling the techniques that transform AI into a virtual artist capable of generating stunning artworks.

10.4.1 The Fusion of Creativity and Algorithms: Art generation with deep learning isn't just about mimicking human artists: it's about harnessing the inherent creativity of algorithms to produce original, awe-inspiring creations. We delve into the process of how algorithms comprehend artistic styles, patterns, and elements to weave together digital masterpieces that captivate and inspire.

The Essence of Style: Neural Style Transfer: Neural Style Transfer is a bridge between art and algorithms. We explore how this technique leverages convolutional neural networks to infuse images with the aesthetic essence of famous artworks. By merging content and style, the algorithmic brush strokes of Neural Style Transfer give rise to unique, hybrid creations that merge human and AI creativity.

The Dance of Pixels: Variational Autoencoders: Variational Autoencoders (VAEs) redefine art generation as a dance of pixels. We uncover how VAEs encode the essence of images into a latent space and then decode it to craft diverse and imaginative creations. This dynamic interplay between encoding and decoding sparks the birth of original artworks that intrigue the human eye.

The Harmonic Convergence: GANs: Generative Adversarial Networks (GANs) orchestrate a harmonious convergence between a generator and a discriminator. We unveil the dance of competition and collaboration that unfolds as the generator creates artworks and the discriminator critiques them. This symbiotic relationship births artistic masterpieces that seamlessly blend human aesthetics with algorithmic ingenuity.

10.4.2 Artistic Style Transfer: The Palette of Aesthetics: The canvas of artistic style transfer is imbued with a rich palette of aesthetics. We delve into the intricacies of defining and capturing artistic styles, exploring how content and style loss functions collaborate to shape the algorithm's creativity. The result is a process where AI transforms mundane images into artworks resonating with the aesthetics of iconic painters.

Content Loss: Weaving the Fabric of Content: Content loss forms the foundation of style transfer, guiding the algorithm to retain the underlying structure of the original image. We dissect how content loss functions quantify the semantic similarity between the original image and the stylized creation, ensuring that the essence of the subject is preserved even amidst stylistic transformations.

Style Loss: Capturing the Soul of Art: Style loss delves into the very soul of artistry, extracting the patterns, textures, and strokes that define a particular style. We delve into how style loss functions measure the discrepancies between the Gram matrices of the original image and the style reference, culminating in the algorithm's ability to infuse artworks with the visual language of artistic giants.

10.4.3 Unleashing Creativity: Generative Adversarial Networks (GANs): Generative Adversarial Networks (GANs) elevate art generation into a realm of unbounded creativity. We embark on a journey through the GAN architecture, from the generator that paints the canvas of imagination to the discriminator that critiques its strokes. This adversarial dance of creation and critique results in artworks that span the spectrum of realism and abstraction.

The Generator: Breathing Life into Canvases: The generator is the AI artist—a network that conjures art from noise. We demystify how the generator crafts images through a process of upsampling, convolution, and activation. It evolves with each brushstroke, learning from both its successes and critiques, to conjure an ever-evolving gallery of digital artistry.

The Discriminator: The Art of Critique: The discriminator plays the role of the art critic—an AI that evaluates the authenticity and quality of the generated art. We dive into how the discriminator distinguishes between real artworks and AI-generated ones, honing its discernment through adversarial interactions. Its critiques propel the generator towards creating art that not only captivates the eye but also deceives the AI's keen judgment.

10.4.4 Creative Synthesis: The Blend of Styles: Art generation transcends mere replication: it's the synthesis of styles that evokes intrigue. We explore techniques that enable the blending of artistic styles, producing hybrids that spark new perspectives and emotions. By infusing algorithms with the capacity to combine stylistic elements, we witness the birth of art that defies categorization and stimulates curiosity.

Neural Style Blending: Hybrid Artistry: Neural Style Blending marries the aesthetics of multiple artworks, producing hybrids that bridge artistic worlds. We dissect how this technique leverages neural networks to map features from multiple styles onto a single canvas, resulting in visual creations that encapsulate the essence of different artists within a single frame.

Style Interpolation: Artistic Transitions: Style Interpolation is the symphony of transition—a technique that seamlessly morphs between different styles. We uncover how style interpolation leverages latent spaces to blend the artistic DNA of two styles, enabling AI to craft artworks that evolve from one stylistic influence to another, painting a vivid narrative of transformation.

10.4.5 Beyond Replication: The Evolution of Art: The culmination of our exploration is not just the replication of existing art but the evolution of new art forms. We delve into the philosophy of AI-generated art, discussing how it challenges traditional definitions of creativity, authorship, and artistic expression. The chapter concludes by peering into the future, where AI's artistic journey is boundless and its contributions to the world of art continue to shape human perceptions of creativity.

10.5 Project

Unsolved Project

Suppose you're working on a creative project that involves generating art using deep learning techniques. To successfully complete this project, you need to understand the entire process, from gathering and preprocessing data to training a deep learning model and producing artistic outputs. Before starting, study the following: the process of image classification to understand data handling and model training, the techniques used in natural language processing to gain insights into text handling and sentiment analysis, reinforcement learning concepts to learn about model training and optimization, and the specific methods used in creative applications of deep learning for art generation. This preparation will help you design and implement an innovative art generation project using deep learning.

10.6 Lab Activity

Unsolved Lab Activity

Design and implement a deep learning model for art generation (e.g., neural style transfer, GAN-based art creation).

Task: Choose an art generation technique (e.g., neural style transfer, GANs). Collect or use an existing dataset of images. Implement the chosen model using a deep learning framework, train the model, and generate new artworks. Document the entire process, including data preparation, model architecture, training procedure, and examples of generated artworks. Provide insights into the challenges faced and how they were overcome.

Exercises

Exercise 1 – Multiple Choice Questions

1. In an image classification project, what is the purpose of data augmentation?
   A) Reducing image resolution
   B) Increasing overfitting
   C) Introducing controlled variations
   D) Normalizing pixel values
2. Which phase of model development ensures that the model generalizes well to unseen data?
   A) Data Collection
   B) Model Architecture Selection
   C) Training and Validation
   D) Deployment
3. What is the primary role of fine-tuning in the image classification project?
   A) Increasing overfitting
   B) Tweaking hyperparameters
   C) Adjusting architectures
   D) Enhancing model performance
4. In natural language processing, what is the purpose of tokenization during data preprocessing?
   A) Removing punctuation
   B) Transforming text into numerical representations
   C) Organizing textual data
   D) Augmenting data
5. Which technique is used to convert textual data into numerical vectors for machine learning models in NLP?
   A) TF-IDF
   B) Data augmentation
   C) Normalization
   D) Stopping words

Exercise 2 – True/False

1. The Image Classification Project involves building a model that can categorize images into different classes.
2. Sentiment Analysis in Natural Language Processing focuses on identifying the main topics of a text.
3. Answer: False (Sentiment Analysis focuses on determining the sentiment expressed in the text, such as positive, negative, or neutral)
4. Reinforcement Learning Projects typically involve training models to make decisions by learning from trial and error.

Review Questions

1. What are the key steps involved in data preprocessing for an image classification project, and why are they important?
2. Explain the concept of data augmentation in image classification and its role in improving model performance.
3. How does the choice of model architecture impact the success of an image classification project?
4. What is the purpose of the training and validation phases in model development for image classification?
5. What are the common evaluation metrics used to assess the performance of an image classification model, and what do they measure?
6. Describe the significance of fine-tuning in enhancing the performance of an image classification model.
7. How does the deployment phase transform a trained image classification model into a practical solution with real-world impact?
8. Why is data preprocessing essential in natural language processing, and what are some common techniques used in this phase?
9. Explain the process of feature extraction and representation in NLP and its significance for machine learning models.
10. What types of model architectures are commonly used for sentiment analysis in natural language processing, and how do they work?
11. What are the key evaluation metrics for assessing the accuracy of sentiment analysis models, and what do they measure?
12. How can fine-tuning be applied to improve the performance of sentiment analysis models in NLP?
13. Describe the deployment phase and real-world applications of sentiment analysis models in NLP.
14. What is the fundamental concept behind reinforcement learning, and how does it differ from other machine learning paradigms?
15. Explain the roles of agents, environments, actions, and rewards in the context of reinforcement learning.
16. How does the Markov Decision Process (MDP) framework govern the decision-making process of a game-playing agent in reinforcement learning?
17. What are state transitions in an MDP, and why are they crucial for an agent's learning process?
18. Discuss the significance of rewards in reinforcement learning and their role in shaping an agent's strategy.
19. What is the Exploration-Exploitation dilemma in reinforcement learning, and how do agents balance these two aspects?
20. How do Deep Q-Networks (DQNs) combine deep learning and reinforcement learning, and what advantages do they offer in game-playing scenarios?
21. What is the goal of art generation with deep learning, and how does it differ from traditional art creation?
22. Explain the concept of Neural Style Transfer in art generation and how it merges content and style.
23. What role do Variational Autoencoders (VAEs) play in generating original artworks, and how do they work?
24. Describe the architecture and purpose of Generative Adversarial Networks (GANs) in creating art with deep learning.
25. How does the discriminator in a GAN contribute to the generation of high-quality art?

26. What are the key techniques for blending artistic styles in art generation, and how do they work?
27. How does art generation with deep learning challenge traditional notions of creativity and authorship?

Answers

Exercise 1- 1.C 2.C 3.D 4.A 5.A
Exercise 2- 1)True, 2) False, 3) True

Online Resources

Online Exam Paper:
Link: https://forms.gle/Q6jvD9gwAEZSELKA8
QR Code:

Chapter 10 Videos Playlist:
Link: https://www.youtube.com/playlist?list=PLzlh_31VWEFqtOWfUgu46KO0TCkSyHyXi
QR Code:

Chapter 11: Optimization and Training Techniques

11. Gradient Descent and Its Variants: Navigating the Optimization Landscape: In the realm of machine learning and optimization, few concepts are as fundamental and powerful as gradient descent. At its core, gradient descent is an optimization algorithm used to minimize (or maximize) functions iteratively. It plays a pivotal role in training machine learning models by finding the optimal parameters that result in the best model performance. Over time, various variants of gradient descent have been developed to enhance its efficiency, speed, and applicability to a wide range of scenarios.

11.1 Understanding Gradient Descent: Before delving into its variants, let's establish a foundational understanding of gradient descent. The concept draws inspiration from the way a ball rolls down a hill—seeking the lowest point in the terrain. In the context of optimization, the "hill" represents the loss function, which quantifies how well a model's predictions match the actual data.

The Gradient Descent Process: Gradient descent begins with initializing a set of parameters for a model. It then calculates the gradient of the loss function with respect to these parameters. The gradient indicates the direction of the steepest increase in the loss function. However, we are interested in finding the direction of the steepest decrease to reach the minimum of the loss function. Thus, the algorithm moves the parameters in the opposite direction of the gradient, adjusting them iteratively to minimize the loss.

The Variants Unveiled: Now that we have a grasp of the foundational gradient descent process, let's explore the variants that have been developed to tailor the optimization process for different scenarios.

11.1.1 Stochastic Gradient Descent (SGD): Standard gradient descent uses the entire dataset to compute the gradient at each iteration, making it computationally expensive, especially for large datasets. SGD addresses this by randomly selecting a subset (mini-batch) of the data for each iteration. This not only reduces computation time but also introduces a level of noise that can help escape local minima and find a more optimal solution.

11.1.2 Mini-Batch Gradient Descent: Mini-batch gradient descent strikes a balance between the extremes of batch gradient descent and SGD. It divides the data into small batches and computes the gradient based on each batch. This combines the advantages of faster convergence (compared to full-batch) and the noisy exploration (akin to SGD).

11.1.3 Batch Gradient Descent: This is the vanilla gradient descent approach that computes the gradient using the entire dataset in each iteration. While it guarantees a more stable convergence, it can be computationally expensive and unsuitable for large datasets.

11.1.4 Momentum: Momentum is an extension that accelerates gradient descent by incorporating past gradients' information. It introduces a "velocity" term that guides the optimization process. This helps to smooth out the optimization trajectory and speed up convergence, particularly in areas with flat gradients.

11.1.5 Adaptive Learning Rate Methods (e.g., AdaGrad, RMSprop, Adam): These methods adjust the learning rate for each parameter based on historical gradient information. AdaGrad adapts the learning rate to the frequency of updates for each parameter, making large updates for infrequent parameters and small updates for frequently updated ones. RMSprop and Adam further refine this idea by incorporating exponential moving averages of past gradients and squared gradients, respectively. These methods are effective in speeding up convergence and handling different scales of parameters.

11.1.6 Nesterov Accelerated Gradient (NAG): NAG is a modification of momentum-based gradient descent. It accounts for the momentum effect when calculating the gradient, allowing for a more accurate approximation of the parameter's future value. This often results in faster convergence.

11.1.7 Adaptive Moment Estimation (Adam): Adam combines ideas from momentum and adaptive learning rates. It maintains both a running average of past gradients and a running average of past squared gradients. This helps the algorithm adaptively adjust the learning rate while also incorporating momentum-like behavior.

11.1.8 Rprop (Resilient Propagation): Unlike methods that rely on gradient information, Rprop only uses the sign of the gradient to update parameters. It adjusts the step size based on the sign of the gradient change between iterations. Rprop is particularly useful when dealing with functions that have flat or undefined gradients.

11.1.9 Choosing the Right Variant: The choice of gradient descent variant depends on factors such as the dataset size, the characteristics of the loss landscape, and computational resources. While some variants might perform exceptionally well for certain problems, they might struggle with others. Experimentation and tuning are crucial to finding the most suitable optimization algorithm.

11.2 Learning Rate Scheduling Strategies: Navigating the Training Process: In the realm of machine learning and optimization, the choice of a learning rate—the step size at which an optimization algorithm adjusts model parameters—plays a crucial role in determining the efficiency and effectiveness of the training process. Learning rate scheduling strategies, a subset of optimization techniques, aim to dynamically adjust the learning rate during training to achieve faster convergence and improved model performance. In this section, we delve into various learning rate scheduling strategies and explore their impact on training neural networks.

11.2.1 The Importance of Learning Rate: Before delving into learning rate scheduling, it's essential to understand the significance of the learning rate in the optimization process. A learning rate that's too small can lead to slow convergence, prolonging the training process. On the other hand, a learning rate that's too large might cause the optimization process to overshoot the optimal solution or even diverge. Finding the right balance is crucial for efficient and effective training.

11.2.2 Adaptive Learning Rate Scheduling: While manually adjusting the learning rate can be effective, modern optimization techniques leverage the power of adaptive learning rate scheduling. These methods automatically adjust the learning rate based on the progress of the optimization process and the characteristics of the loss landscape.

11.2.3 Learning Rate Warmup: Learning rate warmup is a strategy that involves gradually increasing the learning rate at the beginning of training before applying the scheduled decay. This approach can help overcome the problem of slow initial progress, especially in cases where the learning rate starts off too low. By allowing the optimization process to explore a broader range of solutions initially, warmup can accelerate convergence.

11.2.4 Cyclical Learning Rates: Cyclical learning rates involve periodically oscillating the learning rate between low and high values. This exploration-exploitation approach helps the optimization process escape local minima and saddle points. The learning rate periodically switches between a lower bound and an upper bound, allowing the model to explore different regions of the loss landscape.

11.2.5 Selecting the Right Strategy: The choice of a learning rate scheduling strategy depends on factors such as the dataset size, model architecture, and optimization landscape. Experimentation is key to finding the most suitable strategy for a given problem. Combining learning rate scheduling with other optimization techniques, such as gradient clipping and batch normalization, can further enhance training stability and performance.

learning rate scheduling strategies are essential tools in the optimization toolkit for training neural networks and machine learning models. These strategies help strike a balance between rapid convergence and avoiding overshooting or divergence. By intelligently adapting the learning rate over time, practitioners can navigate the training process effectively, leading to faster convergence and improved model performance.

11.3 Batch Normalization and Layer Normalization: Enhancing Neural Network Training: In the realm of deep learning, the architecture and optimization of neural networks are paramount to achieving high-performance models. Two techniques that have significantly improved the training process and convergence of neural networks are Batch Normalization and Layer Normalization. These techniques tackle the challenge of internal covariate shift and help stabilize and accelerate the training process. In this section, we delve into the concepts of Batch Normalization and Layer Normalization and explore their benefits.

11.3.1 The Challenge of Internal Covariate Shift: Internal covariate shift refers to the change in the distribution of network activations (outputs of intermediate layers) during training. As layers update their weights, the distribution of inputs to subsequent layers shifts, which can slow down training. This is because each layer must continuously adapt to the changing distribution of inputs from the previous layer.

11.3.2 Batch Normalization: Batch Normalization (BN) is a technique introduced to mitigate the challenges posed by internal covariate shift. It operates by normalizing the input of each layer in a mini-batch to have zero mean and unit variance. The normalized values are then scaled and shifted using learnable parameters to reintroduce the representation power of the layer.

Benefits of Batch Normalization:

Improved Convergence: Batch Normalization helps maintain a stable distribution of inputs to each layer, allowing for smoother and faster convergence during training.

Regularization Effect: Batch Normalization introduces a form of regularization, reducing the reliance on techniques like dropout or L2 regularization.

Higher Learning Rates: The stabilization effect of Batch Normalization often enables the use of higher learning rates, speeding up the optimization process.

Reduced Sensitivity to Weight Initialization: The technique makes networks less sensitive to the choice of initial weights, making it easier to train deep networks.

11.3.3 Layer Normalization: While Batch Normalization operates on mini-batches, Layer Normalization (LN) extends the concept to operate on individual training examples within a mini-batch. Each example's features are normalized independently across the features of that example. This can be particularly useful in scenarios where batch sizes are small or when applying neural networks to tasks like natural language processing.

Benefits of Layer Normalization: Layer Normalization offers several notable advantages:

Applicability to Variable-Length Sequences: In tasks that involve sequences of varying lengths—such as natural language processing or speech recognition—Layer Normalization shines. Its adaptability to sequences of different lengths makes it a suitable choice for these applications.

Reduced Dependencies on Batch Size: Layer Normalization's instance-level normalization means that it operates effectively even with smaller batch sizes. This makes it a more robust choice when working with limited data.

Stabilization in Recurrent Networks: Recurrent Neural Networks (RNNs) can be prone to vanishing or exploding gradients. Layer Normalization helps stabilize the activations within RNNs, aiding in convergence and enabling the training of deeper recurrent models.

11.4 Regularization: Dropout and L1/L2 Regularization: In the pursuit of creating effective and generalizable machine learning models, the problem of overfitting often arises. Overfitting occurs when a model learns to perform exceedingly well on the training data but struggles to generalize to new, unseen data. Regularization techniques serve as valuable tools to mitigate overfitting by introducing constraints on the model's complexity. In this section, we delve deeply into two prominent regularization techniques: Dropout and L1/L2 Regularization.

11.4.1 The Problem of Overfitting: Before diving into regularization techniques, it's crucial to understand the challenge of overfitting. Overfitting arises when a model becomes too tailored to the training data, capturing noise and irrelevant patterns rather than true underlying relationships. This results in poor generalization to new data, undermining the model's performance on real-world tasks.

11.4.2 Dropout Regularization: Dropout is a powerful and innovative regularization technique that operates within the network architecture itself. It involves randomly "dropping out" a fraction of neurons during each training iteration. This implies that the dropped neurons are excluded from both the forward and backward pass of that iteration.

How Dropout Works: During each training iteration, Dropout deactivates neurons with a certain probability. This effectively simulates training a multitude of different architectures in parallel. At test time, when dropout is not applied, the model's predictions are averaged over all possible subnetworks created during training.

Benefits of Dropout:

Regularization: Dropout serves as a form of regularization by preventing neurons from becoming overly specialized to certain features. It encourages the network to learn more robust and generalizable features.

Ensemble Effect: The dropout process creates an ensemble of subnetworks, each contributing to the final prediction. This ensemble-like behavior often leads to better generalization performance.

Reduced Co-Adaptation: Dropout discourages co-adaptation of neurons, where certain neurons become overly reliant on the presence of other specific neurons. This results in more balanced learning across the network.

11.4.3 L1 and L2 Regularization: L1 and L2 Regularization are techniques that introduce a penalty term to the loss function based on the magnitudes of the model's weights. These regularization terms discourage excessively large weight values and encourage a simpler model.

L1 Regularization (Lasso): L1 regularization adds the sum of the absolute values of the model's weights to the loss function. This encourages many weights to become exactly zero, effectively enforcing feature selection and yielding sparse models.

L2 Regularization (Ridge): L2 regularization introduces the sum of the squared values of the model's weights to the loss function. It doesn't force weights to become exactly zero, but it discourages excessively large weights, leading to more balanced feature contributions.

Benefits of L1/L2 Regularization:

Simplification of Models: L1/L2 regularization encourages models to prioritize important features and downplay irrelevant ones, resulting in simpler, more interpretable models.

Prevention of Overfitting: By controlling the magnitude of weights, L1/L2 regularization reduces the likelihood of overfitting by curbing the model's ability to fit noise in the training data.

Improved Generalization: Regularization techniques lead to models that generalize better to new, unseen data by reducing overfitting.

11.4.4 Choosing the Right Regularization Technique: The choice between Dropout and L1/L2 regularization depends on various factors, including the architecture, dataset size, and the complexity of the problem. Experimentation and validation are crucial to determine which technique works best for a given task.

11.4.5 Conclusion: Regularization techniques like Dropout and L1/L2 regularization play a pivotal role in maintaining model generalization and preventing overfitting. By adding constraints to the learning process, these techniques enable the creation of models that capture meaningful patterns and can apply those patterns to new, unseen data, ultimately leading to more reliable and accurate machine learning models.

11.5 Project

Unsolved Project

Suppose you're developing a deep learning model and want to optimize its performance using various training techniques. To achieve this, you need to understand gradient descent and its variants, learning rate scheduling strategies, normalization techniques, and regularization methods. Before starting your model development, research the following: the basics of gradient descent and its different variants, various learning rate scheduling strategies to adjust the learning rate during training, the roles of batch normalization and layer normalization in stabilizing and accelerating training, and the application of regularization techniques such as dropout, L1, and L2 regularization to prevent overfitting. This foundational knowledge will help you effectively optimize and train your deep learning model.

11.6 Lab Activity

Unsolved Lab Activity

Implement dropout, L1 regularization, and L2 regularization in a neural network and evaluate their effects on model performance.

Task: Train a neural network on a dataset (e.g., MNIST) using a deep learning framework. Apply dropout, L1 regularization, and L2 regularization separately and observe their effects on the training and validation performance. Document the implementation process, track the training loss and accuracy, and compare the results using visualizations.

Exercises

Exercise 1 – Multiple Choice Questions

1. What is the primary goal of gradient descent in machine learning?
   a) To maximize functions iteratively
   b) To minimize functions iteratively
   c) To find the global maximum of the loss function
   d) To make predictions with high accuracy
2. In the context of optimization, what does the "hill" represent in gradient descent?
   a) The learning rate
   b) The model parameters
   c) The loss function
   d) The gradient
3. Which variant of gradient descent randomly selects a subset of the data for each iteration?
   a) Batch Gradient Descent
   b) Mini-Batch Gradient Descent
   c) Stochastic Gradient Descent (SGD)
   d) Momentum
4. How does Mini-Batch Gradient Descent differ from Batch Gradient Descent?
   a) It computes the gradient using the entire dataset in each iteration.
   b) It randomly selects a subset (mini-batch) of the data for each iteration.
   c) It adjusts the learning rate based on historical gradient information.
   d) It incorporates past gradients' information to speed up convergence.
5. What is the primary advantage of using Momentum in gradient descent?
   a) It guarantees a more stable convergence.
   b) It reduces computation time.
   c) It introduces a "velocity" term to accelerate convergence.
   d) It adjusts the learning rate based on historical gradient information.

Exercise 2 – True/False

1. Gradient Descent is a method used to minimize the loss function in machine learning models.
2. Learning rate scheduling strategies are used to adjust the learning rate dynamically during the training process.
3. Dropout is a technique used in batch normalization to prevent overfitting.

Review Questions

1. What is the fundamental goal of gradient descent, and how does it relate to machine learning optimization?
2. How does gradient descent mimic the behavior of a ball rolling down a hill in the context of optimization?
3. Explain the core steps of the gradient descent process and why adjusting parameters in the opposite direction of the gradient is important.
4. Compare and contrast Stochastic Gradient Descent (SGD), Mini-Batch Gradient Descent, and Batch Gradient Descent. When might you choose one over the others?
5. What role does the learning rate play in gradient descent, and how do adaptive learning rate methods improve optimization efficiency?
6. Describe the concept of momentum in gradient descent and how it affects the optimization trajectory.
7. How do adaptive learning rate methods like AdaGrad, RMSprop, and Adam adapt the learning rate for each parameter?
8. What are the advantages of Nesterov Accelerated Gradient (NAG) over traditional momentum-based gradient descent?
9. Explain the significance of learning rate scheduling strategies and how techniques like learning rate warmup and cyclical learning rates contribute to faster convergence in neural network training.

Answers

Exercise 1- 1.b 2.c 3.c 4.b 5.c
Exercise 2- 1) True, 2) True, 3) False

Online Resources

Online Exam Paper:

Link: https://forms.gle/ZnPMf8iTcwyCDJUX9
QR Code:

Chapter 11 Videos Playlist:
Link: https://www.youtube.com/playlist?list=PLzlh_31VWEFqjY6Py6i6rcFEIBD1Z4ti9
QR Code:

Chapter 12: Natural Language Processing (NLP) with Deep Learning

12.1 Word Embeddings: Word2Vec, GloVe, FastText: In the realm of natural language processing (NLP) and deep learning, the representation of words is a pivotal challenge. Traditional approaches relied on one-hot encoding, which represents words as binary vectors, lacking semantic relationships. Word embeddings revolutionized this landscape by capturing word semantics and syntactic patterns. In this section, we delve into three prominent word embedding techniques: Word2Vec, GloVe, and FastText.

12.1.1 Word Embeddings: A Foundation for NLP: Word embeddings are dense vector representations of words in a continuous space. Unlike one-hot encodings, which are sparse and lack semantic information, word embeddings capture semantic relationships and contextual information. Each dimension in the embedding space encodes a specific aspect of meaning, allowing for meaningful algebraic operations.

12.1.2 Word2Vec: Capturing Word Context: In the realm of natural language processing and the quest to empower machines with a deeper understanding of words and their meanings, the Word2Vec technique stands as a pivotal breakthrough. Developed by a team led by Tomas Mikolov, Word2Vec introduces the concept of learning word embeddings—a way to represent words in a continuous vector space—from vast text corpora. The underlying principle of Word2Vec is grounded in the idea that words that appear in similar contexts tend to share similar meanings.

Intuition behind Word2Vec: The driving force behind Word2Vec's innovation lies in its ability to grasp the intrinsic relationships between words by analyzing the way they are used together in sentences and documents. The technique operates under the assumption that words that frequently appear together or are used in similar contexts are likely to have related meanings or semantic connections.To put it simply, Word2Vec tries to capture the "you shall know a word by the company it keeps" idea. Words that often appear together, such as "apple" and "fruit," or "car" and "road," are likely to be related in meaning. Word2Vec aims to map these relationships in a dense, continuous vector space where words with similar contextual meanings are positioned close to each other.

Word2Vec Architectures: CBOW and Skip-gram:

Word2Vec offers two primary architectures: Continuous Bag of Words (CBOW) and Skip-gram. Each architecture addresses the word-context relationship from a different angle, contributing to a holistic understanding of word semantics.

Continuous Bag of Words (CBOW): In the CBOW architecture, the goal is to predict a target word based on its context—surrounding words within a certain window. This architecture is like a language model aiming to understand a word from its neighboring linguistic environment.

Skip-gram: On the other hand, the Skip-gram architecture does the reverse. It tries to predict the context words given a target word. Skip-gram is akin to a "fill-in-the-blank" game where the model tries to predict the missing words in a sentence.

Semantic Relationships and Arithmetic with Word Embeddings: One of the most intriguing outcomes of Word2Vec is its ability to imbue word embeddings with semantic relationships. The vector space created by Word2Vec embeddings captures these relationships, enabling algebraic operations that reflect semantic associations. For instance, by subtracting the vector for "man" from "king" and adding the vector for "woman," the result is a vector close to the embedding for "queen." This computational analogy showcases the impressive semantic understanding achieved by Word2Vec embeddings.

Conclusion: Word2Vec stands as a groundbreaking technique in the realm of natural language processing and deep learning. By learning embeddings that represent words based on their context, Word2Vec has enabled machines to capture semantic relationships and contextual nuances of language. The resulting embeddings facilitate a wide range of language-related tasks and empower models to understand and generate human-like text. The innovation introduced by Word2Vec serves as a cornerstone for the development of more advanced techniques in the field of word embeddings and natural language understanding.

12.1.3 GloVe: Global Vectors for Word Representation: In the quest to enhance word representations that capture both the intricacies of meaning and the interplay of language, GloVe (Global Vectors for Word Representation) emerges as a novel approach that marries the concepts of global and local context information. Crafted by Jeffrey Pennington, Richard Socher, and Christopher D. Manning, GloVe sets out to establish a bridge between these contextual dimensions, ultimately yielding embeddings that embody the global structure of word relationships.

Constructing Word Embeddings through Co-occurrence: The methodology at the core of GloVe is distinct from its predecessors like Word2Vec. GloVe leverages the co-occurrence statistics of words in a corpus—a reflection of how often words appear together. This co-occurrence matrix serves as a foundation for GloVe's learning process. By transforming this matrix, GloVe seeks to preserve the global context and capture the nuanced interplay between words. GloVe's approach takes the form of a matrix factorization problem. It aims to uncover latent factors that contribute to word co-occurrences. The underlying intuition is that words with similar meanings tend to share similar co-occurrence patterns across the entire corpus.

Balancing Local and Global Context: An intriguing facet of GloVe is its adeptness at harmonizing the strengths of local context (as exhibited by Word2Vec) with the overarching global context of co-occurrence patterns. This equilibrium often leads to embeddings that adeptly capture both semantic and syntactic relationships.

12.1.4 FastText: Subword Information: In the dynamic landscape of word embeddings, FastText emerges as an extension of the Word2Vec paradigm, devised by Piotr Bojanowski and a team of researchers. FastText introduces an innovative perspective by embracing subword information—a realm beyond whole words.

Harnessing Subword-Level Insights: FastText delves into the subword realm by representing words as collections of character n-grams. These subword units capture morphological intricacies and smaller linguistic elements. By considering these sub word components, FastText can grasp the morphological diversity of languages and handle out-of-vocabulary words more effectively.

The Strength of Sub word-Level Embeddings: FastText's power lies in its capacity to address rare or unseen words. It constructs embeddings for such words by composing the embeddings of their sub word constituents. This strategy enhances the robustness of the embeddings and fosters a richer understanding of language.

12.1.5 Choosing the Right Word Embedding: The choice between Word2Vec, GloVe, and FastText depends on various factors, such as the size of the dataset, the nature of the task, and the need for handling morphological complexity. Experimentation and evaluation are key to determining the most suitable word embedding technique for a given NLP task.

12.1.6 Conclusion: Word embeddings have revolutionized the field of NLP, enabling machines to understand semantic relationships and contextual nuances of words. Word2Vec, GloVe, and FastText are three influential techniques that have paved the way for more effective language understanding and generation in a wide range of NLP applications. Understanding the strengths and nuances of each technique is essential for harnessing the power of word embeddings in deep learning.

12.2 Recurrent Neural Networks for Text Generation: In the realm of natural language processing (NLP), generating coherent and contextually relevant text is a formidable challenge. Recurrent Neural Networks (RNNs), a class of neural networks designed to capture sequential information, have emerged as a powerful tool for tackling text generation tasks. In this section, we explore how RNNs are harnessed for text generation, their architecture, training process, and their applications in various NLP domains.

12.2.1 The Role of RNNs in Text Generation: Text generation involves producing sequences of words that convey meaningful and coherent information. This task requires understanding the context and dependencies between words, making it a natural fit for RNNs. RNNs have an innate ability to capture sequential information and maintain a memory of previous states, making them well-suited for tasks where the order of elements matters, such as language modeling and text generation.

12.2.2 Architecture of Recurrent Neural Networks: The fundamental architecture of an RNN involves processing sequential data step by step. At each time step, the RNN takes in an input, updates its internal state, and produces an output. This output can be used as a prediction for the next word in text generation tasks.

However, traditional RNNs suffer from vanishing and exploding gradient problems, limiting their ability to capture long-range dependencies. To address these issues, variants like Long Short-Term Memory (LSTM) and Gated Recurrent Unit (GRU) were introduced. These architectures incorporate mechanisms to better control the flow of information through the network, allowing RNNs to capture longer dependencies.

12.2.3 Training RNNs for Text Generation: Training an RNN for text generation involves providing the network with sequences of words and training it to predict the next word in the sequence. The loss function guides the network to minimize the difference between its predictions and the actual next words. The goal is to make the network learn the statistical patterns and dependencies in the training data, enabling it to generate coherent and contextually appropriate text during inference.

12.2.4 Applications of RNNs in Text Generation: The versatility of Recurrent Neural Networks (RNNs) extends beyond their ability to capture sequential information—they have become a linchpin in various text generation tasks, reshaping the landscape of natural language processing. Here, we explore the manifold applications of RNNs in text generation, from crafting grammatically sound sentences to engaging in dynamic dialogues.

Language Modeling: At the heart of text generation lies the task of language modeling. RNNs excel in learning the intricate distribution of words in a language. By understanding the probabilities of word sequences, RNNs can generate coherent and grammatically correct sentences that emulate the patterns observed in the training data. This fundamental application forms the basis for many other text generation tasks.

Machine Translation: In the realm of multilingual communication, RNNs have been harnessed for the monumental task of machine translation. Neural machine translation systems utilize RNNs to decode input sentences in one language and generate corresponding translations in another. This process involves capturing not only linguistic nuances but also the contextual subtleties that ensure faithful and accurate translations.

Caption Generation: The marriage of images and language is a realm where RNNs shine. Caption generation, a task of automatically generating descriptive textual explanations for images, is enriched by the sequential nature of RNNs. By analyzing the visual content and weaving it into coherent captions, RNNs enhance image understanding and make visual content more accessible to those who rely on textual descriptions.

Dialog Generation: The aspiration to foster human-like interactions with machines has given rise to chatbots and virtual assistants. Here, RNNs play a pivotal role in dialog generation. By learning from vast conversational datasets, RNN-based chatbots can craft contextually relevant and engaging responses, driving more meaningful interactions and enhancing user experiences.

Text Summarization: Taming the vast sea of information is a challenge that RNNs embrace through text summarization. These networks can be trained to distill lengthy texts into concise summaries that encapsulate the core points. This application has profound implications across domains where information overload is a concern, such as news aggregation, research paper analysis, and content curation.

12.2.5 Challenges and Future Directions: Despite the remarkable strides made by RNNs in text generation, challenges persist on the horizon. Repetitive or nonsensical text output can arise from the limitations of model learning, and training RNNs is

computationally demanding due to their sequential nature. Researchers are navigating these obstacles by delving into innovative techniques.
Attention mechanisms, which allow the model to focus on specific parts of the input sequence, have brought significant improvements. Moreover, the rise of transformer architectures, which emphasize parallelization and long-range dependencies, has sparked a new era in text generation.

12.2.6 Conclusion: RNNs have reshaped the landscape of text generation across diverse domains. From language modeling to enabling multilingual communication and from crafting engaging dialogues to summarizing vast troves of information, RNNs stand as a cornerstone of natural language processing. As researchers forge ahead, harnessing attention mechanisms, transformers, and novel approaches, the future of text generation appears promising, holding the potential to produce even more sophisticated, coherent, and contextually rich textual outputs.

12.3 Transformer Models for Language Understanding: The field of natural language processing has witnessed a transformative shift with the advent of Transformer models. These architectures have redefined the way machines understand language by introducing attention mechanisms that allow for parallel processing and long-range dependencies. In this section, we delve into the revolutionary impact of Transformer models on language understanding, their architecture, mechanisms, and their contributions to various NLP tasks.

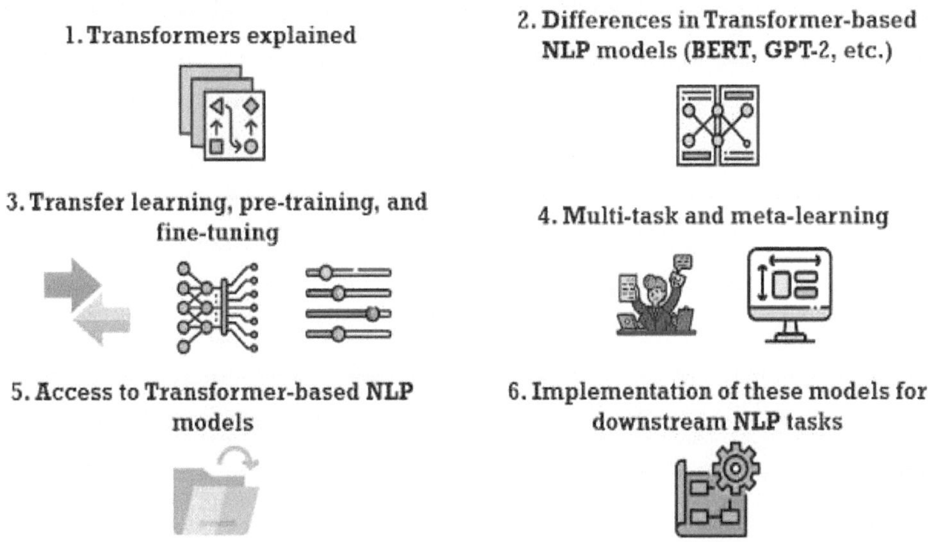

12.3.1 The Rise of Transformers: Traditional sequence-to-sequence models, like RNNs and LSTMs, were instrumental in language tasks. However, they suffered from issues like vanishing gradients and sequential processing bottlenecks. The Transformer architecture, introduced by Vaswani et al., disrupted this paradigm by leveraging self-attention mechanisms to process sequences in parallel, enabling the efficient handling of long-range dependencies.

12.3.2 Architecture of Transformer Models: The emergence of Transformer models marked a watershed moment in the field of natural language processing, introducing a revolutionary architecture that reimagines how machines understand and generate language. At the core of this innovation lies a meticulously designed architecture that consists of two pivotal components: the Encoder and the Decoder. These elements, interconnected by the potency of multi-head self-attention layers, have unlocked the potential for unparalleled language understanding. Let's dive into the intricate design and mechanics of the Transformer architecture.

Components of the Transformer Architecture:

Encoder: The Encoder is the first half of the Transformer architecture responsible for processing the input sequence. It scrutinizes each word's representation and gathers contextual information by leveraging the self-attention mechanism. This mechanism endows the model with the remarkable ability to weigh the importance of each word in relation to the others, transcending the limitations of sequential processing. Consequently, the Encoder captures intricate contextual relationships within the input sequence.

Decoder: Positioned as the counterpart to the Encoder, the Decoder assumes the role of generating the output sequence based on the comprehended input. Like the Encoder, the Decoder encompasses multi-head self-attention layers. However, it introduces additional attention mechanisms to focus on the Encoder's output. This dynamic allows the Decoder to distill the contextual information accumulated during the encoding phase and wield it to generate coherent and contextually informed output sequences.

Multi-Head Self-Attention: The crux of the Transformer's prowess lies in its self-attention mechanism. This mechanism empowers each word to selectively attend to other words within a sequence. The multi-head variant extends this capability by running the self-attention process in parallel multiple times, each with learned weightings. This innovative approach enables the model to capture various aspects of relationships within the input, enhancing its capacity for nuanced understanding.

Layer Composition and Enhancement: Each layer within both the Encoder and the Decoder is a fusion of two sub-layers: multi-head self-attention and feed-forward neural networks. These sub-layers are augmented with residual connections to ensure the preservation of learned information and gradients during training. Additionally, layer normalization is employed to stabilize the learning process by normalizing inputs across dimensions. The combination of these sub-layers, residual connections, and layer normalization forms the bedrock of each layer's functionality. It imbues the Transformer architecture with the ability to process and model intricate dependencies across sequences efficiently and effectively.

Enhancing Language Understanding: By capitalizing on the synergistic interplay between the Encoder and Decoder, and the ingenious utilization of multi-head self-attention, Transformers transcend the limitations of earlier sequence-based models. This architecture unlocks the potential for capturing long-range dependencies, processing sequences in parallel, and generating coherent and contextually informed language output.

12.3.3 Self-Attention Mechanism: The revolutionary impact of Transformer models in natural language processing can be traced back to a fundamental innovation: the self-attention mechanism. This ingenious mechanism lies at the heart of Transformers, propelling their ability to understand contextual relationships and dependencies within sequences of words. Let's delve into the intricate workings of self-attention and explore how it drives the unparalleled capabilities of Transformer models.

Weighing Importance Through Attention: At its core, the self-attention mechanism empowers each word in a sequence to evaluate the importance of other words in relation to itself. This transformative process enables the model to recognize the significance of different words and their roles within the context of the sequence.

Calculating Attention Scores: The essence of self-attention lies in calculating attention scores that quantify the relevance of each word to every other word in the sequence. These scores are computed by considering pairwise relationships between words and are determined based on learned parameters.

Aggregating Representations: Once attention scores are computed, the mechanism proceeds to aggregate the representations of all words according to these scores. Words with higher attention scores contribute more to the aggregated representation, effectively focusing the model's attention on the most relevant words in the context.

Multi-Head Attention: The innovation of multi-head attention elevates the self-attention mechanism's capabilities. In multi-head attention, the self-attention process is replicated multiple times in parallel, each with distinct learned weightings. This setup allows the model to simultaneously focus on different aspects of the input, enhancing its capacity to capture nuanced relationships.

Versatility and Contextual Understanding: The self-attention mechanism underpins the Transformer's ability to understand the contextual nuances of language. By enabling words to collaboratively weigh each other's significance, Transformers excel in capturing long-range dependencies, relationships, and the intricate interplay of words within a sequence.

The self-attention mechanism constitutes the bedrock upon which the Transformer's transformative capabilities are built. By allowing words to evaluate and consider the importance of their peers, self-attention empowers the model to discern contextual nuances and dependencies within sequences. The subsequent introduction of multi-head attention further enriches this process, fostering a deeper understanding of different aspects of the input. The profound implications of the self-attention mechanism have permeated numerous natural language processing tasks, paving the way for more accurate, contextually aware, and versatile language models.

12.3.4 Benefits of Transformer Models: The transformative power of Transformer models in the realm of language understanding cannot be overstated. This novel architecture has ushered in a new era of capabilities, redefining how machines process and comprehend natural language. Let's explore the pivotal benefits that the Transformer architecture has bestowed upon language understanding tasks:

Parallel Processing: One of the defining advantages of Transformer models is their ability to process words in parallel. Unlike traditional models like Recurrent Neural Networks (RNNs), which require sequential processing, Transformers can simultaneously analyze all words in a sequence. This parallelism accelerates both training and inference, significantly reducing computational time and enabling faster model development.

Long-Range Dependencies: The advent of self-attention within the Transformer architecture has revolutionized the handling of long-range dependencies. Transformers excel at capturing relationships between distant words in a sequence. This enhanced contextual awareness empowers the models to understand the broader context and capture intricate nuances even when words are far apart. Consequently, Transformers are well-suited for tasks that demand a deep understanding of context.

Scalability: The modular design of Transformers endows them with remarkable scalability. The architecture can be adapted and fine-tuned for a wide range of tasks without necessitating substantial architectural overhauls. This inherent flexibility makes Transformers a versatile tool that can be harnessed across various language understanding tasks, from sentiment analysis to language translation, with minimal adjustments.

Pretrained Models: Pretraining large Transformer models on massive text corpora has unlocked a powerful avenue for transfer learning. Models like BERT (Bidirectional Encoder Representations from Transformers) and GPT (Generative Pretrained Transformer) are pretrained on extensive datasets, learning rich contextual representations. These pretrained models can then be fine-tuned on task-specific data, resulting in better performance, even when faced with limited labeled data.

12.3.5 Applications of Transformer Models: The profound impact of Transformer models extends across an array of natural language processing tasks, catapulting the field forward with their unprecedented capabilities:

Machine Translation: The prowess of Transformer models, exemplified by models like BERT and GPT, has enabled state-of-the-art results in machine translation. By learning contextual representations, these models deliver more accurate and nuanced translations.

Question Answering: Transformers shine in question-answering tasks. Their ability to capture relevant information from a passage and generate precise answers has led to significant advancements in question-answering systems.

Text Classification: Pretrained Transformer models have demonstrated their potential for text classification tasks. By learning contextual information, they can be fine-tuned to classify text into various categories, such as sentiment analysis or topic categorization.

Named Entity Recognition: Identifying entities like names, dates, and locations within text is vital for information extraction. Transformers leverage their contextual understanding to excel in named entity recognition tasks.

12.3.6 Future Directions: The relentless march of innovation within the field of natural language processing (NLP) ensures that the trajectory of Transformer models is far from stagnant. As the NLP community surges forward, envisioning new horizons and tackling complex challenges, several intriguing avenues for enhancing Transformer models are emerging on the horizon. Let's peer into the future of Transformers and explore the fascinating directions that ongoing research is uncovering.

Architectural Advancements: The drive to construct even more powerful architectures is a focal point of ongoing research. This entails refining existing Transformer components and devising novel structures that can better capture intricate linguistic relationships and further enhance the models' capabilities. By designing architectures that more adeptly understand and manipulate language, researchers aim to elevate the quality of generated outputs and the depth of language comprehension.

Innovative Training Strategies: The mechanisms through which Transformers are trained continue to evolve. Researchers are delving into innovative training strategies that can expedite convergence, improve generalization, and address challenges like catastrophic forgetting. Techniques such as curriculum learning, self-training, and reinforcement learning are being explored to empower Transformers with the ability to learn more efficiently and effectively from data.

Multimodal Fusion: The fusion of text with other modalities, such as images, audio, and video, is gaining traction. Researchers are investigating methods to seamlessly integrate multimodal information into Transformer models, enabling them to comprehend and generate content that combines various forms of data. This direction holds great promise for applications that require a holistic understanding of diverse information sources.

Efficiency and Scalability: As models grow in complexity, the need for efficiency and scalability becomes increasingly crucial. Researchers are working on techniques to make Transformer models more resource-efficient, enabling them to run on devices with limited computational power. Moreover, the development of techniques to scale up training and inference processes while maintaining model quality remains an active area of exploration.

Interpretable and Explainable Models: The 'black-box' nature of complex models like Transformers has sparked interest in creating more interpretable and explainable versions. Researchers are working on methods that can provide insights into the model's decision-making process, making it easier for users to understand why a certain output was generated. This interpretability is crucial for building trust and understanding in AI-driven applications.

Customization and Domain Adaptation: Tailoring Transformer models to specific domains or applications is another burgeoning direction. Researchers are investigating ways to adapt pretrained models to specialized tasks and domains with limited labeled data. By enabling models to learn from domain-specific information, these adaptations can lead to better performance in specialized tasks.

Continual Learning: The ability of Transformers to adapt to new information over time is a topic of active research. Researchers are exploring techniques that facilitate continual learning, where models can learn from new data while retaining their knowledge from previous tasks. This direction is crucial for creating models that can adapt and evolve as they encounter new information.

As the NLP community pushes the boundaries of innovation, the future of Transformer models appears dazzlingly dynamic. With architectural advancements, innovative training strategies, multimodal fusion, efficiency enhancements, interpretability efforts, and domain adaptation, the trajectory of Transformers is poised to redefine language understanding and generation. The relentless pursuit of excellence in NLP will continue to unveil new frontiers and applications, fueling the evolution of Transformer models into even more versatile and powerful language technologies.

12.4 BERT and Pre-trained Language Models: The landscape of natural language processing underwent a seismic shift with the advent of BERT (Bidirectional Encoder Representations from Transformers) and other pre-trained language models. These models, built upon the Transformer architecture, have redefined how machines understand and generate human language. In this section, we delve into the significance of BERT and pre-trained language models, their architecture, and their transformative impact on various NLP tasks.

12.4.1 The Power of Pre-trained Language Models: In the ever-evolving landscape of natural language processing (NLP), the emergence of pre-trained language models has ignited a transformation that challenges conventional machine learning approaches. The power of these models lies in their ability to revolutionize the way machines understand language, unleashing a new era of capabilities that transcend traditional limitations. This section delves into the profound impact of pre-trained language models and how they have democratized NLP by harnessing the potency of generic language representations.

The Traditional Learning Paradigm: Historically, machine learning models were heavily reliant on task-specific labeled data for training. This approach demanded considerable resources and time to curate extensive datasets, annotate them, and subsequently fine-tune models for specific tasks. This laborious process often hindered the scalability of NLP applications and restricted innovation to domains with ample labeled data available.

Paradigm Shift: Pre-trained Language Models: Pre-trained language models have engineered a paradigm shift by learning generic language representations from vast text corpora. This learning phase, referred to as "pre-training," equips the model with a comprehensive understanding of language nuances, syntax, semantics, and context. The acquired knowledge is stored in the form of contextualized embeddings that capture the intricate relationships between words.

Fine-Tuning for Task-Specific Mastery: The transformative potential of pre-trained language models truly shines in the fine-tuning phase. Once equipped with generic language understanding, these models can be fine-tuned using a comparatively small amount of task-specific labeled data. This process leverages the contextual embeddings to adapt the model's knowledge to the nuances of a particular task, effectively personalizing its capabilities.

Democratizing NLP: The impact of pre-trained language models extends far beyond the realm of academia and research. By eliminating the stringent dependence on massive labeled datasets for every new task, these models have democratized NLP. Developers, regardless of their domain, can now harness the potential of NLP technologies without the steep data requirements that earlier hindered progress.

Breakthroughs across Domains: This democratization of NLP has facilitated breakthroughs across diverse domains. From healthcare and finance to education and entertainment, pre-trained language models have enabled the development of sophisticated applications that comprehend and generate human language. This inclusive approach has paved the way for innovative solutions in fields previously untouched by NLP advancements.

Conclusion: The power of pre-trained language models lies in their ability to break down barriers to entry in NLP. By learning generic language representations from extensive text data, they pivot the focus from data collection to efficient adaptation. This transformative approach has catalyzed a paradigm shift in NLP, reshaping how machines understand and generate language, and fostering a new era of accessibility, innovation, and progress.

12.4.2 BERT: Bidirectional Contextual Representations: Among the constellation of pre-trained language models, one star shines particularly bright: BERT (Bidirectional Encoder Representations from Transformers). BERT's groundbreaking approach to language understanding has redefined the landscape of NLP and exemplifies the power of contextualized word embeddings.

A Revolution in Contextual Understanding: BERT's key innovation lies in its ability to understand language in a profoundly contextual manner. Unlike previous models that considered only preceding words (unidirectional context) to predict the next word, BERT introduces a paradigm shift by embracing a bidirectional approach. It processes words in both directions, absorbing context from both preceding and succeeding words. This alteration enables BERT to capture rich and intricate contextual relationships that were previously beyond the reach of NLP models.

The Essence of Contextualized Word Embeddings: BERT's architecture, built upon the foundation of Transformers, facilitates the creation of contextualized word embeddings. Each word's representation is molded by the presence of other words in its vicinity. This contextualization empowers BERT to generate embeddings that encapsulate the subtleties of how a word's meaning shifts based on its context.

Unleashing Nuanced Language Relationships: The ability to capture context from both directions transforms BERT into a formidable engine for understanding nuanced language relationships. It can comprehend idiomatic expressions, polysemous words, and intricate sentence structures with remarkable accuracy. BERT's contextual embeddings reflect the diverse ways in which words interconnect and influence each other within sentences.

A Versatile Powerhouse: BERT's prowess in contextual understanding positions it as a versatile tool for an array of NLP tasks. Its contextualized embeddings enable it to excel in tasks like text classification, question answering, sentiment analysis, and more. The fine-tuning process allows BERT to adapt to specific tasks, harnessing its contextual prowess to generate task-specific insights.

Conclusion: BERT's bidirectional contextual representations have propelled NLP into a new era of understanding. By harnessing the power of contextualized word embeddings, BERT captures language nuances that were previously challenging for models to grasp. Its impact reverberates across diverse NLP applications, underscoring the potential of pre-trained language models to enhance language comprehension, generation, and communication.

12.4.3 Architecture of BERT: At the core of BERT's transformative capabilities lies its architectural foundation, rooted in the renowned Transformer model. This architecture has paved the way for BERT's contextual understanding, enabling it to revolutionize natural language processing. Let's explore the architecture that underpins BERT's power and the unique training process that propels its capabilities.

Transformer Model Framework: BERT inherits its architecture from the Transformer model, a breakthrough development that unleashed parallelism and contextual understanding in NLP. This architecture consists of layers of multi-head self-attention mechanisms and feed-forward neural networks, meticulously designed to capture intricate relationships within sequences of words.

Multi-Head Self-Attention: BERT's multi-head self-attention is a pivotal component that enables the model to weigh the importance of different words in context. By considering various contextual viewpoints, BERT is adept at discerning the nuanced relationships between words, contributing to its contextualized understanding of language.

Feed-Forward Neural Networks: The feed-forward neural networks within BERT's architecture further refine the representations learned through self-attention. These networks process the contextually enriched embeddings and extract higher-level features, enhancing the model's capacity to understand complex language nuances.
Two-Step Training Process: BERT's training process comprises two distinct phases: pre-training and fine-tuning. During pre-training, BERT learns contextual representations from massive amounts of text data. This phase imparts BERT with a rich understanding of language, capturing syntactic, semantic, and contextual relationships.
Fine-Tuning for Task Mastery: The fine-tuning phase tailors BERT's acquired knowledge to specific tasks. Task-specific labeled data is used to adapt BERT's pre-trained contextual embeddings to the nuances of the target task. This personalized adaptation empowers BERT to excel across a diverse spectrum of NLP tasks.
12.4.4 Contributions of BERT: The contributions of BERT to the field of NLP are nothing short of revolutionary. Its architectural innovations and training methodology have catalyzed breakthroughs across a plethora of tasks, transcending the limitations of traditional NLP approaches.
Contextual Embeddings for Nuanced Understanding: BERT's contextual embeddings represent a monumental leap in capturing language nuances. By assimilating contextual cues from surrounding words, BERT can discern polysemy, idiomatic expressions, and intricate linguistic constructs. This contextual understanding enhances its comprehension of language subtleties.
Robustness across Tasks: BERT's pre-trained models serve as a foundation for myriad NLP tasks. Its contextualized embeddings enable it to excel in tasks that involve semantics, context, and linguistic relationships. From sentiment analysis to named entity recognition, BERT's robustness across tasks showcases its versatility.
State-of-the-Art Performance: BERT's pre-trained models have consistently set new benchmarks in NLP tasks. Their ability to capture context and relationships has translated into state-of-the-art performance in domains ranging from question answering to text classification. BERT's contributions have redefined excellence in NLP benchmarks.
A Paradigm Shift: In summary, BERT's architecture and training process have ignited a paradigm shift in NLP. Its contextual prowess and adaptability have unleashed transformative potential, democratizing NLP and enabling machines to comprehend and generate human language with unprecedented accuracy and sophistication.
12.4.5 Expanding the Horizon: Beyond BERT: The success of BERT has paved the way for an array of pre-trained language models. RoBERTa, XLNet, and T5 (Text-to-Text Transfer Transformer) are just a few examples that have built upon BERT's foundation, introducing improvements in architecture, training strategies, and fine-tuning techniques. These models continue to push the boundaries of language understanding.
12.4.6 Democratizing NLP: Pre-trained language models have democratized access to advanced NLP capabilities. Developers and researchers can leverage these models to build powerful applications without needing to train from scratch. This accessibility has sparked innovation across industries, from healthcare to finance, driving the rapid adoption of NLP technologies.
12.4.7 Conclusion: The emergence of BERT and pre-trained language models has revolutionized the field of natural language processing. By learning rich contextual representations from vast text corpora, these models have elevated the capabilities of machines in understanding and generating human language. The architecture, versatility, and transformative impact of BERT and its successors underscore the power of pre-trained language models in reshaping the way we interact with and comprehend language in the digital age.

12.5 Project

Unsolved Project

Suppose you're working on a project to develop a natural language processing (NLP) application using deep learning techniques. To create an effective application, you need to understand word embeddings, recurrent neural networks for text generation, transformer models for language understanding, and pre-trained models like BERT. Before starting the development, research the following: the role and functioning of word embeddings such as Word2Vec, GloVe, and FastText; the use of recurrent neural networks (RNNs) in text generation; the architecture and applications of transformer models in language understanding; and the implementation and benefits of using pre-trained models like BERT. This preparation will enable you to design and implement a powerful NLP application using state-of-the-art deep learning techniques.

12.6 Lab Activity

Unsolved Lab Activity

Implement an RNN-based model to generate text using a given dataset (e.g., Shakespeare's plays or song lyrics).
Task: Use a deep learning framework to implement an RNN-based text generation model. Train the model on a chosen dataset, generate new text samples, and document the implementation process, including data preprocessing, model architecture, training procedure, and generated text examples.

Exercises

Exercise 1 – Multiple Choice Questions

1. What problem did traditional one-hot encoding of words in NLP struggle with?
   A. Capturing word semantics
   B. Parallel processing
   C. Sequential information
   D. Sparse representations
2. What are word embeddings?
   A. Binary vectors representing words
   B. Dense vector representations of words
   C. Sparse representations of words
   D. Sequential models of words
3. What aspect of meaning does each dimension in word embeddings encode?
   A. Semantic relationships
   B. Syntactic patterns
   C. Sequential order
   D. Pronunciation
4. Who developed the Word2Vec technique?
   A. Geoffrey Hinton
   B. Yann LeCun
   C. Tomas Mikolov
   D. Richard Socher
5. What does the CBOW architecture in Word2Vec aim to predict?
   A. A target word's context
   B. The next word in a sequence
   C. A word's syntactic pattern
   D. Semantic relationships

Exercise 2 – True/False

1. Word2Vec, GloVe, and FastText are all methods used for generating word embeddings.
2. Recurrent Neural Networks (RNNs) are not suitable for text generation tasks.
3. BERT is an example of a pre-trained language model designed to improve language understanding.

Review Questions

1. What is the key challenge traditional one-hot encoding of words in NLP faced with?
2. How do word embeddings differ from one-hot encodings in terms of representation?
3. What information do word embeddings capture that one-hot encodings lack?
4. Who is credited with the development of the Word2Vec technique?
5. What is the primary idea behind Word2Vec's approach to learning word embeddings?
6. Explain the intuition behind Word2Vec's approach to capturing word context.
7. What are the two primary architectures of Word2Vec, and how do they differ in their approach?
8. How does Word2Vec enable semantic relationships and arithmetic operations with word embeddings?
9. In what way does GloVe differ from Word2Vec in terms of its methodology?
10. What is the significance of balancing local and global context in GloVe?
11. How does FastText differ from Word2Vec in its approach to representing words?
12. What advantage does FastText offer in handling rare or unseen words?
13. What factors influence the choice between Word2Vec, GloVe, and FastText for NLP tasks?
14. Why are Recurrent Neural Networks (RNNs) well-suited for text generation tasks?
15. What are the challenges traditionally associated with training RNNs for text generation?
16. In what applications have Recurrent Neural Networks (RNNs) made significant contributions?
17. How do Transformer models address the limitations of traditional sequence-to-sequence models like RNNs?
18. What are the key components of the Transformer architecture, and what roles do they play?
19. Explain the concept of multi-head self-attention in Transformer models.
20. What is the role of the self-attention mechanism in the success of Transformer models?
21. How do Transformer models excel in processing sequences with long-range dependencies?
22. What are some of the benefits of Transformer models, particularly in terms of parallel processing?
23. What is the significance of pretraining in pre-trained language models like BERT?
24. How does fine-tuning personalize the capabilities of pre-trained language models for specific tasks?
25. What democratizing effect have pre-trained language models had on the field of NLP?
26. What are some examples of domains that have benefited from the democratization of NLP due to pre-trained language models?
27. What are the key strengths and advantages of pre-trained language models over traditional machine learning approaches in NLP?
28. How does the emergence of pre-trained language models like BERT impact the need for extensive labeled datasets?
29. In what ways have pre-trained language models contributed to innovation in various domains?
30. What is the future potential and significance of pre-trained language models in the field of NLP?

Answers

Exercise 1- 1.A 2.B 3.A 4.C 5.A
Exercise 2- 1) True, 2) False, 3) True

Online Resources

Online Exam Paper:
Link: **https://forms.gle/E9hs6LDiTihD2sTk8**
QR Code:

Chapter 12 Videos Playlist:
Link: **https://www.youtube.com/playlist?list=PLzlh_31VWEFo0stlv2Y_9sSBtHfid7ioq**
QR Code:

Chapter 13: Computer Vision Applications

13.1 Object Detection and Localization: Object detection and localization form the cornerstone of computer vision, enabling machines to identify and locate objects within images or videos. This pivotal task has applications spanning from autonomous vehicles to medical imaging and security surveillance. In this section, we delve into the concepts of object detection and localization, exploring the methodologies and techniques that have revolutionized computer vision.

13.1.1 Understanding Object Detection: In the realm of computer vision, object detection stands as a pivotal task that empowers machines to comprehend visual scenes by identifying and localizing multiple objects within images or video frames. This task transcends the boundaries of mere image classification, where models assign a single label to an entire image. Instead, object detection ventures into the intricate domain of recognizing diverse objects and furnishing vital information about their precise positions.

The fundamental essence of object detection lies in its ability to discern and label multiple objects coexisting within a single image. By extracting meaningful features from visual data, object detection models unveil a spectrum of objects present in the scene. Each detected object is not only assigned a class label indicating its identity but also accompanied by essential spatial information that pinpoints its location within the image.

13.1.2 The Challenge of Localization: The journey of accurate object detection is intrinsically intertwined with the concept of object localization. While identifying objects is indispensable, knowing where they exist within the image is equally vital. This prompts the demand for precise localization, a process that entails defining the spatial boundaries of detected objects.

Localization involves outlining the detected objects using bounding boxes—rectangular frames encapsulating the objects' extents. These bounding boxes act as a visual marker, providing a clear indication of where the object is situated within the image. In scenarios where objects vary in size, orientation, or pose, accurate localization becomes a critical factor to ensure the proper interpretation of visual content.

The significance of precise localization is particularly evident in applications like autonomous vehicles, where the detection of pedestrians, other vehicles, or obstacles necessitates a detailed understanding of their positions. In such cases, the ability to accurately place bounding boxes around objects directly impacts the safety and efficiency of autonomous systems.

the tandem of object detection and localization forms the bedrock of computer vision's ability to comprehend visual data. By identifying multiple objects and determining their precise spatial coordinates, these processes provide a holistic view of visual scenes. This understanding fuels a wide range of applications, from enhancing road safety through autonomous vehicles to streamlining inventory management in retail.

13.1.3 Methodologies for Object Detection: The intricate task of object detection and localization has spurred the development of various methodologies, each with its unique approach to comprehending visual scenes. These methodologies can be broadly categorized into two distinct groups, each bearing its own strengths, challenges, and applications.

Single-Stage Detectors: Single-stage detectors represent a class of methodologies that tackle object detection in a single prediction step. These detectors directly predict both the class of an object and the corresponding bounding box coordinates that encapsulate it within an image. This streamlined approach offers efficiency and speed, making single-stage detectors well-suited for real-time applications where speed is a priority. YOLO (You Only Look Once) is a prime example of a single-stage detector. YOLO divides the image into a grid and associates each grid cell with potential objects. For each grid cell, YOLO predicts class probabilities and bounding box coordinates. While YOLO is fast and efficient, it might encounter challenges in accurately localizing objects, especially when objects overlap or have complex shapes. Another noteworthy single-stage detector is SSD (Single Shot Multi Box Detector). SSD employs a series of convolutional layers to predict class scores and bounding box offsets for objects of different scales. By analyzing multiple layers at varying resolutions, SSD aims to improve accuracy while maintaining efficiency.

Two-Stage Detectors: Two-stage detectors, in contrast, follow a more elaborate two-step process. The first stage involves generating a set of region proposals—potential object locations—within the image. The second stage then refines these proposals by predicting the precise class labels and bounding box coordinates. This approach can achieve higher accuracy, making it well-suited for tasks demanding meticulous localization. A prominent example of a two-stage detector is Faster R-CNN (Region Convolutional Neural Network). Faster R-CNN introduces a region proposal network (RPN) that generates potential object regions using anchor boxes. The subsequent refinement stage fine-tunes these proposals, enhancing both object classification and localization accuracy. Going a step further, Mask R-CNN extends Faster R-CNN to include the capability to segment object instances by predicting pixel-wise masks. This extension proves valuable in tasks where object boundaries and segmentation are crucial, such as instance segmentation.

Conclusion: The choice between single-stage and two-stage detectors depends on the specific demands of the application. Single-stage detectors offer speed and efficiency, while two-stage detectors prioritize precision and accuracy. As computer vision continues to advance, the methodologies for object detection and localization evolve, opening doors to improved techniques that cater to a diverse range of applications.

13.1.4 Challenges and Advances: The pursuit of accurate object detection and localization is not without its challenges. These challenges arise due to the diverse and dynamic nature of real-world visual scenes. Some of the key challenges include:

Variations in Object Characteristics: Objects can exhibit variations in size, shape, pose, and appearance. These variations pose difficulties in defining consistent detection and localization strategies across different instances of the same object class.

Occlusions: Objects in an image may be partially obscured by other objects, leading to challenges in detecting and accurately localizing occluded objects.

Cluttered Backgrounds: Complex and cluttered backgrounds can hinder object detection by causing false positives or obscuring the objects of interest.

Lighting Conditions: Variations in lighting conditions can alter an object's appearance, impacting its detectability and making it challenging to generalize across different lighting scenarios.

Scale and Perspective Changes: Objects can appear at different scales and orientations, demanding algorithms that are robust to changes in perspective.

In response to these challenges, the field of object detection and localization has witnessed significant advances driven by innovative techniques:

Anchor-Based Methods: To handle variations in object sizes and shapes, anchor-based methods propose predefined bounding box shapes and scales at different locations within the image. This approach enhances the model's adaptability to objects of varying proportions.

Attention Mechanisms: Incorporating attention mechanisms, inspired by natural human perception, enables models to focus on relevant parts of the image. Attention mechanisms enhance both the accuracy of detection and the localization of objects.

Transformers: Transformer architectures, known for their success in natural language processing, have been applied to object detection. These architectures capture contextual relationships between objects and their surroundings, contributing to more accurate detection results.

13.1.5 Applications: The impact of object detection and localization extends across various domains, revolutionizing the way machines perceive visual information:

Autonomous Vehicles: Object detection is pivotal for real-time navigation in autonomous vehicles, enabling them to detect pedestrians, vehicles, traffic signs, and obstacles, ensuring safe journeys.

Surveillance Systems: In security and surveillance, accurate detection and localization of unauthorized intruders, suspicious activities, or potential threats are vital for maintaining public safety.

Medical Imaging: Object detection in medical imaging aids in locating and classifying anomalies, tumors, and other abnormalities, facilitating accurate diagnosis and treatment.

Retail: The retail industry benefits from object detection in inventory management, theft prevention, and optimizing the shopping experience through personalized recommendations.

Industrial Automation: Detecting defects or deviations in manufacturing processes ensures product quality, reduces waste, and maintains production efficiency.

The versatility of object detection and localization allows it to make profound contributions across numerous sectors, enhancing safety, efficiency, and decision-making.

despite the challenges posed by the complexities of real-world visual data, the field of object detection and localization continues to advance, driven by ingenious techniques and applications that are transforming industries and enhancing various aspects of our lives.

13.1.6 Future Prospects: As technology advances, object detection and localization are poised for further evolution. The integration of deep learning with attention mechanisms, transformers, and generative models promises more accurate and robust detection. The fusion of computer vision with other modalities like natural language processing could open doors to even more sophisticated applications.

13.1.7 Conclusion: Object detection and localization are bedrocks of computer vision, revolutionizing industries and enhancing various sectors. With methodologies ranging from single-stage to two-stage detectors, and applications spanning from autonomous vehicles to healthcare, the strides made in this field are reshaping how machines perceive and interact with the visual world. As technology marches forward, the future holds the promise of even more accurate, efficient, and intelligent object detection and localization systems.

13.2 Semantic Segmentation and Instance Segmentation: In the realm of computer vision, semantic segmentation and instance segmentation are fundamental tasks that delve deeper into understanding visual content. These tasks go beyond mere object detection by assigning each pixel in an image to a particular class or instance, enabling machines to comprehend and delineate the intricate details of scenes. In this section, we explore the concepts, methodologies, and applications of semantic and instance segmentation.

13.2.1 Semantic Segmentation: Classifying Pixels: In the realm of computer vision, semantic segmentation stands as a powerful technique that goes beyond conventional object detection. This task involves the comprehensive classification of each pixel within an image into predefined categories or classes. These classes often correspond to objects or regions of interest, enabling machines to grasp the intricate details of visual scenes. Unlike object detection, which draws bounding boxes around objects, semantic segmentation provides a fine-grained analysis that yields a pixel-wise labeling of the entire image.

The significance of semantic segmentation lies in its ability to grant machines a profound understanding of the visual content. By labeling each pixel with its corresponding class, the model acquires a nuanced comprehension of the objects present, as well as the various regions and elements that constitute the image. This fine-grained analysis contributes to a more holistic interpretation of the scene, enabling machines to differentiate between different objects and accurately discern background elements.

13.2.2 Instance Segmentation: Identifying Instances: Building upon the foundation of semantic segmentation, instance segmentation takes the concept to the next level by addressing the challenge of object instances within the same class. While semantic segmentation classifies pixels into object categories, instance segmentation goes further by distinguishing between individual instances of the same object class.

In essence, instance segmentation assigns a unique label to each instance of an object. This allows the model not only to recognize different objects but also to separate them even when they overlap or appear adjacent to each other in the scene. The result is a comprehensive understanding of the spatial arrangement of objects, unearthing details that are crucial for tasks requiring precise object separation.

Instance segmentation holds particular importance in scenarios where accurately identifying and differentiating between individual instances is essential. For instance, in counting objects within an image or analyzing object interactions, the ability to separate overlapping instances becomes a critical factor.

In summary, semantic segmentation and instance segmentation are two integral techniques in the field of computer vision, each contributing to the understanding and interpretation of visual scenes at different levels of granularity. While semantic segmentation classifies pixels into meaningful categories, instance segmentation takes the analysis further by untangling the complexities of overlapping object instances. These techniques collectively empower machines to perceive and interpret the visual world with remarkable detail and accuracy.

13.2.3 Methodologies for Semantic and Instance Segmentation: The pursuit of accurate semantic and instance segmentation has led to the development of methodologies that harness the capabilities of convolutional neural networks (CNNs), known for their adeptness in capturing spatial features. These networks are tailored to address the unique challenges posed by segmentation tasks and come in various architectures that span the spectrum from semantic to instance segmentation.

Semantic Segmentation Methodologies: U-Net is an architecture that has gained prominence in semantic segmentation. Its distinctive U-shaped design incorporates both down sampling and up sampling paths. The down sampling path captures context by progressively reducing spatial dimensions, while the up sampling path restores spatial details. This architecture excels at capturing fine-grained details and context simultaneously.

FCN (Fully Convolutional Network) is another foundational architecture for semantic segmentation. FCN transforms fully connected layers into convolutional layers, enabling end-to-end pixel-wise prediction. It employs skip connections to combine low-level and high-level features, enhancing segmentation accuracy.

Deep Lab is an architecture that employs dilated convolutions to address the challenges of capturing object boundaries and contextual information. Dilated convolutions expand the receptive field without losing spatial resolution, making it adept at both local and global information capture.

Instance Segmentation Methodology

Mask R-CNN stands out as a groundbreaking methodology for instance segmentation. An extension of Faster R-CNN, Mask R-CNN introduces the prediction of pixel-wise masks for each detected object instance. By combining object detection and mask prediction, Mask R-CNN enables machines to not only discern object instances but also segment them at the pixel level.

13.2.4 Challenges and Advances: Semantic and instance segmentation tasks are not without challenges, and researchers have continually pushed the boundaries to meet these challenges head-on. Some key challenges include:

Object Occlusions: When objects overlap or occlude each other, accurate segmentation becomes complex.

Fine Details: Capturing intricate details within objects, such as fine textures or boundaries, demands sophisticated techniques.

Ambiguous Boundaries: Objects with ambiguous or ill-defined boundaries present difficulties in accurate segmentation.

To address these challenges, researchers have introduced advanced techniques:

U-Net Architecture: U-Net's architecture, with its emphasis on both context and spatial details, is particularly effective in handling fine details.

Dilated Convolutions: Dilated convolutions, employed in architectures like Deep Lab, enhance the network's ability to capture object boundaries while considering broader context.

Mask R-CNN: By extending Faster R-CNN to predict pixel-wise masks, Mask R-CNN excels in instance segmentation, even in the presence of occlusions and intricate details.

the methodologies for semantic and instance segmentation represent a fusion of architectural ingenuity and technical innovation. These techniques have revolutionized how machines perceive and understand visual scenes, enabling tasks that demand high-level granularity and accuracy. As computer vision continues to evolve, advancements in segmentation methodologies continue to reshape our interaction with visual information.

13.2.5 Applications: The capabilities of semantic and instance segmentation extend far beyond the realm of computer vision research, permeating diverse domains with their transformative potential. These techniques have ushered in a new era of understanding and interacting with the visual world. Here are some notable applications where semantic and instance segmentation play a pivotal role:

Autonomous Vehicles: Semantic and instance segmentation are integral components of the sensory apparatus in autonomous vehicles. These techniques enable vehicles to discern and interpret their surroundings with exceptional precision. Semantic segmentation aids in the analysis of road scenes by identifying road markings, traffic signs, and various types of vehicles. Instance segmentation goes a step further, allowing vehicles to differentiate between individual vehicles and other objects, ensuring safe navigation and decision-making.

Medical Imaging: In the realm of medical imaging, semantic and instance segmentation contribute significantly to diagnostic accuracy and patient care. These techniques enable the segmentation of organs, tissues, and anomalies within medical images. Semantic segmentation helps in the accurate delineation of different structures, aiding in treatment planning and surgery. Instance segmentation is particularly valuable for distinguishing between multiple instances of the same structure, such as identifying individual tumors within an organ.

Agriculture: Agriculture stands to benefit from the precision of semantic and instance segmentation. These techniques facilitate the identification of crops, weeds, and disease-affected areas within agricultural landscapes. By accurately segmenting these elements, farmers can optimize irrigation, pesticide application, and crop management, leading to more efficient and sustainable farming practices.

Augmented Reality: In the realm of augmented reality (AR), semantic and instance segmentation serve as the bridge between the real and virtual worlds. These techniques enable AR systems to understand and interact with real-world scenes. By segmenting the scene into different objects and regions, AR systems can seamlessly integrate virtual elements, such as digital characters or information overlays, into the environment, enhancing user experiences and interactions.

13.2.6 Future Prospects: As the field advances, techniques like self-supervised learning and generative adversarial networks (GANs) hold the potential to improve segmentation accuracy and robustness. Furthermore, the fusion of segmentation with other tasks, such as depth estimation or video understanding, promises to unlock new frontiers in computer vision.

Semantic and instance segmentation transcend traditional object detection by providing a comprehensive understanding of images, down to pixel-level details. These tasks have transformed applications ranging from autonomous systems to medical diagnostics, enriching our interaction with the visual world and propelling computer vision into new dimensions of accuracy and insight.

13.3 Face Recognition and Verification: Face recognition and face verification are groundbreaking applications of computer vision and machine learning that have revolutionized various sectors, from security to entertainment. These technologies leverage the distinctiveness of facial features to identify individuals and determine whether two faces belong to the same person. In this section, we delve into the intricacies of face recognition and verification, exploring the methodologies, challenges, and real-world applications.

13.3.1 Face Recognition: Identifying Individuals: In the realm of computer vision, face recognition stands as a remarkable achievement, leveraging the distinctiveness of facial features to automatically identify individuals. This technology holds immense potential across a spectrum of applications, from security to personalized user experiences. The process involves a sophisticated interplay of algorithms and techniques that enable machines to decipher and differentiate individuals based on their facial attributes.

At its core, face recognition is a process of analyzing the intricate characteristics of a person's face to create a unique identifier, often referred to as a faceprint. This faceprint encapsulates various facial features, including the arrangement of eyes, nose, mouth, and the overall structure of the face. These features are extracted and encoded into a numerical representation that captures the distinctiveness of an individual's face.

The magic of face recognition unfolds when this faceprint is compared against a database containing known faces. The comparison process involves intricate algorithms that measure the similarity between the provided faceprint and those in the database. This similarity score serves as a metric for identification, enabling the system to determine whether the given face corresponds to any known individual in the database.

To achieve this high level of accuracy, face recognition systems harness a range of techniques:

Feature Extraction: This involves isolating and extracting salient facial features, such as eyes, nose, and mouth. These features are crucial for capturing the unique characteristics of an individual's face.

Representation Learning: Through sophisticated neural network architectures, face recognition systems learn to create meaningful and compact representations of facial attributes. These learned representations, or embeddings, capture the essence of an individual's face in a numerical form.

Pattern Recognition: Face recognition algorithms excel at recognizing patterns within the extracted features and embeddings. This involves learning complex relationships among facial attributes that enable accurate identification.

The culmination of these techniques results in a system that can accurately match a provided face to a known individual, even in the presence of varying lighting conditions, facial expressions, and angles.

In essence, face recognition is a testament to the convergence of computer vision, machine learning, and pattern recognition. Its applications are diverse, ranging from unlocking smartphones to enhancing security in public spaces. As the technology continues to advance, the potential for face recognition to reshape industries and our daily lives is undeniable. However, as with any technological advancement, ethical considerations and privacy concerns are vital elements in its responsible development and deployment.

13.3.2 Face Verification: Confirming Identity: Face verification is a powerful concept within the realm of computer vision that revolves around confirming the identity of individuals based on their facial features. Unlike face recognition, which involves identifying individuals from a database of known faces, face verification is a binary decision-making process that determines whether two face images belong to the same person. This technology serves as a cornerstone for authentication and access control, finding applications in secure facilities, digital devices, and beyond.

At its essence, face verification is akin to a digital version of the classic "spot the difference" game. It assesses the similarity between two provided face images and determines whether they indeed depict the same individual. This process involves a nuanced interplay of algorithms designed to capture and compare the unique characteristics of facial attributes.
Here's how face verification works:

Feature Extraction: Just like in face recognition, the process begins with feature extraction. Key facial landmarks, such as the eyes, nose, and mouth, are isolated and encoded into numerical representations.

Embedding Creation: These representations are transformed into embeddings, which are compact numerical vectors that capture the essence of the facial attributes. Embeddings enable quantitative comparison and assessment of similarity.

Comparison: The embeddings of the two provided face images are compared. Algorithms calculate a similarity score that reflects how closely the embeddings align. This score serves as a metric for determining whether the faces belong to the same individual.

Decision: The comparison score is then evaluated against a predefined threshold. If the score surpasses the threshold, the faces are deemed to belong to the same person. If not, they are considered different.

The applications of face verification are diverse and impactful. It finds extensive use in modern-day security systems, where access to secure areas or digital devices is contingent upon confirming one's identity. For instance, smartphones equipped with facial recognition technology employ face verification to unlock the device securely and swiftly. Similarly, secure facilities employ this technology to regulate access to restricted areas.
One of the defining strengths of face verification is its binary nature. It doesn't require an exhaustive database of known faces: instead, it focuses on the comparison between two face images. This simplicity and efficiency make face verification an attractive solution for various applications where the goal is to ensure secure access while minimizing false positives and negatives.

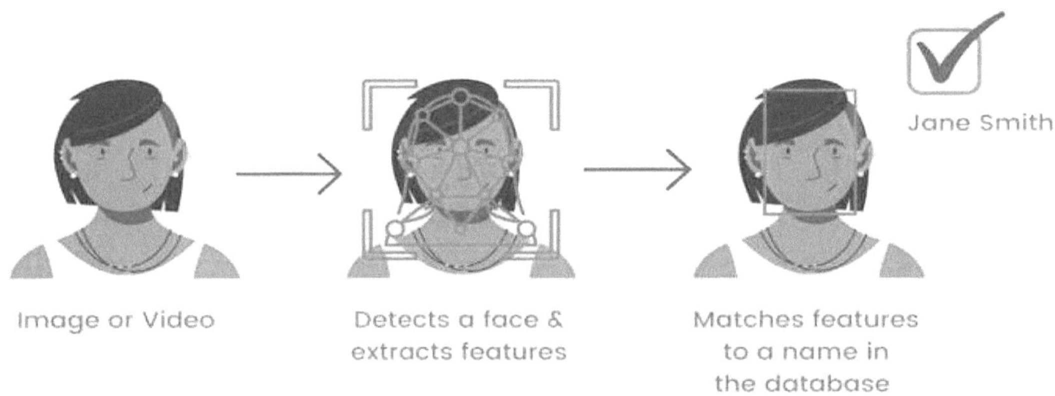

face verification exemplifies the synergy between computer vision and security, delivering a streamlined and effective means of confirming identity. As technology evolves, and the demand for secure and frictionless authentication rises, face verification's role in safeguarding digital and physical spaces becomes increasingly prominent. However, the ethical considerations surrounding privacy, consent, and data security must be at the forefront of its development and implementation.

13.3.3 Methodologies for Face Recognition and Verification: The landscape of face recognition and verification has witnessed a paradigm shift, propelled by the leaps and bounds made in deep learning and neural network architectures. Among these, Convolutional Neural Networks (CNNs) have emerged as the cornerstone due to their exceptional ability to capture intricate features within images. These advancements have paved the way for innovative methodologies that enhance the accuracy and robustness of face recognition and verification systems. Two noteworthy methodologies are Siamese Networks and the Triplet Loss.

Siamese Networks: Learning Embeddings: Siamese Networks stand as an ingenious approach to the challenges of face recognition and verification. These networks consist of twin subnetworks that share identical weights and architectures. The crux of their function lies in their ability to learn to generate similar feature embeddings for images of the same person while producing dissimilar embeddings for images of different individuals.
The process unfolds as follows:

Input Pairs: Siamese Networks take pairs of face images as input. Each pair comprises two images, one belonging to the same individual (a positive pair) and the other to a different person (a negative pair).

Shared Architecture: The twin subnetworks share the same set of weights. This architecture ensures that the embeddings generated for both images within a pair are produced using the same learned parameters.

Embedding Generation: Each image in the pair is fed through the shared architecture, generating a unique embedding for each. These embeddings aim to encapsulate the essential features of the facial attributes.

Distance Calculation: The embeddings are then compared using a distance metric, such as the Euclidean distance. The goal is for the embeddings of positive pairs to be closer to each other and those of negative pairs to be farther apart.

Siamese Networks inherently learn to distinguish between individuals by encouraging the network to recognize subtle differences and similarities in facial attributes. This learning process culminates in an embedding space where similar faces are clustered together, while dissimilar faces are separated by a margin.

Triplet Loss: Optimizing Embedding Space: The Triplet Loss methodology tackles the challenge of face verification by focusing on optimizing the embedding space generated by neural networks. The concept is rooted in the idea of reducing the distance between embeddings of images belonging to the same individual while increasing the distance between embeddings of images from different individuals.

Here's how Triplet Loss works:

Triplet Formation: For each training sample, three images are selected: an anchor image, a positive image (of the same person as the anchor), and a negative image (of a different person).

Embedding Generation: The selected images are passed through the network, generating embeddings for each.

Distance Calculation: The distance between the anchor embedding and the positive embedding is minimized, while the distance between the anchor embedding and the negative embedding is maximized.

The objective is to create an embedding space where similar faces are brought closer together, and distinct faces are pushed apart. The optimization process encourages the network to learn discriminative features that enable accurate identification and verification.

The methodologies of Siamese Networks and the Triplet Loss exemplify the ingenious ways in which deep learning and neural networks are reshaping the landscape of face recognition and verification. These techniques harness the power of similarity learning to create embedding spaces that inherently capture the unique characteristics of individuals. As these methodologies evolve and become integrated into real-world applications, the potential to enhance security, convenience, and personalized experiences grows, underpinned by the meticulous learning of facial attributes and relationships.

13.3.4 Challenges and Advances in Face Recognition and Verification: While face recognition and verification technologies have witnessed remarkable progress, they are not without their share of challenges. The intricacies of human faces, combined with environmental and societal factors, introduce complexities that demand innovative solutions. Fortunately, advances in deep learning and neural network architectures have paved the way for addressing these challenges head-on.

Variability in Pose and Lighting: One of the foremost challenges in face recognition and verification is the variability introduced by changes in pose and lighting conditions. When individuals are captured from different angles or under varying lighting setups, the resulting images can differ significantly from one another. This variance can hinder the accurate matching of faces, impacting the performance of recognition and verification systems.

Advances: Modern face recognition systems employ convolutional neural networks (CNNs) that are adept at capturing invariant features regardless of pose and lighting. Data augmentation techniques, such as rotating, flipping, and altering lighting conditions during training, enable networks to learn robust representations that can handle pose and lighting variations.

Aging: The natural process of aging introduces another layer of complexity to face recognition and verification. Over time, facial features change due to factors like wrinkles, sagging skin, and changes in hairline. This poses a challenge for systems attempting to match faces of the same individual at different ages.

Advances: Researchers are developing methods that can learn to distinguish between age-related changes and inherent facial features. Training models on a diverse range of ages and capturing face images across different stages of life aid in building models that are more resilient to the effects of aging.

Ethnicity and Gender Bias: The issue of bias in face recognition systems, particularly concerning ethnicity and gender, has garnered significant attention. Biases present in training data can lead to inaccuracies and unfair treatment, disproportionately affecting individuals from certain ethnicities or genders.

Advances: Researchers are actively working on reducing biases in training data and developing techniques that can mitigate these biases during model training. Adversarial training, where the model is trained to be robust against biased signals, and data augmentation that ensures balanced representation across different groups are steps toward addressing this challenge.

Advances in Deep Learning: The advances in deep learning techniques have played a pivotal role in improving the accuracy and robustness of face recognition and verification systems. The use of large datasets for training and the emergence of more sophisticated architectures, such as Siamese Networks and Triplet Loss, have enabled models to learn intricate facial features and relationships.

Advances: Transfer learning, where pre-trained models are fine-tuned on smaller datasets, accelerates the training process and improves the performance of models. Additionally, adversarial training and domain adaptation techniques enhance the generalization capabilities of models, making them more effective in real-world scenarios.

Conclusion: Face recognition and verification have traversed a remarkable journey, from challenges rooted in human variability to the innovative solutions emerging from the realm of deep learning. The ongoing advances in the field continue to propel these technologies toward higher accuracy, robustness, and fairness. As these systems become integral to various applications, from security to personal devices, it is imperative to navigate these challenges with a steadfast commitment to ethical considerations, data privacy, and the responsible deployment of these transformative technologies.

13.3.5 Applications of Face Recognition and Verification: The advancements in face recognition and verification technologies have paved the way for transformative applications across a multitude of domains. These technologies, rooted in the understanding of facial attributes and the intricacies of human faces, are reshaping industries and enhancing various facets of our lives.

Security and Surveillance: Perhaps one of the most impactful applications, face recognition and verification have revolutionized security and surveillance. These technologies enable the automatic identification of individuals in public spaces, transportation hubs, and critical infrastructures. By instantly matching faces against databases of known individuals or persons of interest, security personnel can swiftly respond to potential threats and enhance public safety.

User Authentication: In the realm of digital devices and platforms, face verification is a stalwart for secure and seamless user authentication. Smartphones and laptops equipped with facial recognition technology allow users to unlock their devices with a simple glance. This convenience is complemented by the robust security offered by the technology, making unauthorized access significantly more challenging.

Social Media: Face recognition's impact extends to the realm of social media, simplifying the organization and tagging of photos. Recognizing faces within images enables platforms to automatically suggest tags for individuals present in photos. This streamlines the process of identifying and interacting with images, enhancing the overall user experience.

Emotion Detection: Beyond identification, face recognition technologies also contribute to understanding emotions. By analyzing facial expressions and micro-expressions, these systems can discern emotions such as happiness, sadness, surprise, and anger. This capability finds applications in fields like marketing, where understanding customer reactions can drive effective campaigns, and psychology, aiding in emotion research and analysis.

Access Control and Attendance Management: Face recognition has revolutionized access control systems, both in physical spaces and digital platforms. It enables organizations to grant access based on verified identity, streamlining entry to secure areas. Additionally, face recognition systems can be employed for attendance management, automating attendance tracking in educational institutions and workplaces.

13.3.6 Ethical Considerations: While face recognition and verification offer remarkable benefits, they raise ethical concerns related to privacy, surveillance, and bias. Striking a balance between technological advancement and safeguarding individual rights is crucial in the development and deployment of these technologies.

Conclusion

Face recognition and verification have redefined the way we interact with technology, offering seamless authentication and enhanced security. As these technologies continue to evolve, their impact on industries, personal security, and social interactions is set to grow. Balancing innovation with ethical considerations remains pivotal as we navigate this transformative landscape.

13.4 Style Transfer and Image-to-Image Translation: The realm of computer vision isn't solely confined to recognition and understanding: it also delves into the creative and artistic domain. Style transfer and image-to-image translation are two captivating subfields that bring a touch of artistry to the world of visual processing. These techniques enable the transformation of images, imbuing them with new styles, characteristics, or even converting them into entirely different forms. Let's explore the fascinating world of style transfer and image-to-image translation.

13.4.1 Style Transfer: Bridging Art and Reality: Art has the unique power to evoke emotions, provoke thoughts, and transport us to different realms of imagination. On the other hand, the realm of computer vision and image processing delves into the manipulation and understanding of visual data. In a captivating convergence of these worlds, the technique of style transfer emerges as a bridge between the realms of art and reality. It breathes life into images by seamlessly merging the content of one image with the artistic style of another, yielding visually captivating and harmonious results.

Unleashing Creativity Through Fusion: At its core, style transfer involves imbuing the content of one image with the unique stylistic characteristics of another image. This fusion goes beyond the mere combination of pixels: it encapsulates the essence of artistic expression. The process encompasses two primary components:

Content Features: These are the structural and semantic elements that define the essence of the scene or subject in an image. They include shapes, objects, and their arrangements.

Style Features: These are the intricate details that constitute an artist's distinct style – brushstrokes, color palette, texture, and patterns.

The art of style transfer lies in the delicate balance of these features, which results in an image that retains its original content while embodying the artistic style of another.

The Intricacies of Style Transfer: Underlying the process of style transfer are neural network architectures that encode and decode the features of images. The content features of the source image are extracted and combined with the style features of the reference image. Through a process of optimization, the final image emerges – a harmonious blend that seamlessly integrates content and style.

For example, one could take a photograph of a cityscape and infuse it with the distinctive brushstroke patterns of a renowned painter. The outcome is an image that appears to have transcended photography, merging the artistic strokes of the painter with the real-world elements of the cityscape.

A Gateway to Artistic Exploration: Style transfer transcends the confines of traditional artistic mediums, enabling artists and enthusiasts to experiment with novel visual aesthetics. Photographers, painters, and digital artists can collaborate across genres, creating images that harmoniously fuse the artistic expressions of different mediums.

Moreover, style transfer is not limited to the art world. It can find application in fields like design, advertising, and visual communication, where captivating visuals are essential for conveying messages and eliciting emotions.

Style transfer stands as a testament to the boundless creativity that technology can unlock. By bridging the realms of art and reality, it invites us to explore new dimensions of visual expression and storytelling. As technology continues to evolve, style transfer holds the promise of enriching our visual experiences and broadening our understanding of the dynamic interplay between art and technology.

13.4.2 Image-to-Image Translation: Navigating Visual Realms: The canvas of reality often contains distinct visual realms – each with its own unique characteristics, colors, and forms. Yet, what if we could traverse these realms, transcending the boundaries of the visual spectrum? Image-to-image translation is the key that unlocks this possibility, allowing us to bridge the chasm between disparate visual domains and embark on a journey of transformative creativity.

A Metamorphosis of Visual Concepts: At its core, image-to-image translation is the art of metamorphosis. It takes images from one domain and transmutes them into the language of another. Sketches are endowed with realistic textures, daytime scenes transition into nightscapes, and satellite images morph into comprehensible maps.

The process is a marvel of modern neural networks. It involves training a model using pairs of images – one from the source domain and another from the target domain. Through intricate layers of computation, the model learns the intricate relationships between the two domains. Armed with this knowledge, it can then generate images that seamlessly traverse the boundaries of reality and perception.

Beyond the Horizon of Reality: Image-to-image translation transcends the confines of the ordinary, enabling transformations that often appear magical. It empowers us to see the world through new lenses, revealing hidden facets and uncharted territories.

The applications are as diverse as they are fascinating:

Art and Design: Artists can harness image-to-image translation to conjure fantastical scenes and render abstract concepts into visual reality.

Urban Planning: Transforming satellite images into detailed maps aids in urban development, resource allocation, and environmental analysis.

Fashion and Interior Design: Converting sketches into photorealistic representations aids in envisioning and designing clothing and spaces.

Virtual Reality: Bridging visual domains enriches immersive experiences, transporting users to worlds that seamlessly blend reality and imagination.

Navigating the Unseen Realms: As the field of image-to-image translation continues to evolve, researchers are exploring ways to enhance its capabilities. Techniques for guiding the translation process and achieving more precise transformations are on the horizon. Multimodal translation, which extends the concept to other sensory domains, holds the potential to create truly immersive experiences that engage multiple senses simultaneously.

In essence, image-to-image translation is a testament to the boundless potential of technology to reshape how we perceive and interact with the visual world. It invites us to journey beyond the horizon of reality, unlocking realms of creativity and exploration that were once confined to our imagination.

13.4.3 Challenges and Innovations in Visual Transformation: The journey of visual transformation through style transfer and image-to-image translation is one of innovation and creativity, but it is not without its challenges. As technology seeks to bridge the realms of art and reality, it encounters hurdles that must be overcome to ensure the fidelity and coherence of the transformed images.

Preserving Content and Style: In the realm of style transfer, the challenge lies in preserving the original content of an image while seamlessly infusing it with a new artistic style. Achieving this balance necessitates the extraction and alignment of both content and style features. The intricate dance between these features demands sophisticated models that can understand and represent the essence of images across different domains.

Coherence in Translation: Image-to-image translation, while magical in its concept, faces the challenge of maintaining coherence and realism during transformation. As images traverse between visual domains, artifacts, distortions, and unintended alterations can arise, leading to perceptual inconsistencies. Ensuring that the translated images remain faithful to their intended concepts requires a deep understanding of both the source and target domains.

Harnessing Deep Learning Architectures: The landscape of deep learning architectures has undergone a profound transformation, leading to innovations that address the challenges of visual transformation. Generative Adversarial Networks (GANs) have emerged as a cornerstone, pitting a generator against a discriminator to produce images that are increasingly difficult to distinguish from real ones. Variational Autoencoders (VAEs), on the other hand, facilitate the generation of images while navigating latent spaces of variation.

A Leap in Quality and Realism: The integration of GANs and VAEs has marked a significant advancement in the quality of style transfer and image-to-image translation results. These architectures have the power to capture the intricate nuances of style, the essence of content, and the transitions between visual domains. Through adversarial training and probabilistic modeling, they bring forth images that evoke the magic of creative transformation while maintaining realism and coherence.

Future Horizons: As the fields of style transfer and image-to-image translation continue to evolve, the path ahead holds promise and excitement. Fine-tuning models, guiding transformations, and enhancing interpretability are areas of active exploration. Furthermore, advancements in generative models may lead to even greater levels of creativity and control, enabling users to craft images that fuse their imagination with the capabilities of technology.

In the realm of visual transformation, challenges are met with innovative solutions, and every advance brings us closer to realizing the dreams of artists, creators, and enthusiasts who seek to blend the boundaries of art and reality.

13.4.4 Applications of Visual Transformation: The transformative powers of style transfer and image-to-image translation ripple across various domains, reshaping the way we perceive and interact with the visual world. From unleashing artistic creativity to revolutionizing practical applications, these technologies have left an indelible mark on the canvas of innovation.

Artistry Unleashed: The realm of art has witnessed a renaissance through style transfer. Artists, photographers, and creators of all kinds are embracing the potential to merge diverse artistic styles, culminating in images that defy traditional boundaries. The canvas is no longer confined to a single aesthetic – it is a realm where the strokes of Van Gogh dance with the contours of a photograph, creating new dimensions of visual expression.

Cinematic Marvels: Image-to-image translation has found its way into the world of cinema and visual effects. Mundane scenes can be transmuted into fantastical landscapes, unlocking the doors to unprecedented storytelling. The realms of science fiction and fantasy are no longer bound by the constraints of reality, as technology grants filmmakers the power to weave the fabric of imagination into the tapestry of the screen.

Urban Evolution: The practical applications of these technologies are equally compelling. Architecture and urban planning benefit from the translation of satellite images into informative maps, offering insights into spatial distribution, land use, and infrastructure. The blueprint of cities comes to life, facilitating informed decisions for sustainable urban development.

Designing New Realities: In the world of fashion and design, style transfer becomes a tool for creating unique patterns, textures, and visual elements. Designers can seamlessly blend different aesthetics, resulting in garments and spaces that push the boundaries of creativity. The marriage of digital innovation and design intuition breathes life into concepts that were once confined to the realm of imagination.

As style transfer and image-to-image translation continue to evolve, their applications will undoubtedly expand. The journey of visual transformation is an invitation to explore uncharted territories, where art, imagination, and technology coalesce to redefine the possibilities of the visual landscape.

13.4.5 Future Directions: As the technologies of style transfer and image-to-image translation evolve, researchers are exploring ways to make these processes more controllable and customizable. The ability to guide the style transfer process or achieve precise translations opens up new opportunities for creative expression and problem-solving. Additionally, advancements in multimodal translation could lead to even more dynamic transformations between visual and other modalities, further blurring the boundaries between reality and imagination.

13.5 Project

Unsolved Project

Suppose you're working on a project that involves applying deep learning techniques to various computer vision tasks. To achieve this, you need to understand object detection and localization, semantic and instance segmentation, face recognition and verification, and style transfer and image-to-image translation. Before starting your project, research the following: methods for object detection and localization, techniques for semantic and instance segmentation, algorithms for face recognition and verification, and approaches for style transfer and image-to-image translation. This foundational knowledge will equip you with the skills needed to implement and integrate these computer vision applications effectively.Top of Form

13.6 Lab Activity

Unsolved Lab Activity

Implement an object detection model using a deep learning framework on a given dataset (e.g., COCO or Pascal VOC).

Task: Use a deep learning framework (e.g., TensorFlow or PyTorch) to implement an object detection model. Train the model on a dataset such as COCO or Pascal VOC. Document the implementation process, including data preprocessing, model architecture, training procedure, and evaluation metrics. Provide visualizations of the detected objects in sample images.

Exercises

Exercise 1 – Multiple Choice Questions

1. What is the primary focus of object detection and localization in computer vision?
   A. Identifying image backgrounds
   B. Detecting and labeling multiple objects
   C. Image classification
   D. Camera calibration
2. What is the significance of accurate object localization in computer vision?
   A. It helps in image classification.
   B. It provides a holistic view of visual scenes.
   C. It ensures efficient image compression.
   D. It speeds up object detection.
3. Which type of detector is known for its speed and efficiency but may face challenges in precise object localization?
   A. YOLO (You Only Look Once)
   B. SSD (Single Shot MultiBox Detector)
   C. Faster R-CNN
   D. Mask R-CNN
4. What does SSD (Single Shot MultiBox Detector) aim to improve while maintaining efficiency?
   A. Speed
   B. Object classification accuracy
   C. Object localization accuracy
   D. Image resolution
5. In which application is precise object localization particularly important for ensuring safety and efficiency?
   A. Image compression
   B. Autonomous vehicles
   C. Image classification
   D. Medical imaging

Exercise 2 – True/False

1. Object detection is only about identifying the presence of objects in an image.
2. Semantic segmentation assigns a label to each pixel of an image, while instance segmentation differentiates between different instances of the same object class.
3. Face recognition and face verification are the same processes in computer vision.

Review Questions

1. What are the key applications of object detection and localization in computer vision?
2. How does object detection differ from image classification, and why is it important?
3. Explain the significance of precise object localization in computer vision.
4. What information is provided by object detection models beyond class labels?
5. Describe the challenges involved in accurate object localization.
6. Provide examples of applications where precise object localization is critical.
7. What are single-stage detectors, and what advantages do they offer in object detection?
8. Explain the concept of anchor-based methods in object detection.
9. How do two-stage detectors differ from single-stage detectors, and what are their strengths?
10. What is Mask R-CNN, and how does it extend the capabilities of Faster R-CNN?
11. What is semantic segmentation, and how does it differ from object detection?
12. Why is fine-grained analysis important in semantic segmentation?
13. Describe the concept of instance segmentation and its applications.
14. How does instance segmentation differ from semantic segmentation?
15. Explain the methodologies used in semantic segmentation, such as U-Net and Deep Lab.
16. What are the challenges faced in semantic and instance segmentation tasks?
17. How do dilated convolutions enhance the performance of segmentation models?
18. In what domains do semantic and instance segmentation find practical applications?
19. What is the primary goal of face recognition, and how does it work?
20. How do face recognition systems create unique identifiers for individuals?
21. Explain the process of comparing a faceprint to a database of known faces in face recognition.
22. What are some key applications of face recognition technology?
23. How does face verification differ from face recognition, and what is its primary use?
24. Describe the steps involved in face verification, including feature extraction and decision-making.

25. What advantages does face verification offer in terms of authentication and access control?
26. What are some ethical considerations associated with face recognition and verification technologies?
27. How do Siamese Networks and the Triplet Loss enhance face recognition and verification systems?

Answers

Exercise 1- 1.B 2.B 3.A 4.B 5.B
Exercise 2- 1) False, 2) True, 3) False

Online Resources

Online Exam Paper:
Link: **https://forms.gle/yhu7u1tTgTgGXEWx9**
QR Code:

Chapter 13 Videos Playlist:
Link: **https://www.youtube.com/playlist?list=PLzlh_31VWEFoVGOwBkc_B4CbIR0Zen-my**
QR Code:

Chapter 14: Time Series Analysis with Deep Learning

14.1 Time Series Forecasting using RNNs: Time series data is a treasure trove of insights, and predicting future values based on historical patterns is crucial for decision-making. Recurrent Neural Networks (RNNs) have emerged as a potent tool for time series forecasting due to their aptitude for capturing sequential information.

14.1.1 Unraveling Temporal Patterns: At the heart of time series forecasting lies the exploration of temporal patterns. These patterns are the building blocks of predictability, hinting at the trends, seasonality, and dependencies that underlie the data. RNNs, with their recurrent connections, excel at understanding and leveraging these temporal relationships. Unlike traditional methods, RNNs can consider not only the current input but also the historical context, enabling them to capture nuances that would otherwise remain hidden.

14.1.2 The Anatomy of an RNN: The architecture of an RNN mirrors the flow of time itself. It processes input sequences one step at a time, updating its hidden state with each new input. This hidden state acts as a memory of the past, retaining information about previous time steps. This memory is crucial for understanding the sequential dynamics that shape time series data.

14.1.3 Long Short-Term Memory (LSTM) and Gated Recurrent Units (GRUs): While basic RNNs are capable of capturing short-term dependencies in time series data, they often struggle with long-range dependencies due to the vanishing gradient problem. This limitation is where specialized architectures like Long Short-Term Memory (LSTM) and Gated Recurrent Units (GRUs) come into play.

Long Short-Term Memory (LSTM): Long Short-Term Memory (LSTM) is a breakthrough architecture that overcomes the limitations of traditional RNNs in capturing long-range dependencies. The vanishing gradient problem, where gradients diminish as they propagate backward in time, hampers the ability of basic RNNs to remember distant context. LSTMs address this by introducing specialized memory cells that selectively store and update information over time.

LSTM units consist of three gates: the input gate, the forget gate, and the output gate. The input gate regulates the flow of new information into the memory cell, the forget gate determines what information to discard from the cell's memory, and the output gate controls the information that gets passed to the next time step. This gating mechanism enables LSTMs to capture and retain relevant information while discarding noise, making them adept at modeling both short-term and long-term dependencies.

Gated Recurrent Units (GRUs): Gated Recurrent Units (GRUs) are a sibling architecture to LSTMs, designed to address the same vanishing gradient problem. GRUs simplify the LSTM architecture by combining the memory cell and hidden state into a single unit. They have two gates: the reset gate and the update gate.

The reset gate determines which information from the previous time step to forget, while the update gate controls how much of the previous hidden state to consider in the current time step. GRUs strike a balance between complexity and performance, making them computationally efficient while still capturing short-term and long-term dependencies effectively.

14.1.4 Unveiling Future Trends: Time series forecasting using RNNs is a two-step process that begins with training and culminates in prediction. In the training phase, historical data is fed into the network, enabling it to learn underlying temporal patterns and dependencies. Once trained, the network applies its learned knowledge to predict future values iteratively.

During prediction, the network generates one step ahead at a time, using the predicted value as input for the next step. This iterative process unveils future trends, capturing patterns, seasonality, and fluctuations. These insights empower decision-makers to plan and act proactively, leveraging the predictive power of RNNs to navigate uncertainty and make informed choices.

14.1.5 Beyond the Basics: As the field of time series forecasting evolves, innovations are constantly pushing the boundaries of what's possible. Attention mechanisms have emerged as a powerful tool to enhance the accuracy of predictions. These mechanisms allow RNNs to dynamically focus on relevant time steps while downplaying noise, thereby improving the model's ability to capture and forecast subtle patterns within the data.

Hybrid models that combine RNNs with other techniques further elevate the capabilities of time series forecasting. These models might incorporate external factors, such as economic indicators or weather data, into the forecasting process. By leveraging the strengths of different methodologies, hybrid models provide a holistic approach to understanding and predicting complex temporal dynamics.

14.1.6 The Tapestry of Possibilities: Time series forecasting using RNNs weaves a tapestry of possibilities across diverse industries. In finance, RNNs predict stock prices, enabling investors to make informed decisions. In healthcare, they forecast patient admissions, assisting in resource allocation. From energy to manufacturing, RNNs help organizations anticipate demand and optimize operations.

As artificial intelligence continues to advance, our ability to decipher the intricacies of time series data grows stronger. The evolution of algorithms and computing power empowers us to unravel deeper insights from the temporal fabric of information. In an era of uncertainty, time series forecasting stands as a beacon of strategic planning and proactive decision-making, enabling us to navigate the future with newfound clarity.

14.2 Temporal Convolutional Networks (TCNs): Temporal Convolutional Networks (TCNs) represent a groundbreaking approach to time series analysis, offering an alternative to traditional Recurrent Neural Networks (RNNs). TCNs leverage the power of convolutional layers to capture temporal dependencies, making them highly effective for tasks like time series forecasting, sequence classification, and more.

14.2.1 Embracing Convolutional Power: Temporal Convolutional Networks (TCNs) harness the potent capabilities of convolutional layers, which have demonstrated their prowess in capturing intricate spatial hierarchies within images. In the context of TCNs, these convolutional layers are ingeniously adapted to operate along the temporal dimension of sequential data. This adaptation enables TCNs to immerse themselves in the temporal dynamics of sequences, uncovering and representing the underlying patterns and dependencies encoded within the data.

Convolutional layers are renowned for their aptitude in recognizing local features in images, such as edges and textures. When transposed to the realm of time series data, these layers shine a light on short-term temporal dependencies, unraveling the temporal intricacies that weave the fabric of sequences. This union of convolutional power with temporal context equips TCNs with a unique vantage point for time series analysis.

14.2.2 Dilated Convolutions for Wider Insights: A hallmark feature of TCNs is the integration of dilated convolutions, also referred to as atrous convolutions. Dilated convolutions endow TCNs with the ability to grasp wide-spanning contexts without succumbing to the pitfalls of excessive parameter inflation.

Conventionally, increasing the receptive field of a neural network layer necessitates a corresponding increase in the number of parameters. However, dilated convolutions bypass this trade-off by incorporating gaps within the convolutional filter. These gaps allow the convolutional layer to accumulate information from a broader temporal scope without proportionally augmenting parameter count.

This innovation empowers TCNs to capture long-range dependencies that are pivotal for comprehending intricate temporal patterns. By avoiding the vanishing and exploding gradient challenges that can impede the training of recurrent architectures, TCNs rise as formidable contenders for modeling sequences characterized by extended temporal relationships.

In essence, the utilization of dilated convolutions within TCNs manifests as a strategic choice, enabling these networks to transcend the limitations of traditional convolutional layers and recurrent structures. This unique architectural component fuels TCNs' capability to unveil hidden temporal nuances within sequential data, marking a significant stride forward in time series analysis.

14.2.3 Parallelism for Faster Computation: TCNs introduce parallelism to time series analysis. Unlike RNNs that process sequences sequentially, TCNs can process multiple time steps in parallel. This parallelism accelerates training and prediction times, making TCNs efficient and suitable for real-time applications.

14.2.4 Applications and Advantages: Temporal Convolutional Networks (TCNs) have showcased their mettle across an array of time series tasks, earning a reputation for superiority in certain domains. These applications span the breadth of time-related challenges, showcasing TCNs' versatility and effectiveness.

In time series forecasting, TCNs have emerged as formidable contenders. Their inherent capability to capture intricate patterns, including seasonality and subtle variations, makes them adept at uncovering the hidden rhythms within historical data. By leveraging dilated convolutions to discern long-range dependencies, TCNs provide a robust platform for generating accurate predictions of future trends.

Sequence classification benefits from TCNs' prowess as well. Their knack for comprehending contextual information equips them to excel in tasks that demand understanding sequential nuances. TCNs exhibit an ability to dissect sequences and identify key elements, making them well-suited for tasks such as text classification, speech recognition, and sentiment analysis.

One of TCNs' remarkable virtues lies in their ability to offer stability during training. The vanishing gradient problem, which has haunted traditional recurrent architectures, is mitigated by TCNs' incorporation of dilated convolutions. This stability not only accelerates training but also bolsters the reliability of predictions, making TCNs an attractive option for industries where precision and timely decisions are paramount.

14.2.5 Limitations and Ongoing Research: However, TCNs are not a universal panacea for all time series challenges. While they shine in tasks where capturing long-range dependencies is essential, there are scenarios where recurrent architectures like RNNs might still hold an edge. Tasks that heavily rely on modeling sequential dynamics, such as machine translation or music generation, could potentially benefit more from RNNs' intrinsic understanding of sequential relationships.

Ongoing research delves into understanding the precise niches where TCNs can shine brightest. Researchers are exploring the boundaries of TCNs' applicability and refining their capabilities through hybrid models that amalgamate TCNs with other architectures. These hybrid models seek to harness the strengths of different approaches to create synergistic solutions that cater to a diverse spectrum of time series challenges.

Temporal Convolutional Networks offer a fresh perspective on time series analysis, capitalizing on convolutional power and dilated convolutions to capture temporal patterns and dependencies. Their applications span forecasting and classification, and while they're not universally superior, ongoing research seeks to carve out their ideal domains while exploring hybrid models that meld the best of various approaches.

14.2.6 Empowering Temporal Analysis: Temporal Convolutional Networks have carved a niche in the landscape of time series analysis. Their ability to capture long-range dependencies, exploit parallelism, and offer stable training makes them a powerful tool for diverse applications. As the field of artificial intelligence continues to evolve, TCNs stand as a testament to innovation and the quest for more efficient and effective methods of understanding temporal data.

14.3 Applications in Finance and Stock Market Prediction: The world of finance is a realm where timely insights and accurate predictions hold immense value. In recent years, the marriage of machine learning techniques and financial data has opened doors to transformative applications, particularly in the domain of stock market prediction. The integration of sophisticated algorithms, such as time series forecasting and deep learning, has propelled the financial landscape into an era of data-driven decision-making.

14.3.1 Unveiling Trends and Patterns: The applications of machine learning in finance extend beyond routine tasks. Time series analysis, a cornerstone of machine learning, is instrumental in understanding and uncovering hidden trends and patterns within financial data. Techniques like moving averages, exponential smoothing, and autoregressive integrated moving average (ARIMA) models provide insights into historical performance and short-term trends.

14.3.2 Deep Learning and Stock Market Prediction: The allure of deep learning models, particularly Recurrent Neural Networks (RNNs) and Temporal Convolutional Networks (TCNs), lies in their ability to capture intricate temporal dependencies within financial data. By analyzing historical stock prices, trading volumes, and other relevant factors, these models can generate forecasts that aid traders, investors, and financial analysts in making informed decisions.

RNNs can identify complex patterns and relationships in time series data, enabling them to make predictions with a grasp of both short-term fluctuations and long-term trends. TCNs, on the other hand, harness the power of dilated convolutions to capture extended temporal dynamics, making them ideal for forecasting in scenarios with a mix of short and long-term influences.

14.3.3 Risk Management and Portfolio Optimization: Beyond prediction, machine learning plays a pivotal role in risk management and portfolio optimization. Algorithms can assess the risk associated with different investments and construct portfolios that balance risk and reward. This helps investors diversify their holdings and manage their exposure to market volatility.

14.3.4 Challenges and Future Directions: While the integration of machine learning in finance holds immense promise, it is not without its challenges. Financial markets are influenced by a multitude of factors, including global events, economic indicators, and human behavior. Navigating these complexities demands models that are both accurate and adaptable.

The future of machine learning in finance lies in harnessing its potential to create predictive models that encompass a broader range of factors. Hybrid models that combine traditional quantitative analysis with cutting-edge deep learning techniques could provide a holistic view of market dynamics.

the application of machine learning techniques in finance, particularly in stock market prediction, is revolutionizing the way decisions are made in this complex and dynamic domain. The ability to unveil trends, predict market movements, manage risks, and optimize portfolios showcases the transformative power of data-driven insights in shaping the financial landscape.

14.4 Health Monitoring and Disease Prediction: In the realm of healthcare, the fusion of machine learning and medical data has ushered in a new era of personalized health monitoring and disease prediction. With the abundance of patient data and the advancements in machine learning algorithms, healthcare professionals are now equipped with powerful tools to enhance diagnosis, treatment, and patient care.

14.4.1 Leveraging Data for Insights: Health monitoring has evolved from occasional check-ups to continuous and real-time monitoring, thanks to the integration of machine learning algorithms and data-driven approaches. This advancement allows healthcare professionals to gain deeper insights into an individual's health status and make informed decisions for better patient care.

Continuous Data Collection: Health monitoring involves the continuous collection of various types of data from patients. This data can include vital signs such as heart rate, blood pressure, body temperature, respiratory rate, and more. Wearable devices, such as smartwatches and fitness trackers, play a crucial role in collecting this data throughout the day, even during routine activities and sleep.

Physiological Parameters: Machine learning algorithms are adept at processing physiological data to detect anomalies and trends. For example, they can analyze heart rate variability to identify signs of stress or fatigue. By monitoring sleep patterns, algorithms can provide insights into sleep quality and identify sleep disorders.

Comprehensive Health Overview: By combining data from multiple sources, machine learning models can generate a comprehensive overview of an individual's health. This can include assessing physical activity levels, tracking caloric expenditure, and even monitoring emotional well-being through sentiment analysis of text data.

14.4.2 Disease Prediction and Early Detection: Machine learning has the potential to revolutionize disease prediction and early detection, ushering in a new era of proactive and personalized healthcare.

Analyzing Complex Data: Machine learning models excel at processing and analyzing complex and multidimensional data. By considering various factors such as genetic information, lifestyle choices, medical history, and environmental factors, these models can identify subtle patterns and correlations that might not be apparent through traditional methods.

Identifying Precursors: Early signs of diseases often manifest in subtle ways that might go unnoticed by patients and even clinicians. Machine learning models can identify precursors or risk factors that indicate an increased likelihood of developing specific conditions. For example, changes in biomarkers, irregularities in heart rate patterns, or fluctuations in glucose levels can provide valuable insights.

Personalized Preventive Strategies: Armed with predictive insights, healthcare professionals can develop personalized preventive strategies for individuals at risk. These strategies might include lifestyle modifications, dietary recommendations, and targeted screenings. By intervening early, the progression of diseases can be slowed down or even prevented.

Transforming Healthcare: Disease prediction and early detection not only improve patient outcomes but also have the potential to reduce healthcare costs by minimizing the need for intensive treatments and hospitalizations. Additionally, the focus shifts from reactive care to proactive and preventive measures, ultimately leading to healthier populations.

In the realm of health monitoring and disease prediction, machine learning has the capacity to transform healthcare into a more personalized, data-driven, and proactive field, empowering individuals to take control of their health and enabling healthcare professionals to make more informed decisions. However, it's essential to address challenges related to data privacy, model interpretability, and ethical considerations to ensure the responsible and ethical use of these technologies in healthcare.

14.4.3 Precision Medicine: Machine learning also plays a crucial role in precision medicine, tailoring treatments to individual patients based on their unique genetic makeup, medical history, and other factors. By analyzing vast amounts of genomic and clinical data, machine learning models can identify the most effective treatment options and predict how patients will respond to different therapies. This not only enhances patient outcomes but also reduces the trial-and-error approach to treatment.

14.4.4 Challenges and Ethical Considerations: The integration of machine learning into health monitoring and disease prediction brings both opportunities and challenges. Addressing these challenges and ensuring ethical considerations are paramount for the responsible deployment of these technologies.

Data Privacy and Security: Health data is sensitive and private, and maintaining patient confidentiality is crucial. Ensuring robust data encryption, secure storage, and strict access controls are necessary to protect patient information from breaches.

Biases in Data: Biases in training data can lead to skewed predictions, particularly if certain demographic groups are underrepresented. It's essential to address these biases to ensure that predictions are accurate and equitable for all patient populations.

Informed Consent: Using patient data for machine learning requires informed consent. Patients must understand how their data will be used, and their consent should be obtained in a transparent and comprehensible manner.

Interpretability: Machine learning models used in healthcare need to be interpretable. Healthcare professionals must be able to understand and explain how predictions are generated to make informed decisions.

Patient Autonomy: While predictive models can provide valuable insights, patients must retain the right to make their own healthcare decisions. Predictions should complement, not replace, clinical judgment.

Bias Mitigation: Machine learning models can inadvertently perpetuate biases present in the training data. Continuous monitoring and active efforts to identify and mitigate biases are essential to ensure equitable healthcare outcomes.

Regulatory Compliance: Healthcare is subject to stringent regulations and compliance requirements. Machine learning models must adhere to these regulations, including those related to data protection and medical device classification.

14.4.5 Future Directions: The future of health monitoring and disease prediction through machine learning holds great promise. To further harness this potential, several directions are being explored:

Multimodal Data Integration: Integrating data from diverse sources, such as electronic health records, wearable devices, and genomics, can provide a holistic view of an individual's health and enable more accurate predictions.

Explainable AI: Developing models that provide transparent explanations for their predictions is crucial for gaining trust from healthcare professionals and patients.

Personalized Treatment: Machine learning can help tailor treatment plans based on individual patient profiles, optimizing interventions and improving patient outcomes.

Continuous Monitoring: Real-time monitoring using wearable devices and sensors can provide a continuous stream of data for analysis, enabling timely interventions.

Collaboration: Collaboration between data scientists, clinicians, and regulatory bodies is essential to ensure that machine learning models align with medical best practices and ethical standards. The integration of machine learning into health monitoring and disease prediction has the potential to revolutionize healthcare by enabling earlier interventions, personalized treatments, and more proactive patient care. However, responsible development, transparency, and collaboration are key to realizing these benefits while addressing challenges and ethical considerations.

14.5 Project

Unsolved Project

Suppose you're developing a project focused on time series analysis using deep learning techniques. To effectively analyze and predict time series data, you need to understand time series forecasting with RNNs, temporal convolutional networks (TCNs), and their applications in various fields such as finance and health monitoring. Before starting, research the following: the use of recurrent neural networks (RNNs) for time series forecasting, the structure and advantages of temporal convolutional networks (TCNs), specific applications in finance, such as stock market prediction, and the use of deep learning for health monitoring and disease prediction. This preparation will provide you with the necessary knowledge to build a robust time series analysis model for your project.

14.6 Lab Activity

Unsolved Lab Activity

Understand and apply deep learning techniques for time series analysis, including RNNs, Temporal Convolutional Networks (TCNs), and their applications in finance, stock market prediction, health monitoring, and disease prediction.

Exercises

Exercise 1 – Multiple Choice Questions

1. What is the primary purpose of time series forecasting?
   a. Data visualization
   b. Identifying outliers
   c. Predicting future values
   d. Clustering historical data
2. Why are Recurrent Neural Networks (RNNs) suitable for time series forecasting?
   a. They excel at image recognition
   b. They capture sequential information
   c. They require no historical data
   d. They eliminate temporal patterns
3. What is the role of the hidden state in an RNN?
   a. It stores input data
   b. It updates with each new input
   c. It discards historical context
   d. It hampers data understanding
4. Which problem do Long Short-Term Memory (LSTM) networks address?
   a. Short-term memory
   b. Vanishing gradient
   c. Input gate regulation
   d. Sequential data processing
5. How many gates do LSTM units typically consist of?
   a. One
   b. Two
   c. Three
   d. Four

Exercise 2 – True/False

1. Recurrent Neural Networks (RNNs) are commonly used for time series forecasting due to their ability to handle sequential data.
2. Temporal Convolutional Networks (TCNs) are not suitable for tasks requiring long-term memory retention.
3. Time series analysis with deep learning can be effectively applied to health monitoring and disease prediction.

Review Questions

1. What is the primary advantage of using Recurrent Neural Networks (RNNs) in time series forecasting?
2. How do RNNs differ from traditional methods when it comes to understanding temporal patterns?
3. What is the role of the hidden state in an RNN, and why is it important for time series analysis?
4. How do Long Short-Term Memory (LSTM) networks address the vanishing gradient problem?
5. Explain the functions of the three gates in LSTM units: input gate, forget gate, and output gate.
6. What is the key difference between LSTM and Gated Recurrent Units (GRUs)?
7. How do GRUs simplify the architecture compared to LSTMs, and what trade-offs are made?
8. Describe the two gates in a GRU and their respective functions.
9. Why are Temporal Convolutional Networks (TCNs) considered computationally efficient for time series analysis?
10. How do dilated convolutions in TCNs help capture long-range dependencies without increasing parameter count?
11. What is the advantage of parallelism in TCNs when compared to traditional RNNs?
12. In which domains have TCNs proven to be effective for time series tasks?
13. What is the vanishing gradient problem, and how do TCNs help mitigate it?
14. What are some limitations of TCNs in certain scenarios compared to RNNs?

Answers

Exercise 1- 1.c 2. b 3.b 4.b 5.c
Exercise 2- 1) True, 2) False, 3) True

Online Resources

Online Exam Paper:
Link: https://forms.gle/UAjAbnvufLoJyk9q6
QR Code:

Chapter 14 Videos Playlist:
Link: https://www.youtube.com/playlist?list=PLzlh_31VWEFolAEMzd64gYh0Sa4_qsemC
QR Code:

Chapter 15: Deep Learning in Healthcare

15.1 Medical Image Analysis and Diagnosis: Medical image analysis and diagnosis using machine learning have transformed the field of healthcare by enhancing the accuracy and efficiency of medical imaging interpretation. Machine learning techniques have enabled healthcare professionals to extract valuable insights from various medical images, aiding in disease diagnosis, treatment planning, and patient care.

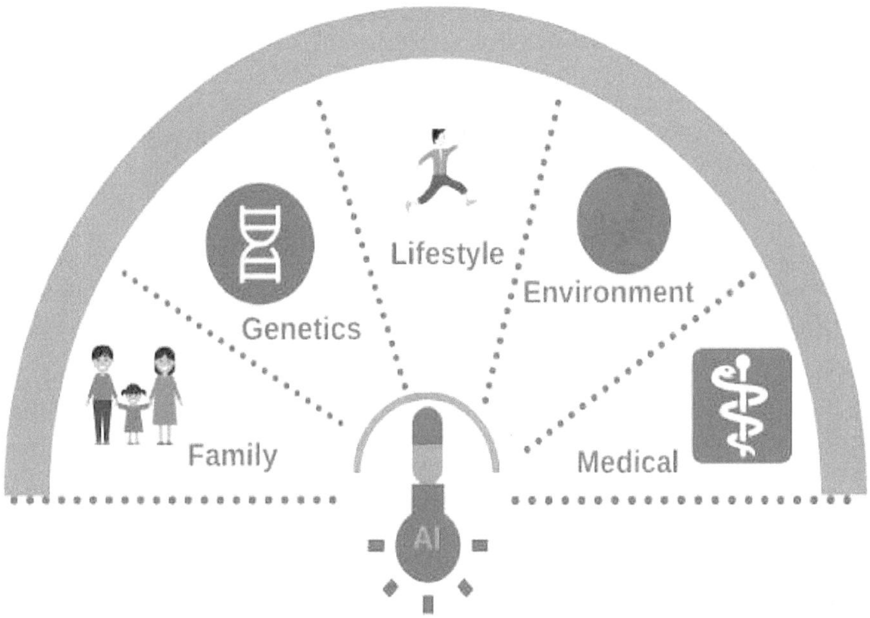

15.1.1 Extracting Information from Images: Medical images are a treasure trove of crucial information, but their complexity often exceeds the capacity of the human eye to analyze comprehensively. This is where machine learning steps in, leveraging its ability to process vast amounts of visual data. By employing various algorithms and techniques, machine learning extracts intricate patterns, textures, and features from medical images that hold valuable diagnostic insights.

15.1.2 Automated Diagnosis: The realm of medical diagnosis has been significantly enhanced by the capabilities of machine learning. Through extensive training on diverse datasets, machine learning models learn to differentiate between various categories within medical images. For instance, consider chest X-rays. A machine learning model, meticulously trained on a multitude of X-ray images, can swiftly classify them as either normal or indicative of specific respiratory conditions such as pneumonia or lung cancer.

The introduction of automated diagnosis not only accelerates the diagnostic process but also alleviates the burden on healthcare professionals. By providing rapid preliminary assessments, machine learning allows doctors to focus their expertise on more intricate cases, ultimately leading to improved patient care and outcomes.

15.1.3 Segmentation and Localization: In the realm of medical image analysis, segmentation plays a pivotal role in pinpointing and defining specific structures or regions of significance within an image. This involves the precise delineation of objects of interest, a task that can be exceptionally intricate and time-consuming when performed manually. Machine learning algorithms, armed with the capacity to comprehend intricate patterns, excel in this domain. For instance, they can adeptly segment tumors in MRI scans or discern intricate blood vessels in retinal images. Such segmentation is vital for ensuring accurate diagnosis and formulating effective treatment strategies.

15.1.4 Quantitative Analysis: The quantitative analysis of medical images marks another watershed application of machine learning. It involves extracting precise measurements and metrics from images—information that is often challenging to derive through manual examination. This capability becomes especially pertinent when tracking disease progression over time. Imagine the context of cancer patients: machine learning can accurately monitor changes in tumor size across various scans, providing objective data for medical professionals to assess the efficacy of treatments. By offering quantitative insights, machine learning empowers healthcare providers with robust evidence to make informed decisions for patient care.

15.1.5 Personalized Treatment Planning: One of the most transformative aspects of medical image analysis powered by machine learning is its capacity to facilitate personalized treatment planning. Each patient's medical journey is unique, and machine learning leverages the intricate details extracted from medical images to guide tailored treatment strategies. Whether it's mapping out the optimal surgical approach, customizing radiation therapy, or designing post-treatment monitoring protocols, the insights gleaned from these analyses enhance healthcare providers' ability to make informed decisions aligned with individual patients' needs.

15.1.6 Challenges and Advances: While the potential benefits of medical image analysis with machine learning are vast, the field does not come without its challenges:

Data Availability: The availability of labeled medical image datasets can be limited, hampering the development of accurate and generalizable models.

Interpretability: In medical contexts, interpretability is paramount. Understanding the rationale behind a machine learning model's decisions is crucial for building trust and facilitating effective collaboration between clinicians and algorithms.

Ethical Considerations: Handling sensitive patient data requires stringent adherence to ethical and privacy standards to ensure patient confidentiality and data security.

Advancements in deep learning architectures, transfer learning techniques, and data augmentation have significantly improved the performance of medical image analysis models. However, successful integration of these models into clinical practice necessitates interdisciplinary collaboration between data scientists, medical professionals, and radiologists. By synergizing their expertise, these stakeholders can develop models that are not only accurate but also clinically meaningful and impactful.

15.1.7 Future Directions: The trajectory of medical image analysis and diagnosis is on a path of continuous innovation and transformation. Several exciting future directions are poised to redefine healthcare practices:

Multimodal Fusion: The integration of information from diverse imaging modalities, such as combining MRI and PET scans, holds the promise of providing a more comprehensive and accurate assessment of a patient's condition. This fusion of data can lead to a more holistic understanding of diseases and guide treatment strategies.

Explainable AI: As machine learning models become more sophisticated, the ability to explain their decision-making becomes increasingly vital in the medical field. Developing models that not only make accurate predictions but also provide transparent explanations for their decisions is essential for building trust and facilitating collaboration between human experts and algorithms.

Real-time Analysis: The advancement of technology is enabling real-time image analysis, which can have a transformative impact during surgical procedures, emergency situations, and critical care scenarios. Immediate insights drawn from medical images can guide healthcare professionals in making rapid and informed decisions.

Predictive Analysis: Machine learning models are evolving to not only diagnose current medical conditions but also predict future disease risks. By analyzing imaging data alongside other patient information, these models can provide early warnings about potential health issues, enabling proactive interventions and personalized preventive strategies.

Precision Medicine: The future of medical image analysis envisions a shift toward precision medicine, where treatment plans are tailored to each individual's unique characteristics. Machine learning models can help identify subtle patterns and markers in medical images that predict how a specific patient will respond to different treatments, leading to more effective and personalized care.

As these directions unfold, the collaboration between data scientists, medical professionals, regulatory bodies, and technology experts will be paramount in realizing the full potential of machine learning in revolutionizing medical image analysis and diagnosis. The fusion of cutting-edge technology with the expertise of healthcare practitioners has the potential to reshape patient care and outcomes on a global scale.

15.2 Predictive Modeling for Patient Outcomes: Predictive modeling for patient outcomes leverages the power of machine learning to forecast the future health status of individuals based on a variety of factors, including medical history, genetic data, lifestyle, and environmental influences. This approach enables healthcare professionals to anticipate potential risks, intervene early, and provide personalized care plans to improve patient outcomes.

15.2.1 Personalized Prognosis: The realm of predictive modeling in healthcare has transcended general population trends to provide personalized prognoses for individual patients. This paradigm shift is made possible by harnessing the power of machine learning to analyze extensive patient data, encompassing electronic health records, medical images, genetic information, and lifestyle details. Through this intricate analysis, machine learning models are capable of generating forecasts that take into account the unique attributes of each patient.

This transformative capability enables healthcare providers to craft treatment plans that are finely tuned to an individual's genetic predispositions, medical history, and lifestyle choices. By recognizing and accounting for these intricate factors, predictive models empower healthcare professionals to anticipate the trajectory of a patient's health journey with unprecedented precision. This shift towards personalized prognosis promises a seismic change in healthcare by moving away from the one-size-fits-all approach to a tailor-made strategy that acknowledges the diversity of patients' characteristics.

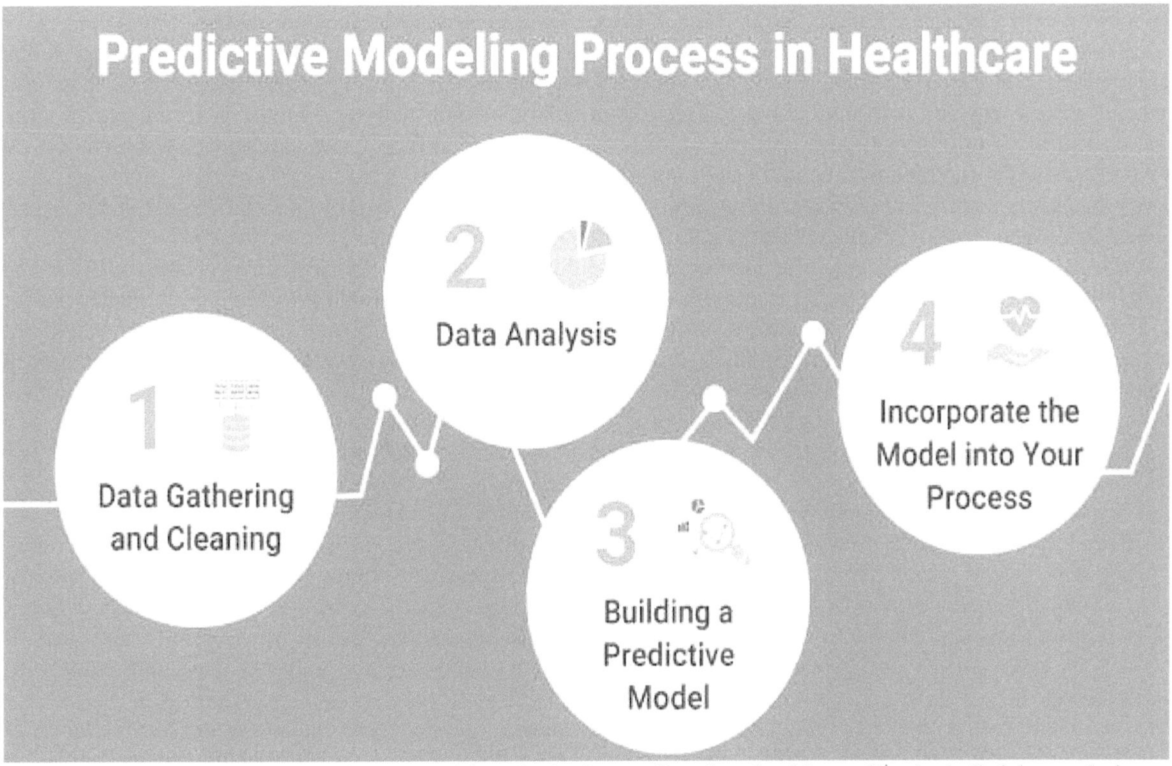

15.2.2 Early Intervention: Unveiling Opportunities: At the heart of modern healthcare lies the belief that early intervention is paramount. This is where predictive modeling emerges as a potent tool, orchestrating a symphony of data analysis to identify individuals who stand on the precipice of developing specific health conditions. By delving into historical patient data and uncovering hidden patterns, machine learning models can uncover subtle shifts that might herald the onset of a disease.

The magic of this lies in its potential for early detection. By identifying these telltale signs, healthcare professionals are empowered to initiate preventive measures or interventions before a condition spirals into a more advanced stage. This early intervention holds the key to avoiding severe complications, reducing the need for invasive treatments, and ultimately improving patient outcomes.

The profound impact of early intervention is far-reaching. It not only mitigates the personal suffering of patients but also alleviates the burden on healthcare systems. The preventive approach made possible by predictive modeling aligns perfectly with the vision of a healthcare system that prioritizes proactive care and places patients at the center of their own well-being journey.

15.2.3 Treatment Optimization: Tailoring Care: Predictive modeling's impact on healthcare reaches a zenith with its ability to optimize treatment strategies down to an individualized level. This concept is a revelation, as machine learning models, armed with a wealth of patient data and treatment outcomes, can orchestrate a symphony of insights to predict precisely how a patient will respond to various therapeutic approaches.

This optimization translates to a reduction in the trial-and-error ordeal that often accompanies healthcare decisions. By leveraging the patterns gleaned from similar cases, predictive models can guide healthcare professionals towards the most effective treatment options for a particular patient. This not only expedites the path to recovery but also minimizes the risk of adverse effects, sparing patients from unnecessary discomfort.

The very essence of treatment optimization lies in its potential to revolutionize healthcare by making it more precise, efficient, and patient-centric. Gone are the days of generic treatment plans: instead, healthcare is embracing an era of personalized care that considers an individual's unique attributes, from genetic makeup to medical history. This movement towards tailored care embodies the pinnacle of healthcare's evolution—a journey that strives to deliver the best possible outcomes to every patient.

15.2.4 Challenges and Considerations: The landscape of predictive modeling for patient outcomes is a tantalizing realm of possibilities, yet it is not devoid of challenges and considerations that demand meticulous attention. These challenges, while formidable, are integral to ensuring that the potential benefits are harnessed responsibly and effectively.

Data Quality and Integration: The Backbone of Reliable Predictions: At the heart of predictive modeling lies the imperative of data quality and integration. The accuracy and reliability of predictions hinge on the availability of high-quality and comprehensive datasets. However, in the modern healthcare ecosystem, data is sourced from a plethora of disparate sources—ranging from electronic health records that store clinical observations to wearable devices that track patient activity, and even genetic databases that harbor genetic profiles. Integrating these varied data sources into a unified framework is no small feat. The complexity lies not only in data formats but also in addressing data gaps, inconsistencies, and biases. Robust strategies for data cleaning, preprocessing, and harmonization become paramount to ensure that the predictive models are built on a strong foundation of accurate and meaningful data.

Ethical and Privacy Concerns: Safeguarding Patient Trust: The ethical considerations in predictive modeling are profound, especially in a domain as sensitive as healthcare. Handling patient data—much of which is inherently personal and private—calls for meticulous attention to ethical and privacy concerns. Patient consent is a cornerstone, ensuring that data usage aligns with patient preferences and respects their autonomy. Data anonymization techniques must be employed to strip data of personally identifiable information, reducing the risk of re-identification. Striking a delicate balance between data utility and privacy preservation is paramount to uphold patient trust and adhere to ethical standards. Moreover, navigating the complex regulatory landscape, such as complying with regulations like GDPR in Europe or HIPAA in the United States, is essential to ensure that data usage remains lawful and respectful of patient rights.

Interpretability: Bridging the Trust Gap: The adoption of predictive models in clinical settings is intrinsically linked to their interpretability. Many advanced machine learning models, while offering exceptional predictive performance, suffer from a "black-box" nature, meaning that the rationale behind their predictions is not readily understandable to humans. In healthcare, where decisions directly impact patient well-being, this lack of transparency poses a substantial barrier to adoption. To build trust and confidence among healthcare professionals, models need to shed their opacity and offer explanations for their predictions. Ensuring interpretability is a multidisciplinary challenge that requires the development of techniques to visualize and explain model decisions, thereby bridging the gap between the technical intricacies of machine learning and the practical domain knowledge of clinicians.

Clinical Validation: Ensuring Real-World Reliability: The journey of a predictive model from conception to clinical implementation demands rigorous validation. While promising results within controlled environments are encouraging, the real-world complexity of patient populations and healthcare settings necessitates thorough clinical validation. Models need to be tested on diverse patient cohorts, spanning various demographics, clinical conditions, and treatment scenarios. This validation ensures that the predictions hold relevance beyond the training data and can be generalized to new cases. Rigorous validation is an essential step to demonstrate the reliability, accuracy, and practical utility of predictive models in guiding clinical decisions.

In the pursuit of harnessing predictive modeling for patient outcomes, addressing these challenges and considerations is pivotal. Collaboration between data scientists, healthcare professionals, ethicists, legal experts, and technology stakeholders is vital to ensure that the potential benefits are maximized while upholding ethical standards, patient privacy, and the clinical relevance of these models. The road may be complex, but it is a path that holds the promise of transforming healthcare into a realm of personalized, informed, and effective interventions.

15.2.5 Future Implications: Predictive modeling for patient outcomes is poised to revolutionize healthcare by enabling personalized, proactive, and efficient patient care. As machine learning techniques continue to advance, models will become more accurate and precise, leading to improved patient outcomes, reduced healthcare costs, and a shift towards a preventive and patient-centered approach to healthcare delivery. However, collaboration between data scientists, clinicians, and healthcare stakeholders is essential to navigate the challenges and unlock the full potential of predictive modeling in healthcare.

15.3 Drug Discovery and Bioinformatics: Unveiling New Frontiers in Medicine: The realms of drug discovery and bioinformatics have undergone a revolutionary transformation with the infusion of machine learning techniques. These cutting-edge approaches have the potential to expedite the arduous process of identifying potential drugs, understanding their mechanisms, and optimizing their efficacy. Here, we delve into the intricate landscape of drug discovery and bioinformatics, exploring their implications for the future of medicine.

15.3.1 In Silico Exploration of Molecular Space: Accelerating Drug Discovery Through Virtual Exploration: In the dynamic landscape of drug discovery, the convergence of machine learning and molecular science has revolutionized the traditional paradigms. The arduous and often serendipitous nature of identifying potential drug candidates is now undergoing a transformative shift. This shift is epitomized by the concept of "in silico exploration," where machine learning techniques serve as the compass guiding scientists through the vast and intricate molecular space.

Tradition Meets Innovation: Traditionally, drug discovery involved painstakingly synthesizing and testing chemical compounds in the lab—a process that could take years and yield limited success. The cost in terms of time, resources, and human effort was substantial. Machine learning disrupts this traditional approach by offering a virtual playground for scientists to explore the molecular universe using computational algorithms.

Predictive Power Unleashed: Central to this revolution is the predictive power of machine learning models. These models are trained on large datasets that encompass information about molecular structures, properties, and biological interactions. Leveraging this knowledge, machine learning algorithms can swiftly analyze massive chemical libraries, predicting the likelihood of molecules binding to specific target proteins.

Navigating the Chemical Space: Imagine an immense landscape with countless molecules, each holding the potential to be a groundbreaking drug. Machine learning techniques act as navigational tools, helping scientists pinpoint molecules that exhibit desired characteristics—such as strong binding affinity, low toxicity, and favorable pharmacokinetics. This predictive approach expedites the identification of potential "hits" that warrant further investigation.

Virtual High-Throughput Screening: In the past, high-throughput screening involved laboriously testing numerous compounds in the lab. Machine learning turns this process on its head by conducting virtual high-throughput screening. Predictive models can rapidly evaluate thousands of molecules in silico, highlighting the most promising candidates for experimental validation.

A Leap in Efficiency and Innovation: The in silico exploration of molecular space significantly accelerates the drug discovery timeline. It minimizes the trial-and-error aspect of traditional methods and empowers scientists to make data-driven decisions. This not only saves time and resources but also encourages innovation by allowing researchers to explore unconventional molecular structures that might have been overlooked using conventional approaches.

A Glimpse into the Future: As machine learning algorithms continue to evolve, so does their capability to predict molecular interactions and properties with greater accuracy. This paves the way for more efficient drug discovery pipelines, reduced costs, and the identification of novel therapeutic agents that could transform patient care.

In the vast expanse of the molecular world, machine learning acts as a guiding light, illuminating the path to potential drugs with unprecedented speed and precision. The fusion of computational prowess and molecular insights heralds a new era in drug discovery—one that holds the promise of transforming the future of medicine.

15.3.2 Predicting Molecular Interactions: At the heart of drug discovery lies the intricate dance of molecular interactions. Machine learning techniques, particularly deep learning architectures, excel at deciphering these complex interactions. Predictive models can assess the binding affinity between a drug candidate and its target protein, enabling researchers to prioritize molecules with the highest likelihood of success. Additionally, machine learning can forecast potential adverse effects and off-target interactions, guiding the selection of drug candidates with a higher safety profile.

15.3.3 Biomarker Discovery and Personalized Medicine: Bioinformatics, driven by machine learning, has catalyzed the discovery of biomarkers—indicators that provide insights into disease progression, treatment response, and patient prognosis. By analyzing multi-omics data—genomics, transcriptomics, proteomics—machine learning models can uncover patterns that correlate with specific diseases or treatment outcomes. These biomarkers not only enhance diagnostic accuracy but also pave the way for personalized medicine, where treatments are tailored to individual patients based on their molecular profiles.

15.3.4 Accelerating Drug Design and Optimization: The iterative process of drug design and optimization is a hallmark of drug discovery. Machine learning expedites this process by predicting the properties of potential drug candidates, such as solubility, bioavailability, and toxicity. These predictions guide chemists in selecting compounds with favorable profiles, streamlining the path from lead identification to clinical trials. Moreover, generative models, such as generative adversarial networks (GANs), offer the possibility of generating entirely new molecular structures with desired properties.

15.3.5 Challenges and Ethical Considerations: The synergy of machine learning and drug discovery ushers in a new era of possibilities, but this journey is not without challenges and ethical considerations. As scientists harness the power of computational models to expedite drug development, they are also navigating a landscape fraught with intricate complexities.

Data: The Bedrock of Accuracy: The effectiveness of machine learning models in drug discovery hinges on the quality, quantity, and diversity of data. Ensuring that datasets accurately represent the chemical and biological space is imperative to avoid biases and ensure the generalizability of models. However, accessing such comprehensive and unbiased datasets can be a challenge.

The Enigma of Interpretability: As machine learning models unlock potential drug candidates, the need for interpretability becomes paramount. Understanding the reasoning behind a model's predictions—particularly in the realm of molecular interactions—is crucial for building trust and making informed decisions. The complex nature of some models poses challenges in rendering their decision-making processes intelligible.

Ethical Dilemmas: A Balancing Act: The rapid pace of in silico drug discovery raises ethical questions that demand careful consideration. Who owns the discoveries generated by machine learning models? How does one navigate patenting when algorithms play a significant role? Balancing innovation with ethical concerns about intellectual property and open access to data requires thoughtful solutions.

The Bridge from Virtual to Reality: While predictive models can suggest potential drug candidates, their efficacy and safety must be validated in the real world. Clinical trials remain the gold standard for demonstrating a drug's effectiveness. Ensuring that in silico predictions seamlessly transition to meaningful clinical outcomes requires meticulous validation, bridging the virtual world of algorithms with the reality of patient care.

A Holistic Approach: Navigating these challenges necessitates a multidisciplinary approach. Collaboration between data scientists, chemists, biologists, clinicians, and ethicists is essential to ensure that the benefits of machine learning in drug discovery are maximized while mitigating potential pitfalls.

Towards an Ethical Horizon: The ethical considerations of machine learning in drug discovery mirror those in other fields. Striking the right balance between technological innovation, patient welfare, and regulatory compliance is a shared responsibility. As the boundaries of what's possible continue to expand, the ethical horizon must be continually redefined to ensure that this brave new world is one of positive impact and responsible progress.

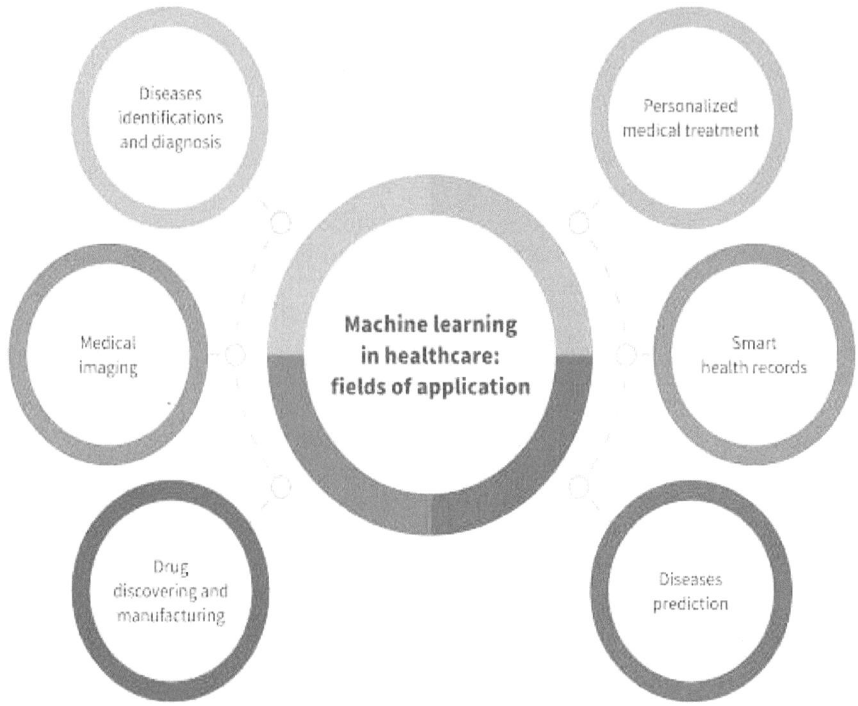

15.4 Ethical Challenges and Privacy Concerns in AI and Healthcare: The integration of artificial intelligence (AI) into healthcare has ushered in transformative possibilities, yet it also brings forth a tapestry of ethical challenges and privacy concerns. While the potential benefits of AI in healthcare are substantial, navigating this complex landscape requires a delicate balance of innovation and ethical considerations.

Patient Privacy: A Precious Asset: The cornerstone of healthcare ethics, patient privacy, is paramount in the era of AI-driven healthcare. The utilization of patient data, ranging from medical records to genetic information, necessitates stringent measures to safeguard against unauthorized access, breaches, and misuse. Striking a harmonious balance between leveraging patient data for medical advancements and protecting individual privacy is a foundational ethical challenge. Robust data security protocols, informed consent procedures, and adherence to regulatory frameworks such as the Health Insurance Portability and Accountability Act (HIPAA) are imperative to ensure the sanctity of patient information.

Transparency and Interpretability: A fundamental ethical consideration in AI is transparency – the ability to understand the reasoning behind AI-driven decisions. The "black-box" nature of certain AI algorithms poses challenges in healthcare contexts. Ethical frameworks should emphasize the development of AI systems that provide transparent explanations for their predictions and recommendations. This transparency not only fosters trust between healthcare professionals and AI technologies but also allows clinicians to validate and contextualize the AI's suggestions within the broader clinical context.

Bias and Fairness: AI models, when trained on biased or incomplete datasets, can inadvertently perpetuate biases in healthcare practices. These biases can lead to inaccurate diagnoses, treatment disparities, and unequal patient outcomes. An ethical approach demands that AI models are trained on diverse and representative datasets, mitigating the risk of reinforcing existing healthcare disparities. Rigorous testing for fairness ensures that AI technologies do not exacerbate societal inequalities.

Clinical Decision-Making: A Collaborative Endeavor: The integration of AI into clinical decision-making introduces intricate ethical dimensions. While AI can offer valuable insights, it should complement rather than supplant the expertise of healthcare professionals. Ensuring that clinical decisions involve human judgment preserves the human-centric nature of patient care and avoids undue reliance on algorithmic recommendations.

Ownership and Accountability: The accountability for AI-generated recommendations or decisions raises essential ethical questions. Clarity regarding the ownership of AI-generated insights and the accountability for their outcomes is vital. An ethical framework must delineate the roles and responsibilities of healthcare professionals, AI developers, and institutions to ensure patient safety and the well-being of individuals.

Regulatory Oversight: Balancing Innovation and Patient Safety: Regulatory frameworks play a pivotal role in governing AI in healthcare. Striking the delicate balance between promoting innovation and ensuring patient safety requires adaptable regulatory oversight. Rigorous testing, validation, and approval processes are indispensable to prevent the premature deployment of inadequately tested AI models.

A Compassionate Ethos: Guiding the Future: In the midst of advancing AI technologies, a compassionate ethos must remain the cornerstone of AI-driven healthcare. Patient welfare, privacy, and equitable access to care should be the guiding principles of every AI-related decision. By addressing ethical challenges and privacy concerns head-on, the healthcare community can harness the potential of AI while safeguarding individual rights and well-being. In doing so, the transformative power of AI can be harnessed responsibly and ethically to shape the future of healthcare.

15.5 Project

Unsolved Project

Suppose you're developing a comprehensive project that explores the applications of deep learning in healthcare. To ensure a thorough understanding and effective implementation, you need to study various areas such as medical image analysis and diagnosis, predictive modeling for patient outcomes, drug discovery and bioinformatics, and the ethical challenges and privacy concerns associated with these technologies. Before starting your project, research the following: techniques for medical image analysis and diagnosis using deep learning, methods for predictive modeling to forecast patient outcomes, approaches in drug discovery and bioinformatics leveraging deep learning, and the ethical and privacy challenges that arise in the healthcare domain. This foundational knowledge will enable you to create a well-rounded and impactful healthcare project using deep learning.

15.6 Lab Activity

Unsolved Lab Activity

Implement a deep learning model for medical image classification using a dataset (e.g., chest X-rays for pneumonia detection). **Task:** Use a deep learning framework (e.g., TensorFlow or PyTorch) to implement and train a CNN for classifying medical images. Train the model on a dataset such as chest X-rays for pneumonia detection. Document the implementation process, including data preprocessing, model architecture, training procedure, and performance evaluation. Provide visualizations of the model's predictions and evaluation metrics.

Exercises

Exercise 1 – Multiple Choice Questions

1. What role does machine learning play in medical image analysis and diagnosis?
   a) Enhancing the accuracy and efficiency of medical imaging interpretation
   b) Replacing healthcare professionals in diagnosis
   c) Reducing the need for medical imaging
   d) None of the above
2. How does machine learning extract valuable insights from medical images?
   a) By making medical images less complex
   b) By processing vast amounts of visual data and identifying patterns
   c) By generating new medical images
   d) By simplifying medical images
3. What is one significant application of machine learning in medical diagnosis mentioned in the chapter?
   a) Predicting future diseases
   b) Classifying chest X-rays
   c) Reducing the need for doctors
   d) Enhancing medical imaging devices
4. How does automated diagnosis benefit healthcare professionals?
   a) It replaces healthcare professionals in diagnosis.
   b) It accelerates the diagnostic process and reduces their workload.
   c) It makes healthcare professionals obsolete.
   d) It increases the complexity of medical diagnosis.
5. What is the purpose of segmentation in medical image analysis?
   a) To simplify medical images
   b) To pinpoint and define specific structures within an image
   c) To reduce the resolution of medical images
   d) To increase the size of medical images

Exercise 2 – True/False

1. Drug discovery does not benefit from the application of deep learning techniques.
2. Ethical challenges and privacy concerns are important considerations when applying deep learning in healthcare.
3. Bioinformatics does not involve the use of deep learning for analyzing biological data.

Review Questions

1. What are some of the ways in which machine learning has transformed healthcare, according to the chapter?
2. How does machine learning assist in extracting valuable insights from medical images?

3. Provide an example of how machine learning can be used for automated diagnosis in healthcare.
4. How does the introduction of automated diagnosis benefit healthcare professionals and patients?
5. Explain the role of segmentation in medical image analysis and its importance.
6. Why is quantitative analysis of medical images significant in healthcare, and how does machine learning contribute to it?
7. How does machine learning enable personalized treatment planning in healthcare?
8. What are some of the challenges mentioned in the chapter regarding medical image analysis with machine learning?
9. Describe one of the future directions discussed in the chapter for medical image analysis.
10. What is the concept of "Explainable AI," and why is it important in healthcare?
11. In drug discovery, what does "in silico exploration" involve, and how does it benefit the process?
12. How does machine learning expedite drug discovery, and what advantages does it offer over traditional methods?
13. What ethical considerations are associated with the use of patient data in AI-driven healthcare, as discussed in the chapter?
14. Why is transparency and interpretability important in AI-driven healthcare, and how can it be achieved?
15. What challenges and considerations are involved in ensuring fairness in AI models used in healthcare, and why is this important?

Answers

Exercise 1- 1. a 2. b 3. b 4. b 5. b
Exercise 2- 1) False, 2) True, 3) False

Online Resources

Online Exam Paper:
Link: https://forms.gle/fsvwzcMTCnT7NEdp6
QR Code:

Chapter 15 Videos Playlist:
Link: https://www.youtube.com/playlist?list=PLzlh_31VWEFqzFujVB1fyRrtLRQijacv0
QR Code:

Chapter 16: Generative Adversarial Networks (GANs) Variants

16.1 Conditional GANs for Controlled Image Generation: Conditional Generative Adversarial Networks (cGANs) represent a significant advancement in the field of generative models, enabling controlled and targeted image synthesis. This section delves into the intricacies of cGANs, exploring their architecture, training process, and applications in generating images with specific attributes.

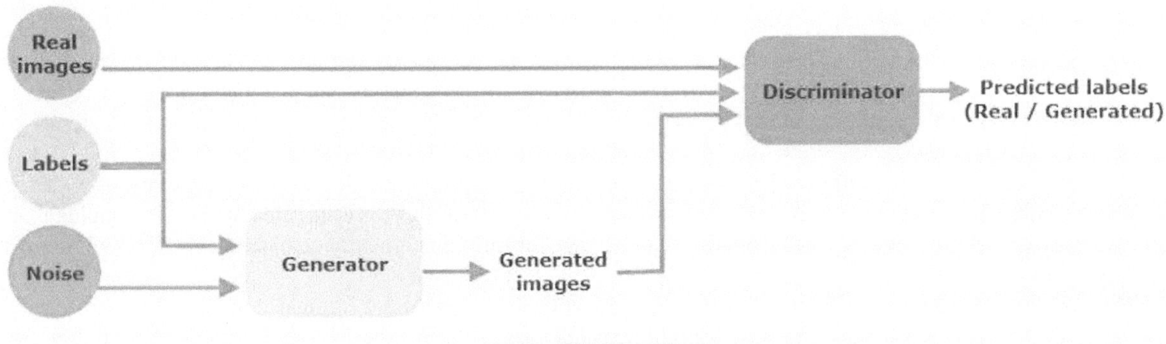

Conditional GAN

16.1.1 Unveiling Conditional Generative Adversarial Networks: Conditional Generative Adversarial Networks (cGANs) introduce a transformative dimension to the GAN framework by enabling controlled and targeted image generation. This section unveils the concept of cGANs, shedding light on how they extend the capabilities of traditional GANs.

At the core of cGANs is the notion of conditional generation. Unlike traditional GANs, where the generator creates images solely from random noise, cGANs introduce an additional layer of information. This information, referred to as conditional labels, serves as guidance for the image generation process. By conditioning both the generator and the discriminator on these labels, cGANs open the door to generating images that align with specific attributes, characteristics, or classes.

16.1.2 The Architecture of Conditional GANs: The architecture of cGANs follows the fundamental structure of conventional GANs, consisting of a generator and a discriminator engaged in an adversarial interplay. However, the true innovation of cGANs lies in the integration of conditional information into this architecture.

The generator, responsible for creating images, now receives two types of inputs: random noise and conditional labels. The random noise serves as the traditional source of creativity, while the conditional labels guide the generator in producing images with specific attributes or features. This integration empowers the generator to synthesize images that meet predefined criteria, such as generating images of a particular object category or style. On the other side of the adversarial spectrum, the discriminator's role is enhanced in cGANs. It not only evaluates the authenticity of generated images but also considers the correctness of their associated conditional attributes. This means that the discriminator not only seeks to differentiate between real and fake images but also ensures that the generated images align with the desired attributes encoded in the conditional labels. The marriage of conditional labels with the generator-discriminator interplay in cGANs offers a powerful framework for controlled image generation. This architecture enables the creation of images that go beyond randomness, opening avenues for tailored and attribute-guided synthesis. As we explore further, we'll delve into the training process, applications, challenges, and advancements in the realm of conditional GANs.

16.1.3 Training Conditional GANs: Training cGANs involves optimizing both the generator and discriminator simultaneously. The generator aims to create images that not only fool the discriminator but also adhere to the desired conditional attributes. The discriminator's goal is to accurately distinguish between real and generated images while correctly classifying their attributes. This adversarial interplay leads to the development of a generator capable of producing images with precise attributes.

16.1.4 Controlled Image Generation with cGANs: The power of cGANs lies in their ability to generate images with specific attributes. This has diverse applications, including image-to-image translation, style transfer, and even text-to-image synthesis. By conditioning the generator on attributes such as facial expressions, poses, or object categories, cGANs enable the creation of images tailored to predefined criteria.

16.1.5 Challenges and Advances in Conditional GANs: Conditional Generative Adversarial Networks (cGANs) hold immense promise, but they also grapple with challenges that impact their performance and effectiveness. One of the most significant challenges is mode collapse, a phenomenon where the generator produces a limited range of similar-looking images regardless of the input conditions. This undermines the diversity and richness of generated outputs, limiting the overall utility of cGANs.

Addressing mode collapse and improving the quality and diversity of generated images has driven notable advancements in the field. Progressive training techniques, for instance, introduce a gradual complexity increase during training, allowing the generator to learn a wider range of features and attributes progressively. This approach mitigates mode collapse by preventing the generator from getting stuck in suboptimal solutions. Additionally, attention mechanisms have been integrated into cGANs, enabling the generator to focus on specific regions of the image and capture finer details. These mechanisms enhance the overall realism and coherence of the generated content.

Furthermore, researchers have developed novel loss functions that encourage diverse image generation. Loss functions, like Wasserstein distance or feature matching loss, guide the generator to produce images that not only fool the discriminator but also exhibit a richer variety of attributes. These advances collectively contribute to overcoming challenges and elevating the capabilities of cGANs, pushing the boundaries of what they can achieve in controlled image generation.

16.1.6 Beyond Images: Conditional GANs in Various Domains: While cGANs are widely recognized for their prowess in image generation, their influence goes far beyond the realm of images alone. The concepts and principles that underpin cGANs extend naturally to various other domains, opening doors to creativity and innovation across different media. In audio synthesis, for example, cGANs can be conditioned on musical attributes to generate diverse and intricate compositions. By guiding the generator with specific musical characteristics, such as tempo, style, or instruments, cGANs can create music that resonates with desired moods or genres. Similarly, in text generation, cGANs can produce written content with specific tones, topics, or writing styles, revolutionizing content creation and storytelling.

Beyond static media, the influence of cGANs expands to dynamic domains like videos. By conditioning on video attributes such as scene settings or characters, cGANs can manipulate video content in unprecedented ways. This includes tasks like changing weather conditions, altering backgrounds, or even transforming the appearance of characters, all while maintaining temporal coherence.

16.1.7 Ethical Considerations and Future Prospects: As with any technology, ethical considerations are crucial in the deployment of cGANs. Ensuring that generated content respects societal norms and values is paramount. Looking ahead, the future of conditional GANs holds promises of even more sophisticated attribute control, enhanced diversity, and seamless integration into creative workflows.

The use of Conditional GANs for Controlled Image Generation represents a significant leap in the realm of generative models, enabling the creation of customized and targeted visual content. This chapter has provided an in-depth exploration of cGANs, their architecture, training, applications, challenges, and potential ethical implications. With cGANs, the world of creative image synthesis is undergoing a transformative evolution.

16.2 CycleGAN and Unpaired Image Translation: CycleGAN, short for Cycle-Consistent Generative Adversarial Network, is a groundbreaking model that excels in unpaired image-to-image translation. Unlike paired image translation, where corresponding images in different domains are required for training, CycleGAN is designed to work with unpaired data, making it exceptionally versatile for a wide range of applications.

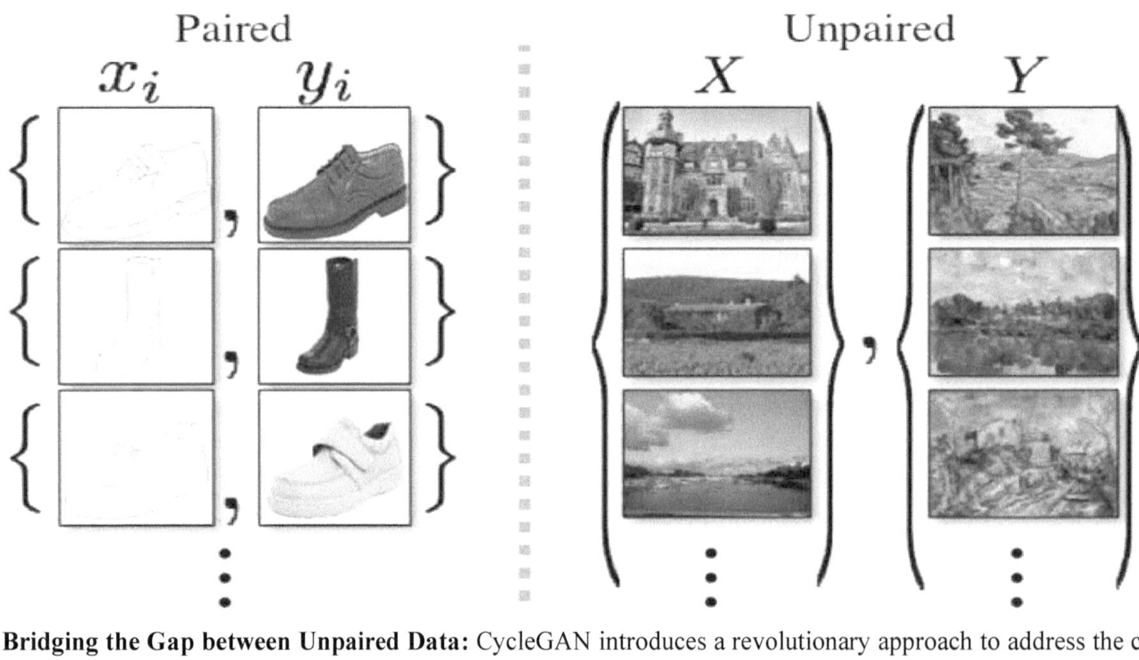

16.2.1 Bridging the Gap between Unpaired Data: CycleGAN introduces a revolutionary approach to address the challenge of translating images between two distinct domains, even when direct correspondences between individual images are unavailable. This innovation holds profound implications for various applications, ranging from artistic transformations to domain adaptation in computer vision. In the realm of unpaired image translation, the conventional supervised learning paradigm, which relies on paired images for training, falls short. CycleGAN addresses this limitation by leveraging unpaired datasets, where images from different domains lack direct one-to-one correspondence. This opens up the possibility of translating images across diverse domains that might not share the same objects, scenes, or viewpoints. The core breakthrough of CycleGAN lies in its ability to learn mappings between these unpaired domains, effectively discovering shared characteristics and relationships. Here's how it works: Given two sets of images from distinct domains, let's call them "Domain A" and "Domain B," CycleGAN employs two key components: generators and discriminators. The generators, denoted as

"Generator A" and "Generator B," are responsible for translating images from Domain A to Domain B and vice versa. The discriminators, "Discriminator A" and "Discriminator B," evaluate the authenticity of the translated images in their respective domains. What makes CycleGAN truly remarkable is the incorporation of cycle-consistency. This principle ensures that the translated images can be "cycled" back to the original domain with minimal loss of information. In other words, if an image from Domain A is translated to Domain B and then translated back to Domain A, it should resemble the original image as closely as possible. This introduces a form of self-supervision, as no paired data is needed for training this cycle-consistency aspect. The cycle-consistency loss enforces the alignment of the original image and the image reconstructed through the translation cycle. By minimizing the discrepancies between the two, CycleGAN encourages the generators to capture the essential shared features and semantics between the domains.

16.2.2 Architecture and Working Principles: The architecture of CycleGAN is ingeniously designed to enable unpaired image translation and enforce cycle-consistency. Comprising two generators and two discriminators, CycleGAN orchestrates a dynamic interplay between these components to achieve remarkable image transformations.

Generators: The heart of CycleGAN lies in its generators, denoted as "Generator A" and "Generator B." Each generator is responsible for translating images from one domain to the other. For instance, Generator A transforms images from Domain A to Domain B, and Generator B performs the reverse translation. These generators are implemented as deep neural networks, often utilizing convolutional layers. Their role is to learn the intricate mapping between the domains, capturing shared features and relationships.

Discriminators: To ensure the authenticity of both real and translated images, CycleGAN employs discriminators, "Discriminator A" and "Discriminator B." Discriminator A evaluates the realism of images in Domain A, while Discriminator B assesses images in Domain B. These discriminators act as adversarial networks, distinguishing between real images and images generated by the corresponding generators. The adversarial training process drives the generators to produce translations that closely resemble authentic images.

Cycle-Consistency Loss: The ingenious concept of cycle-consistency underpins CycleGAN's transformative capabilities. This is achieved through a loss term that enforces the coherence between the original and translated images. When an image from Domain A is translated to Domain B using Generator A and then back to Domain A using Generator B, it should ideally resemble the original image. The cycle-consistency loss measures the dissimilarity between the original image and its reconstructed counterpart, guiding the generators to produce consistent and meaningful translations.

The training process of CycleGAN involves a delicate balance between the generators and discriminators. As the generators strive to create convincing translations, the discriminators sharpen their ability to distinguish between authentic and translated images. This adversarial dynamic culminates in a state where the translated images are not only perceptually convincing but also possess attributes consistent with the target domain.

CycleGAN's architecture and working principles enable the model to learn the intricate correspondences and shared attributes between unpaired domains. By leveraging adversarial training and cycle-consistency, it navigates the challenge of unpaired data translation, leading to the creation of meaningful and accurate cross-domain image transformations. This unique approach has revolutionized the field of image translation and holds promise for applications spanning art, design, and various scientific domains.

16.2.3 Applications of CycleGAN: CycleGAN's versatility has led to its application in a myriad of domains. One prominent use is in artistic style transfer, where CycleGAN can transform photographs into artwork imitating the styles of famous painters. This technique offers a fresh perspective on merging photography and art, generating visually captivating results.

Another notable application is domain adaptation, especially relevant in computer vision tasks. For instance, CycleGAN can be used to adapt images from a synthetic domain (e.g., computer-generated images) to match the characteristics of a real-world domain. This is particularly valuable for scenarios where collecting sufficient labeled data in the target domain is challenging.

16.2.4 Challenges and Future Directions: CycleGAN's innovative approach to unpaired image translation has opened new avenues in the field of machine learning, but it also faces challenges and promises exciting future directions.

Challenges: Achieving perfect cycle-consistency across diverse and complex datasets can be demanding. Variations in image content, style, and context may lead to translation discrepancies that deviate from ideal cycle-consistency. Ensuring that the translated images preserve the intended attributes while being faithful to the original poses a continuous challenge. Additionally, handling domain-specific nuances and avoiding artifacts in translations require careful optimization.

Refining Cycle-Consistency: Future advancements might focus on refining the cycle-consistency concept. This involves developing techniques to handle cases where strict cycle-consistency may not be feasible or desirable. Models could be designed to allow controlled deviations from perfect cycle-consistency while maintaining the essence of the original image.

Attribute-Guided Translations: Incorporating additional information or attributes into the translation process is a promising avenue. By explicitly conditioning the translation on specific attributes, such as style, lighting, or content, models could achieve more precise and controlled image transformations. This could be especially valuable in scenarios where fine-grained control over the translation process is essential.

Hybrid Models: The fusion of CycleGAN with other advanced techniques holds potential for addressing existing challenges. Combining CycleGAN with attention mechanisms, semantic segmentation, or other state-of-the-art methods could enhance the quality and fidelity of translated images. These hybrid models could offer finer control over the translation process and enable the preservation of important image details.

Multimodal Translation: Extending CycleGAN to handle multimodal data, such as translating images to text descriptions or vice versa, is an exciting direction. This would broaden the scope of applications and facilitate seamless interactions between different types of data.

Interdisciplinary Applications: The principles of CycleGAN could be applied to domains beyond visual imagery. Expanding its concepts to other domains, such as audio, text, or even scientific simulations, could lead to breakthroughs in interdisciplinary research.

In essence, the challenges faced by CycleGAN pave the way for dynamic advancements in image translation and beyond. As researchers delve deeper into refining its mechanisms and extending its capabilities, the future of unpaired image translation looks promising, with applications that touch art, design, communication, and scientific exploration.

16.2.5 Redefining Image Translation: CycleGAN's ability to perform unpaired image translation expands the boundaries of what is achievable with generative models. By bridging the gap between diverse image domains, CycleGAN opens doors to innovative applications that redefine how we perceive and manipulate visual content.

16.3 StyleGAN and High-Quality Image Synthesis: Generative Adversarial Networks (GANs) have transformed the landscape of image generation, and StyleGAN stands as a remarkable innovation within this realm. With its ability to synthesize high-quality and diverse images, StyleGAN has become a powerhouse in the field of machine learning and creative content generation.

16.3.1 The Evolution of Image Synthesis: The emergence of StyleGAN signifies a significant leap forward in the realm of image synthesis, particularly within the context of Generative Adversarial Networks (GANs). While earlier iterations of GANs focused on generating images based on random noise, StyleGAN introduces a revolutionary approach rooted in style-based techniques. This paradigm shift introduces novel concepts that not only enhance image quality but also empower creators with a new level of control over the generated content. Traditional GANs learned to generate images by transforming random noise into visual patterns. However, StyleGAN transcends this conventional approach by embracing the idea of disentangled representation. This concept revolutionizes how images are synthesized by allowing the model to understand and manipulate distinct components of an image independently. These components include both content and style, providing a dual layer of manipulation that was previously unattainable.

At the heart of this evolution lies the realization that images are composed of multiple attributes that contribute to their appearance. Content attributes capture the essence of the object or scene depicted, while style attributes encompass characteristics such as color, texture, and lighting. StyleGAN harnesses this insight to separate the manipulation of content and style, enabling creators to modify one aspect without impacting the other. This disentangled representation not only leads to improved image quality but also introduces a higher degree of flexibility, granting artists and designers unprecedented control over the creative process.

In essence, StyleGAN's evolution represents a departure from the limitations of generating images from noise alone. By allowing for the independent manipulation of content and style, it opens doors to a new era of artistic expression and content creation. This advancement has profound implications not only within the realm of machine learning but also in various creative fields where image generation plays a pivotal role.

16.3.2 Anatomy of StyleGAN: The fundamental architecture of StyleGAN is composed of two key components: the generator and the discriminator. These components work in tandem to produce high-quality images that exhibit an unprecedented level of control over style and appearance. The generator in StyleGAN employs a progressive growing strategy. It begins by generating low-resolution images and then progressively refines them to higher resolutions. This approach ensures that the generated images are of exceptional quality, as they are constructed in a manner that pays attention to both global structures and intricate details. However, the true innovation lies in the concept of the mapping network. This network operates within the latent space, which is a multidimensional space that encodes the variations in content and style of the images. The mapping network's role is to manipulate this latent space to exert precise control over the style and appearance of the generated images. By altering the latent space in a deliberate manner, creators can achieve fine-tuned adjustments to various attributes such as colors, textures, and patterns. This unique ability to separate and manipulate content and style attributes is a cornerstone of StyleGAN's exceptional capabilities. Complementing the generator is the discriminator. The discriminator's primary function is to evaluate the realism of the generated images. It acts as the critical judge, providing feedback to the generator about the quality and authenticity of the images it produces. This feedback loop is essential for the iterative improvement of the generator's performance. As the generator receives guidance from the discriminator's assessments, it fine-tunes its approach to generate images that not only exhibit high-quality visuals but also satisfy the criteria of realism and authenticity.

In essence, the architecture of StyleGAN is a testament to its complexity and innovation. By combining a progressive growing approach, a sophisticated mapping network, and a discriminating feedback mechanism, StyleGAN offers a transformative platform for image synthesis that empowers creators with an unprecedented level of control and artistic expression. This architecture forms the foundation upon which StyleGAN's remarkable image generation capabilities are built.

16.3.3 Disentangled Latent Space: One of StyleGAN's standout features is its disentangled latent space. By separating the latent code into different components, StyleGAN enables users to modify individual attributes without affecting others. This empowers artists and designers to manipulate specific characteristics of an image, such as its pose, expression, or lighting, without altering the overall content.

16.3.4 Challenges and Advances: The journey of StyleGAN, while revolutionary, is not without its challenges, some of which revolve around interpretability and fine-grained control. These challenges highlight the complexity inherent in manipulating the multifaceted latent space and fine-tuning the intricate aspects of image generation.

Interpreting the latent space can be a complex endeavor. While StyleGAN's mapping network empowers users to control various attributes, comprehending the exact relationships between changes in the latent space and resulting image modifications can be intricate. Artists and creators might find themselves in a realm of trial and error, seeking the right combination of latent space alterations to achieve the desired visual effects. This challenge underscores the need for improved interpretability tools and techniques that provide clearer insights into the latent space's behavior.

Fine-grained control over image attributes is another area that presents challenges. While StyleGAN allows for impressive control over various aspects of style and appearance, achieving precise adjustments to specific elements can still be a nuanced process. For instance, generating images with specific textures or patterns might require intricate manipulation of the latent space. Artists may need to delve deep into the mechanics of StyleGAN to produce images that align precisely with their artistic visions. On the bright side, the field of interpretability is advancing rapidly, with researchers and practitioners developing methods to visualize and understand the latent space's intricate dynamics. These advances could empower users to navigate the latent space more intuitively, accelerating the process of creating images with desired attributes. Moreover, user-friendly interfaces and tools could simplify the process of controlling StyleGAN. As the technology matures, developers might create intuitive software that allows artists to interact with the latent space in a more intuitive and straightforward manner. This democratization of access to StyleGAN's capabilities could expand its user base and make its powerful image generation capabilities more accessible to a broader spectrum of creators.

While challenges related to interpretability and fine-grained control persist, advances in interpretability techniques and user-friendly interfaces hold the promise of overcoming these obstacles. The journey of refining StyleGAN is ongoing, and the fusion of technical innovation and user-centric design could ultimately unlock even more of its artistic potential.

16.3.5 Creative Applications: The profound impact of StyleGAN reverberates far beyond the confines of research laboratories. Its transformative capabilities have unleashed a wave of creative applications, revolutionizing art, entertainment, and design landscapes.

Artistry Unleashed: Artists, both seasoned and emerging, have embraced StyleGAN as a potent tool for crafting captivating and surreal artworks. By harnessing the disentangled representation and fine-grained control, artists can breathe life into their visions like never before. The latent space becomes a canvas of exploration, allowing for the synthesis of imagery that defies conventional artistic boundaries. From dreamlike landscapes to abstract forms, StyleGAN empowers artists to transcend the limitations of reality and venture into the realms of imagination.

Design Enchantment: StyleGAN's prowess extends to the world of design. Designers leverage its capabilities to produce visuals that resonate with viewers on a profound level. In advertising, fashion, and branding, StyleGAN-generated images possess a photorealistic quality that captivates and engages. The fusion of technical precision and artistic ingenuity opens up new avenues for crafting visuals that leave a lasting impact. From creating eye-catching product advertisements to designing cutting-edge fashion concepts, StyleGAN amplifies the designer's creative toolkit.

Visualizing Virtual Realities: The high-quality images produced by StyleGAN hold immense promise in virtual reality and gaming. The ability to generate detailed and lifelike visuals enhances the immersive experience for users. Virtual worlds come alive with realism, textures, and depth, enriching the user's engagement and sense of presence. Architects and creators in the architectural visualization realm also benefit from StyleGAN's capabilities, as it aids in rendering realistic environments that resonate with clients and stakeholders.

The myriad applications of StyleGAN illuminate its versatility as a tool that transcends academic research and permeates the realms of creativity and expression. Artists, designers, and creators from diverse domains find themselves equipped with a new medium through which they can manifest their visions. As the technology continues to evolve, the boundaries of what can be achieved with StyleGAN remain boundless, making it an indispensable ally in the pursuit of creative excellence.

16.3.6 The Future of StyleGAN: As StyleGAN continues to evolve, its future holds exciting possibilities. Advances in controlling the disentangled latent space could lead to even finer artistic control. Incorporating feedback mechanisms that allow users to guide image generation in real-time could democratize the creative process further. Collaborations between artists, researchers, and technology developers will likely shape the future of high-quality image synthesis and push the boundaries of what is creatively possible.

16.4 GANs for Data Augmentation and Anomaly Detection: The innovative prowess of Generative Adversarial Networks (GANs) extends beyond image generation, penetrating domains like data augmentation and anomaly detection. These applications showcase GANs' adaptability to enhance data availability and uncover hidden irregularities.

16.4.1 Amplifying Data Augmentation: In the realm of data augmentation, GANs emerge as a potent tool to expand the horizons of training datasets. Data scarcity often poses a challenge in machine learning, hindering model performance. GANs counter this by generating synthetic data that complements existing samples. By learning the underlying data distribution, GANs craft new instances that align seamlessly with real data, boosting the diversity and size of training sets.

16.4.2 Anomaly Detection Unveiled: The power of GANs extends to anomaly detection—a critical facet in various industries, from finance to cybersecurity. GANs excel in learning normal data patterns, enabling them to detect anomalies that deviate from established norms. By employing a GAN to model normal data distribution, any deviation from the learned pattern flags as an anomaly. This technique, known as "anoganomaly," holds promise for identifying fraudulent transactions, network intrusions, or defective products.

16.4.3 Challenges and Progress:

Challenges:

Data Realism and Diversity in Augmentation: GANs generate synthetic data, but ensuring the realism and diversity of these samples is challenging. There's a risk of generating unrealistic or biased data that doesn't accurately represent the true distribution.

Anomaly Detection Ambiguities: Anomaly detection using GANs can result in false positives and negatives. Variations in normal data can be mistaken for anomalies, impacting the reliability of the detection process.

Progress:

Refining Data Augmentation with Self-Attention: Advances in GAN architectures incorporate self-attention mechanisms to enhance data augmentation. Self-attention helps the generator focus on crucial regions in the data, improving the quality of generated samples.

Controlled Generation for Augmentation: Progress in GAN research allows for explicit control over generated samples' attributes. This control ensures that generated data aligns with specific characteristics, addressing the challenge of data diversity.

Hybrid Models for Anomaly Detection: Combining GANs with traditional anomaly detection techniques leads to hybrid models. These models leverage the discriminative power of GANs and the well-established attributes of other methods, enhancing anomaly detection accuracy.

Addressing Anomaly Detection Challenges: Research focuses on fine-tuning GAN architectures to reduce false positives and negatives. By refining how GANs distinguish anomalies from normal data, accuracy in anomaly detection improves.

The challenges GANs encounter in data augmentation and anomaly detection are being met with innovative solutions and continuous research. These advancements not only mitigate the difficulties but also enhance the practicality and effectiveness of using GANs in these critical domains.

16.4.4 Embracing Future Possibilities: The future of GANs in data augmentation and anomaly detection is promising. Evolving GAN architectures promise more precise control over generated data, enabling data augmentation that aligns with specific use cases. For anomaly detection, models that handle varying levels of anomaly severity and adapt to dynamic data environments are on the horizon.

Incorporating GANs into these domains offers an ingenious way to transcend data limitations and unravel hidden insights. As the field advances, GAN-powered data augmentation and anomaly detection stand as potent tools driving accuracy and robustness in various applications.

16.5 Project

Unsolved Project

Suppose you're working on a project that involves exploring and implementing various Generative Adversarial Network (GAN) variants for different applications. To successfully complete this project, you need to understand conditional GANs for controlled image generation, CycleGAN for unpaired image translation, StyleGAN for high-quality image synthesis, and the use of GANs for data augmentation and anomaly detection. Before starting, research the following: the principles and implementation of conditional GANs, the workings and applications of CycleGAN for translating images between domains without paired examples, the architecture and capabilities of StyleGAN for generating high-quality images, and the applications of GANs in data augmentation and detecting anomalies. This preparation will equip you with the necessary knowledge to develop and experiment with various GAN variants in your project.

16.6 Lab Activity

Unsolved Lab Activity

Implement a Conditional GAN for generating images based on specific conditions (e.g., MNIST digits with class labels).

Task: Use a deep learning framework (e.g., TensorFlow or PyTorch) to implement and train a Conditional GAN on a dataset like MNIST. The model should generate images based on specific class labels (e.g., generating specific digits). Document the implementation process, including data preprocessing, model architecture, training procedure, and visualizations of generated images.

Exercises

Exercise 1 – Multiple Choice Questions

1. What is the primary innovation introduced by Conditional Generative Adversarial Networks (cGANs)?
   A. Disentangled representation
   B. Progressive growing strategy
   C. Random noise generation
   D. Discriminator feedback
2. In the context of cGANs, what are conditional labels used for?
   A. Guiding the generator in creating random noise
   B. Providing feedback to the discriminator
   C. Enabling control over specific attributes in image generation
   D. Defining the architecture of the generator
3. How does CycleGAN address the challenge of translating images between unpaired domains?
   A. It relies on direct correspondences between individual images.
   B. It leverages unpaired datasets and cycle-consistency.
   C. It uses supervised learning with paired images.
   D. It employs a single generator for all translations.
4. What is the role of the mapping network in StyleGAN?
   A. To generate high-resolution images
   B. To evaluate the realism of generated images
   C. To manipulate the latent space for style control
   D. To separate content and style attributes
5. What does the term "cycle-consistency" refer to in the context of CycleGAN?
   A. The consistency between the generator and discriminator
   B. The ability to cycle between different domains without loss of information
   C. The quality of generated images
   D. The interpretability of the latent space

Exercise 2 – True/False

1. Conditional GANs can be used for controlled image generation by conditioning on additional information such as class labels.
2. CycleGAN is designed to perform paired image translation, requiring a direct mapping between input and output images.
3. StyleGAN is known for its ability to generate high-quality and realistic images by controlling the style at different levels of the image generation process.

Review Questions

1. What distinguishes Conditional Generative Adversarial Networks (cGANs) from traditional GANs?
2. How do conditional labels influence the image generation process in cGANs?
3. What is the primary role of the discriminator in cGANs?
4. How does the architecture of cGANs differ from conventional GANs?
5. What are some applications of Conditional GANs mentioned in the text?
6. What is mode collapse in the context of cGANs, and why is it a challenge?
7. How does progressive training mitigate mode collapse in cGANs?
8. What is the purpose of attention mechanisms in cGANs, and how do they enhance image generation?
9. What are some novel loss functions mentioned in the text that encourage diverse image generation in cGANs?
10. In what domains beyond images can Conditional GANs (cGANs) be applied?
11. What are the ethical considerations discussed in the deployment of cGANs?
12. How does CycleGAN address the challenge of translating images between unpaired domains?
13. What is the role of the mapping network in StyleGAN, and how does it affect image generation?
14. What is cycle-consistency, and why is it important in CycleGAN?
15. How does StyleGAN allow for fine-grained control over image attributes, and what are some challenges associated with it?
16. What are some creative applications of StyleGAN mentioned in the text?
17. How do GANs address the challenge of data scarcity in machine learning?
18. How can GANs be used for anomaly detection, and what is "anoganomaly"?
19. What is the primary function of the discriminator in GANs used for anomaly detection?
20. What is the main challenge mentioned in using GANs for anomaly detection?

Answers

Exercise 1- 1.A 2.C 3.B 4.C 5.B 6.A 7.B 8.B 9.A 10 .C 11 .C 12 .C 13 .D 14 .B 15 .C
Exercise 2- 1) True, 2) False, 3) True

Online Resources

Online Exam Paper:
Link: https://forms.gle/CGUD36yhTHbLqfeHA
QR Code:

Chapter 16 Videos Playlist:
Link: https://www.youtube.com/playlist?list=PLzlh_31VWEFoWA6HvdBx7D2LyRuXUXXzd
QR Code:

Chapter 17: Interpreting and Visualizing Deep Learning Models

17.1 Activation Maximization and Feature Visualization: Activation Maximization and Feature Visualization are techniques that offer insights into the inner workings of deep neural networks by unveiling the patterns and features they have learned. These methods provide a window into the representations that neural networks develop, helping researchers and practitioners understand what information is being captured at different layers of the network.

17.1.1 Decoding Neural Network Representations: In the realm of deep learning, neural networks are known for their ability to automatically learn intricate features and representations from input data. However, understanding exactly what these neural networks have learned and how they make decisions can be quite challenging due to their complex and non-linear nature. This is where the concept of Activation Maximization comes into play, offering a method to unravel the inner workings of these networks.

Activation Maximization Process: Activation Maximization is a technique used to gain insights into the type of input data that triggers specific neurons or layers within a neural network to produce strong activations. This is achieved through an iterative process of modifying an input data instance, often an image, in a way that maximizes the activation of a chosen neuron.

Choosing a Target Neuron: The process begins by selecting a neuron of interest within the neural network. This could be a neuron in any layer, and researchers often choose neurons that correspond to specific features or patterns they want to understand.

Generating Initial Input: An initial input data instance, such as a random noise image or a blank canvas, is chosen as the starting point.

Iterative Modification: The input image is iteratively updated to enhance its response to the chosen neuron. This is achieved by adjusting the pixel values of the image in a way that gradually increases the neuron's activation.

Gradient Ascent: The key idea is to use gradient ascent to update the image in the direction that maximizes the neuron's activation. The gradient indicates how sensitive the neuron's activation is to changes in the input image.

Repeating the Process: Steps 3 and 4 are repeated for a certain number of iterations or until the activation of the chosen neuron reaches a predefined threshold.

Unveiling Neuron Preferences: Activation Maximization essentially attempts to decode what visual patterns or features the chosen neuron is "looking for" in an input image to become highly active. For instance, if the chosen neuron corresponds to detecting edges, the process might generate images that exhibit strong edges, as this is what the neuron responds to.

Insights and Applications: Activation Maximization provides a way to gain an understanding of the kinds of visual features that certain neurons or layers in a neural network have learned to recognize. It can be particularly useful in interpreting convolutional neural networks (CNNs), where individual neurons often specialize in detecting specific textures, shapes, or patterns.

By unveiling the preferences of neurons, researchers can get a glimpse into the network's thought process and use this knowledge to verify if the network is focusing on the right features for a given task. This technique is a powerful tool for improving model interpretability, fine-tuning network architectures, and addressing issues related to biases and erroneous activations.

17.1.2 Probing Features in Convolutional Networks: Feature Visualization complements Activation Maximization by providing a broader perspective on the features extracted by convolutional neural networks (CNNs). This involves visualizing the patterns that trigger individual neurons or channels in a CNN. By generating images that elicit strong responses from specific neurons, researchers can gain an understanding of the hierarchical and increasingly complex features that the network captures as information flows through its layers.

17.1.3 Uncovering Network Understanding: Activation Maximization and Feature Visualization have emerged as powerful techniques that go beyond the surface-level performance of neural networks. They delve into the inner workings of these complex models, offering insights that contribute to a deeper understanding of their learned representations and behaviors. Here's how these techniques uncover the hidden layers of network understanding:

Interpreting Network Responses: Neural networks, especially deep and convolutional architectures, can be seen as black boxes due to their complex transformations of input data. Activation Maximization and Feature Visualization act as a window into these black boxes, revealing what specific neurons or layers within the network respond to. By generating images that maximally activate a certain neuron, researchers can infer the kinds of patterns or concepts the network has learned to recognize.

Exploring Features and Biases: These techniques enable researchers to explore the features that trigger strong activations in neurons. For instance, in image classification tasks, they can reveal whether certain neurons respond more to textures, shapes, or colors. This exploration can also expose potential biases in the network's learning process. If a neuron in an image classifier consistently activates for a certain demographic group, it might indicate the presence of unintended biases in the training data.

Model Validation and Debugging: Activation Maximization and Feature Visualization act as tools for model validation and debugging. If a network trained for a specific task produces unexpected activations during visualization, it could indicate that the network has learned unintended associations or that its behavior diverges from what was intended. This helps researchers identify where the model might be making mistakes or drawing upon inappropriate features.

Improving Generalization: Understanding what features the network is focused on can lead to improvements in generalization. If a network relies on superficial features that are not relevant to the task, it might struggle to generalize to new data. By visualizing the activated features, researchers can refine the network's architecture or training data to ensure that it prioritizes meaningful and task-relevant representations.

Ethical Considerations: While these techniques are powerful tools for understanding neural networks, they also bring ethical considerations to the forefront. Revealing biases or sensitive features might expose the vulnerabilities of a model, potentially leading to misuse or unintended consequences. Striking a balance between transparency and potential risks is essential when applying Activation Maximization and Feature Visualization.

Empowering Responsible AI: Activation Maximization and Feature Visualization empower researchers to create more responsible and transparent AI systems. By shining a light on the learned representations, biases, and reasoning of neural networks, these techniques contribute to the broader goal of building AI that is not only accurate but also accountable, fair, and aligned with human values.

17.1.4 Challenges and Future Applications: While Activation Maximization and Feature Visualization offer a captivating window into the inner workings of neural networks, they also pose challenges and hold the promise of future applications. Here's exploration of these aspects:

Interpretation Subjectivity: The interpretations derived from Activation Maximization and Feature Visualization are subject to interpretation themselves. Researchers often need domain expertise to decipher the meaning of activated features. What might seem like an abstract pattern to one person could hold crucial significance to another. This subjectivity underscores the importance of collaboration between machine learning experts and domain specialists.

Balancing Interpretability and Realism: Generated images from Activation Maximization might not always resemble realistic examples. They could exhibit exaggerated or unrealistic features that the network responds to. Balancing interpretability with realism is an ongoing challenge. Ensuring that the generated images align with real-world data while still highlighting the features of interest is a delicate balance that researchers need to strike.

Guiding Model Improvements: One potential future application of Activation Maximization and Feature Visualization lies in guiding model improvements. By understanding what features or concepts a neural network struggles to capture, researchers can modify the model architecture or training data to address these shortcomings. This iterative process can result in more robust and accurate models.

Debugging and Bias Detection: These techniques can serve as valuable tools for debugging and detecting biases within neural networks. If certain neurons consistently activate for biased or undesirable features, it prompts a deeper investigation into the training data and potential biases that might have seeped into the model's representations.

Education and Outreach: Activation Maximization and Feature Visualization have educational potential as well. They can serve as tangible examples to explain the concept of learned representations in neural networks to non-experts. Visualizing the features that neural networks focus on can help bridge the gap between technical jargon and intuitive understanding.

Responsible AI Development: As AI continues to integrate into various aspects of society, responsible development becomes crucial. Activation Maximization and Feature Visualization can play a role in building AI systems that are not only accurate but also transparent and fair. Understanding what drives a neural network's decisions allows for more informed discussions about potential biases and ethical considerations.

Evolving Techniques: The field of Activation Maximization and Feature Visualization continues to evolve. Researchers are exploring new methods to make generated images more interpretable and aligned with real-world data. Advances in explainable AI and visualization techniques will likely enhance the accuracy and meaningfulness of the insights obtained from these methods.

Ethics and Privacy: As these techniques provide deep insights into neural network behavior, ethical considerations come to the forefront. Revealing the inner workings of models might expose vulnerabilities or sensitive associations. Striking a balance between transparency and potential risks is vital to ensure responsible use.

In essence, Activation Maximization and Feature Visualization hold the potential to reshape how we understand, interpret, and improve neural networks. By harnessing the power of visualization, we gain a clearer understanding of the representations learned by these complex models, paving the way for more robust and accountable artificial intelligence systems.

17.2 Grad-CAM and Saliency Maps: In the realm of interpretability and visualizing the decision-making process of neural networks, techniques like Grad-CAM and Saliency Maps have emerged as powerful tools. Let's delve deeper into their significance and workings:

17.2.1 Understanding Network Decisions: Grad-CAM (Gradient-weighted Class Activation Mapping) and Saliency Maps offer insights into why a neural network makes certain predictions by highlighting the areas of an input image that contribute most to a particular decision. These techniques provide a window into the inner workings of complex models, shedding light on the features and patterns that capture the network's attention.

17.2.2 Grad-CAM: Unveiling Activation Importance: Grad-CAM operates by analyzing the gradients flowing into the final convolutional layer of the network. It assigns importance scores to each neuron's activation in this layer, based on how much the final prediction would change if that activation were modified. By upscaling these importance scores and overlaying them on the original image, Grad-CAM highlights regions that significantly influence the network's decision.

17.2.3 Saliency Maps: Visualizing Sensitivity: Saliency Maps provide a powerful tool for gaining insights into the decision-making process of neural networks. By examining the sensitivity of individual pixels in an input image, Saliency Maps offer a means to understand the key factors influencing a network's predictions. Here's a deeper exploration of how Saliency Maps function and their significance in interpreting neural network decisions:

The Gradients of Influence: At the core of Saliency Maps lies the concept of gradients. In the realm of neural networks, gradients indicate how the predicted class score changes in response to alterations in the values of the input image's pixels. Essentially, gradients express the sensitivity of the network's prediction to variations in pixel intensities.

Unveiling Influential Pixels: To construct a Saliency Map, gradients are computed for every pixel in the input image. These gradients act as a guide to identify which pixels have the most significant impact on the final prediction. Pixels that contribute substantially to the prediction receive higher gradient values.

Mapping the Intensity of Impact: With the computed gradients in hand, the Saliency Map is crafted. This map serves as a visual representation where the intensity of each pixel corresponds to the magnitude of its gradient. In simpler terms, pixels with larger gradients are emphasized more prominently in the Saliency Map.

Spotting Decision-Making Regions: Analyzing the resulting Saliency Map provides a direct view into the regions of the input image that play a pivotal role in shaping the network's prediction. Bright areas on the map indicate regions that exert a strong influence on the prediction outcome, while darker regions signify less influential portions.

Unlocking Interpretability and Beyond: Saliency Maps yield several key applications within the realm of deep learning:

Interpretable Insights: They offer a clear avenue to understanding why a neural network arrives at a specific decision, providing valuable insights to both experts and stakeholders.

Model Debugging: When a model produces unexpected outputs, Saliency Maps can unveil the specific image regions responsible for driving such outcomes.

Bias Detection: By examining the emphasis or neglect of certain image areas, Saliency Maps can potentially uncover biases within the network.

Visualizing Attention: In architectures featuring attention mechanisms, these maps illuminate the aspects of the input that draw attention from different parts of the model.

Challenges and Future Refinements: However, the utility of Saliency Maps does come with challenges:

Pixel-Level Interpretation: Interpreting pixel-level contributions can be subjective and require domain knowledge for meaningful insights.

Complex Networks: For intricate networks with multifaceted interactions, Saliency Maps might not capture all nuances of decision-making.

Enhancing Robustness: Researchers are actively exploring ways to bolster the robustness of Saliency Maps to variations in inputs, as well as improving their consistency across different samples.

In the journey toward explainable AI, Saliency Maps serve as an accessible and intuitive method to uncover the decision-making mechanisms of neural networks. As techniques evolve, they continue to bridge the divide between complex model behaviors and human comprehension.

17.2.4 Applications and Benefits: Grad-CAM and Saliency Maps are versatile tools with a range of applications, contributing to a deeper understanding of neural networks and their performance. Here's a closer look at how these techniques are applied and the benefits they bring:

Interpretability and Insights:

Understanding Model Decisions: Both Grad-CAM and Saliency Maps help reveal the reasoning behind a model's predictions. This understanding is crucial for building trust and identifying potential biases or errors.

Biomedical Imaging: In medical imaging, these techniques assist doctors in comprehending why a model diagnoses certain conditions. This transparency is vital for medical professionals to make informed decisions.

Model Evaluation and Debugging:

Diagnosing Errors: When a model produces unexpected or incorrect outputs, Grad-CAM and Saliency Maps act as diagnostic tools. They enable researchers to identify if the model is focusing on irrelevant or misleading features.

Bias Detection: By visualizing attention, these techniques can uncover any biased behaviors in the model's predictions, helping researchers rectify potential ethical issues.

Transfer Learning and Model Improvement:

Transferability Assessment: Grad-CAM and Saliency Maps assist in assessing the transferability of a pre-trained model. Understanding which regions the model deems important in different tasks aids in optimizing transfer learning.

Feature Improvement: Researchers can use these maps to identify underrepresented features or areas that the model should focus on more, thereby enhancing the model's feature recognition capabilities.

Communication and Education:

Teaching and Learning: Grad-CAM and Saliency Maps facilitate the educational process by showing students and enthusiasts how neural networks arrive at decisions. This visual aid simplifies complex concepts and demystifies AI behaviors.

Ethical Considerations and Accountability:

Bias Mitigation: These techniques help address potential biases in AI models by revealing where they focus their attention. Addressing such biases is crucial for building fair and just AI systems.

Regulatory Compliance: In sectors like finance and healthcare, where model decisions have significant consequences, these techniques provide a way to justify and explain AI-driven decisions to regulatory bodies.

Benefits:

Transparency: Grad-CAM and Saliency Maps contribute to model transparency by revealing which parts of an input influence the model's decision.

Trust: Understanding why a model makes certain predictions builds trust among users, stakeholders, and the general public.
Model Improvement: By identifying areas of focus or biases, these techniques guide researchers in refining models for better performance and fairness.
As AI continues to integrate into various aspects of our lives, the applications and benefits of Grad-CAM and Saliency Maps make them indispensable tools for ensuring transparency, accountability, and informed decision-making in the deployment of AI systems.
17.2.5 Challenges and Evolving Techniques: While Grad-CAM and Saliency Maps have proven to be powerful tools for understanding neural network decisions, they are not without challenges. As these techniques evolve, researchers are actively addressing limitations and developing new strategies to enhance their effectiveness. Here are some of the challenges they face and the evolving techniques being explored:
Sensitivity to Input:
Challenge: Grad-CAM and Saliency Maps can be sensitive to minor variations in input data. Small changes in input can lead to different saliency patterns, which may not always align with human intuition.
Evolving Technique: Researchers are working on methods to make these techniques more robust to input variations. This involves exploring ways to reduce the impact of noise in input data on the generated saliency maps.
Complex Networks and Interpretability:
Challenge: In intricate network architectures like transformers, where information flows in complex ways, Grad-CAM and Saliency Maps might struggle to provide meaningful insights. The intricacy of these architectures can hinder accurate attribution of feature importance.
Evolving Technique: Researchers are investigating techniques that are specifically tailored to complex architectures, allowing for more accurate visualization of feature importance within these networks.
Negative Gradients and Comprehensive Insights:
Challenge: Existing techniques focus primarily on positive gradients, indicating regions that contribute positively to a prediction. However, overlooking negative gradients can provide an incomplete picture of feature importance.
Evolving Technique: Evolving techniques are exploring ways to incorporate both positive and negative gradients. By considering the complete gradient spectrum, these techniques aim to provide a more comprehensive understanding of feature relevance.
Integration into Decision-making:
Challenge: Currently, Grad-CAM and Saliency Maps primarily serve as visualization tools after model predictions have been made. Integrating these techniques directly into the decision-making process of neural networks remains a challenge.
Evolving Technique: Future directions involve developing methods to integrate saliency information into the network's architecture, allowing models to dynamically adjust their focus on specific features based on their relevance to the task.
As the field of interpretability continues to advance, addressing these challenges and refining techniques like Grad-CAM and Saliency Maps will contribute to building more transparent, trustworthy, and accountable AI systems. These evolving techniques hold the potential to provide clearer insights into neural network behavior, enhancing our understanding of AI decision-making processes.
17.3 Lime and SHAP: Model Explanation Techniques: In the realm of model explanation and interpretability, techniques like LIME (Local Interpretable Model-agnostic Explanations) and SHAP (SHapley Additive exPlanations) have gained prominence. These techniques offer insights into the inner workings of complex machine learning models, enabling us to understand how individual predictions are influenced by input features. Let's delve into these model explanation techniques:
17.3.1 LIME: Local Interpretable Model-agnostic Explanations: LIME stands for Local Interpretable Model-agnostic Explanations, and it is a pioneering technique in the field of model explanation and interpretability. LIME addresses a fundamental challenge in understanding the decisions of complex machine learning models, especially black-box models, by providing local and interpretable explanations for individual predictions.
The Core Idea: At the heart of LIME lies the concept of approximating the behavior of a complex model within a local neighborhood of a specific data point. The central motivation is that a complex model's behavior can be simplified and understood within a constrained region. LIME achieves this by generating a set of perturbed samples around the instance of interest.
Steps of LIME:
Data Perturbation: LIME starts by creating perturbed samples of the original instance by introducing slight variations to the input features. These perturbations simulate how the model might respond to small changes in the input.
Model Prediction: The perturbed samples are then presented to the black-box model, and their corresponding predictions are recorded. This step captures the model's behavior within the local region surrounding the original instance.
Surrogate Model: LIME constructs a simpler, interpretable surrogate model using the perturbed samples and their corresponding predictions. This surrogate model serves as a proxy for the black-box model's behavior within the local region.
Feature Importance: The surrogate model is now interpretable, which means its predictions can be easily understood. LIME uses the surrogate model to estimate the importance of each input feature in influencing the model's prediction. The features that contribute the most to the prediction within the local neighborhood are highlighted as the main drivers of the decision.
Benefits and Applications:

Local Explanations: LIME provides insights into why a specific instance received a particular prediction. This is particularly useful for explaining individual instances without needing to interpret the entire model.
Model Debugging: LIME can help identify whether a model's prediction is based on relevant features or if it's sensitive to noise or irrelevant information.
Trust and Transparency: In high-stakes applications like healthcare or finance, LIME offers transparency by explaining why a certain decision was made, enhancing user trust.

Challenges and Considerations:

Local Scope: LIME provides explanations within a local region, which may not capture the entire model's behavior. Generalizing these local explanations to the entire model can be challenging.
Surrogate Model Assumption: The surrogate model may not perfectly capture the complex model's behavior, leading to some degree of approximation.
Hyperparameter Tuning: LIME involves tuning parameters like the number of perturbed samples and the complexity of the surrogate model, which can impact the quality of explanations.

In Conclusion:

LIME is a versatile tool that bridges the gap between complex models and human understanding. It enables us to gain insights into the factors that drive individual predictions, enhancing transparency, trust, and accountability in machine learning systems.

17.3.2 SHAP: SHapley Additive exPlanations: SHAP, inspired by cooperative game theory, aims to attribute the contribution of each feature to a model's prediction. Building on the concept of Shapley values, which assign a value to each player in a coalition game, SHAP provides a unified framework for feature attribution. It computes the average contribution of each feature across all possible feature permutations and quantifies how much each feature deviates from the expected average. This results in a comprehensive explanation for individual predictions, highlighting the role of each feature in the context of the entire feature set.

17.3.3 Applications and Benefits: Both LIME and SHAP offer valuable insights in various applications, revolutionizing the way we understand and interact with complex machine learning models:

Model Debugging:

These techniques play a crucial role in identifying whether a model's predictions are based on relevant features or if they are picking up noise or biases present in the data. By explaining why certain predictions are made, LIME and SHAP facilitate the process of diagnosing and improving model behavior.

Trust and Accountability:

LIME and SHAP provide transparency to users by offering understandable explanations for model predictions. This transparency is especially vital in critical domains such as healthcare and finance, where understanding the rationale behind predictions is essential for decision-making.

Bias Detection:

These techniques can uncover hidden biases within models by revealing the contribution of different features to predictions. By highlighting biased or unfair decisions, LIME and SHAP contribute to building more equitable and just AI systems.

17.3.4 Challenges and Ongoing Research: While LIME and SHAP offer significant benefits, they are not without challenges:

Complex Models:

Explaining complex models accurately can be challenging. Creating surrogate models that capture the full complexity of the original model's behavior is not always straightforward.

High-Dimensional Data:

Interpreting models with a large number of features can be overwhelming. Visualizing explanations for high-dimensional data poses its own set of complexities.

Quantitative Comparison:

Comparing explanations across different models or instances is challenging due to the lack of standardized metrics. Quantitative assessment of the quality and consistency of explanations remains an ongoing research area.

17.3.5 Future Directions: As LIME and SHAP continue to evolve, research is focused on addressing these challenges and extending their applicability:

Ensemble Explanations: Combining explanations from multiple techniques can provide a more comprehensive and reliable understanding of model behavior. Ensemble approaches can potentially enhance the robustness and accuracy of explanations, especially in scenarios where a single technique might fall short.
Explaining Deep Learning Models: Adapting LIME and SHAP to explain deep learning models, such as neural networks, is an active area of research. Techniques are being developed to effectively capture the complex interactions within deep learning architectures and provide interpretable explanations.
User-Friendly Interfaces: As LIME and SHAP gain traction in real-world applications, efforts are being made to develop user-friendly tools and interfaces. These interfaces aim to simplify the process of applying LIME and SHAP, making them accessible to a broader range of users without extensive technical expertise.

In essence, LIME and SHAP are dynamic techniques that continue to evolve, shaping the landscape of interpretable and transparent AI systems while addressing the challenges that arise along the way. Sure, here's the information in the format you provided:

17.4 Visualizing Network Architectures and Attention:

17.4.1 Insight into Network Behavior: Understanding the intricate behavior of neural network architectures is a pivotal aspect of their development, analysis, and enhancement. Visualizing network architectures offers a window into the underlying mechanisms by which information traverses through the layers. This visualization empowers researchers and practitioners with a deeper comprehension of the internal dynamics of complex models.

In the realm of deep learning, where models often consist of numerous interconnected layers, deciphering how data is transformed and processed at each stage is far from trivial. Visualizing network architectures breaks down this complexity, allowing us to observe the transformations that occur as data progresses through the network. By gaining insights into how different layers respond to various patterns and features, developers can fine-tune models for optimal performance.

Furthermore, visualizations shed light on the flow of gradients during the backpropagation process, showcasing how information is adjusted in response to training signals. This transparency aids in diagnosing issues such as vanishing gradients, exploding gradients, or ineffective weight updates.

In essence, visualizing network architectures serves as a powerful tool for unraveling the inner workings of neural networks. It not only enhances our understanding of their behavior but also facilitates their improvement, making it an indispensable aspect of modern deep learning research and practice.

17.4.2 Visualizing Convolutional Neural Networks (CNNs): Visualizing Convolutional Neural Networks (CNNs) is a pivotal endeavor for unveiling the inner workings of these specialized architectures. CNNs excel in image analysis, but comprehending how they identify features and patterns within images is a complex task. Visualizations aid in demystifying this process, offering insights into the learned features and their significance.

One technique employed in visualizing CNNs is feature visualization. This approach generates images that activate specific filters in the network. By iteratively modifying an input image to maximize the activation of a chosen filter, researchers can understand what kind of visual patterns that filter responds to. This process effectively allows us to visualize the preferences of individual filters, revealing edges, textures, or more complex structures that they detect.

Class Activation Maps (CAM) are another vital visualization tool for CNNs. CAMs identify the regions within an input image that are influential in predicting a specific class. This technique offers a spatial understanding of which parts of an image contribute most significantly to a certain classification decision. By overlaying these maps on the original image, researchers can validate whether the network is attending to the correct features for its predictions.

17.4.3 Attention Mechanisms: Insight into Learning: Attention mechanisms have transformed the landscape of sequence-to-sequence tasks, particularly in models like transformers. These mechanisms allow for the visualization of which portions of the input sequence receive heightened attention during processing. This visualization offers a window into how the model understands and learns the relationships between different elements in the sequence.

In tasks like language translation, attention mechanisms reveal which words in the source sentence the model emphasizes when generating the translation. This not only provides insight into the linguistic context but also helps identify potential biases or misinterpretations. By visualizing attention distributions, researchers can diagnose whether the model allocates appropriate focus to relevant elements and identify cases where improvements are needed.

In summary, the visualization of CNNs and attention mechanisms brings transparency to the decision-making processes of complex neural architectures. These techniques empower researchers to gain deeper insights into how these networks learn and make predictions, leading to enhanced model understanding, validation, and improvement.

17.4.4 Interactive Model Exploration: Interactive model exploration tools bring a new dimension to understanding neural network architectures and attention mechanisms. These tools empower users to engage with models in real-time, fostering experimentation, debugging, and a deeper comprehension of how networks operate.

With interactive visualization tools, users can manipulate various parameters, observe changes in real-time, and gain immediate feedback on network responses. This interactivity facilitates a hands-on approach to exploring network behavior, enabling researchers and practitioners to probe different scenarios, validate assumptions, and refine models more effectively.

17.4.5 Challenges and Future Developments: While the benefits of visualizing network architectures and attention mechanisms are substantial, several challenges persist:

Complexity: As neural architectures become more intricate, simplifying these complex structures for visualization without compromising the essence of their behavior poses a challenge. Developing techniques to distill complex networks into understandable visual representations remains a subject of ongoing research.

Scalability: With the proliferation of larger and more sophisticated models, visualizations need to handle massive networks efficiently. Ensuring that visualization tools can cope with the scale of modern architectures is crucial for their practical applicability.

Interpretability: Converting visualizations into actionable insights demands careful interpretation. Balancing the sophistication of visual representations with their interpretability is essential to ensure that the insights gained from visualizations translate into meaningful decisions and improvements.

As these challenges are addressed, the field of interactive model exploration is expected to flourish further, contributing to the democratization of neural network understanding and enhancing the efficiency of model development and analysis.

17.5 Project

Unsolved Project

Suppose you're tasked with developing a project focused on interpreting and visualizing deep learning models to understand how they make decisions. To achieve this, you need to explore activation maximization and feature visualization, Grad-CAM and saliency maps, model explanation techniques like LIME and SHAP, and methods for visualizing network architectures and attention mechanisms. Before starting your project, research the following: the use of activation maximization and feature visualization to understand what neurons in a network are detecting, the implementation of Grad-CAM and saliency maps to highlight important regions in input data, techniques like LIME and SHAP for explaining model predictions, and methods for visualizing the architecture of deep learning models and attention mechanisms. This foundational knowledge will help you interpret and visualize your deep learning models effectively.

17.6 Lab Activity

Unsolved Lab Activity

Implement activation maximization to visualize the features learned by a specific layer in a pre-trained CNN model (e.g., VGG16).

Task: Use a deep learning framework (e.g., TensorFlow or PyTorch) to implement activation maximization for visualizing features learned by a specific layer in a pre-trained CNN model like VGG16. Document the implementation process, including data preprocessing, model setup, and visualizations of the maximized activations.

Exercises

Exercise 1 – Multiple Choice Questions

1. What is the primary purpose of Activation Maximization in deep neural networks?
   - A. To improve model accuracy
   - B. To unravel the inner workings of networks
   - C. To reduce model complexity
   - D. To increase training speed
2. In Activation Maximization, what is the first step in the process?
   - A. Iterative Modification
   - B. Gradient Ascent
   - C. Choosing a Target Neuron
   - D. Generating Initial Input
3. What does Gradient Ascent in Activation Maximization indicate?
   - A. How sensitive the neuron's activation is to input changes
   - B. How to decrease neuron activation
   - C. The pixel values of the input image
   - D. The number of iterations required
4. How does Activation Maximization help in interpreting convolutional neural networks (CNNs)?
   - A. It reduces the number of neurons in a CNN.
   - B. It visualizes the training data.
   - C. It uncovers the preferences of neurons in CNNs.
   - D. It speeds up the training process.
5. What is one potential application of Activation Maximization?
   - A. Reducing model complexity
   - B. Model validation and debugging
   - C. Enhancing model training speed
   - D. Generating random images

Exercise 2 – True/False

1. Grad-CAM and saliency maps are techniques used to visualize the areas in an image that influence a deep learning model's predictions.
2. Lime and SHAP are model explanation techniques that help in interpreting the predictions made by deep learning models.
3. Activation maximization is a technique used to minimize the activation of neurons in a neural network to understand what features they respond to.

Review Questions

1. What are Activation Maximization and Feature Visualization, and what purpose do they serve in deep neural networks?
2. Describe the process of Activation Maximization and how it helps unveil neural network representations.
3. How is the target neuron chosen in Activation Maximization, and why is this important?
4. Explain the role of gradient ascent in Activation Maximization and its significance.
5. What kind of insights can be gained by using Activation Maximization on specific neurons in a neural network?
6. In what types of neural networks, particularly, is Activation Maximization useful for interpretation, and why?
7. How can Activation Maximization be employed for model interpretability and validation?
8. What ethical considerations should be kept in mind when applying Activation Maximization and Feature Visualization?
9. How do Activation Maximization and Feature Visualization contribute to responsible AI development?
10. What challenges and potential future applications are associated with Activation Maximization and Feature Visualization?

11. What are Grad-CAM and Saliency Maps, and what insights do they provide into neural network decision-making?
12. Explain how Grad-CAM operates and how it highlights regions in an image.
13. How do Saliency Maps function, and what is the significance of gradients in this context?
14. What are some practical applications of Grad-CAM and Saliency Maps in understanding neural networks?
15. What challenges are associated with Saliency Maps, especially when dealing with complex network architectures?
16. How can Grad-CAM and Saliency Maps contribute to model debugging and bias detection?
17. What role do LIME and SHAP techniques play in model explanation and interpretability, and how do they work?

Answers

Exercise 1- 1. B 2. C 3. A 4. C 5. B
Exercise 2- 1) True, 2) True, 3) False

Online Resources

Online Exam Paper:
Link: https://forms.gle/Av4K262afcZ4GrtG7
QR Code:

Chapter 17 Videos Playlist:
Link: https://www.youtube.com/playlist?list=PLzlh_31VWEFq_uQErBGm5pIfg1qdc6Fuc
QR Code:

Chapter 18: Multi-modal Learning and Fusion

18.1 Audio-Visual Fusion for Speech Recognition: Audio-visual fusion, a powerful cross-modal technique, has emerged as a dynamic approach for enhancing speech recognition systems by combining both auditory and visual information. This fusion leverages the complementary nature of audio and visual cues to improve the accuracy and robustness of speech recognition in various real-world scenarios.

18.1.1 The Power of Multimodal Fusion: Audio-visual fusion taps into the inherent redundancy of information present in both auditory and visual signals. While audio conveys linguistic content, visual cues from lip movements and facial expressions provide additional context. By merging these modalities, the system gains a more comprehensive understanding of spoken content, resulting in enhanced recognition performance.

18.1.2 Mechanisms of Fusion: Audio-visual fusion involves integrating audio and visual features at different stages of the speech recognition pipeline:

Early Fusion: At the input stage, audio and visual features are combined to create a joint representation, which is then fed to the recognition system. This approach captures the combined information from the start, aiding in robust feature extraction.

Late Fusion: In this approach, individual audio and visual recognizers process their respective modalities independently. The outputs are then combined at a later stage, such as during language modeling or decision fusion. This method preserves the modality-specific processing while exploiting the complementarity of the cues.

Intermediate Fusion: This technique involves fusing features at intermediate layers within a neural network architecture. Modality-specific networks process audio and visual data separately until a certain layer, where the representations are combined before further processing. This approach balances modality-specific learning with integrated representation.

18.1.3 Enhanced Robustness and Accuracy: In the realm of speech recognition, the integration of audio and visual information through fusion holds the promise of enhanced robustness and accuracy. This advantage becomes particularly evident in challenging scenarios characterized by noisy environments or audio signal corruption. In such conditions, the audio component of speech might suffer from distortions, making it difficult for conventional speech recognition systems to accurately decipher the spoken content.

Visual cues, such as lip movements, offer a distinct advantage in these circumstances. Unlike audio signals, visual cues tend to remain relatively resilient to various forms of audio distortion. This resilience arises from the fact that lip movements are not directly influenced by background noise or acoustic interference. As a result, they can provide a consistent and reliable source of information for deciphering spoken words even in conditions where the audio signal is compromised.

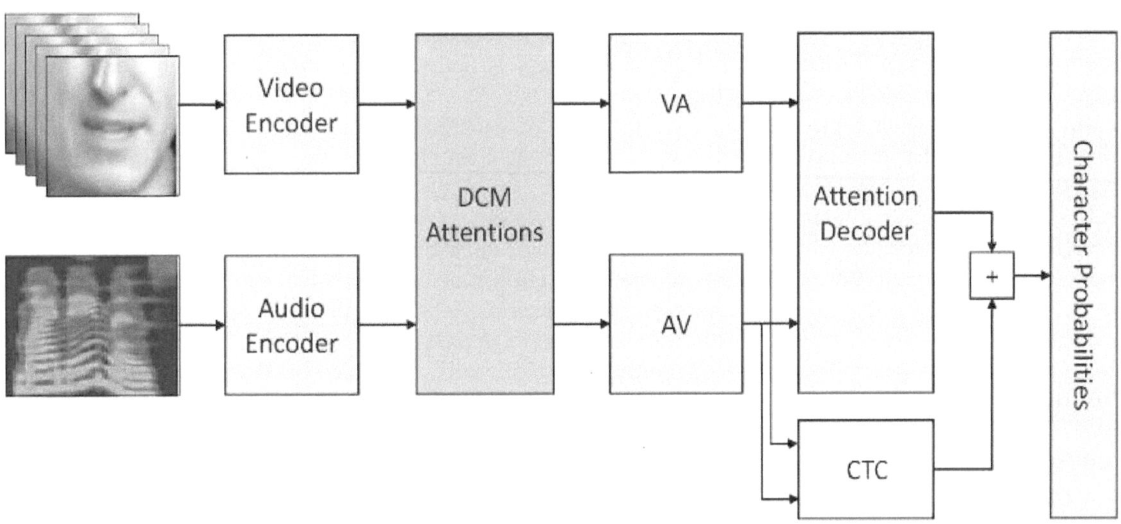

18.1.4 Applications and Benefits: The concept of audio-visual fusion has wide-ranging applications across different domains, owing to its ability to leverage the strengths of both modalities. Some notable applications and benefits include:

Noisy Environments: In environments characterized by high levels of background noise, such as crowded public spaces or industrial settings, audio-visual fusion proves invaluable. The incorporation of lip movements and facial expressions helps disentangle speech content from the surrounding noise, leading to more accurate and reliable speech recognition outcomes.

Speaker Identification: Visual cues, especially lip movements, play a crucial role in speaker identification and discrimination. In scenarios where multiple speakers are present, audio-visual fusion aids in distinguishing individual speakers based on their unique lip patterns, contributing to more accurate speaker identification systems.

Multilingual Speech Recognition: Different languages possess distinct acoustic characteristics that can challenge conventional audio-only recognition systems, especially for languages that are less familiar to the system. Audio-visual fusion capitalizes on the universal nature of visual cues like lip movements, offering a supplementary channel for recognizing and distinguishing speech in languages with unfamiliar audio characteristics.

18.1.5 Challenges and Future Directions: While audio-visual fusion offers numerous benefits, it also presents certain challenges that researchers are actively working to address:

Data Synchronization: Effective fusion relies on precise alignment between audio and visual data. Variations in audio-visual synchronization can impact the accuracy of fusion, making the development of techniques for robust synchronization a priority.

Real-world Variability: Different speakers exhibit variations in lip movements, facial expressions, and speaking styles. Adapting fusion models to accommodate this variability is essential for achieving reliable and consistent results across various speakers and scenarios.

Looking ahead, future directions for audio-visual fusion involve leveraging more advanced neural network architectures for joint modeling, exploring novel fusion mechanisms, and refining synchronization techniques. As technology evolves, audio-visual fusion stands poised to reshape the landscape of speech recognition, offering improved accuracy and resilience in an array of practical applications.

18.2 Multi-modal Sentiment Analysis: Sentiment analysis, the task of determining the emotional tone or attitude expressed in text, has gained significant attention in the field of natural language processing. However, human communication is inherently multi-modal, involving not only text but also visual and auditory cues. Multi-modal sentiment analysis aims to leverage this diversity of information by incorporating text, images, and audio to gain a more comprehensive understanding of sentiment.

18.2.1 Fusion of Text and Visual Modalities: Multi-modal sentiment analysis begins with the fusion of different modalities to create a unified representation of the input data. In the case of text and visual information, techniques like late fusion and early fusion are employed. Late fusion involves separately processing each modality and then combining the results at a later stage, while early fusion integrates the modalities at an earlier processing stage. This fusion allows the model to capture the synergistic effects of different modalities, leading to improved sentiment prediction.

18.2.2 Audio-Visual Fusion: Audio-visual sentiment analysis extends the multi-modal approach to include auditory cues, such as tone of voice, laughter, and speech rate. These cues can provide valuable insights into the speaker's emotions and attitudes. Integrating audio-visual information requires specialized architectures that can process both auditory and visual signals simultaneously. This fusion can be particularly powerful in scenarios where visual cues might be ambiguous or insufficient on their own.

18.2.3 Challenges and Benefits: Multi-modal sentiment analysis, particularly when incorporating audio-visual fusion, offers a spectrum of challenges and benefits:

Challenges:

Data Collection and Labeling: Gathering and labeling multi-modal data can be intricate. Different modalities may require diverse annotation approaches, and subjectivity in sentiment labeling across modalities can lead to inconsistencies.

Fusion Complexity: Integrating textual, visual, and auditory information requires intricate architectures that can handle the heterogeneity of these signals. Ensuring that the fusion process is both effective and interpretable adds another layer of complexity.

Interpretability: Understanding the individual contribution of each modality to the final sentiment prediction can be challenging. Interpreting the combined effect of text, visual cues, and auditory signals is a nuanced task.

Benefits:

Improved Performance: The integration of auditory cues in sentiment analysis can significantly boost accuracy. Tone of voice, speech rate, and other audio features can offer unique insights that complement textual and visual cues.

Real-world Applicability: Human interactions are inherently multi-modal. Models that can grasp sentiments across various modalities are more aligned with real-world communication scenarios, enhancing their practicality.

Enhanced Robustness: In situations where textual or visual cues might be ambiguous or insufficient, auditory cues can provide an additional layer of information. This enhanced robustness is particularly valuable in real-world, noisy environments.

18.2.4 Future Directions: The trajectory of multi-modal sentiment analysis is poised to evolve along the following exciting directions:

Continued Research and Innovation: The exploration of novel architectures, fusion techniques, and learning strategies is expected to persist. Researchers will continue to refine existing methodologies and devise innovative approaches to enhance sentiment prediction across modalities.

Integration of Contextual Understanding: The incorporation of contextual information represents a promising avenue. Understanding the context in which sentiment is expressed can profoundly impact the accuracy of predictions. Models capable of comprehending contextual cues and their influence on sentiment dynamics are likely to emerge.

Domain Adaptation and Multilingualism: Extending the capabilities of multi-modal sentiment analysis to various domains and languages remains a central focus. Adapting models to different contexts and linguistic nuances will enable their broader applicability and relevance across global communication scenarios.

As technology advances and data availability grows, the convergence of textual, visual, and auditory information for sentiment analysis is poised to redefine our understanding of human communication, emotions, and attitudes. By harnessing the strengths of diverse modalities, future multi-modal sentiment analysis systems hold the promise of unlocking new dimensions of insights and applications.

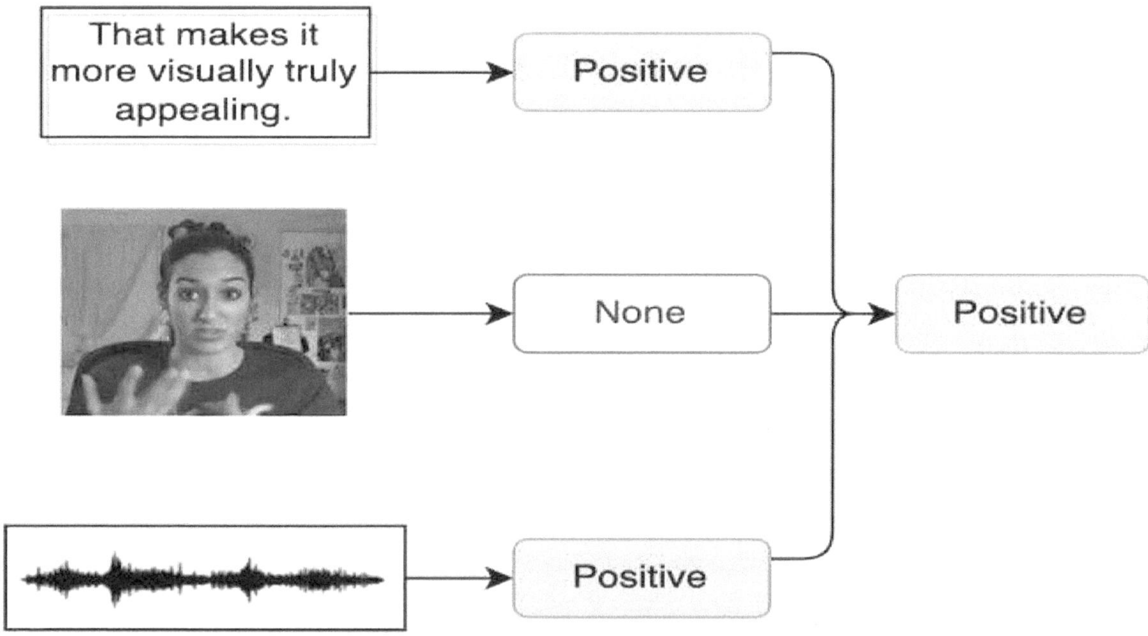

18.3 Fusion of Text, Image, and Audio Data: In the era of multimodal data, combining text, image, and audio information offers a comprehensive understanding of complex content. The fusion of these modalities leverages their unique strengths, enhancing various AI tasks such as understanding context, sentiment analysis, and information retrieval. This fusion enables AI systems to operate more holistically, mimicking human-like comprehension across multiple senses.

18.3.1 Enhanced Contextual Understanding: Fusing text, image, and audio data enriches contextual understanding. Language might lack the nuances to convey complete meaning, but images and audio offer complementary layers. For instance, in news analysis, understanding an article's sentiment is bolstered by analyzing accompanying images and the tone of spoken words in related audio content.

18.3.2 Multi-Modal Sentiment Analysis Reimagined: The fusion of text, image, and audio opens new dimensions in sentiment analysis. Instead of considering each modality in isolation, models can analyze how text sentiment aligns with visual cues, like facial expressions or objects present in images, as well as auditory cues such as tone and intonation. This multi-modal approach promises a deeper understanding of sentiment nuances.

18.3.3 Improved Information Retrieval: In the realm of information retrieval, the fusion of text, image, and audio data offers a transformative approach. Traditional keyword-based search engines excel at matching search terms to textual content, but they often struggle to decipher the context and intent behind a user's query. This is where multi-modal fusion steps in to enhance the accuracy and relevance of search results. By integrating multiple modalities, such as text, image, and audio, search engines gain a more holistic understanding of user queries. This allows them to go beyond simple keyword matching and delve into the nuanced context and intent of the query. For instance, consider a user searching for "best hiking trails." A traditional search engine might retrieve results based solely on the keyword "hiking trails," potentially overlooking the user's specific intent. However, by analyzing the context of the query alongside relevant images and audio, a multi-modal search engine can discern whether the user is looking for beginner-friendly trails, scenic routes, or perhaps trails suitable for a family outing.

Multi-modal information retrieval involves interpreting not only the textual query but also related visual and auditory cues. Visual content, such as images, can offer insights into the user's preferences, while audio cues, like speech intonation, may indicate urgency or excitement. By amalgamating these cues, multi-modal search engines deliver results that are aligned with the user's true information needs, resulting in a more personalized and satisfying search experience.

18.3.4 Challenges and Opportunities:

Challenges:

Complex Architecture: Designing models capable of effectively processing and fusing multiple modalities is a demanding task. The architecture must accommodate the unique characteristics of each modality and seamlessly integrate their information. This often leads to intricate and resource-intensive architectures, increasing computational demands.

Data Integration: Integrating diverse data types is a critical challenge. Textual data, images, and audio have distinct representations and formats, requiring careful preprocessing and alignment. Data quality discrepancies and variations further complicate the integration process.

Interpretability: Interpreting the contribution of each modality to model decisions is a complex issue. Understanding why a certain result was produced requires disentangling the individual effects of each modality, which can be challenging in complex models.

Opportunities:

Enhanced Understanding: Multi-modal fusion enables AI systems to glean a richer understanding of content by capturing nuances that might be overlooked when considering a single modality in isolation.

Robustness: By drawing from multiple sources, multi-modal models become more robust to noise, ambiguity, and inconsistencies in data. They can make informed decisions even when individual modalities are unclear or conflicting.

Innovative Applications: The fusion of modalities unlocks innovative applications across various domains. Educational platforms can provide interactive learning experiences that combine text, images, and audio. Entertainment platforms can create immersive experiences that engage users through a blend of sensory cues.

As research and development in multi-modal fusion progress, the challenges are being met with innovative solutions, and the benefits are increasingly being realized in applications that demand a comprehensive understanding of diverse content. The journey toward seamlessly integrating text, image, and audio data continues to pave the way for more intelligent, versatile, and human-like AI systems.

18.3.5 Future Prospects: The fusion of text, image, and audio data is poised to shape the future of AI and information processing in exciting and transformative ways. As technology and research continue to advance, several promising prospects emerge on the horizon:

Advancements in Architectures: A significant focus of future research will center on refining and innovating architectures that facilitate effective multi-modal fusion. These architectures will aim to strike a balance between computational efficiency and high-performance fusion, enabling AI systems to seamlessly process and understand diverse data types.

Human-like Comprehension: As multi-modal models become more sophisticated, their ability to comprehend and interpret content across different modalities will approach human-like levels. AI systems will be better equipped to understand context, nuances, and intent, leading to more accurate and contextually relevant responses.

Creative Applications: The fusion of text, image, and audio data will open the doors to innovative applications across various domains. In education, interactive learning experiences that leverage multiple modalities will enhance engagement and comprehension. In the entertainment industry, AI-powered platforms will craft personalized experiences that blend textual, visual, and auditory elements, immersing users in captivating narratives. Healthcare platforms could benefit from comprehensive content analysis, leading to more accurate diagnostics and personalized treatment recommendations.

Enhanced Accessibility: Multi-modal fusion has the potential to make technology more accessible to diverse users. Voice assistants that understand spoken commands enriched with contextual visual cues can cater to users with different communication preferences and abilities.

Cross-domain Insights: The fusion of modalities can facilitate cross-domain insights, allowing AI systems to connect information across different fields. For example, medical researchers could leverage multi-modal models to correlate medical literature, patient records, and medical images for more accurate diagnoses.

Ethical Considerations: As AI systems gain deeper insights into human communication and behavior through multi-modal fusion, ethical considerations surrounding privacy, consent, and potential biases will become more crucial than ever. Striking a balance between technological advancement and ethical responsibility will be paramount.

Interdisciplinary Collaboration: The fusion of text, image, and audio data inherently involves expertise from various domains, including natural language processing, computer vision, and audio analysis. Collaborative efforts between researchers and experts from these domains will drive advancements and innovation in multi-modal fusion.

the future of multi-modal fusion holds the promise of more intelligent, adaptable, and contextually aware AI systems that can seamlessly integrate and comprehend diverse forms of human communication and expression. As these prospects become reality, they will not only reshape how we interact with technology but also revolutionize the way AI systems understand and engage with the world around them.

18.4 Challenges and Benefits of Multi-modal Learning: The integration of multi-modal data, which involves combining information from various sources such as text, images, and audio, presents a range of challenges and benefits in the realm of machine learning. Understanding these aspects is essential for effectively harnessing the power of multi-modal learning to improve the accuracy and robustness of AI systems.

Challenges:

Data Heterogeneity: Multi-modal data comes in diverse formats, scales, and quality levels. Integrating and preprocessing data from different sources can be complex, requiring careful handling to ensure compatibility.

Feature Alignment: Aligning features from different modalities to effectively capture relevant information can be intricate. Discrepancies in feature scales and distributions need to be addressed to enable meaningful fusion.

Data Synchronization: In tasks involving temporal data, such as video and audio fusion, ensuring accurate synchronization is crucial. Misalignment can lead to incorrect interpretations and degraded fusion outcomes.

Model Complexity: Designing models that can seamlessly fuse data from multiple modalities while maintaining high performance demands sophisticated architectures. This complexity can result in increased computational requirements.

Interpretability: As models grow in complexity and involve multiple modalities, understanding how they arrive at decisions becomes challenging. Interpreting the individual contributions of each modality can require specialized techniques.

Labeling and Annotation: Ground truth labels that encompass multiple modalities can be challenging to create, as they might involve subjective judgments. Ensuring consistency and reliability across modalities is crucial.

Benefits:

Comprehensive Information: Multi-modal learning facilitates a comprehensive understanding of data by leveraging the strengths of each modality. Combining multiple sources of information leads to a more holistic representation of underlying patterns.

Robustness to Noise: Utilizing information from various modalities can enhance model robustness. When one modality contains noise or inaccuracies, other modalities can compensate, resulting in more reliable predictions.
Improved Performance: The fusion of modalities often leads to enhanced model performance. Multi-modal models can outperform their single-modal counterparts by leveraging diverse cues for decision-making.
Contextual Understanding: Multi-modal learning enables models to better comprehend context and capture intricate nuances that might be missed when considering only a single modality. This is particularly relevant in tasks involving human communication.
Reduced Ambiguity: In scenarios where a single modality might be ambiguous or lacking, combining multiple modalities can provide a clearer and more definitive representation, reducing uncertainty.
Real-world Applicability: Human interaction and communication involve multiple modalities, such as speech, text, and images. Multi-modal models are better equipped to handle real-world scenarios where understanding and generating content across modalities are essential.
Innovative Applications: The fusion of modalities opens up new avenues for innovation in various fields. Applications can range from healthcare and education to entertainment and beyond, enriching user experiences and capabilities.
In navigating the challenges and leveraging the benefits of multi-modal learning, researchers and practitioners contribute to advancing AI systems' capabilities. Such systems can better understand and interact with the world, paving the way for more sophisticated and comprehensive AI applications.

18.5 Project

Unsolved Project

Suppose you're developing a project that leverages multi-modal learning and data fusion techniques to enhance the performance of machine learning models. To achieve this, you need to understand audio-visual fusion for speech recognition, multi-modal sentiment analysis, the fusion of text, image, and audio data, and the challenges and benefits of multi-modal learning. Before starting your project, research the following: methods for combining audio and visual data to improve speech recognition accuracy, techniques for performing sentiment analysis using multiple data modalities, strategies for effectively fusing text, image, and audio data, and the various challenges and benefits associated with multi-modal learning. This foundational knowledge will enable you to develop a robust and innovative multi-modal learning project.

18.6 Lab Activity

Unsolved Lab Activity

Implement a multi-modal fusion model that combines text, image, and audio data for a specific task (e.g., multi-modal classification or retrieval).
Task: Use a deep learning framework to implement and train a multi-modal fusion model for a specific task, such as multi-modal classification or retrieval. Document the implementation process, including data preprocessing, model architecture, training procedure, and performance evaluation. Provide examples of the model's outputs.

Exercises

Exercise 1 – Multiple Choice Questions

1. What is the primary objective of audio-visual fusion in speech recognition?
   A. To replace auditory information
   B. To eliminate visual cues
   C. To combine auditory and visual information for improved recognition
   D. To focus solely on linguistic content
2. How does audio-visual fusion enhance speech recognition in challenging environments?
   A. By distorting audio signals
   B. By providing an additional source of background noise
   C. By leveraging the resilience of visual cues to audio distortion
   D. By reducing the importance of audio cues
3. Which of the following fusion techniques combines audio and visual features at the input stage?
   A. Early Fusion
   B. Late Fusion
   C. Intermediate Fusion
   D. Advanced Fusion
4. In late fusion, when are individual audio and visual recognizers combined?
   A. At the input stage
   B. During language modeling
   C. At the recognition system's output
   D. Never
5. What advantage does late fusion offer over early fusion?

A. Early fusion is computationally simpler.
B. Late fusion captures combined information from the start.
C. Late fusion preserves modality-specific processing.
D. Early fusion is more interpretable.

Exercise 2 – True/False

1. Multi-modal learning can only combine two types of data, such as text and images.
2. Audio-visual fusion for speech recognition involves integrating both audio and visual inputs to improve speech recognition accuracy.
3. One of the benefits of multi-modal learning is that it can help in understanding more complex patterns by leveraging different data types.

Review Questions

1. What is the primary purpose of audio-visual fusion in speech recognition, and how does it achieve this goal?
2. Explain how audio and visual cues complement each other in audio-visual fusion for speech recognition.
3. Describe the concept of early fusion in audio-visual fusion and its advantages.
4. In the context of audio-visual fusion, what is late fusion, and when are individual audio and visual recognizers combined?
5. What is the key advantage of late fusion over early fusion in audio-visual fusion?

Answers

Exercise 1- 1. C 2. C 3. A 4. C 5. C
Exercise 2- 1) False, 2) True, 3) False

Online Resources

Online Exam Paper:
Link: https://forms.gle/Ga1Gd8iGjS1ZsUdi7
QR Code:

Chapter 18 Videos Playlist:
Link: https://www.youtube.com/playlist?list=PLzlh_31VWEFoBRXgt-MvHWzmbmKrh1wgI
QR Code:

Chapter 19: Auto ML and Neural Architecture Search

19.1 Automated Machine Learning (Auto ML) Pipelines: Automated Machine Learning (Auto ML) pipelines represent a transformative approach to streamlining and optimizing the machine learning model development process. These pipelines automate various stages, from data preprocessing to model selection and hyperparameter tuning, allowing data scientists and developers to focus on high-level tasks while minimizing the manual effort required for model building.

19.1.1 The Evolution of Auto ML Pipelines: Auto ML pipelines emerged as a response to the growing complexity of machine learning projects. Traditionally, building machine learning models involved several time-consuming and iterative steps, including data preprocessing, feature engineering, model selection, hyperparameter tuning, and evaluation. Auto ML pipelines aim to automate these steps, reducing the need for manual intervention and expertise.

19.1.2 Components of Auto ML Pipelines: Auto ML pipelines are composed of several interconnected components that collaboratively automate the entire process of developing machine learning models:

Data Preprocessing: This initial step involves preparing the raw data for model training. Auto ML pipelines handle tasks like imputing missing values, scaling features to similar ranges, and encoding categorical variables into numerical formats. Ensuring clean and well-preprocessed data is essential for accurate model training.

Feature Engineering: Automated feature engineering techniques are employed to extract relevant information from the data. These methods can automatically select the most important features, transform existing features, and even generate new features based on patterns in the data. Feature engineering plays a critical role in improving model performance by providing the algorithm with more meaningful inputs.

Model Selection: Auto ML pipelines explore a diverse range of machine learning algorithms and models to determine the optimal one for a specific problem. This involves training multiple models with varying architectures and parameters. The pipeline evaluates their performance and selects the model that best fits the data and exhibits the highest predictive accuracy.

Hyperparameter Tuning: Hyperparameters are configuration settings that control how a machine learning model is trained. They significantly impact a model's performance, and finding the optimal values is a crucial step. Auto ML pipelines automate the process of searching for the best hyperparameters using techniques such as grid search, random search, and more advanced optimization methods like Bayesian optimization.

Ensemble Learning: Ensembling involves combining the predictions of multiple models to create a more accurate and robust final prediction. Auto ML pipelines can automatically construct ensembles by selecting and blending the outputs of the best-performing individual models. Ensemble methods can enhance generalization and mitigate overfitting.

Evaluation and Validation: Auto ML pipelines utilize various validation techniques, such as cross-validation, to assess a model's performance on unseen data. These techniques help estimate how well the model is expected to perform in real-world scenarios. Validation ensures that the selected model is not overfitting to the training data and can generalize to new instances.

Auto ML pipelines orchestrate these components seamlessly, relieving developers and data scientists from the burden of manually performing each step. This automation accelerates the model development process, improves efficiency, and allows practitioners to focus on higher-level tasks, such as problem formulation and domain expertise.

19.1.3 Benefits of Auto ML Pipelines: Automated Machine Learning (Auto ML) pipelines provide a range of advantages that contribute to more efficient and effective model development:

Time Efficiency: Auto ML significantly accelerates the process of building machine learning models. By automating data preprocessing, feature engineering, model selection, and hyperparameter tuning, developers can rapidly iterate and experiment with different approaches, saving valuable time.

Reduced Expertise Barrier: Auto ML pipelines democratize machine learning by enabling individuals with varying levels of expertise to create models. You don't need to be a machine learning expert to utilize Auto ML tools, making AI development more accessible to a broader audience.

Optimized Performance: Auto ML systematically explores a diverse array of models, algorithms, and hyperparameter configurations. This exhaustive search increases the likelihood of finding the best-performing model, leading to improved predictive accuracy and generalization.

Consistency and Reproducibility: Auto ML enforces consistency in the model development process. The automated nature of the pipeline ensures that every iteration follows the same set of preprocessing steps, feature engineering techniques, and validation methods. This consistency enhances reproducibility and makes it easier to track and compare different models.

Resource Optimization: Auto ML pipelines can be customized to utilize computing resources efficiently. Depending on the available resources, you can adjust the complexity of the search. For instance, you can limit the exploration to certain algorithms or allocate more computational power to speed up hyperparameter tuning.

Focus on Domain Expertise: By automating routine tasks, Auto ML allows data scientists and domain experts to concentrate on more strategic aspects of model development, such as defining the problem, understanding the data's domain-specific nuances, and interpreting results.

Reduced Human Bias: The automation of various steps in the model development process minimizes the potential for human bias. Auto ML operates based on algorithms and predefined rules, reducing the risk of subjective decisions influencing the model.

Scalability: Auto ML pipelines can be scaled up to handle large datasets and complex modeling tasks. They can also be applied across various domains and industries, making them suitable for a wide range of applications.

Overall, Auto ML pipelines democratize machine learning, streamline development workflows, and improve the quality of models, making them an invaluable asset in today's data-driven landscape.

19.1.4 Challenges and Considerations: While Automated Machine Learning (Auto ML) pipelines offer significant advantages, they also present challenges and considerations that need to be addressed:

Model Interpretability: The automated nature of Auto ML can result in complex models that are difficult to interpret. Interpreting and explaining the decisions made by such models can be a challenge, especially in applications where transparency and accountability are critical.

Domain Expertise: Although Auto ML simplifies the process of model development, domain expertise remains essential. Understanding the problem context, data characteristics, and nuances is crucial for effectively defining the problem, selecting appropriate features, and interpreting results accurately.

Overfitting: Automated model selection and hyperparameter tuning can lead to overfitting if not carefully managed. Auto ML might exhaustively search for the best-performing model on the training data, which could result in models that perform well on training data but poorly on unseen data.

Data Quality: Auto ML pipelines heavily depend on the quality of the input data. No amount of automation can compensate for poor-quality or biased data. Ensuring data cleanliness, completeness, and fairness remains a critical consideration.

Resource Constraints: While Auto ML can optimize performance, it may require substantial computational resources, both in terms of memory and processing power. This can limit its practicality in resource-constrained environments.

Black-Box Models: Some Auto ML tools might generate models that are essentially black boxes, lacking transparency in their decision-making process. This can be problematic in applications where regulatory compliance, interpretability, and accountability are important.

Transferability: Models created by Auto ML pipelines might not be easily transferable to different domains or datasets. A model that performs well on one dataset might not generalize effectively to another dataset with different characteristics.

Human Oversight: Although Auto ML automates many tasks, human oversight is still required. Humans need to define the problem, make informed decisions about data preprocessing, and validate the final model's performance.

Cost: While Auto ML can save time, it might come with additional costs, particularly when using cloud-based solutions or specialized software. The cost-effectiveness of using Auto ML should be carefully evaluated against the benefits it brings.

Ethical Considerations: As with any AI technology, ethical considerations are paramount. Auto ML should be used responsibly, considering issues like data privacy, fairness, and potential bias in model predictions.

19.1.5 Future Directions: As Auto ML continues to evolve, future directions include:

Interpretable Auto ML: Developing techniques to create interpretable models within automated pipelines.

Domain-Specific Solutions: Customizing Auto ML pipelines for specific industries and domains to address unique challenges and requirements.

Integration with Deployment: Seamless integration of Auto ML pipelines with deployment platforms for rapid deployment of models in real-world scenarios.

Automated Machine Learning pipelines represent a promising advancement that accelerates model development, making AI more accessible and efficient across various industries and applications.

19.2 Hyperparameter Optimization and Bayesian Methods: Hyperparameter optimization is a critical aspect of machine learning model development, aiming to find the best combination of hyperparameters that maximize a model's performance. Bayesian methods provide an efficient and intelligent approach to hyperparameter optimization, offering advantages over traditional grid search or random search techniques.

19.2.1 The Importance of Hyperparameters: : Hyperparameters play a pivotal role in shaping the behavior and performance of machine learning models. Unlike the model's internal parameters, hyperparameters are not learned during the training process: instead, they are set by the developer before training begins. These parameters govern various aspects of the learning process and greatly influence the model's ability to generalize, converge, and achieve optimal performance on the task at hand. In essence, hyperparameters act as configuration settings that guide how the model learns from the data. They impact the model's capacity, regularization, and optimization strategy. Selecting appropriate hyperparameters is a critical task, as they can significantly impact the model's effectiveness and efficiency. Poor choices of hyperparameters can lead to models that underfit, overfit, converge slowly, or fail to reach satisfactory performance.

19.2.2 Challenges in Hyperparameter Optimization: The process of finding the best hyperparameters is challenging due to several reasons:

Dimensionality and Search Space: Hyperparameters often exist in multi-dimensional spaces, where each dimension represents a different configuration setting. The search space can be vast and complex.

Computational Resources: Exhaustively exploring the entire search space is computationally expensive and time-consuming, especially as the number of hyperparameters increases.

Optimal Configurations: Optimal hyperparameter settings might not be intuitive or directly derivable from the problem domain, requiring an exploratory approach.

Trade-offs: Hyperparameters might have trade-offs, where tuning one hyperparameter for improved performance might negatively impact another aspect of the model.

19.2.3 Bayesian Hyperparameter Optimization: Bayesian methods offer a sophisticated approach to hyperparameter optimization. They treat the hyperparameter optimization process as a probabilistic model, iteratively updating beliefs about which hyperparameters are likely to yield optimal performance. Bayesian optimization balances the exploration of different hyperparameter configurations with the exploitation of promising regions of the search space. The core idea of Bayesian optimization is to build a surrogate probabilistic model that estimates the objective function's behavior as a function of the hyperparameters. This surrogate model guides the selection of hyperparameter configurations to evaluate, focusing on areas with high predicted utility. By using probabilistic models like Gaussian Processes, Bayesian optimization efficiently estimates the performance landscape and adapts its exploration strategy based on observed outcomes. This approach is particularly useful when evaluating configurations can be time-consuming or expensive, as it intelligently selects the most informative configurations to assess.

19.2.4 Advantages of Bayesian Methods: Bayesian hyperparameter optimization offers a range of advantages that contribute to its popularity and effectiveness in fine-tuning machine learning models:

Efficiency: Bayesian methods excel in efficiently exploring the hyperparameter search space. Unlike exhaustive grid search, where every combination is evaluated, Bayesian methods make informed decisions about which hyperparameters to try next. By intelligently selecting configurations that are likely to yield valuable insights, Bayesian optimization reduces the number of trials required to identify optimal hyperparameters. This efficiency is particularly valuable when evaluating configurations is time-consuming or computationally expensive.

Adaptability: Bayesian methods are adaptive in nature. As they evaluate different hyperparameter configurations, they continuously update their beliefs about the objective function's behavior. This adaptability allows them to refine their exploration strategy based on observed outcomes. If certain regions of the search space show promise, Bayesian methods direct their focus towards those areas. This dynamic adjustment enables efficient convergence towards optimal configurations, even in complex and noisy search spaces.

Exploration-Exploitation Balance: One of the strengths of Bayesian methods is their ability to strike a balance between exploration and exploitation. Exploration involves sampling hyperparameters from underexplored regions to gain a comprehensive understanding of the search space. Exploitation entails focusing on regions that show potential for optimal performance. Bayesian optimization inherently manages this trade-off by using a probabilistic surrogate model to guide the exploration of both well-known and less-explored regions.

Model Flexibility: Bayesian optimization is flexible in terms of the surrogate models it can incorporate. Gaussian Processes (GPs) are a popular choice due to their ability to capture uncertainty and provide probabilistic estimates of the objective function's behavior. GPs enable Bayesian methods to not only predict the optimal configurations but also quantify the uncertainty associated with those predictions. This information is valuable in guiding the exploration process, as it helps identify regions where further evaluation might lead to improved results.

19.2.5 Challenges and Considerations: Despite its advantages, Bayesian hyperparameter optimization faces certain challenges and considerations that practitioners should be aware of:

Computational Complexity: While Bayesian methods are designed for efficient optimization, they can still demand substantial computational resources, especially when evaluating complex machine learning models or working with large datasets. The process of fitting surrogate models, updating beliefs, and selecting new configurations can require significant processing power and time.

Surrogate Models: Selecting an appropriate surrogate model, such as Gaussian Processes, and configuring its hyperparameters can impact the optimization process. The choice of surrogate model affects the accuracy of predictions and uncertainty estimates, ultimately influencing the efficiency of the optimization process.

High-Dimensional Spaces: As the number of hyperparameters increases, the search space becomes high-dimensional. In such spaces, optimization algorithms may face challenges in efficiently exploring the vast parameter combinations. Curse of dimensionality can lead to increased computational costs and make it harder to find optimal configurations.

Local Optima: Bayesian optimization, like other optimization methods, is susceptible to getting stuck in local optima, particularly in non-convex search spaces. This can prevent the discovery of globally optimal configurations and necessitates the use of exploration techniques to mitigate this issue.

Initial Sampling: The choice of initial hyperparameter configurations for evaluation can significantly impact the performance of Bayesian optimization. Poor initial sampling might lead to suboptimal exploration of the search space, resulting in slower convergence or convergence to suboptimal solutions.

Hyperparameter Dependencies: Hyperparameters often exhibit dependencies, where the optimal setting of one hyperparameter might depend on the value of another. Bayesian optimization algorithms may struggle to capture complex dependencies, potentially leading to suboptimal configurations.

Scalability: Scaling Bayesian optimization to handle large-scale problems can be challenging. As the search space grows, the computational demands of evaluating configurations and updating surrogate models can increase, affecting optimization efficiency.

Practitioners should carefully consider these challenges when applying Bayesian hyperparameter optimization. Addressing these issues may involve a combination of algorithmic improvements, careful selection of surrogate models, thoughtful initialization strategies, and domain-specific knowledge.

19.2.6 Future Directions

Bayesian hyperparameter optimization continues to be an active area of research, with ongoing efforts to improve efficiency and scalability. Integrating Bayesian methods with other techniques, like neural architecture search and Auto ML, could lead to more powerful and comprehensive optimization strategies.

19.3 Neural Architecture Search (NAS): Neural Architecture Search (NAS) is a cutting-edge technique that automates the process of designing and optimizing neural network architectures. It involves using algorithms or approaches to explore and evaluate a large space of possible network architectures, searching for the configuration that yields the best performance on a specific task.

19.3.1 Motivation for Neural Architecture Search: The motivation driving the development and adoption of Neural Architecture Search (NAS) is rooted in addressing the challenges associated with manual and resource-intensive design of neural network architectures. Traditional methods of architecting neural networks rely heavily on human expertise, experimentation, and trial-and-error. However, as the complexity of deep learning models increases, the process becomes more intricate and time-consuming. The key motivations for NAS include:

Automation and Efficiency: Creating effective neural network architectures demands exploring a vast space of possible configurations. NAS automates this process, drastically reducing the need for human intervention. This automation speeds up the architecture design phase, enabling rapid experimentation and iteration.

Resource Optimization: Manual architecture design often requires significant computational resources and expert time. NAS algorithms are designed to optimize architectures efficiently, leveraging computational power to explore a wider range of architectures than feasible manually.

Architecture Innovation: NAS encourages the exploration of unconventional and innovative architectures that might not be readily considered through traditional design methods. By automating the search process, NAS has the potential to uncover novel architectural designs that can lead to breakthroughs in performance and efficiency.

Scalability: As neural network models grow in complexity and size, manual design becomes increasingly challenging. NAS provides a scalable solution to designing architectures for models with thousands or even millions of parameters.

Generalization: NAS can contribute to the development of architectures that generalize well across different tasks and datasets. By automating the process and considering a broad range of configurations, NAS has the potential to discover architectures that perform well on various problems.

19.3.2 NAS Approaches: NAS encompasses various approaches, each with its unique characteristics and strategies:

Exhaustive Search: This approach involves systematically evaluating all possible architectures within a predefined search space. While comprehensive, this method is computationally expensive and impractical for large-scale architectures due to the exponential growth of possibilities.

Random Search: Randomly sampling architectures from the search space is a simpler and less resource-intensive approach. However, it lacks optimization direction and might miss valuable architectural configurations.

Reinforcement Learning (RL)-based NAS: This method formulates architecture design as a reinforcement learning problem. An RL agent learns to generate architectures through interactions with a simulated environment. The agent's reward is based on the architecture's performance on a validation dataset.

Evolutionary Algorithms: Inspired by natural evolution, this approach treats the search for architectures as a genetic algorithm. Architectures undergo mutation and crossover operations over generations, with the most promising ones advancing.

Gradient-based Methods: These methods use gradient-based optimization to modify hyperparameters or architectural elements in pursuit of optimal configurations. This approach often requires treating the architecture as a differentiable function.

Each NAS approach addresses the challenge of searching for optimal architectures by leveraging various techniques, balancing computational efficiency, and search effectiveness. The choice of approach depends on factors such as the complexity of the architecture and available computational resources.

19.3.3 Benefits of Neural Architecture Search: Neural Architecture Search (NAS) brings forth a range of benefits that contribute to the advancement of deep learning and model design:

Automated Design: NAS significantly reduces the manual effort required for designing neural network architectures. This automation frees up researchers and engineers from the tedious and time-consuming process of architecture crafting, allowing them to focus on higher-level tasks.

Efficiency: Automated search algorithms explore the architectural space more comprehensively and efficiently than manual trial-and-error methods. This efficiency enables the discovery of architectures that can outperform manually designed ones, leveraging computational power to its fullest extent.

Enhanced Performance: NAS has the potential to discover architectures with improved performance compared to manually designed ones. By exploring a wider range of configurations, NAS algorithms can uncover design choices that lead to superior accuracy and generalization on various tasks.

Customization: NAS can customize architectures for specific tasks, datasets, or problem domains. This adaptability ensures that the network's structure aligns with the inherent characteristics of the task, potentially boosting overall performance.

Innovation: NAS encourages the exploration of unconventional and innovative architectural configurations. It provides a platform for researchers to experiment with new ideas and paradigms, leading to architectural breakthroughs that might not be intuitive to human designers.

Time Savings: The automated nature of NAS expedites the architecture design process. This acceleration is particularly valuable in scenarios where rapid prototyping and experimentation are essential.

Scalability: As the complexity of neural networks continues to increase, manual design becomes impractical for large-scale models. NAS scales naturally to handle architectures with thousands or even millions of parameters.

Democratization of Design: NAS democratizes the process of architecture design, making it accessible to individuals with varying levels of expertise. This democratization accelerates innovation by allowing a broader range of individuals to contribute to architecture development.

Overall, the benefits of NAS extend beyond efficiency and performance improvements to revolutionizing the way neural network architectures are conceived and optimized.

19.3.4 Challenges and Considerations: Despite its benefits, Neural Architecture Search (NAS) is not without challenges and considerations. These factors highlight the complexity and limitations of the NAS process:

Search Space Complexity: The architecture search space can be extremely large and complex, with numerous design choices and hyperparameters to consider. This complexity can lead to increased search times and require more computational resources.

Computational Resources: Many NAS approaches demand substantial computational power and time. Running multiple architecture evaluations and training iterations can be resource-intensive, limiting the accessibility of NAS to researchers with access to high-performance computing infrastructure.

Overfitting: During the architecture search process, there's a risk of overfitting the validation dataset. The search algorithm might identify architectures that perform well on the validation set but fail to generalize to new, unseen data.

Transferability: Architectures discovered through NAS may be highly specialized to the training dataset and task. These architectures might not generalize well to other datasets or tasks, limiting their applicability and transferability.

Lack of Interpretability: Some NAS methods generate architectures that are highly complex and lack human interpretability. Understanding the rationale behind the chosen architectures can be challenging, hindering insights into their functioning.

Hyperparameter Optimization: NAS often involves tuning various hyperparameters of the search process itself. Poor choices in these hyperparameters can impact the effectiveness of the search and lead to suboptimal architectures.

Limited Understanding of Architecture: While NAS can identify high-performing architectures, it might not provide a deep understanding of why a particular architecture works well. This lack of understanding can hinder further optimization or customization.

Benchmarking and Evaluation: Properly benchmarking NAS results can be difficult, as the selection of appropriate datasets, tasks, and evaluation metrics requires careful consideration.

Human Expertise: Despite automation, human expertise remains crucial in guiding the NAS process, selecting appropriate search spaces, and interpreting the results.

Ethical Considerations: The increasing role of automated design in neural architectures raises ethical considerations, such as the potential for biased or unfair model designs that perpetuate societal inequalities.

Considering these challenges is essential for effectively utilizing NAS and maximizing its benefits while acknowledging its limitations in the context of deep learning model design.

19.3.5 Future Directions: Future directions in NAS involve addressing its challenges:

Search Space Reduction: Developing techniques to reduce the complexity of the search space, making the optimization process more efficient.

Transfer Learning: Improving the transferability of discovered architectures by training them on diverse datasets.

Efficiency Improvements: Designing NAS algorithms that require fewer computational resources while maintaining the quality of discovered architectures.

Interpretable Architectures: Enhancing the interpretability of NAS-generated architectures to provide insights into the network's decision-making process.

Neural Architecture Search continues to evolve as a powerful tool for automating the design of neural network architectures, promising to shape the future of deep learning model development.

19.4 Balancing Automation and Expertise in Model Design: In the realm of deep learning, finding the right equilibrium between automated tools and human expertise when designing models is a crucial consideration. While automated techniques like Automated Machine Learning (Auto ML) and Neural Architecture Search (NAS) offer speed and efficiency gains, it's important to acknowledge the challenges and considerations that underscore the significance of human involvement in the process.

Complex Problem Domains: Automated tools might encounter difficulties when dealing with complex or specialized problem domains. Human experts possess domain-specific knowledge that can provide guidance in crafting models tailored to intricate scenarios.

Model Interpretability: Automated methods may generate complex models that lack interpretability. Human expertise is indispensable in crafting models that not only deliver accurate results but are also comprehensible and explainable.

Data Understanding: Human experts are capable of comprehending data deeply, including its context and potential biases. This understanding is crucial for selecting relevant features, addressing data quality issues, and ensuring that the model's performance is impartial.

Problem Formulation: Accurately defining the problem and its objectives requires human involvement. Experts are adept at identifying relevant metrics, setting target performance thresholds, and considering the trade-offs among various objectives.

Handling Edge Cases: Automated tools might struggle with handling infrequent or exceptional cases that hold significance in real-world applications. Human expertise can identify and address these cases, ensuring that the model performs reliably across diverse scenarios.
Ethical Considerations: Ensuring the ethical utilization of AI necessitates human oversight. Complex ethical aspects such as bias, fairness, and privacy demand expert judgment to make responsible decisions.
Model Customization: Automated methods might not fully encapsulate the precise requirements of a project. Human experts can fine-tune models based on distinct constraints, preferences, and specific business needs.
Innovations and Creativity: Human creativity serves as a catalyst for innovation. Expertise empowers the exploration of unconventional solutions, fostering the development of pioneering model architectures and methodologies.
Model Deployment and Monitoring: Constructing a model is just the initial phase. Human expertise is indispensable for deploying models in real-world settings, monitoring their performance, and making necessary adaptations.
Ethical Responsibility: Ultimately, humans bear the responsibility for the repercussions of AI systems. Human experts guarantee that models align with ethical standards and societal values.
The process of balancing automation and expertise entails capitalizing on automated tools to expedite model design while harnessing human insights for vital decision-making, validation, and customization. Collaborative efforts that synergize the advantages of automation and human expertise are likely to yield the most favorable outcomes in the design of deep learning models.

19.5 Project

Unsolved Project

Suppose you're developing a project focused on leveraging automated machine learning (AutoML) and neural architecture search (NAS) to streamline and optimize the model design process. To successfully execute this project, you need to understand AutoML pipelines, hyperparameter optimization methods, NAS, and the balance between automation and human expertise in model design. Before starting, research the following: the construction and utilization of AutoML pipelines to automate machine learning workflows, hyperparameter optimization techniques such as Bayesian methods to improve model performance, the principles and implementation of NAS for discovering optimal neural network architectures, and the benefits and limitations of balancing automated tools with expert knowledge in designing machine learning models. This foundational knowledge will help you create a well-rounded project that effectively uses automation to enhance model design and performance.

19.6 Lab Activity

Unsolved Lab Activity

Implement an AutoML pipeline using a chosen framework (e.g., Auto-Keras) for a specific task (e.g., image classification or text classification).
Task: Use an AutoML framework (e.g., Auto-Keras) to implement and train a model for a specific task, such as image classification or text classification. Document the implementation process, including data preprocessing, model selection, training procedure, and performance evaluation. Provide examples of the model's predictions and evaluation metrics.

Exercises

Exercise 1 – Multiple Choice Questions

1. What is the primary goal of Automated Machine Learning (Auto ML) pipelines?
   A. Automating feature engineering
   B. Automating data preprocessing
   C. Automating model deployment
   D. Automating data collection
2. Why did Auto ML pipelines emerge as a response to traditional machine learning processes?
   A. To increase manual intervention
   B. To streamline and automate the process
   C. To reduce data preprocessing
   D. To simplify feature engineering
3. Which of the following is NOT a component of Auto ML pipelines?
   A. Data Preprocessing
   B. Model Selection
   C. Data Collection
   D. Hyperparameter Tuning
4. Why is clean and well-preprocessed data essential for accurate model training in Auto ML?
   A. It speeds up the training process.
   B. It reduces the need for hyperparameter tuning.
   C. It improves model performance.
   D. It eliminates the need for feature engineering.
5. What is the role of feature engineering in Auto ML?
   A. Selecting the best machine learning algorithms
   B. Imputing missing values in the data
   C. Transforming existing features to improve model performance
   D. Deploying machine learning models

Exercise 2 – True/False

1. Automated Machine Learning (Auto ML) Pipelines are designed to automate the entire machine learning process.
2. Hyperparameter Optimization using Bayesian Methods is considered less efficient than random search methods.
3. Neural Architecture Search (NAS) is a process to automatically design neural network architectures.

Review Questions

1. What are Auto ML pipelines, and how do they streamline the machine learning model development process?
2. Why did Auto ML pipelines emerge as a solution to the challenges of traditional machine learning model development?
3. List and explain the key components of Auto ML pipelines.
4. Why is data preprocessing an essential step in Auto ML, and what tasks does it typically involve?
5. How does feature engineering contribute to improving model performance in Auto ML?
6. Describe the process of model selection in Auto ML pipelines and why it's crucial.
7. What are hyperparameters, and why are they important in machine learning?
8. How does Auto ML handle hyperparameter tuning, and what are some common techniques used for this purpose?
9. What is ensemble learning in Auto ML, and how does it benefit model performance?

Answers

Exercise 1- 1. B 2. B 3. C 4. C 5. C
Exercise 2- 1) True, 2) False, 3) True

Online Resources

Online Exam Paper:
Link: https://forms.gle/c6dqcHLaZbyRS72BA
QR Code:

Chapter 19 Videos Playlist:
Link: https://www.youtube.com/playlist?list=PLzlh_31VWEFpgOq2KvtilNQE7K-bW8OY9
QR Code:

Chapter 20: Quantum Machine Learning and Deep Learning

20.1 Introduction to Quantum Computing: Quantum computing is a cutting-edge field at the intersection of computer science, physics, and mathematics that explores the potential of quantum mechanics to revolutionize computation. Unlike classical computers, which process data using bits (0s and 1s), quantum computers use quantum bits or qubits, which can exist in multiple states simultaneously due to the principles of superposition and entanglement.

20.1.1 Quantum Bits (Qubits): A classical bit can be either 0 or 1, representing the simplest unit of information. Quantum bits, or qubits, however, can exist in a superposition of both 0 and 1 states simultaneously. This property allows quantum computers to process a vast amount of information in parallel, potentially offering exponential speedup for certain problems.

20.1.2 Superposition and Entanglement: Superposition is a foundational principle in quantum mechanics that enables qubits to exist in multiple states simultaneously. This property forms the basis for quantum parallelism, which is the core of quantum computing's power. By leveraging superposition, quantum computers can consider and compute many possible solutions simultaneously, significantly speeding up certain types of computations. Entanglement is another remarkable phenomenon that arises in quantum systems involving multiple qubits. When qubits become entangled, the state of one qubit becomes intrinsically correlated with the state of another, regardless of the distance between them. This correlation is so strong that changing the state of one entangled qubit instantaneously affects the state of the other, even if they are separated by large distances. Entanglement is a unique feature of quantum systems that defies classical intuition and plays a crucial role in quantum computing's potential to outperform classical computers.

Both superposition and entanglement are fundamental properties that distinguish quantum computing from classical computing. These properties underlie the potential of quantum computers to solve problems that are currently intractable for classical machines, particularly in areas such as cryptography, optimization, and simulation.

20.1.3 Quantum Gates and Circuits: Just as classical computers use logic gates to process and manipulate bits, quantum computers use quantum gates to operate on qubits. Quantum gates perform transformations on qubits, such as changing their state or creating entanglement. Quantum circuits are sequences of these gates that encode and manipulate quantum information to perform computations.

20.1.4 Quantum Parallelism: Quantum parallelism is one of the cornerstone principles that underlie the revolutionary potential of quantum computing. Unlike classical computers that process calculations sequentially, quantum computers exploit the inherent properties of qubits, such as superposition, to perform computations in parallel across multiple possible states. In classical computing, solving complex problems often requires trying different solutions sequentially, one after another. This process can be time-consuming and computationally intensive, especially for problems with a large search space. Quantum parallelism, on the other hand, allows quantum computers to explore multiple potential solutions simultaneously. By manipulating qubits in a superposition of states, quantum computers can perform operations on all possible solutions at once.

Imagine a problem involving searching through a list of items to find a specific one. In classical computing, each item must be checked one after another. In contrast, a quantum computer with qubits in superposition could effectively check all items at once, dramatically reducing the time needed to find the solution. This potential for exponential speedup in certain problems makes quantum parallelism a powerful and intriguing aspect of quantum computing.

20.1.5 Quantum Computing vs. Classical Computing: Quantum computing and classical computing are not mutually exclusive: each has its strengths and weaknesses. Quantum computers excel in solving specific types of problems that are challenging for classical computers. These problems include tasks like factoring large numbers, simulating quantum systems, and solving optimization problems. Quantum computers offer the potential for significant speedup in these domains due to their ability to leverage quantum parallelism and other quantum properties. However, for everyday tasks and problems that do not exhibit quantum behavior, classical computers remain highly efficient and practical. Classical computers have been optimized for decades to perform general-purpose computing tasks, and they are well-suited for a wide range of applications, from web browsing and word processing to data analysis and scientific simulations.

In essence, quantum computing and classical computing represent complementary tools in the realm of computation. Quantum computing's power lies in its ability to tackle certain complex problems more efficiently, while classical computing continues to be the workhorse for most tasks due to its maturity and versatility. As quantum computing technology advances, it holds the potential to revolutionize various industries and scientific fields by addressing challenges that are currently beyond the reach of classical computers.

20.1.6 Quantum Hardware: Quantum hardware forms the physical foundation of quantum computing systems. Constructing stable and functional quantum systems is a formidable challenge due to the delicate nature of quantum states. These states are highly susceptible to environmental disturbances, which can cause decoherence – the loss of quantum information – and hinder the proper operation of quantum algorithms. As a result, quantum hardware requires specialized engineering techniques to create, control, and maintain qubits while preserving their coherence.

Several physical implementations of qubits have been explored, each with its own advantages and challenges:

Superconducting Circuits: Qubits are implemented using superconducting electronic circuits. These circuits operate at extremely low temperatures, close to absolute zero, to minimize noise and decoherence. Superconducting qubits are known for their fast gate operations and scalability.

Trapped Ions: Ions are trapped using electromagnetic fields and manipulated using lasers. Trapped ion qubits have long coherence times and high fidelity gates, making them well-suited for quantum computation.

Topological Qubits: These qubits are based on topological properties of exotic states of matter. They are designed to be inherently robust against certain types of errors, which is crucial for fault-tolerant quantum computation.

Photonic Qubits: Quantum information is encoded in photons, making use of their intrinsic quantum properties such as polarization and entanglement. Photonic qubits are suitable for long-distance quantum communication.

Creating and maintaining stable qubits is just one aspect of quantum hardware. Quantum computers also require components like cryogenic systems for cooling, control electronics for precise manipulation, and error correction mechanisms to mitigate the effects of decoherence and errors.

20.1.7 Quantum Algorithms: Quantum algorithms are specifically designed to harness the power of quantum computation for solving problems more efficiently than classical algorithms. Quantum algorithms take advantage of quantum parallelism, superposition, and entanglement to process information in unique ways. Some notable quantum algorithms include:

Shor's Algorithm: Shor's algorithm is a breakthrough algorithm for factoring large numbers into their prime factors. This poses a significant challenge for classical computers but has important implications for cryptography and number theory.

Grover's Algorithm: Grover's algorithm speeds up the process of searching an unsorted database. It can find the desired item in roughly the square root of the number of items, providing a quadratic speedup compared to classical search algorithms.

Quantum Fourier Transform: The quantum Fourier transform is a fundamental operation in many quantum algorithms. It efficiently transforms the basis states of qubits into their superposition states, enabling algorithms like Shor's to function.

Quantum algorithms are still an active area of research, and finding new algorithms that provide quantum advantage for a broader range of problems remains a goal. As quantum hardware advances, the potential impact of these algorithms on cryptography, optimization, simulation of quantum systems, and other domains becomes increasingly significant.

20.1.8 Quantum Computing's Potential Impact: Quantum computing's potential impact spans various fields, including cryptography, optimization, material science, drug discovery, and artificial intelligence. While practical large-scale quantum computers are still in development, advancements in this field hold the promise of revolutionizing industries and solving problems that are currently intractable for classical computers.

20.2 Quantum Neural Networks: Quantum neural networks (QNNs) are a hybrid computational framework that combines principles from quantum computing and traditional artificial neural networks. These networks aim to leverage the unique properties of quantum systems, such as superposition and entanglement, to enhance the capabilities of machine learning tasks. QNNs hold promise for solving certain problems that classical neural networks struggle with, such as complex optimization tasks and quantum data analysis.

20.2.1 Quantum Neurons: Quantum neurons are the fundamental units of computation in a Quantum Neural Network (QNN). They play a role analogous to classical neurons in traditional artificial neural networks. However, quantum neurons harness the unique properties of quantum systems, such as superposition and entanglement, to perform computations that can potentially outperform classical counterparts for certain tasks.

Qubits as Quantum Neurons: In a QNN, each quantum neuron is represented by a qubit. A qubit can exist in a superposition of states, which enables it to simultaneously hold multiple pieces of information. This superposition property forms the basis of quantum parallelism, allowing quantum neurons to process multiple inputs and states in parallel.

Quantum Gates: The behavior of quantum neurons is determined by quantum gates. These gates are quantum operations that manipulate the state of the qubits. Quantum gates perform various transformations on the qubit's quantum state, altering the probabilities of measuring different outcomes when the qubit is measured. Quantum gates include operations like Pauli-X, Pauli-Y, Pauli-Z, Hadamard, and others.

Superposition and Entanglement: Quantum neurons can exist in superposition states, meaning they can simultaneously represent multiple classical states. This property enables quantum neurons to process multiple inputs at once, potentially speeding up computations for certain tasks. Additionally, entanglement can occur between qubits, creating correlations between their states that can be exploited for specific computations.

20.2.2 Quantum Layers: Similar to classical neural networks, QNNs are constructed in layers. Quantum layers are the building blocks of a QNN, and they consist of interconnected quantum neurons that process input data using quantum gates. These layers are responsible for performing computations and transformations on the quantum data.

Quantum Computation within Quantum Layers: Within a quantum layer, quantum gates are applied to the qubits representing the input data. These gates perform quantum operations that manipulate the qubit states, transforming the input data in a quantum-mechanical way. The quantum gates allow the QNN to capture complex relationships within the data using quantum parallelism.

Hybrid Quantum-Classical Computation: Quantum layers are often followed by classical layers in a QNN. Classical layers process the outputs of the quantum layers using traditional computation methods. This hybrid approach leverages both quantum and classical processing capabilities to bridge the gap between quantum computations and classical computations, allowing for more flexible and effective information processing.

Overall Architecture: A typical QNN consists of multiple quantum layers followed by classical layers, forming a hybrid architecture. The outputs of the quantum layers are passed to the classical layers for further processing and interpretation, enabling the QNN to perform complex computations that leverage the advantages of both quantum and classical computation.

20.2.3 Quantum Neural Networks: Training and Learning: Quantum Neural Networks (QNNs) require training processes that adapt their parameters to perform specific tasks. While similar to classical neural network training, QNN training involves certain quantum-specific considerations due to the unique properties of quantum systems.

Parameterized Quantum Circuits: QNNs are often implemented as parameterized quantum circuits, where the gates' parameters are trainable variables. These circuits are designed to perform specific quantum computations based on the task at hand.

Quantum Variational Circuits: Variational Quantum Circuits (VQCs) are a common type of QNN used for training. They consist of layers of gates with trainable parameters. During training, these parameters are adjusted to minimize a specified loss function, similar to classical neural network optimization.

Gradient Descent in Quantum Circuits: To update the trainable parameters of quantum gates, optimization methods like gradient descent are used. Quantum gradients are computed by estimating the change in the quantum circuit's output with respect to the gate parameters.

Hybrid Quantum-Classical Optimization: Due to the hybrid nature of QNNs, training often involves both quantum and classical optimization steps. The quantum part evaluates the quantum circuits' outputs, while the classical part computes gradients and updates parameters using classical optimization techniques.

Measurement and Feedback: After applying quantum gates, measurements are performed on the qubits to obtain classical outcomes. These outcomes are used to compute the loss function and update the parameters of the quantum gates to improve the network's performance.

Challenges: Quantum systems are sensitive to noise and errors, which can affect training. Mitigating these issues is a challenge in quantum machine learning. Additionally, as quantum hardware is still in the early stages of development, training large-scale QNNs can be resource-intensive.

20.2.4 Applications of Quantum Neural Networks: QNNs have several promising applications across various domains:

Quantum Data Analysis: QNNs can analyze and process quantum data generated by quantum systems. This is crucial for fields like quantum chemistry, where understanding complex quantum states is essential for simulating molecular behaviors and designing new materials.

Optimization Problems: Quantum systems naturally excel at optimization tasks due to their ability to explore multiple solutions simultaneously. QNNs can be applied to solve optimization problems in fields such as supply chain management, financial modeling, and logistics.

Quantum Machine Learning: QNNs can process and analyze quantum data, enabling applications in quantum machine learning. Quantum state tomography, which aims to reconstruct unknown quantum states from measurements, is an example of a task where QNNs can be beneficial.

Hybrid Quantum-Classical Learning: Many real-world problems involve both classical and quantum data. QNNs can be integrated into larger hybrid models that combine classical and quantum computations, allowing them to tackle complex problems that require the strengths of both paradigms.

Quantum Generative Models: QNNs can be used to create quantum generative models that learn to simulate complex quantum systems. These models have applications in quantum simulations and quantum materials research.

It's important to note that the development of QNNs is still an active area of research, and their practical applications are evolving as quantum computing technologies advance.

20.2.5 Challenges and Future Directions: While Quantum Neural Networks (QNNs) offer exciting possibilities, they also face several challenges and uncertainties. Here are some of the challenges and potential future directions for QNNs:

Noise and Error Mitigation: Quantum systems are susceptible to noise and errors due to interactions with their environment. Noise-induced errors can significantly impact the performance of QNNs. Developing effective error mitigation techniques and quantum error correction methods is crucial to ensure the reliability of QNNs in practical applications.

Limited Quantum Resources: Current quantum hardware is limited in terms of qubit coherence, connectivity, and gate fidelity. These limitations restrict the complexity and scalability of QNNs. Future advancements in quantum hardware technology, such as improved qubit coherence times and more reliable gates, will be essential for realizing the full potential of QNNs.

Quantum Advantage: Demonstrating a clear quantum advantage, where QNNs outperform classical counterparts, remains a challenge. Identifying problem domains and tasks where QNNs provide significant speedup or improved solutions compared to classical methods is essential to establish their practical value.

Hybrid Approaches: Integrating classical and quantum computations in a hybrid manner is a promising direction. Combining the strengths of classical machine learning techniques with the computational power of QNNs can lead to more robust and efficient solutions for complex problems.

Algorithm and Architecture Design: Developing quantum algorithms and architectures that effectively leverage quantum parallelism and entanglement for specific tasks is a challenging research area. Optimizing the design of quantum circuits, choosing suitable gates, and determining appropriate initialization strategies are crucial for QNN performance.

Education and Expertise: Quantum computing is a rapidly evolving field, and expertise is limited. The development of QNNs requires a deep understanding of both quantum mechanics and machine learning. Efforts to educate researchers and practitioners in both domains will be essential for advancing QNN research.

Quantum Software Tools: As QNNs become more accessible, the development of user-friendly quantum software tools and platforms will be crucial. These tools should provide abstraction layers and intuitive interfaces to facilitate the design, simulation, and optimization of QNNs.

Benchmarking and Evaluation: Establishing benchmark datasets and evaluation metrics for QNNs is important for comparing different models and approaches. This will help the community understand the capabilities and limitations of QNNs and track progress over time.

In the future, as quantum hardware and software technologies continue to advance, QNNs hold the potential to revolutionize various fields, from optimization and materials science to cryptography and artificial intelligence. Addressing the challenges and pursuing innovative research directions will play a vital role in realizing the practical benefits of QNNs.

20.3 Quantum Data Encoding and Processing:

20.3.1 Quantum Data Encoding: Quantum data encoding is a crucial step in quantum computing that involves the representation of classical or quantum information using qubits, which are the fundamental building blocks of quantum systems. Qubits possess unique properties, such as superposition and entanglement that make quantum computing distinct from classical computing. Various techniques are employed to encode information into qubits, allowing for the manipulation and processing of quantum data. Let's delve deeper into the techniques used for quantum data encoding:

Basis Encoding: Basis encoding is a fundamental technique used in quantum data encoding. In this approach, classical information is mapped onto quantum states that correspond to classical bits: |0? And |1? In the context of quantum mechanics, |0? And |1? Are the computational basis states. A qubit in state |0? Represents a classical bit '0', while a qubit in state |1? Represents a classical bit '1'. These two states are orthogonal, meaning they are distinct and can be unambiguously distinguished from each other. One of the key features of quantum mechanics is superposition. This property allows qubits to exist in a linear combination of states. For example, a qubit can exist in a superposition |?? = a|0? + ß|1?, where a and ß are complex coefficients that define the qubit's state. This superposition enables the representation of information in multiple states simultaneously, providing a quantum advantage for certain types of computations.

Amplitude Encoding: Amplitude encoding is another quantum data encoding technique that leverages the concept of superposition. In amplitude encoding, the information is encoded into the amplitudes of quantum states. Unlike basis encoding, where information is associated with specific basis states, amplitude encoding allows information to be distributed across multiple states in a coherent way.

In amplitude encoding, a qubit can exist in a superposition of states with varying amplitudes. For example, a qubit can be in a state |?? = a|0? + ß|1?, where a and ß are complex numbers that determine the qubit's amplitudes. The magnitudes of a and ß encode the information, and their phases determine the relative weights of the states. Amplitude encoding is particularly valuable for quantum algorithms that exploit interference effects. Quantum algorithms often involve manipulating the amplitudes of quantum states to enhance constructive interference (when amplitudes align) and suppress destructive interference (when amplitudes cancel out). This allows quantum algorithms to amplify correct solutions and suppress incorrect ones, leading to efficient computations.

Phase Encoding: Phase encoding is a quantum data encoding technique that utilizes the phase of quantum states to represent information. In phase encoding, the information is encoded by manipulating the relative phase between different quantum states. This technique is particularly relevant in quantum algorithms that involve complex interference patterns, such as the Quantum Fourier Transform (QFT).

In phase encoding, a qubit's state can be represented as |?? = a|0? + e^(i?)|1?, where a and e^(i?) are complex numbers that determine the qubit's amplitudes and phase, respectively. The phase ? encodes information and contributes to the interference effects that quantum algorithms exploit. By manipulating the phase of qubit states, quantum algorithms can enhance constructive interference for correct solutions and suppress destructive interference for incorrect ones, leading to more efficient computations.

20.3.2 Quantum Data Processing: Quantum data processing involves performing operations on encoded quantum states to perform computations. Quantum gates are the fundamental units of quantum data processing, analogous to classical logic gates. Quantum gates manipulate the quantum states of qubits, allowing for operations such as changing states, creating entanglement between qubits, and applying phase shifts. Quantum circuits are constructed by arranging sequences of quantum gates to execute specific computations.

20.3.3 Applications of Quantum Data Encoding and Processing:

Quantum Algorithms: Quantum data encoding and processing are central to various quantum algorithms. Examples include Shor's algorithm for factoring large numbers and Grover's algorithm for search. These algorithms leverage quantum properties like superposition and entanglement to achieve exponential speedup over classical algorithms for specific tasks.

Quantum Simulations: Quantum computers excel at simulating complex quantum systems, such as molecules and materials, which classical computers struggle to simulate accurately. Quantum simulations enable the study of chemical reactions, material properties, and physical phenomena with unprecedented accuracy.

Optimization: Quantum computing shows promise in solving optimization problems efficiently. Quantum annealing, a specialized form of quantum computation, encodes optimization problems into quantum states and evolves the system to find optimal solutions. This approach is particularly suited for solving combinatorial optimization problems.

Machine Learning: Quantum data encoding and processing have applications in quantum machine learning. Quantum neural networks utilize quantum encoding techniques to represent features, and quantum gates for processing information. Quantum machine learning explores the potential for quantum systems to enhance certain machine learning tasks.

20.3.4 Challenges and Future Directions: Efficient quantum data encoding and processing are crucial for the success of quantum computing. Challenges include maintaining qubit coherence to prevent errors, minimizing errors during gate operations, and developing robust techniques for encoding and manipulating quantum information. Advances in quantum hardware, quantum error correction methods, and quantum algorithms drive the exploration of new applications and approaches for harnessing the capabilities of quantum data encoding and processing.

20.4 Applications in Quantum Chemistry and Optimization: Quantum computing holds significant promise for applications in quantum chemistry and optimization, offering the potential to address complex problems that are challenging for classical computers.

20.4.1 Quantum Chemistry: Quantum chemistry involves the study and simulation of molecular behavior, electronic structures, and chemical reactions at the quantum level. Quantum computers have the capability to simulate molecular systems with a level of accuracy and efficiency that surpasses classical computational methods. This has profound implications for a range of scientific and practical applications, including drug discovery, materials science, and catalysis.

Molecular Simulation: One of the key applications of quantum computing in quantum chemistry is molecular simulation. Quantum computers can simulate molecular interactions, electronic structures, and properties with a precision that was previously unattainable with classical methods. This capability enables researchers to predict the behavior of molecules in various environments, facilitating the design of new materials with specific properties. For instance, in drug discovery, understanding the interactions between drug molecules and biological targets at the quantum level can lead to the development of more effective therapeutic compounds.

Quantum Dynamics: Quantum dynamics simulations focus on the exploration of chemical reactions and energy transfer processes occurring at the quantum level. These simulations involve modeling complex reaction mechanisms, understanding reaction pathways, and predicting reaction rates. Quantum computers excel at simulating quantum dynamics, offering insights into the behavior of chemical systems that are difficult to achieve using classical simulations. These insights have implications for fields such as chemistry, physics, and materials science.

20.4.2 Optimization: Optimization problems, which involve finding the best possible solution from a set of alternatives, are pervasive across industries and disciplines. Quantum computing's inherent property of quantum parallelism offers the potential to solve complex optimization problems more efficiently than classical methods, particularly for certain classes of problems.

Combinatorial Optimization: Combinatorial optimization involves finding the optimal arrangement or configuration of elements from a finite set of possibilities. Classical computers often struggle with combinatorial optimization problems due to their exponential nature. Quantum computing offers innovative solutions through quantum annealing and quantum algorithms like the Quantum Approximate Optimization Algorithm (QAOA). These approaches leverage the quantum parallelism to explore multiple possible solutions simultaneously, potentially leading to more efficient optimization outcomes. The combination of quantum chemistry and optimization applications has the potential to drive advancements in various scientific and industrial domains. However, challenges such as quantum error correction, scalability, and the need for hybrid quantum-classical approaches remain to be addressed. As quantum hardware continues to improve and quantum algorithms mature, the impact of quantum computing on these applications is expected to grow, opening new avenues for exploration and discovery.

Traveling Salesperson Problem: The Traveling Salesperson Problem (TSP) is a classic optimization challenge that involves finding the shortest possible route that visits a set of cities and returns to the starting city. Quantum algorithms offer a unique advantage in solving the TSP by exploring multiple paths simultaneously, a feat that classical algorithms struggle with due to the problem's combinatorial nature. Quantum approaches can provide near-optimal solutions more rapidly, making them applicable to real-world scenarios in route optimization, logistics, and resource allocation.

Portfolio Optimization: Portfolio optimization is a critical task in finance, where the goal is to select a combination of assets that maximizes returns while minimizing risk. Quantum algorithms excel in efficiently searching through an extensive array of potential asset combinations to identify portfolios that strike the optimal balance between risk and reward. By harnessing quantum parallelism, these algorithms can navigate the vast solution space more effectively than classical counterparts.

20.4.3 Challenges and Future Directions: While quantum chemistry and optimization applications hold immense potential, several challenges must be addressed to fully realize their benefits:

Quantum Error Correction: Quantum computers are susceptible to errors due to environmental factors, such as noise and decoherence. The development of robust quantum error correction techniques is pivotal to ensure the accuracy and reliability of quantum computations for complex problems.

Scalability: Scaling up quantum systems to handle larger and more intricate problems is a significant challenge. Quantum hardware improvements are essential to enable the processing of real-world datasets and to tackle more complex instances of quantum chemistry and optimization tasks.

Hybrid Approaches: To bridge the gap between current quantum computing capabilities and practical applications, researchers are exploring hybrid approaches that combine quantum and classical computations. These hybrid quantum-classical methods leverage the strengths of both paradigms, offering a more practical and accessible route to solving complex problems in quantum chemistry and optimization.

As quantum hardware continues to advance and error correction techniques mature, the domains of quantum chemistry and optimization are on the brink of transforming industries that rely on complex simulations and efficient solutions. The ability of quantum computers to tackle these challenges more efficiently and accurately holds the potential to revolutionize scientific research, industry practices, and technological innovations.

20.5 Project

Unsolved Project

Suppose you're developing a project to explore the intersection of quantum computing and machine learning. To create a comprehensive project, you need to understand the basics of quantum computing, quantum neural networks, quantum data encoding and processing, and their applications in fields like quantum chemistry and optimization. Before starting, research the following: an introduction to quantum computing principles and how it differs from classical computing, the structure and functioning of quantum neural networks, methods for encoding and processing data in quantum systems, and specific applications of quantum machine learning in quantum chemistry and optimization problems. This foundational knowledge will enable you to develop an insightful project that investigates the potential of quantum computing in enhancing machine learning and deep learning techniques.

20.6 Lab Activity

Unsolved Lab Activity

Implement a quantum algorithm for a quantum chemistry or optimization problem using a quantum computing framework. Demonstrate the solution to a specific problem.

Task: Use a quantum computing framework to implement a quantum algorithm for a specific problem in quantum chemistry or optimization. For example, use the VQE to find the ground state energy of a molecule or the QAOA to solve a combinatorial optimization problem. Document the implementation process, including problem setup, algorithm implementation, execution, and results. Provide visualizations of the solution and performance metrics.

Exercises

Exercise 1 – Multiple Choice Questions

1. What is the fundamental unit of information in classical computing?
   a. Quantum bits
   b. Superposition
   c. Entanglement
   d. Classical bits
2. How do quantum bits (qubits) differ from classical bits?
   a. They can exist in multiple states simultaneously
   b. They are always in either state 0 or 1
   c. They are larger in size
   d. They cannot be entangled
3. Which of the following quantum properties allows qubits to exist in multiple states simultaneously?
   a. Quantum gates
   b. Superposition
   c. Classical computing
   d. Entanglement
4. What is the phenomenon where changing the state of one entangled qubit instantaneously affects the state of another, regardless of the distance between them?
   a. Quantum entanglement
   b. Quantum gates
   c. Classical computing
   d. Superposition
5. What role do quantum gates play in quantum computing?
   a. They perform calculations sequentially
   b. They create classical bits
   c. They manipulate qubits
   d. They are used for classical encryption

Exercise 2 – True/False

1. Quantum computing is unrelated to optimization problems.
2. Quantum machine learning has applications in quantum chemistry.
3. The introduction to quantum computing is not necessary for understanding quantum neural networks.

Review Questions

1. What are the fundamental differences between quantum computing and classical computing?

2. How do qubits differ from classical bits in terms of their state representation?
3. Explain the concept of superposition in quantum computing and its significance.
4. Describe quantum entanglement and its implications in quantum systems.
5. What role do quantum gates play in quantum computing, and how do they differ from classical logic gates?
6. How does quantum parallelism enable quantum computers to potentially solve problems more efficiently?
7. Provide an example of a problem that can benefit significantly from quantum parallelism.
8. What are some areas where quantum computing excels compared to classical computing?
9. Explain the concept of quantum hardware and its importance in quantum computing.
10. List and briefly describe some physical implementations of qubits mentioned in the chapter.
11. What is the significance of Shor's Algorithm in the context of quantum computing?
12. How does Grover's Algorithm improve the process of searching unsorted databases?
13. What is a Quantum Neural Network (QNN), and how does it differ from classical neural networks?
14. What are quantum neurons, and what unique properties do they leverage in QNNs?
15. Describe the typical architecture of a Quantum Neural Network, including the role of quantum and classical layers.
16. What is the process of training Quantum Neural Networks, and what are some quantum-specific considerations in training?
17. Explain the concept of amplitude encoding in quantum data encoding and its advantages.

Answers

Exercise 1- 1. d 2. a 3. b 4. a 5. c
Exercise 2- 1) False, 2) True, 3) False

Online Resources

Online Exam Paper:
Link: https://forms.gle/SMYeXFtJgs8DhBek9
QR Code:

Chapter 20 Videos Playlist:
Link: https://www.youtube.com/playlist?list=PLzlh_31VWEFoLM-AylnGYzPrqR702cTGV
QR Code:

Chapter 21: Deep Learning in Robotics and Autonomous Systems

21.1 Sensor Fusion and Perception in Robotics: Robotics is the field of designing, constructing, and operating robots to perform various tasks autonomously or semi-autonomously. A fundamental requirement for robots is the ability to perceive and understand their environment accurately. This perception allows them to make informed decisions, navigate safely, and interact effectively with their surroundings. Sensor fusion, a key concept in robotics, involves integrating data from multiple sensors to create a comprehensive and coherent representation of the environment. By combining information from different sources, sensor fusion enhances the robot's ability to interpret its surroundings and perform tasks more efficiently.

21.1.1 Sensor Types in Robotics: To perceive the world around them, robots employ various types of sensors, each capturing different aspects of the environment:

Vision Sensors: Vision sensors, including cameras and depth sensors, play a pivotal role in robotics by providing visual information about the surroundings. Cameras capture images that robots can analyze to identify objects, detect obstacles, and recognize patterns. Depth sensors, such as LiDAR and structured light sensors, estimate the distances to objects in the environment, enabling the creation of 3D maps and enhancing navigation capabilities.

LiDAR Sensors: LiDAR sensors emit laser beams and measure the time taken for these beams to reflect back from objects. This information is used to construct accurate 3D point cloud representations of the environment. LiDAR is crucial for tasks like mapping, localization, and obstacle avoidance, making it a common sensor in autonomous vehicles and robots operating in complex environments.

Radar Sensors: Radar sensors utilize radio waves to detect objects and gather information about their distance, speed, and relative position. These sensors are particularly useful for navigation and detecting objects beyond the line of sight. Radars are valuable in scenarios where weather conditions might impact visibility, such as in autonomous driving during rain or fog.

Inertial Sensors: Inertial sensors, such as accelerometers and gyroscopes, measure the robot's acceleration and rotation rates. These sensors provide essential information about the robot's movement and orientation, helping in tasks like tracking its position and controlling its motion. Inertial sensors are crucial for applications such as navigation and inertial measurement units (IMUs).

Ultrasonic Sensors: Ultrasonic sensors emit sound waves and measure the time taken for these waves to bounce back after hitting objects. These sensors are commonly used for proximity sensing and obstacle detection at close range. They are especially effective in scenarios where robots need to avoid collisions while moving in confined spaces.

21.1.2 Sensor Fusion Techniques: Sensor fusion aims to leverage the strengths of different sensors by combining their data in meaningful ways. There are several techniques for sensor fusion:

Data Level Fusion: Data level fusion involves directly integrating raw sensor data from multiple sources. This method creates a comprehensive dataset that includes information from all sensors. The combined data can provide a more accurate and detailed representation of the environment.

Feature Level Fusion: Feature level fusion focuses on extracting relevant features from the sensor data before combining them. This approach reduces the dimensionality of the data while preserving important information. Feature level fusion is particularly useful when sensors capture different aspects of the same phenomenon.

Decision Level Fusion: Decision level fusion involves aggregating the decisions or outputs of individual sensors' processing pipelines. By combining the results of various sensors, the system can achieve higher confidence and reliability in its perception. Decision level fusion is often used when redundancy and fault tolerance are crucial.

21.1.3 Applications and Benefits: Sensor fusion and perception are pivotal for various applications in robotics:

Autonomous Vehicles: In autonomous vehicles, sensor fusion enables the creation of a detailed and accurate model of the vehicle's surroundings. This information is vital for safe navigation, real-time decision-making, and collision avoidance in dynamic environments.

Robotic Manipulation: Robots equipped with sensor fusion capabilities can manipulate objects with greater precision. The combined data from various sensors help robots identify object shapes, sizes, and positions, enabling successful grasp planning and manipulation.

Search and Rescue: During search and rescue missions, robots with sensor fusion capabilities can navigate hazardous environments and locate survivors. Integration of data from different sensors helps robots map the terrain, detect obstacles, and identify signs of life.

21.1.4 Challenges and Future Directions: While sensor fusion offers significant advantages, challenges persist:

Sensor Noise and Calibration: Dealing with sensor noise and ensuring accurate calibration are ongoing challenges. Accurate sensor data is essential for reliable fusion and accurate perception.

Integration of Multiple Modalities: Efficiently integrating data from multiple sensory modalities, such as vision, LiDAR, and radar, requires advanced algorithms and processing techniques.

Machine Learning and Deep Learning: The integration of machine learning and deep learning techniques can enhance sensor fusion and perception by enabling the system to learn and adapt to complex environments.

Real-time Processing: Real-time processing of fused sensor data is crucial for time-sensitive applications such as autonomous navigation. Ensuring low-latency processing remains a challenge.

As robotics advances, research continues to focus on developing robust and efficient sensor fusion techniques. These techniques, combined with advances in machine learning and sensor technology, will play a crucial role in enhancing robotic perception and enabling robots to operate autonomously in diverse and dynamic environments.

21.2 Reinforcement Learning for Robotic Control: Reinforcement Learning (RL) has emerged as a transformative approach in the field of robotics, enabling robots to learn complex tasks through trial and error. RL leverages interactions with the environment to discover optimal strategies for performing tasks, making it particularly well-suited for robotic control and decision-making. This article delves into the concept of Reinforcement Learning for Robotic Control, its key components, applications, challenges, and future directions.

21.2.1 Understanding Reinforcement Learning: Reinforcement Learning (RL) stands as a pivotal paradigm within the realm of machine learning, particularly relevant to the field of robotics. It offers a mechanism through which an agent, such as a robot, learns to execute actions within a given environment to maximize an aggregate reward. This optimization process forms the basis for the agent's decision-making and action selection, leading to the achievement of specific objectives or tasks. In the context of robotics, this approach holds immense potential for enabling robots to autonomously learn and execute complex tasks through trial and error.

21.2.2 Components of RL: Reinforcement Learning consists of several essential components, each playing a distinct role in the learning and decision-making process:

Agent: The agent embodies the robotic entity that operates within the designated environment. It takes actions based on its current understanding and interacts with the surroundings to accomplish certain goals. These actions are selected in a manner that is expected to lead to the highest possible cumulative reward over time.

Environment: The environment encapsulates the physical or virtual context in which the robot operates. It dictates the agent's experiences and provides feedback based on the actions taken. The environment's response to the agent's actions is crucial in determining the success or failure of a task and, consequently, the rewards or penalties received.

State: A state refers to the representation of the environment's current condition at a given moment. It encompasses all the relevant information necessary for the agent to make informed decisions regarding its subsequent actions. The state acts as a crucial input that guides the agent's action selection process.

Action: Actions encompass the choices made by the agent to interact with the environment. These actions are chosen based on the agent's current state and its objective of maximizing the cumulative reward. The decision-making process revolves around selecting the action that is anticipated to lead to the most favorable outcomes.

Reward: A reward serves as a scalar feedback signal generated by the environment in response to the agent's actions. It quantifies the extent to which the agent's behavior aligns with the desired task objectives. Positive rewards are typically associated with desirable actions, while negative rewards (or penalties) are assigned for undesired outcomes.

As the agent interacts with the environment and receives feedback in the form of rewards, it learns to adjust its behavior over time. Reinforcement Learning harnesses this iterative process of exploration, action, feedback, and adaptation to enable robots to progressively refine their decision-making strategies and achieve improved performance on complex tasks. This paradigm empowers robots to learn autonomously and navigate uncertain environments, making it a cornerstone for enabling intelligent robotic control.

21.2.3 RL Techniques for Robotic Control: Reinforcement Learning offers a spectrum of techniques tailored for the intricate domain of robotic control, each aimed at enhancing a robot's ability to execute tasks autonomously and effectively:

Policy Optimization: Policy optimization centers on the pursuit of the optimal strategy, or policy, that maps various states of the environment to corresponding actions. Through a process of continuous refinement, the policy is iteratively updated to enhance the expected cumulative reward garnered by the robot's actions. Techniques like Proximal Policy Optimization (PPO) and Trust Region Policy Optimization (TRPO) enable the systematic enhancement of policies to achieve performance.

Value-Based Methods: Value-based methods revolve around estimating the value associated with distinct states and the actions that can be taken from those states. Algorithms like Q-learning and Deep Q-Networks (DQN) learn to maximize the anticipated cumulative reward by making informed decisions based on the learned value estimates. These methods pave the way for efficient decision-making even in complex and dynamic environments.

Actor-Critic Models: Actor-Critic models offer a harmonious fusion of policy optimization and value-based approaches. In this framework, the "actor" assumes the role of suggesting actions, while the "critic" evaluates these suggestions and provides feedback regarding their efficacy. The synergistic relationship between these two components enables the agent to iteratively refine its decision-making strategies.

21.2.4 Applications in Robotic Control: The integration of Reinforcement Learning has engendered transformative advancements in the domain of robotic control, fueling progress across diverse applications:

Robotic Manipulation: Reinforcement Learning empowers robots to attain dexterity in manipulating objects by learning complex movements and control techniques. This capability finds utility in tasks such as object grasping, assembly, and delicate manipulation.

Autonomous Navigation: Autonomous navigation is revolutionized as robots learn to dynamically explore environments, avoid obstacles, and successfully reach predetermined goals. This advancement has substantial implications for sectors like autonomous vehicles and mobile robotics.

Drone Flight Control: Reinforcement Learning revolutionizes drone flight control by equipping drones with the capacity to master intricate flight maneuvers and optimize trajectories. This skill is invaluable for tasks ranging from surveillance to package delivery and search and rescue operations.

Human-Robot Interaction: Reinforcement Learning redefines human-robot interaction, facilitating natural and safe collaboration. By enabling robots to adapt their behaviors and actions to align with human preferences and behaviors, RL nurtures seamless cooperation between humans and robots.

21.2.5 Challenges and Future Directions: While the fusion of RL and robotic control has yielded remarkable progress, it is not devoid of challenges that require attention for further advancements:

Sample Efficiency: Reinforcement Learning often necessitates a substantial number of interactions with the environment to learn effectively. Improving sample efficiency is imperative to ensure practical applicability in real-world scenarios.

Safety and Exploration: Balancing the exploration of novel actions with the exploitation of known strategies remains a challenging endeavor, especially in situations where safety is paramount.

Transfer Learning: Research in the realm of transfer learning is pivotal for enabling robots to effectively transfer knowledge gained from one task to excel in another, expediting the learning process and broadening the applicability of RL techniques.

Real-World Robustness: Ensuring the adaptability and robustness of RL policies across diverse conditions, such as varying environmental conditions or object types, is an ongoing pursuit aimed at enhancing the generalizability and reliability of robotic control systems in practical scenarios.

21.3 Sim-to-Real Transfer and Robot Navigation: The fusion of simulated environments and real-world robotics, known as sim-to-real transfer, has emerged as a pivotal paradigm for enhancing the navigation capabilities of robots. This innovative approach leverages the benefits of simulation, such as cost-effectiveness and safety, to prepare robots for real-world challenges:

21.3.1 Sim-to-Real Transfer: Sim-to-real transfer is a groundbreaking approach that capitalizes on simulated environments to enhance the performance of robotic algorithms in real-world applications. This methodology involves training and refining robotic models within simulated environments before deploying them in actual physical scenarios. By doing so, sim-to-real transfer addresses numerous challenges associated with collecting real-world data, safety concerns during experimentation, and the limited availability of real-world training samples. The core objective is to establish a seamless connection between the realm of simulation and the complexities of reality, thereby empowering models trained in simulations to effectively generalize their capabilities to real-world contexts.

21.3.2 Challenges in Sim-to-Real Transfer: The journey of achieving successful sim-to-real transfer is marked by several significant challenges that need to be overcome:

Reality Gap: The "reality gap" symbolizes the disparities that exist between the characteristics of simulated data and those of real-world data. Robots exclusively trained in simulation can often encounter performance discrepancies when deployed in real-world settings. These discrepancies arise due to variations in physical properties, lighting conditions, and other nuanced factors that simulations might fail to capture accurately.

Domain Adaptation: Domain adaptation techniques play a pivotal role in minimizing the disparities between simulated and real-world data distributions. These techniques aim to align the statistical characteristics of simulated and real-world data to ensure that models exhibit robust performance across diverse real-world conditions. Effective domain adaptation facilitates the seamless transition of models from simulation to reality.

Transferability: Ensuring that the knowledge acquired by models in the simulated environment translates effectively to real-world scenarios is a substantial challenge. Models that become overly attuned to the specifics of simulated data can struggle to adapt when faced with unseen real-world situations. Striking the right balance between the richness of simulation-based learning and the transferability to real-world applications is essential for achieving successful sim-to-real transfer.

21.3.3 Sim-to-Real Navigation: The integration of sim-to-real transfer in robot navigation brings forth a transformative paradigm with wide-ranging implications:

Autonomous Vehicles: In the realm of autonomous vehicles, sim-to-real transfer holds immense potential. By training self-driving cars in simulated environments, they can learn complex navigation tasks while minimizing the risks associated with real-world testing. This approach enables them to attain a higher level of competence and safety in navigating intricate road scenarios.

Mobile Robotics: Mobile robots that navigate diverse indoor and outdoor environments can derive significant benefits from simulation-based training. They can learn to navigate through a variety of terrains, tackle obstacles, and adapt to changing conditions before they encounter them in the real world.

Humanoid Robots: Humanoid robots can leverage simulation training to refine their locomotion skills before executing them in real-world environments. This enhances their stability, coordination, and overall performance, facilitating tasks that involve complex and dynamic movements.

21.3.4 Future Directions: The trajectory of sim-to-real transfer and robot navigation is poised for further advancements:

Improved Simulators: Developing more sophisticated and accurate simulators is pivotal for enhancing sim-to-real transfer. These advanced simulators reduce the reality gap by replicating real-world conditions more faithfully, thereby enhancing the adaptability of robots trained in simulations.

Domain Randomization: Domain randomization emerges as a powerful strategy. Robots trained in simulations featuring a diverse array of environmental conditions gain the ability to adapt effectively to a wide spectrum of real-world scenarios, regardless of their complexity.

Reinforcement Learning: Integrating reinforcement learning into the sim-to-real transfer paradigm can catalyze the adaptability of robots. By allowing robots to fine-tune their behaviors based on real-world experiences, this approach enables them to navigate complex and dynamic environments with greater efficiency and effectiveness.

Sim-to-real transfer presents a groundbreaking avenue for elevating the efficacy of robot navigation. From autonomous vehicles to humanoid robots, this approach is poised to reshape navigation capabilities across various domains. With the ongoing evolution of research and the pursuit of innovative strategies, sim-to-real transfer is set to play a pivotal role in shaping the future of robot navigation.

21.4 Challenges and Future Directions in Robotic AI: The landscape of robotic AI is characterized by a multitude of challenges and promising avenues that collectively shape the trajectory of robotics. These challenges reflect the complexities of creating intelligent, adaptable, and ethical robots that seamlessly integrate into our world. At the same time, the future directions point toward the advancements that will define the evolution of robotic AI.

Challenges:

Robustness: Achieving robustness in robotic AI is a cornerstone challenge. The goal is to develop robots that can operate effectively across a spectrum of diverse and unpredictable environments. From bustling urban landscapes to complex industrial settings, robots must be equipped to handle uncertainties, variations, and unexpected situations. Ensuring that AI models and control strategies can adapt to varying conditions without compromising performance or safety remains a significant hurdle.

Safety: Safety stands as a paramount concern as robots interact more closely with humans and dynamic surroundings. The challenge lies in crafting AI algorithms and control mechanisms that not only enable robots to perform tasks effectively but also guarantee safe interactions. This involves creating systems that can predict and prevent potential risks, ensure collision avoidance, and respond intelligently to emergency situations.

Ethical Considerations: With the increasing autonomy of robots, the ethical dimension of robotic AI becomes ever more critical. Addressing questions of responsibility, accountability, and ethical decision-making is a challenge that resonates across various contexts. Robots need to be imbued with AI that aligns with human values, respects privacy, and navigates ethical dilemmas in complex scenarios, all while adhering to legal and societal norms.

Scalability: The scalability challenge centers on developing AI solutions that can seamlessly adapt across a diverse spectrum of applications and environments. Whether it's a small-scale robotic arm in a factory or an autonomous vehicle navigating a city, AI algorithms should be versatile enough to perform effectively across different scales and scenarios. Achieving this adaptability without sacrificing efficiency is a complex undertaking.

Human-Robot Interaction: Creating natural and intuitive ways for humans to interact with robots represents a multifaceted challenge. The goal is to develop AI that enables seamless communication, collaboration, and understanding between humans and robots. This involves not only technical aspects but also cultural, social, and psychological considerations that shape how humans and robots interact in various contexts.

Future Directions: The future of robotic AI is marked by exciting directions that will shape the evolution of robotics:

Explainability and Interpretability: Enhancing the explainability and interpretability of robotic AI models stands as a crucial focus. Researchers are actively exploring methodologies that empower humans to comprehend the decision-making processes of AI systems. By shedding light on how AI arrives at specific choices, this direction cultivates trust and accountability in human-robot interactions.

Lifelong Learning: A pivotal direction in robotic AI is enabling robots to engage in lifelong learning. Beyond initial training, robots will possess mechanisms that facilitate continuous learning and adaptation. This capacity will empower robots to refine their performance, acquire new skills, and navigate evolving environments effectively over time.

Human-Centric Design: The future of robotic AI is anchored in human-centric design principles. Systems will be engineered to prioritize human needs, preferences, and safety considerations. AI algorithms will be crafted to align seamlessly with human values and seamlessly integrate into environments tailored for human interactions.

Cognitive Robotic Systems: Elevating robots to cognitive capabilities is a defining trajectory. Cognitive abilities encompass reasoning, common-sense understanding, and context-aware decision-making. The pursuit of cognitive robotic systems aims to equip robots with the prowess to navigate intricate real-world scenarios with efficiency and sophistication.

Swarm Robotics and Collective Intelligence: Exploration into swarm robotics and collective intelligence holds immense potential. This direction involves robots functioning collaboratively as a cohesive swarm to tackle challenges that may appear insurmountable for individual entities. Harnessing collective intelligence enables robots to accomplish tasks more efficiently and adapt adeptly to dynamic and complex environments.

The future of robotic AI is shaped by these vibrant directions. Advancements in explainability, lifelong learning, human-centric design, cognitive capabilities, and collective intelligence are poised to redefine the landscape of robotics, catalyzing innovations that will enhance the integration of robots into various aspects of our lives.

21.5 Project

Unsolved Project

Suppose you're developing a project that focuses on the application of deep learning in robotics and autonomous systems. To successfully complete this project, you need to understand sensor fusion and perception, reinforcement learning for robotic control, sim-to-real transfer techniques, and the challenges and future directions in robotic AI. Before starting, research the following: methods for sensor fusion and perception to enable robots to interpret and respond to their environments, the use of reinforcement learning to train robots for various control tasks, techniques for transferring models trained in simulation to real-world robotic systems (sim-to-real transfer), and the current challenges and potential future advancements in the field of robotic AI. This foundational knowledge will help you develop a comprehensive project that explores the integration of deep learning with robotics and autonomous systems.

21.6 Lab Activity

Unsolved Lab Activity

Implement a sensor fusion algorithm using data from multiple sensors (e.g., camera, LiDAR, IMU) to improve perception in a robotic system.

Task: Use a deep learning framework (e.g., ROS with TensorFlow or PyTorch) to implement a sensor fusion algorithm. Combine data from multiple sensors, such as a camera, LiDAR, and IMU, to improve perception in a robotic system. Document the implementation process, including data preprocessing, algorithm setup, and performance evaluation. Provide visualizations of the fused sensor data and the improved perception outcomes

Exercises

Exercise 1 – Multiple Choice Questions

1. What is the fundamental requirement for robots to perform tasks autonomously or semi-autonomously?
   a. Robotic construction
   b. Accurate perception and understanding of the environment
   c. Efficient navigation
   d. Effective interaction with humans
2. Sensor fusion in robotics involves:
   a. Combining robots to create a comprehensive robot
   b. Integrating data from multiple sensors to understand the environment
   c. Enhancing the robot's physical construction
   d. Modifying sensor data to suit the robot's needs
3. Which type of sensor is crucial for mapping, localization, and obstacle avoidance in autonomous vehicles and complex environments?
   a. Vision sensors
   b. LiDAR sensors
   c. Radar sensors
   d. Inertial sensors
4. What do radar sensors use to detect objects and gather information about their distance, speed, and relative position?
   a. Laser beams
   b. Radio waves
   c. Sound waves
   d. Ultraviolet light
5. Inertial sensors, such as accelerometers and gyroscopes, provide information about the robot's:
   a. Vision capabilities
   b. Environment
   c. Movement and orientation
   d. Sound perception

Exercise 2 – True/False

1. Sensor fusion is the process of combining data from multiple sensors to improve the perception and understanding of the environment.
2. Reinforcement learning is not applicable for robotic control because it cannot handle dynamic environments.
3. Sim-to-real transfer refers to the technique of training robotic models in simulation environments and applying them in real-world scenarios.

Review Questions

1. What is the primary purpose of robotics in the field of robotics?
2. Explain the significance of accurate perception and understanding of the environment for robots.
3. Define sensor fusion and its role in robotics.
4. Name two types of vision sensors used in robotics and describe their functions.
5. How do LiDAR sensors estimate the distances to objects in the environment, and what are their common applications?
6. What is the primary function of radar sensors in robotics, and in what scenarios are they particularly useful?
7. Briefly explain the role of inertial sensors, such as accelerometers and gyroscopes, in robotic systems.
8. How do ultrasonic sensors work, and for what purposes are they commonly used in robotics?
9. Describe the three main techniques for sensor fusion mentioned in the chapter.

10. In what situations is data level fusion most suitable for sensor fusion?
11. What is feature level fusion, and why is it useful when dealing with multiple sensors?
12. How does decision level fusion enhance the reliability of robotic perception systems?
13. Name three applications of sensor fusion and perception in robotics.
14. What challenges are associated with sensor noise and calibration in robotics?
15. How can machine learning and deep learning techniques enhance sensor fusion and perception in robotic systems?
16. Why is real-time processing of fused sensor data crucial in certain robotic applications?
17. What is the future direction of research in sensor fusion techniques and their impact on robotics?

Answers

Exercise 1- 1. b 2. b 3. b 4. b 5. c
Exercise 2- 1) True, 2) False, 3) True

Online Resources

Online Exam Paper:
Link: https://forms.gle/gj9CoqAHbF7SDECp7
QR Code:

Chapter 21 Videos Playlist:
Link: https://www.youtube.com/playlist?list=PLzlh_31VWEFoYaPQl8wzSWbnECgDfNSRP
QR Code:

Chapter 22: Neuroscience and Cognitive Models in Deep Learning

22.1 Biological Neural Networks: Unveiling the Blueprint: Biological neural networks, which form the foundation of human brain function, serve as the inspiration for artificial neural networks in the field of deep learning. These networks exhibit a remarkable parallelism in their fundamental mechanisms, enabling machines to mimic the complex processes underlying human cognition.

22.1.1 Neurons: The Building Blocks of Intelligence: At the core of the human brain's information processing capabilities are neurons, intricate cells designed to transmit and process signals. Neurons achieve this through the utilization of electrochemical signals known as action potentials. These action potentials travel along the neuron's extended structure called the axon, enabling the transmission of information across the neural network. In the realm of artificial neural networks, a corresponding concept emerges with the introduction of artificial neurons, also known as perceptrons or nodes. These artificial neurons act as information-processing units, mirroring the functionality of biological neurons. Just as their biological counterparts, artificial neurons process and transmit data, fostering communication across different layers of the neural network.

22.1.2 Synapses and Connectivity: The human brain's neural communication relies on synapses, specialized junctions that facilitate the transfer of signals from one neuron to another. These synapses hold the ability to adapt over time, a phenomenon referred to as synaptic plasticity. This plasticity allows synapses to strengthen or weaken in response to the frequency and timing of signals. In deep learning, this concept finds its counterpart in the form of connection weights between artificial neurons. These weights represent the strength of connections and are adjustable during the learning process. This remarkable adaptability permits artificial neural networks to learn intricate patterns and distinctive features from the data they process.

22.1.3 Layers: Mimicking Brain Structure: The intricate organization of the human brain involves the arrangement of neurons into distinct layers, each serving a specific role in the processing hierarchy. Similarly, artificial neural networks are structured with layers, comprising the input layer, hidden layers, and the output layer. Each layer of an artificial neural network progressively processes information in a hierarchical manner, akin to the brain's stratified architecture. This hierarchical processing facilitates the extraction of features at varying levels of abstraction, contributing to the network's capacity to comprehend complex patterns within data.

22.1.4 Activation Functions: Igniting Neural Responses: Biological neurons exhibit activation in response to specific stimuli, a property that artificial neural networks replicate through activation functions. Activation functions operate on the weighted sum of inputs to a node, determining the node's output. Common activation functions, such as the sigmoid function or the rectified linear unit (ReLU), introduce non-linearity into the network's computations. This non-linearity enables artificial neural networks to effectively capture intricate relationships within the data, enhancing their capability to model complex patterns.

22.1.5 Learning Paradigms: Uniting Nature and Machines:

Supervised Learning: Just as learning in the human brain is often guided by external feedback, supervised learning is a cornerstone of training artificial neural networks. This paradigm involves presenting the network with labeled examples, enabling it to learn associations between inputs and corresponding outputs. Through iterative adjustments to connection weights, the network refines its ability to make accurate predictions or classifications.

Unsupervised Learning: Unsupervised learning, aligned with the brain's aptitude for recognizing patterns without explicit guidance, encompasses techniques that enable artificial neural networks to uncover latent structures within data. Techniques such as clustering and autoencoders exemplify this paradigm, allowing networks to identify underlying patterns and relationships.

Reinforcement Learning: Inspired by the brain's reward-based learning mechanisms, reinforcement learning involves training artificial neural networks to make sequential decisions that maximize cumulative rewards. Similar to how the brain associates actions with positive or negative outcomes, reinforcement learning agents learn to take actions that lead to favorable results in a given environment.

Conclusion: The emulation of biological neural networks through artificial counterparts underscores the incredible sophistication of nature's design. By unveiling and adopting the blueprint of biological neural systems, deep learning has propelled the field of artificial intelligence to unprecedented heights. This integration of natural principles and machine innovation has paved the way for advancements that were once relegated to the realm of imagination.

22.1.6 Challenges and Future Prospects: Despite the remarkable advancements in the realm of artificial neural networks, there remain significant challenges in fully replicating the intricacies and efficiency of the human brain's neural networks. These challenges highlight the need for ongoing research and innovation to bridge the gap between artificial and biological intelligence. Moreover, the future prospects in this field hold the promise of creating more biologically plausible models that encompass the rich complexities of the brain's mechanisms.

Challenges in Replicating Biological Neuronal Systems: Artificial neural networks, while powerful, face limitations in several key aspects:

Efficiency: The human brain is a marvel of energy efficiency, capable of processing vast amounts of information while consuming minimal energy. In contrast, artificial neural networks, particularly deep ones, demand significant computational resources and energy consumption. Achieving a similar level of efficiency in artificial systems remains a formidable challenge.

Adaptability and Learning: The brain exhibits an extraordinary ability to adapt, learn, and generalize from a limited set of examples. Current artificial neural networks often require substantial amounts of labeled data to perform well, and they struggle to generalize effectively in novel situations. Improving the adaptability and learning efficiency of artificial systems is an ongoing endeavor.

Robustness and Fault Tolerance: Biological neural networks are remarkably robust, capable of functioning even when individual neurons or connections fail. Artificial neural networks, on the other hand, can be fragile, with performance degrading significantly when certain nodes or connections are compromised. Enhancing the fault tolerance and robustness of artificial networks is a pressing challenge.

Future Prospects and Research Directions: Researchers are actively working to address these challenges and advance the field of artificial neural networks toward greater biological fidelity:

Neuromorphic Computing: Neuromorphic computing aims to create hardware architectures that closely mimic the brain's structure and operation. This approach leverages specialized hardware to accelerate neural network computations while emulating biological processes, potentially leading to substantial improvements in energy efficiency and computational performance.

Spiking Neural Networks (SNNs): Unlike traditional artificial neural networks that rely on continuous-valued activations, SNNs operate on discrete spikes of activity, resembling the firing of biological neurons. SNNs have the potential to achieve higher efficiency and better biological resemblance, making them an active area of research.

Biologically-Inspired Learning Algorithms: Novel learning algorithms draw inspiration from biological learning mechanisms, such as Hebbian learning, spike-timing-dependent plasticity, and homeostatic regulation. Incorporating these mechanisms into artificial networks could lead to more adaptive, lifelong learning systems.

Interdisciplinary Collaboration: Bridging the gap between neuroscience and machine learning involves collaboration between experts in various fields. Neuroscientists provide insights into the brain's functioning, guiding the development of more realistic artificial models.

Ethical and Philosophical Considerations: As artificial neural networks become more advanced and biologically plausible, ethical questions arise regarding the implications of creating systems that exhibit higher levels of intelligence and autonomy. Ensuring responsible development and use of such systems requires careful consideration.

Conclusion: The journey to replicate the complexities of biological neural networks within artificial systems is a challenging yet exciting endeavor. While artificial neural networks have come a long way, their limitations compared to their biological counterparts are evident. However, with ongoing research, innovation, and interdisciplinary collaboration, the field holds the potential to unlock new frontiers in artificial intelligence. The fusion of biology and technology not only advances our understanding of both domains but also paves the way for groundbreaking applications that can reshape industries, enhance human capabilities, and usher in a new era of intelligent machines.

22.2 Spiking Neural Networks: Bridging the Biological Gap: Spiking Neural Networks (SNNs) stand as a pivotal departure from conventional artificial neural networks, aiming to emulate the distinct spiking behavior inherent in biological neurons. By incorporating the discrete and temporally dynamic nature of neural communication, SNNs bridge the gap between artificial and biological intelligence, paving the way for more accurate and efficient information processing.

22.2.1 The Essence of Spikes: At the core of SNNs lies their emulation of the spiking activity observed in biological neurons. Instead of continuous activations, SNNs employ spikes or pulses of activity to communicate information between neurons. This spike-based communication offers a heightened level of precision and efficiency in transmitting information. By adopting this mechanism, SNNs capture the temporal dynamics that characterize neural communication in the human brain, allowing them to model time-dependent processes with an enhanced level of fidelity.

22.2.2 Synaptic Plasticity and Spike-Timing-Dependent Learning: Central to the efficacy of SNNs is the concept of synaptic plasticity, reflecting the ability of synapses to adapt and alter their strengths over time. A prominent facet of synaptic plasticity within SNNs is known as spike-timing-dependent plasticity (STDP). This phenomenon hinges on the precise timing of spikes between interconnected neurons. When a presynaptic spike closely precedes a postsynaptic spike, the synapse's strength is augmented, reinforcing the connection. Conversely, if the order of spikes is reversed, the synapse weakens. This synaptic learning mechanism mirrors the intricate learning processes seen in biological brains.

22.2.3 Event-Driven Computation: Unlike the continuous computational nature of traditional artificial neural networks, SNNs operate under an event-driven paradigm. Neurons within SNNs generate spikes only when the accumulated input surpasses a specific threshold. This approach optimizes computational resources by activating neurons solely when necessary, minimizing energy expenditure. This event-driven strategy closely aligns with the energy-efficient operation observed in the biological brain, where neurons fire selectively to conserve energy.

22.2.4 Applications of Spiking Neural Networks: Spiking Neural Networks (SNNs) emerge as versatile tools with applications spanning various domains, harnessing their unique properties for innovative solutions:

Neuromorphic Vision: SNNs excel in tasks demanding temporal analysis, such as object recognition and motion detection. Their inherent ability to process temporal information aligns seamlessly with the dynamic nature of visual stimuli. This makes SNNs well-suited for real-time visual processing tasks, enabling accurate and efficient identification of objects in complex environments.

Neuromorphic Auditory Processing: SNNs hold the capacity to replicate auditory processing by capturing the intricate temporal dynamics of sound patterns. Just as the human auditory system processes sound over time to discern various auditory features, SNNs can similarly analyze temporal patterns in auditory data. This ability makes SNNs a valuable asset in tasks involving sound recognition, classification, and even speech processing.

Brain-Computer Interfaces: One of the most promising applications of SNNs lies in the development of brain-computer interfaces (BCIs). By capitalizing on the inherent temporal nature of neural communication, SNNs can facilitate direct communication between the brain and external devices. This offers unprecedented potential for individuals with motor disabilities to control devices using their neural activity, opening doors to enhanced mobility and communication.

22.2.5 Neuromorphic Computing: A Paradigm Shift:

The Essence of Neuromorphic Computing: Neuromorphic computing epitomizes a fundamental shift in computational philosophy, centered on hardware architectures that closely emulate the principles of the human brain. Unlike traditional computing, which emphasizes raw processing power, neuromorphic architectures prioritize efficiency, adaptability, and parallelism – mirroring the brain's intricate yet resource-efficient operation.

TrueNorth and SpiNNaker: Pioneering projects, such as IBM's TrueNorth and the University of Manchester's SpiNNaker, stand as exemplary instances of neuromorphic hardware platforms. These platforms exemplify massive parallelism and efficient spike-based communication, traits that align with the brain's information processing strategies. TrueNorth and SpiNNaker offer promise in real-time data processing tasks, paving the way for cognitive tasks that require rapid and dynamic computations.

Neuromorphic vs. Traditional Computing: Neuromorphic computing's distinct advantage lies in its alignment with energy efficiency and suitability for cognitive tasks. In contrast to traditional computing architectures, which follow the von Neumann model, neuromorphic designs accommodate large-scale parallelism and event-based processing – qualities inherent in biological neural systems. Traditional computing architectures struggle to efficiently manage tasks necessitating parallel, real-time, and event-driven processing, further underscoring the significance of the neuromorphic approach.

Ethical and Practical Considerations: As the frontiers of neuromorphic computing expand, ethical considerations come to the fore. The potential to create machines that closely resemble brain functions raises important questions about the ethical implications of such creations. Striking a balance between technological advancement and responsible development becomes imperative to ensure that the benefits of neuromorphic computing are realized without transgressing ethical boundaries. Navigating these considerations ensures that the potential ethical pitfalls are acknowledged and mitigated, ultimately steering the development of neuromorphic computing in a positive and productive direction.

Conclusion: The applications of Spiking Neural Networks and the paradigm shift brought about by neuromorphic computing collectively represent a pivotal advancement in the journey toward intelligent computation. By integrating temporal dynamics, energy efficiency, and cognitive adaptability, these innovations unlock unprecedented capabilities in machine intelligence. Through their novel approaches to information processing, SNNs and neuromorphic architectures propel us closer to systems that not only process data but also mirror the nuanced operations of the human mind. As we continue to explore their potential, these technologies have the capacity to redefine industries, revolutionize computation, and broaden our understanding of what is achievable in the realm of artificial intelligence.

22.3 Connectionism: Unveiling Neural Networks: Connectionism stands as a compelling theoretical framework that unveils the intricate workings of neural networks, offering profound insights into the processes underlying human cognition and learning.

22.3.1 The Essence of Connectionism: Connectionism postulates that the intricacies of complex cognitive processes can be unraveled by dissecting the interconnections between simple processing units. This concept draws a compelling parallel between artificial neural networks and the intricate web of neural connections within the human brain. It suggests that the collective interactions of these interconnected units give rise to the higher-order cognitive functions observed in biological and artificial systems alike.

22.3.2 Neural Networks as Connectionist Models: Artificial neural networks epitomize the connectionist paradigm by mimicking both the structure and operation of biological neural networks. In these networks, nodes or neurons are interlinked through weighted connections that facilitate the transmission and processing of information. By adopting this connectionist approach, researchers can delve into the intricacies of cognitive functions by analyzing the interplay between these elementary processing units. These networks provide a computational framework for understanding how simple elements can collectively produce complex behaviors.

22.3.3 Learning Mechanisms in Connectionist Models: Connectionist models place significant emphasis on the process of learning, which is integral to both biological and artificial systems. Learning within connectionist models entails the adjustment of connection weights in response to experience and external feedback. This adaptive mechanism enables connectionist models to progressively acquire knowledge, generalize patterns from examples, and enhance their performance over time. The iterative nature of learning in connectionist models mirrors the way humans acquire skills and insights through repeated exposure and practice.

22.3.4 Parallel Distributed Processing: Connectionism aligns harmoniously with the concept of parallel distributed processing (PDP), a fundamental feature of neural systems. PDP signifies that information processing occurs simultaneously across interconnected units, akin to the brain's parallel neural pathways. This approach fosters robust and efficient cognition as information is processed in parallel across multiple units. By embracing parallelism, connectionist models capture the efficiency and dynamic nature of information processing seen in biological neural networks.

Conclusion: Connectionism serves as a gateway to understanding the complex interplay of neural networks, learning mechanisms, and cognitive processes. By unveiling the significance of interconnections between simple processing units, connectionism provides insights that bridge the gap between artificial and biological intelligence. The exploration of neural networks within this framework sheds light on the intricate dynamics that contribute to human cognition, learning, and adaptability. Ultimately, connectionism facilitates a deeper comprehension of how the fusion of simple elements in interconnected networks generates the astonishing complexity of intelligence and behavior observed in both natural and artificial systems.

22.3.5 Application in Cognitive Science: The application of connectionism reverberates across diverse domains within cognitive science, casting light on the intricacies of human intelligence and cognition:

Language Processing: Connectionist models emerge as powerful tools for simulating language processing. These models capture how linguistic patterns are acquired, learned, and represented in the brain. By elucidating how simple interconnected units grasp the complexities of language, connectionism offers insights into the cognitive foundations of linguistic abilities.

Memory Formation: The connectionist perspective offers a unique vantage point to delve into the intricate processes of memory formation and retrieval. Through connectionist models, researchers unravel how memories are stored, interconnected, and retrieved. This perspective provides a nuanced understanding of the mechanisms underpinning our ability to retain and recollect information.

Perception and Cognition: Connectionist models provide an invaluable framework for exploring the interplay of perceptual processes and cognitive functions. By simulating the interactions of interconnected nodes, these models shed light on the mechanisms underlying perception, reasoning, decision-making, and problem-solving. This holistic perspective contributes to a comprehensive comprehension of the multifaceted landscape of human cognition.

22.3.6 Biological Learning Mechanisms:

Synaptic Plasticity: In the intricate dance of biological systems, synaptic plasticity takes center stage as a cornerstone of learning. Synaptic plasticity encapsulates the remarkable ability of synapses to alter their strength based on the frequency and timing of neural activity. The forms of synaptic plasticity, such as long-term potentiation (LTP) and long-term depression (LTD), wield significant influence in memory formation and the storage of information. Through these mechanisms, neural connections adapt and solidify, laying the groundwork for learning and cognitive development.

Hebbian Learning: Hebbian learning, an iconic principle in neuroscience, encapsulates the notion that neural connections between neurons strengthen when those neurons fire in synchrony. This principle succinctly captures the essence of associative learning. As neurons engage in synchronous activity, their connections are reinforced, leading to enhanced neural pathways. This phenomenon echoes the brain's strategy of amplifying the connectivity of neurons involved in correlated activities.

Spike-Timing-Dependent Plasticity (STDP): Spike-Timing-Dependent Plasticity (STDP) emerges as a refined mechanism for shaping synaptic connections based on the precise timing of spikes between interconnected neurons. STDP embodies a temporal dimension, where synapses strengthen when a presynaptic neuron fires just before its postsynaptic counterpart, and vice versa. This mechanism elegantly captures the temporal intricacies of neural communication, further mirroring the exquisite timing-dependent adaptations observed in the brain's neural networks.

The journey into connectionism and biological learning mechanisms unravels the very fabric of human intelligence and cognition. By embracing connectionist paradigms, researchers delve into the profound interplay of interconnected processing units. These models transcend the artificial confines of machine learning, echoing the intricate dance of neurons in the human brain. Moreover, the exploration of biological learning mechanisms, including synaptic plasticity, Hebbian learning, and STDP, unveils the astonishing adaptability and plasticity of the brain, fostering a deeper appreciation for the mechanisms that underpin human learning and cognitive growth.

22.4 Bridging the Gap Between AI and Neuroscience: A Synergistic Journey: The convergence of artificial intelligence (AI) and neuroscience marks a remarkable endeavor, fostering a symbiotic relationship that empowers both disciplines. This chapter explores the dynamic interplay between AI and neuroscience, elucidating how each field informs and catalyzes advancements in the other.

22.4.1 Insights from Neuroscience Inform AI: Neuroscience serves as a wellspring of insights that profoundly shape the development of AI systems. The intricate knowledge of neural circuits, learning mechanisms, and sensory processing within the brain offers a blueprint for the design of AI algorithms. The marvel of neural networks, for instance, arises from the emulation of the interconnectedness witnessed among neurons in the brain. This model resonates powerfully in tasks such as image recognition and natural language processing, where neural networks replicate the brain's capacity to decipher intricate patterns and glean meaning from complex data. The insights drawn from neuroscience provide AI with a roadmap to replicate the brain's ability to process and make sense of information.

22.4.2 AI Advances Illuminate Neuroscientific Understanding: The reciprocal relationship between AI and neuroscience manifests in AI's contributions to unraveling the mysteries of the brain. Leveraging the prowess of machine learning and data analysis, AI equips neuroscientists with tools to decipher voluminous datasets emanating from brain imaging and electrophysiological experiments. These analytical tools excel at identifying subtle patterns, forecasting brain activity, and unraveling the intricate neural substrates that underlie cognition and behavior. The insights gleaned from AI-driven analysis offer fresh perspectives on how the brain processes information, and this newfound understanding contributes to the growing mosaic of human cognition.

22.4.3 Brain-Inspired Computing: Neuromorphic AI: Neuromorphic computing emerges as an epitome of the amalgamation between AI and neuroscience. Drawing inspiration from the brain's efficiency and parallel processing, neuromorphic hardware architectures strive to replicate these principles within AI systems. These architectures hold the promise of revolutionizing AI by facilitating real-time processing, cognitive tasks, and brain-computer interfaces that echo the brain's remarkable efficiency and adaptability. The synergy between AI and neuroscience is particularly pronounced in this domain, as AI endeavors to emulate the brain's intricate mechanisms, pushing the boundaries of computational power.

22.4.4 Advancing Brain-Computer Interfaces: The harmonious convergence of AI and neuroscience fuels pioneering developments in brain-computer interfaces (BCIs). These interfaces usher in a new era of direct communication between the brain and external devices, enabling applications like controlling prosthetic limbs or restoring sensory perceptions. AI algorithms decode neural signals, translating intentions into tangible actions. This union between AI and neuroscience bridges the divide between neural activity and meaningful outcomes, exemplifying the profound transformations that arise from interdisciplinary collaboration.

22.4.5 Ethical Considerations and Responsible Innovation: Amid the remarkable progress at the crossroads of AI and neuroscience, ethical considerations take center stage. The intertwining of AI with brain-related applications raises questions about privacy, autonomy, and the implications of cognitive enhancement. Responsible innovation necessitates the careful contemplation of these concerns to ensure that the fusion of AI and neuroscience aligns with societal values, placing the well-being of individuals and society at the forefront.

Conclusion: The journey of bridging the gap between AI and neuroscience underscores the power of interdisciplinary synergy. As AI leverages insights from neuroscience to mimic intricate brain processes, it garners the ability to perform complex tasks with remarkable precision. Simultaneously, AI empowers neuroscience by unraveling neural mysteries through data analysis and modeling. This convergence holds the potential to reshape industries, from healthcare to artificial intelligence itself. Nevertheless, the ethical compass must navigate this journey, ensuring that these advancements are ethically aligned and that the union of AI and neuroscience heralds a future where intelligence and understanding flourish hand in hand.

22.5 Project

Unsolved Project

Suppose you're developing a project that explores the intersection of neuroscience and cognitive models in deep learning. To create a comprehensive project, you need to understand the biological inspiration behind artificial neural networks, spiking neural networks and neuromorphic computing, connectionism and learning in biological systems, and efforts to bridge the gap between AI and neuroscience. Before starting, research the following: how biological neural networks have inspired the development of artificial neural networks, the principles and applications of spiking neural networks and neuromorphic computing, theories of connectionism and how learning occurs in biological systems, and current research and approaches aimed at integrating insights from neuroscience with AI development. This foundational knowledge will enable you to develop a project that effectively examines the synergies between deep learning and neuroscience.

22.6 Lab Activity

Unsolved Lab Activity

Implement a simple artificial neural network inspired by biological principles to perform a basic task (e.g., pattern recognition).

Task: Use a deep learning framework (e.g., TensorFlow or PyTorch) to implement a simple artificial neural network inspired by biological principles. Train the network to perform a basic task, such as pattern recognition. Document the implementation process, including data preprocessing, model architecture, training procedure, and performance evaluation. Provide visualizations of the network's structure and performance.

Exercises

Exercise 1 – Multiple Choice Questions

1. What serves as the inspiration for artificial neural networks in the field of deep learning?
   A. Quantum computing C. Genetic algorithms
   B. Biological neural networks D. Expert systems
2. What do neurons in the human brain use to transmit and process signals?
   A. Electrical currents C. Radio waves
   B. Chemical reactions D. Action potentials
3. What is the extended structure along which action potentials travel in a neuron called?
   A. Axon B. Dendrite

C. Synapse
D. Soma

4. What is the term for artificial neurons in the context of artificial neural networks?
   A. Electrodes
   B. Nodes
   C. Conductors
   D. Transistors
5. What is synaptic plasticity, as described in the chapter?
   A. The ability of neurons to fire rapidly
   B. The strengthening or weakening of synapses over time
   C. A type of action potential
   D. A form of neurotransmitter

Exercise 2 – True/False

1. Spiking Neural Networks are a type of neuromorphic computing inspired by biological neurons.
2. Connectionism focuses on how artificial neural networks can mimic learning processes in biological systems.
3. Bridging the gap between AI and Neuroscience has no relevance in the development of new AI models.

Review Questions

1. What role do biological neural networks play in inspiring artificial neural networks in the field of deep learning?
2. Describe the fundamental mechanism that neurons in the human brain use to transmit and process signals.
3. What is the significance of action potentials in the context of neuron communication?
4. In artificial neural networks, what is the function of artificial neurons, also known as perceptrons or nodes?
5. How do artificial neurons in artificial neural networks mimic the functionality of biological neurons?

Answers

Exercise 1- 1. B 2. D 3. A 4. B 5. B
Exercise 2- 1) True, 2) False, 3) True

Online Resources

Online Exam Paper:
Link: https://forms.gle/Q7z772NBYwpZZrD48
QR Code:

Chapter 22 Videos Playlist:
Link: https://www.youtube.com/playlist?list=PLzlh_31VWEFq0HBRLOOwmyfH7dMevkdSN
QR Code:

Chapter 23: Deep Learning for Edge Devices and IoT

23.1 Challenges of Deploying Deep Learning on Edge: The rapid proliferation of edge devices, encompassing smartphones, Internet of Things (IoT) devices, drones, and autonomous vehicles, has sparked a compelling demand to deploy deep learning models directly onto these devices. However, this ambitious endeavor comes accompanied by an array of intricate challenges that necessitate careful consideration and innovative solutions.

Resource Constraints: Edge devices are inherently characterized by their limited computational power, memory capacity, and energy resources. This presents a fundamental challenge when deploying deep learning models, which often exhibit significant size and complexity. Operating such models efficiently within these resource-constrained environments is a formidable task. Striking a delicate balance between maintaining model accuracy and ensuring resource efficiency becomes an imperative concern.

Latency and Real-time Processing: One of the driving motivations for deploying deep learning on the edge is the imperative to reduce latency, particularly in applications that demand real-time or low-latency responses. Transmitting data to a centralized server for processing introduces delay, which can be detrimental in scenarios such as autonomous driving or real-time image analysis. Deploying deep learning models directly on edge devices aims to mitigate this latency challenge. However, achieving real-time performance on devices with limited computational resources poses a significant hurdle that requires innovative optimizations.

Model Complexity: Deep learning models, especially those boasting numerous layers and parameters, impose substantial computational demands. The intricacy of these models can lead to slow inference times and rapid battery depletion on edge devices. This reality underscores the necessity of optimizing models for efficiency while upholding their performance. Striking a balance between reducing model complexity and maintaining accuracy is essential to ensure seamless operation within edge environments.

Data Privacy and Security: Edge devices frequently process sensitive data locally, raising significant concerns regarding data privacy and security. The prospect of transmitting data to external servers for processing, while addressing some of these concerns, introduces a new set of challenges. Ensuring the protection of data during transmission becomes paramount. Developing robust encryption and secure communication protocols is essential to safeguard sensitive information from potential threats.

Adaptability and Flexibility: Edge environments are characterized by their diversity and dynamism. Deployed devices encounter a wide spectrum of conditions and scenarios. Consequently, deep learning models deployed on edge devices must exhibit adaptability and versatility. Designing models capable of accommodating varying edge contexts without compromising performance presents a formidable challenge. Models must be agile enough to address the evolving nature of edge deployments.

Model Updates and Maintenance: Maintaining up-to-date deep learning models on edge devices presents unique challenges. Limited connectivity and intermittent access to the internet hinder the seamless deployment of updates. Ensuring consistency and accuracy across devices, while navigating these connectivity constraints, necessitates the development of efficient mechanisms for model updates and maintenance.

Heterogeneity of Hardware: The diverse landscape of edge devices introduces a significant challenge in creating universally applicable models that perform optimally across all hardware configurations. Edge devices vary in terms of computational power, memory, and specialized hardware components. Tailoring models to suit diverse hardware architectures while preserving compatibility requires intricate model design and optimization strategies.

Energy Efficiency: A cornerstone consideration for edge devices is energy efficiency, particularly because many are powered by batteries. Deep learning models that consume excessive power can significantly diminish a device's battery life, rendering them less practical for extended use. Designing models that strike a delicate balance between high performance and energy conservation is pivotal in ensuring the viability of deep learning on the edge.

Conclusion: While deploying deep learning on edge devices holds immense potential, it comes with an array of multifaceted challenges. Successfully navigating these challenges requires a holistic understanding of the unique constraints and requirements of edge environments. Innovations in model design, optimization techniques, and secure communication protocols will be pivotal in unlocking the transformative possibilities that deep learning brings to the edge of network architectures. As the fields of AI and edge computing continue to advance, addressing these challenges will play a pivotal role in shaping the future landscape of intelligent edge applications.

23.2 Efficient Model Compression and Quantization: The surge in demand for deploying deep learning models on edge devices has catalyzed the need for novel approaches that optimize the utilization of constrained resources:

Model Compression: Optimizing Model Complexity: Deep learning models, characterized by their intricate architecture and a multitude of parameters, often exceed the resource constraints of edge devices. Model compression techniques intervene to alleviate this challenge. Through mechanisms such as pruning, redundant parameters are identified and removed, leading to a streamlined model. Additionally, architecture search methods facilitate the discovery of efficient network structures that balance performance and resource efficiency. Model compression results in leaner models that occupy minimal memory and impose less computational burden.

Quantization: Enhancing Computational Efficiency: The computational demands of deep learning models, rooted in high-precision floating-point arithmetic, are formidable within the limitations of edge devices. Quantization techniques emerge as a remedy, strategically reducing the precision of numerical values. This process involves converting high-precision floating-point numbers to lower-bit representations, thereby economizing memory usage and computational power. Remarkably, quantization achieves this while preserving a commendable degree of model accuracy.

Distillation: Knowledge Transfer for Compact Models: Distillation introduces an innovative approach by training a smaller model to replicate the behavior of a larger, complex model. This knowledge transfer technique leverages the predictive expertise of the larger "teacher" model to guide the learning of the smaller "student" model. The distilled model not only learns from the original training data but also benefits from the insights embedded in the teacher model's predictions. This results in a compact yet proficient model that capitalizes on the knowledge distilled from its larger counterpart.

Pruning: Trimming Redundancy for Efficiency: Pruning addresses model complexity by systematically identifying and eliminating less impactful connections and parameters. This iterative process progressively refines the model's architecture, progressively excising components with minimal influence on performance. Pruned models maintain a commendable level of accuracy while emerging as viable candidates for deployment on edge devices.

Knowledge Distillation: Compact Models with Expertise: Knowledge distillation harnesses the intelligence of a resource-intensive model to train a more compact counterpart. The smaller model learns not only from training data but also from the probability distribution of the teacher model's predictions. This innovative technique facilitates knowledge transfer, enhancing the smaller model's performance by imbibing the insights of the larger model.

Significance of Efficient Model Compression and Quantization: Efficient model compression and quantization wield profound implications for edge computing:

Resource Optimization: These techniques align deep learning models with the limitations of edge devices, rendering them efficient in terms of computational power and memory usage.

Latency Reduction: Smaller models translate into swifter inference times, fostering real-time applications that hinge on minimal latency.

Energy Efficiency: Leaner models exhibit reduced energy consumption, an attribute critical for the sustained operation of battery-powered edge devices.

Enhanced Accessibility: Efficient models broaden the range of deployable devices, democratizing access to AI capabilities across diverse hardware.

Privacy and Security: The diminished need for data transmission enhances data privacy and security, particularly in scenarios involving sensitive information.

Cost Effectiveness: Reduced computational demands contribute to cost savings in terms of hardware infrastructure and operational expenses.

Conclusion: The realm of edge computing is invigorated by the strides made in efficient model compression and quantization. These strategies epitomize the delicate equilibrium between deep learning model performance and the intricacies of edge environments. As technological frontiers continue to expand, the advancement of model compression and quantization will remain instrumental in realizing an era where intelligent applications thrive on the edge, reshaping sectors spanning healthcare, transportation, smart cities, and beyond.

23.3 Federated Learning in Distributed Edge Environments: As edge computing gains prominence, the demand to deploy deep learning models across distributed edge devices has surged. Federated learning, a revolutionary concept, offers a compelling solution to the challenges of edge deployment:

Federated Learning: Decentralized Model Training: Federated learning reimagines the conventional model training process. Instead of centralizing data in a singular location, federated learning distributes the training process across edge devices. This decentralization is instrumental in preserving data privacy, as sensitive data remains localized and never leaves the edge devices. In this federated paradigm, each edge device contributes to model training using its local data, with only model updates shared between devices and a central server.

Localized Learning: Enhancing Privacy: Federated learning aligns with the principle of data privacy. As sensitive data remains on edge devices, concerns regarding data breaches during transmission are assuaged. This approach empowers individuals to retain control over their data, fostering a sense of ownership and privacy.

Decentralized Training: Addressing Resource Constraints: The resource constraints characteristic of edge devices pose a significant challenge. Federated learning deftly tackles this obstacle by distributing the computational burden across devices. This ensures that the model training process does not overwhelm any individual device, enabling the participation of even resource-constrained devices.

Collaborative Learning: Knowledge Aggregation: In federated learning, each edge device trains a model using its local data. Subsequently, these locally trained models are aggregated into a global model. This collaborative approach capitalizes on the diversity of edge devices, enhancing the model's generalization capabilities.

Communication Efficiency: Minimal Data Transmission: Traditional machine learning involves transmitting large volumes of data to a central server for processing. Federated learning minimizes data transmission by transmitting only model updates. This reduces bandwidth consumption, addressing challenges posed by limited network connectivity.

Challenges and Opportunities: While federated learning presents groundbreaking opportunities, it also entails challenges:

Heterogeneity: Edge devices exhibit diverse hardware and software configurations. Federated learning must accommodate this heterogeneity while maintaining model consistency.

Communication Overhead: Coordinating model updates from numerous edge devices incurs communication overhead. Optimizing communication protocols is vital.
Bias and Fairness: Localized training can introduce biases. Ensuring fairness and avoiding biased models require careful consideration.
Conclusion: Federated learning emerges as a pioneering approach in the deployment of deep learning models in distributed edge environments. By preserving data privacy, addressing resource constraints, and fostering collaboration, this paradigm empowers edge devices to contribute to model training without sacrificing individual privacy. As federated learning continues to evolve, it has the potential to redefine the landscape of AI deployment, enabling a future where intelligent applications seamlessly coexist with edge devices while respecting privacy and harnessing collective intelligence.
23.4 Real-time Object Detection on Resource-constrained Devices: Deploying real-time object detection on resource-constrained devices represents a fascinating intersection of deep learning and edge computing. This chapter delves into the intricacies and methodologies of achieving swift and accurate object detection in such challenging environments.
Real-time Object Detection: A Complex Challenge: Real-time object detection finds applications across domains such as surveillance, autonomous vehicles, and robotics. Edge environments, characterized by limited resources, require intelligent solutions that balance accuracy and efficiency.
Strategies for Real-time Object Detection:
Single Shot Multibox Detector (SSD): SSD is renowned for its speed and accuracy. It employs a series of convolutional layers to predict object classes and bounding boxes at various scales within a single forward pass.
You Only Look Once (YOLO): YOLO's strength lies in its ability to detect objects in real-time by dividing the image into a grid and predicting objects' attributes within each grid cell.
Quantization and Pruning: Quantization reduces model size by converting high-precision weights to lower-bit representations, conserving memory and computational power.
Pruning for Efficiency: Pruning identifies and removes redundant connections, optimizing the model for resource-constrained devices.
Transfer Learning:
Leveraging Pretrained Models: Transfer learning accelerates model training by utilizing pre-trained models on large datasets. Fine-tuning these models on specific object detection tasks boosts efficiency.
One-shot Learning: One-shot learning explores object detection with minimal training data, ideal for resource-constrained settings where data acquisition is limited.

23.5 Project

Unsolved Project

Suppose you're working on a project that involves deploying deep learning models on edge devices and IoT systems. To ensure your project is successful, you need to understand the challenges of deploying deep learning on edge, efficient model compression and quantization techniques, federated learning in distributed edge environments, and real-time object detection on resource-constrained devices. Before starting, research the following: the specific challenges faced when deploying deep learning models on edge devices, techniques for compressing and quantizing models to make them efficient for edge deployment, the principles and applications of federated learning in environments where data is distributed across many devices, and methods for implementing real-time object detection on devices with limited computational resources. This foundational knowledge will help you develop a robust project that addresses the complexities of integrating deep learning with edge devices and IoT systems.

23.6 Lab Activity

Unsolved Lab Activity

Implement a basic deep learning model and deploy it on an edge device (e.g., Raspberry Pi). Evaluate the performance and identify the key challenges faced during deployment.
Task: Use a deep learning framework to implement a basic model (e.g., a simple CNN for image classification) and deploy it on an edge device like a Raspberry Pi. Document the deployment process, including model optimization, setup, and performance evaluation. Identify the key challenges encountered and suggest improvements.

Exercises

Exercise 1 – Multiple Choice Questions

1. What are some of the challenges associated with deploying deep learning models on edge devices?
   a. High computational power
   b. Unlimited memory capacity
   c. Data privacy concerns
   d. Abundant energy resources

2. Why is reducing latency important when deploying deep learning on edge devices?
   a. To save energy
   b. To improve model accuracy
   c. To meet resource constraints
   d. To achieve real-time or low-latency responses

3. What is the primary goal of model compression techniques for edge devices?
   a. Increasing model complexity
   b. Reducing resource constraints
   c. Expanding battery life
   d. Streamlining model size

4. What is the process of converting high-precision numerical values to lower-bit representations to save memory and computational power?
   a. Pruning
   b. Quantization
   c. Distillation
   d. Knowledge transfer

5. Which technique involves training a smaller model to replicate the behavior of a larger, complex model to create a compact yet proficient model?
   a. Pruning
   b. Quantization
   c. Distillation
   d. Knowledge transfer

Exercise 2 – True/False

1. Efficient model compression and quantization are essential techniques for optimizing deep learning models for edge devices.
2. Federated learning is not applicable in distributed edge environments.
3. Real-time object detection is achievable on resource-constrained devices using advanced optimization techniques.

Review Questions

1. What are some examples of edge devices mentioned in the chapter?
2. What are the fundamental challenges when deploying deep learning models on edge devices?
3. Why is resource optimization essential when deploying deep learning on the edge?
4. How does deploying deep learning models directly on edge devices help reduce latency?
5. What is the significance of efficient model compression and quantization for edge computing?

Answers

Exercise 1- 1.c 2.d 3.d 4.b 5.c
Exercise 2- 1) True, 2) False, 3) True

Online Resources

Online Exam Paper:
Link: https://forms.gle/vYhAkzvfVPnrwqVEA
QR Code:

Chapter 23 Videos Playlist:
Link: https://www.youtube.com/playlist?list=PLzlh_31VWEFpmzNKd0azl459J43wkukzP
QR Code:

Chapter 24: Adaptive Learning and Lifelong Learning

24.1 Catastrophic Forgetting and Its Implications: Catastrophic forgetting, a phenomenon observed in neural networks, refers to the tendency of a model to completely forget previously learned information when trained on new, unrelated data. This issue poses significant challenges for lifelong or continual learning scenarios where a model is expected to accumulate knowledge over time without erasing its previous learning experiences. In this section, we delve into the concept of catastrophic forgetting, its causes, and its implications.

24.1.1 Understanding Catastrophic Forgetting: Catastrophic forgetting occurs due to the plasticity of neural networks. When a model is trained on new data, the updates to its weights and parameters can lead to a drastic overwriting of previously learned representations. This can result in the model losing the ability to perform well on tasks it was proficient at before the new training phase.

24.1.2 Causes of Catastrophic Forgetting: One primary cause of catastrophic forgetting is the optimization process used during training, such as stochastic gradient descent (SGD). SGD aims to minimize the loss function on the current task, which can lead to the model drifting away from the optimal solution for past tasks. Additionally, the limited capacity of neural networks can exacerbate forgetting, as the model may have to allocate resources to new tasks at the expense of old ones.

24.1.3 Implications for Continual Learning: Catastrophic forgetting, a phenomenon inherent to neural networks, has significant implications in scenarios involving continual learning. Continual learning refers to the ability of a model to learn from a stream of data over its operational lifetime while retaining knowledge from previously encountered tasks. This capability is crucial in various real-world applications, including autonomous systems, language translation, and medical diagnosis.

In autonomous systems, such as self-driving cars and drones, models need to adapt to new environments and situations they encounter. For instance, an autonomous vehicle should be able to learn from new traffic patterns or road conditions without erasing its past knowledge about driving rules and behaviors. Catastrophic forgetting could cause the vehicle to lose its ability to navigate previously learned routes effectively, compromising safety and reliability.

In the context of language translation, a model might be trained to translate multiple languages. When exposed to new languages, the model should be able to incorporate this knowledge without undermining its proficiency in translating the languages it already learned. Catastrophic forgetting here could lead to incorrect translations in previously mastered languages, which would be undesirable for communication and information dissemination.

Similarly, in the field of medical diagnosis, deep learning models may need to continually learn from new patient data or medical research findings. A model that forgets past medical conditions or symptoms could provide inaccurate diagnoses or treatment recommendations. This could have serious consequences for patient care and safety.

The implications of catastrophic forgetting can be summarized as follows:

Diminished Performance: As the model forgets past knowledge, its performance on tasks it previously excelled at can degrade. This can result in inaccurate predictions, translations, or diagnoses, affecting the overall quality of the system's output.

Reliability Concerns: Models that suffer from catastrophic forgetting may not be dependable in critical situations. For instance, an autonomous vehicle suddenly forgetting its handling of certain road conditions could lead to accidents.

Safety Risks: In safety-critical applications, such as medical diagnosis or autonomous driving, forgetting important information could jeopardize human lives. An incorrect diagnosis or a driving mistake due to forgotten knowledge could have severe consequences.

24.1.4 Mitigation Strategies: Addressing catastrophic forgetting is crucial to ensure the viability and reliability of models in continual learning scenarios. Researchers have proposed several strategies to mitigate this phenomenon and allow models to learn sequentially without compromising their previous knowledge.

Regularization Techniques: Regularization methods, such as Elastic Weight Consolidation (EWC) and Learning without Forgetting (LwF), introduce additional terms into the loss function during training. These terms penalize changes to important parameters learned in previous tasks. By doing so, these techniques encourage the model to preserve its knowledge while adapting to new tasks. The model strikes a balance between learning new information and retaining its prior knowledge.

Replay and Experience Replay: Replay methods involve periodically exposing the model to previously encountered data, effectively allowing it to "replay" past experiences. This refreshes the model's memory of earlier tasks and helps prevent forgetting. Experience replay, commonly used in reinforcement learning, involves storing a buffer of past experiences. During new tasks, the model learns from this buffer in addition to the new data. Both approaches ensure that the model continues to learn from its history.

Architectural Approaches: Architectural solutions focus on designing neural network architectures that can accommodate continual learning without forgetting. Progressive neural networks and neural episodic control are examples of such approaches. Progressive neural networks involve expanding the network's capacity as new tasks are encountered. Neural episodic control involves periodically storing episodes of past experiences and replaying them during training to prevent forgetting.

Transfer Learning and Knowledge Distillation: Transfer learning and knowledge distillation are techniques that leverage knowledge from old tasks to aid in learning new tasks. In transfer learning, a pre-trained model's knowledge is fine-tuned for new tasks while preserving its foundational knowledge. Knowledge distillation involves using a pre-trained model as a "teacher" to guide the learning of a new model, enabling the transfer of knowledge between models.

By employing these mitigation strategies, researchers aim to address the challenges posed by catastrophic forgetting in continual learning scenarios. These strategies ensure that models can adapt to new information while maintaining their ability to perform well on previously learned tasks, thus improving performance, reliability, and safety in applications across various domains.

24.1.5 Future Directions: As the field of deep learning continues to advance, addressing catastrophic forgetting remains a central focus of research due to its critical implications for building adaptive and intelligent AI systems. The development of models that can learn continuously from a stream of data while retaining past knowledge is essential for the progression of AI systems capable of effectively adapting to dynamic environments and evolving tasks. Several future directions and challenges are worth exploring in this context:

Dynamic Task Allocation and Prioritization: Future research might delve into creating models that can dynamically allocate resources to different tasks based on their importance or relevance. This would involve designing mechanisms that enable the model to decide when to devote more learning capacity to a new task while still preserving essential knowledge from previous tasks.

Meta-Learning for Catastrophic Forgetting: Meta-learning involves training models to learn how to learn efficiently across different tasks. Researchers could focus on developing meta-learning algorithms that explicitly tackle the problem of catastrophic forgetting. These algorithms could guide models to retain crucial knowledge even when learning new tasks rapidly.

Interdisciplinary Collaboration: The challenge of catastrophic forgetting extends beyond computer science and deep learning. Collaborations with cognitive science and neuroscience could yield insights into how humans manage to learn new information while retaining old knowledge. Such interdisciplinary efforts could inspire innovative strategies for addressing catastrophic forgetting in AI systems.

Online and Incremental Learning: Online learning involves training models in real time as new data arrives, and incremental learning entails updating models incrementally as new tasks appear. Research might focus on devising approaches that integrate these paradigms while combating catastrophic forgetting. This could involve designing model architectures, loss functions, and training strategies tailored for online and incremental learning.

Ethical and Legal Considerations: AI systems that continually learn and adapt raise ethical concerns. Models that forget important information could potentially make biased or discriminatory decisions due to insufficient training on certain aspects. Research could investigate ways to ensure ethical behavior, transparency, and accountability in models that learn over time.

Benchmarking and Evaluation: Developing standardized benchmarks and evaluation metrics specifically designed to assess models' ability to mitigate catastrophic forgetting will be important. These benchmarks would aid in objectively comparing different mitigation strategies and identifying their strengths and weaknesses.

Real-world Applications: Future research should emphasize applying mitigation strategies for catastrophic forgetting to real-world applications. Validating these strategies in contexts like healthcare, autonomous systems, and financial analysis will demonstrate their practical effectiveness and help deploy more reliable AI systems.

24.2 Continual Learning Strategies and Techniques: Continual learning, the process of enabling models to learn sequentially from a stream of data without forgetting previous knowledge, is a fundamental challenge in deep learning. In this section, we explore various strategies and techniques that researchers have developed to tackle the issue of catastrophic forgetting and facilitate effective continual learning.

24.2.1 Elastic Weight Consolidation (EWC): Elastic Weight Consolidation (EWC) stands as a powerful tool within the realm of continual learning, targeting the challenge of catastrophic forgetting. As neural networks adapt to new tasks, they tend to overwrite previously learned information, leading to degradation in performance on prior tasks. EWC seeks to counteract this phenomenon by introducing an innovative regularization approach.

Concept and Mechanism: EWC introduces a penalty term into the loss function used during training. This term penalizes changes to the model's parameters that were critical for performing well on previous tasks. The idea is to discourage the model from drifting too far away from its previous knowledge while adapting to new tasks. This penalty encourages the model to strike a balance between optimizing for the new task and retaining crucial information from previous tasks.

Parameter Importance and Sensitivity: EWC calculates the importance of each parameter by assessing its sensitivity to the loss function concerning the model's parameters learned in previous tasks. Parameters that had a greater impact on previous tasks are considered more important. By assigning higher importance values to these parameters, EWC ensures that they are protected from drastic changes during training on new tasks.

Balancing Adaptation and Retention: The magic of EWC lies in its ability to balance adaptation and retention. The model remains flexible enough to adapt to new tasks, but it does so while being mindful of the knowledge it has accumulated. The penalty on critical parameters acts as a safeguard against erasing valuable insights from past tasks.

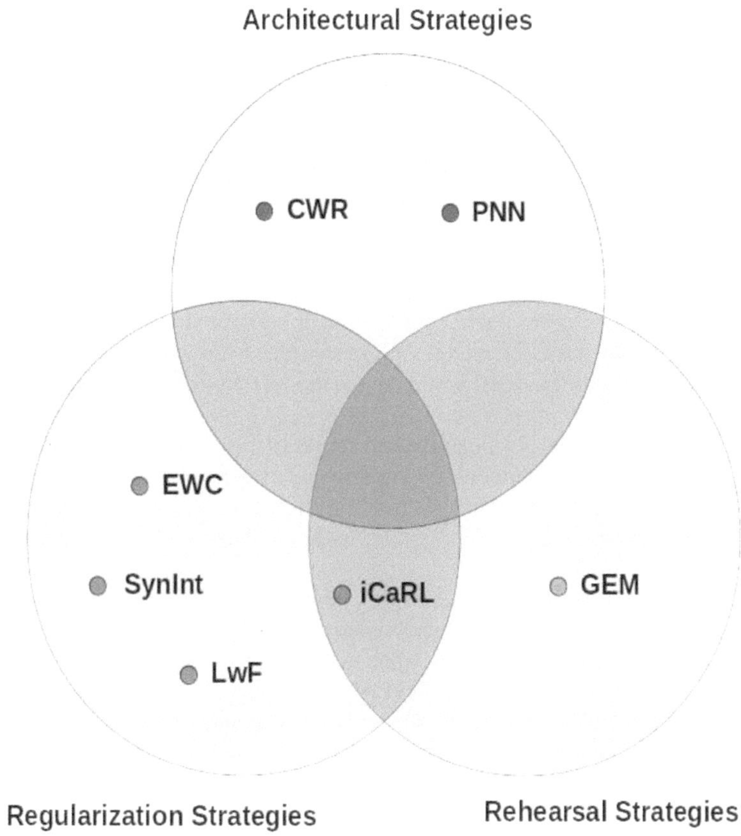

24.2.2 Learning without Forgetting (LwF): Learning without Forgetting (LwF) is a regularization technique with a focus on continual learning scenarios. It addresses the challenge of catastrophic forgetting by leveraging the concept of distillation. Distillation involves transferring knowledge from a pre-trained model (referred to as the "teacher") to a new model (the "student") that is learning a new task.

Distillation: Knowledge Transfer: In LwF, the teacher model guides the learning process of the student model. Specifically, as the student learns to predict the labels for the current task, it also aims to mimic the teacher's predictions on previously learned tasks. This two-fold learning process ensures that the student not only adapts to the new task but also maintains its understanding of previous tasks.

Retaining Past Knowledge: LwF excels at retaining past knowledge. By mimicking the teacher's predictions, the student model effectively transfers insights gained from previous tasks. This mechanism mitigates the risk of forgetting, as the student continually reinforces its understanding of earlier tasks.

Benefits of LwF: Learning without Forgetting offers several benefits. It provides a framework for continual learning where models can sequentially acquire new skills without compromising previously acquired skills. Additionally, LwF does not require access to the original data from previous tasks, making it practical for scenarios where data retention is limited.

Adapting to New Tasks: When confronted with a new task, the student model learns not only from the new data but also from the distilled knowledge of the teacher. This enables the student to adapt more efficiently, utilizing its broader understanding of related tasks.

both Elastic Weight Consolidation (EWC) and Learning without Forgetting (LwF) stand as powerful techniques in the arsenal of continual learning strategies. EWC focuses on preserving critical parameters and balancing adaptation and retention, while LwF leverages distillation to transfer knowledge and maintain a cohesive understanding of past tasks. As the field of deep learning progresses, these techniques contribute to the development of AI systems that can learn continuously and adapt to an ever-changing landscape of tasks and information.

24.2.3 Progressive Neural Networks: Progressive Neural Networks (ProgNNs) represent an innovative approach to mitigating catastrophic forgetting by enabling the model to expand its capacity as it encounters new tasks. Traditional neural networks typically employ a fixed architecture, which can lead to the overwriting of previously acquired knowledge during training on new tasks. ProgNNs address this by dynamically growing the architecture to accommodate additional tasks.

Dynamic Architecture Expansion: In the context of ProgNNs, each new task corresponds to the addition of new neurons or layers to the existing neural network. These new neurons or layers form a task-specific module dedicated to the new task. Consequently, the model's architecture becomes progressively more complex as it accumulates tasks.

Isolation of Knowledge: One of the key features of ProgNNs is the isolation of knowledge. Each task-specific module retains the knowledge acquired during training on its associated task. Since the architecture expands for each task, the knowledge from earlier tasks is compartmentalized and protected from interference during subsequent training.
Transferring Knowledge: Despite the isolation of knowledge, ProgNNs allow for the transfer of knowledge between tasks. While new modules are added to accommodate new tasks, the connections between modules enable information sharing. This transfer mechanism ensures that the model benefits from insights gained across tasks without suffering from catastrophic forgetting.
24.2.4 Experience Replay: Experience replay is a technique commonly employed in reinforcement learning contexts but finds relevance in continual learning scenarios as well. It addresses the challenge of catastrophic forgetting by reintroducing past experiences during the training of new tasks.
Storing Past Experiences: In experience replay, the model maintains a buffer of past experiences, which includes samples from previous tasks. This buffer serves as a reservoir of knowledge that the model can draw from during training on new tasks.
Knowledge Retention: When training on a new task, the model replays samples from the buffer alongside the new task's data. By learning from the historical experiences in addition to the new data, the model retains knowledge about past tasks, preventing catastrophic forgetting.
Limited Data Access: Experience replay is particularly valuable when access to the original data from previous tasks is limited. Instead of relying solely on the available new data, the model can tap into its buffer to reinforce its understanding of past tasks.
Reinforcement Learning Context: While experience replay has been prominently used in reinforcement learning to stabilize learning and improve sample efficiency, its application in continual learning showcases its versatility and effectiveness in addressing the challenges posed by catastrophic forgetting.
both Progressive Neural Networks (ProgNNs) and Experience Replay contribute significantly to the arsenal of strategies for continual learning. ProgNNs' dynamic architecture expansion and isolation of knowledge allow models to adapt to new tasks without erasing old knowledge. Experience replay, on the other hand, capitalizes on the power of historical experiences to enhance knowledge retention when learning new tasks. As the field advances, these techniques play a pivotal role in creating AI systems that can learn continuously and adapt seamlessly to the evolving demands of diverse tasks.
24.2.5 Dynamic Architectures: Dynamic architecture approaches stand as a remarkable solution to the challenge of catastrophic forgetting, emphasizing adaptability to new tasks by evolving the neural network's structure. One noteworthy example is Neural Episodic Control (NEC), a strategy that leverages an episodic memory mechanism to effectively combat forgetting.
Episodic Memory Mechanism: In NEC, the model maintains an episodic memory where it stores episodes of past experiences. An episode typically consists of a sequence of inputs and corresponding outputs from previous tasks. During training on a new task, the model replays episodes from the memory alongside new data. This mechanism enables the model to re-encounter and learn from its historical experiences.
Recalling and Reusing Old Experiences: The power of NEC lies in its ability to recall and reuse old experiences. By revisiting episodes stored in its memory, the model refreshes its understanding of past tasks and reinforces its knowledge. This ensures that previous insights are not lost but rather incorporated into the learning process of new tasks.
24.2.6 Generative Replay: Generative replay emerges as an innovative approach to continual learning, particularly in scenarios where access to original data from previous tasks is limited. This technique involves harnessing the capabilities of generative models, such as Generative Adversarial Networks (GANs), to create synthetic data that resembles past tasks.
Creating Synthetic Data: Generative replay involves training a GAN to generate data samples that resemble those encountered during past tasks. These synthetic samples are mixed with new data from the current task during training. This combined dataset, comprising real and synthetic data, enriches the learning experience of the model.
Preventing Catastrophic Forgetting: Generative replay operates on the principle that exposing the model to a mix of real and synthetic data helps prevent catastrophic forgetting. By revisiting and learning from past experiences through synthetic data, the model retains its understanding of previous tasks, contributing to improved knowledge retention.
24.2.7 Hybrid Methods: Addressing catastrophic forgetting often involves the synergistic integration of multiple strategies. Hybrid methods combine different techniques to create a comprehensive approach that effectively mitigates the phenomenon.
Complementary Strategies: For example, a hybrid approach could combine regularization techniques like Elastic Weight Consolidation (EWC) with experience replay. This combination benefits from the strengths of each technique—regularization for preserving important parameters and experience replay for knowledge retention—and addresses the issue from multiple angles.
24.2.8 Meta-Learning: Meta-learning, or learning to learn, introduces a novel paradigm in the context of continual learning. This approach involves training models on a diverse range of tasks to acquire a generalized learning ability that can be efficiently applied to new tasks.
Broad Generalization: By exposing models to various tasks during training, meta-learning equips them with a broader understanding of different problem domains. This generalized knowledge enables models to adapt quickly and effectively to new tasks while minimizing the risk of catastrophic forgetting.
Transferable Knowledge: Meta-learning is built on the premise that knowledge acquired from one task can be transferred to another. This transferability enables models to leverage insights from past tasks to facilitate learning on new ones, thereby enhancing knowledge retention and adaptability.

the strategies and techniques within the realm of continual learning encompass a spectrum of innovative approaches. Dynamic architectures adapt neural networks to new tasks, episodic memory mechanisms like Neural Episodic Control (NEC) allow models to recall past experiences, and generative replay leverages synthetic data to prevent forgetting. Hybrid methods synergize diverse strategies, and meta-learning introduces a broader understanding that aids rapid adaptation. As research advances, these techniques collectively contribute to the development of AI systems capable of seamless and effective learning in dynamic environments.

24.2.9 Task Prioritization and Scheduling: Task prioritization and scheduling serve as strategic approaches within the realm of continual learning, offering models the ability to manage their learning process effectively. These strategies involve making intelligent decisions about when to learn new tasks and when to revisit old ones, with the overarching goal of mitigating catastrophic forgetting while efficiently adapting to changing demands.

Adapting to Evolving Requirements: In many real-world scenarios, the importance of different tasks can vary over time. Some tasks might remain crucial, while others might lose significance or relevance. Task prioritization and scheduling aim to adapt to evolving requirements by making informed decisions about how much focus to allocate to each task.

Preventing Catastrophic Forgetting: By strategically revisiting and retraining on older tasks, models can prevent catastrophic forgetting. This involves scheduling periodic updates on previous tasks, ensuring that the knowledge accumulated remains fresh and intact, even as the model learns new tasks.

Balancing Learning and Retention: The essence of task prioritization and scheduling lies in striking a balance between learning new tasks and retaining knowledge from previous ones. This balance ensures that the model remains adaptable to new information without losing its proficiency in previously learned tasks.

Importance-Driven Learning: One approach to task prioritization involves assigning importance weights to different tasks. These weights guide the model in deciding how much emphasis to place on each task during training. Tasks deemed more important receive greater attention, helping the model retain its understanding of critical information.

Adaptive Scheduling: Adaptive scheduling involves dynamically adjusting the frequency of learning updates for different tasks based on their current relevance. This approach allows the model to dedicate more resources to tasks that are currently important, while revisiting less crucial tasks less frequently.

Long-Term Knowledge Retention: An effective task prioritization and scheduling strategy aims to ensure long-term knowledge retention. By preventing catastrophic forgetting and consistently updating knowledge, the model maintains its ability to perform well on a wide range of tasks over extended periods.

task prioritization and scheduling strategies offer a nuanced approach to continual learning, enabling models to navigate the complex landscape of tasks and knowledge retention. By intelligently managing the allocation of resources and determining when to learn new tasks and revisit old ones, these strategies contribute to the creation of AI systems that can learn continuously and adapt to changing requirements while preventing the erosion of critical knowledge.

24.3 Elastic Weight Consolidation and Synaptic Intelligence: Continual learning poses a significant challenge in the field of deep learning, with the threat of catastrophic forgetting looming over models as they adapt to new tasks. In this section, we delve into two advanced techniques, Elastic Weight Consolidation (EWC) and Synaptic Intelligence that address this challenge by preserving past knowledge and ensuring the seamless acquisition of new skills.

24.3.1 Elastic Weight Consolidation (EWC): Balancing Adaptation and Retention: Elastic Weight Consolidation (EWC) has emerged as a powerful technique in the realm of continual learning, addressing the challenge of catastrophic forgetting. At its core, EWC introduces a regularization mechanism that delicately balances the adaptation to new tasks while retaining valuable insights from previously learned tasks.

Understanding Catastrophic Forgetting: Catastrophic forgetting occurs when a neural network's training on a new task leads to a significant degradation of its performance on previously learned tasks. This phenomenon is especially problematic when a model needs to learn sequentially from a stream of tasks, as it can result in the loss of accumulated knowledge.

The Role of EWC: EWC acts as a safeguard against catastrophic forgetting. It does so by penalizing significant changes to the parameters that are crucial for performing well on previously learned tasks. This penalty is incorporated into the loss function during training on new tasks, guiding the model to adapt without forsaking its earlier knowledge.

Balancing Adaptation and Retention: One of EWC's core achievements lies in its ability to balance adaptation and retention. When learning a new task, the model naturally updates its parameters to fit the new data distribution. However, EWC ensures that this adaptation doesn't come at the cost of losing knowledge from earlier tasks.

Introducing the Penalty Term: EWC introduces a penalty term in the loss function. This term discourages the model from making drastic changes to parameters that had significant importance for performing well on previous tasks. By penalizing large parameter changes, EWC effectively mandates that the model retain a degree of consistency with its earlier knowledge.

Parameter Importance and Sensitivity: Crucially, EWC doesn't treat all parameters equally. It goes beyond a uniform approach by considering the importance of each parameter for the model's performance on previous tasks. The importance of a parameter is determined by its sensitivity to the loss function with respect to the model's previous parameters.

Protecting Important Parameters: Parameters that were found to have a substantial impact on the performance of past tasks are considered important. These parameters receive a higher level of protection during training on new tasks. This protection prevents the model from making drastic modifications to parameters that hold valuable knowledge.

Preserving Valuable Insights: In essence, EWC strives to prevent the undue erosion of valuable insights gained from previous tasks. By encouraging the model to maintain a certain level of fidelity to its original parameter values, EWC ensures that the knowledge obtained through previous learning experiences remains intact and applicable even as the model continues to learn and adapt.

Elastic Weight Consolidation (EWC) exemplifies a sophisticated technique for achieving effective continual learning. By striking a careful balance between adaptation and retention, EWC introduces a penalty mechanism that protects important parameters from being overwritten during training on new tasks. This strategy helps prevent catastrophic forgetting and contributes to the creation of AI systems that can continuously learn and adapt while retaining a diverse spectrum of knowledge.

24.3.2 Synaptic Intelligence: Dynamically Retained Parameters and Task-Specific Plasticity: Synaptic Intelligence emerges as a nuanced approach to addressing the challenge of catastrophic forgetting, building upon the foundational principles of Elastic Weight Consolidation (EWC). While EWC aims to preserve knowledge by penalizing significant parameter changes, Synaptic Intelligence introduces a more fine-grained strategy to achieve this goal.

The Challenge of Catastrophic Forgetting: Catastrophic forgetting is a critical concern in continual learning. As models learn new tasks, there's a risk that they may overwrite or compromise the knowledge they have accumulated from previous tasks. Synaptic Intelligence offers a solution by selectively preserving the parameters critical for maintaining this knowledge.

Dynamically Retained Parameters: At the heart of Synaptic Intelligence lies the concept of dynamically retained parameters. Instead of treating all parameters uniformly, this technique identifies a subset of important parameters for each task. These parameters are vital for preserving knowledge relevant to that task. The crucial insight here is that not all parameters contribute equally to a task's performance, and therefore, not all need the same level of protection.

Tailored Protection for Knowledge: The identified important parameters are given special treatment during training on new tasks. They are shielded from significant modifications, ensuring that the knowledge crucial for previous tasks remains intact. By dynamically retaining these parameters, Synaptic Intelligence addresses the challenge of preserving knowledge without hindering adaptation.

Task-Specific Plasticity: A noteworthy aspect of Synaptic Intelligence is the concept of task-specific plasticity. Parameters that aren't deemed crucial for past tasks are allowed to undergo more substantial changes. This acknowledges that certain parameters are more adaptable and can be modified without posing a risk to the model's overall performance.

The Role of Adaptive Strategies: Synaptic Intelligence underscores the importance of adopting adaptive strategies in continual learning. By dynamically adjusting the level of protection for different parameters based on their relevance, the technique ensures that the model strikes an optimal balance between adaptation to new tasks and retention of valuable insights.

24.3.3 A Unifying Goal: Preserving Knowledge and Acquiring Skills: Both Elastic Weight Consolidation (EWC) and Synaptic Intelligence share a fundamental goal: preserving past knowledge while allowing models to acquire new skills. These techniques exemplify innovative approaches to addressing catastrophic forgetting in the context of continual learning scenarios.

24.3.4 Synergies and Future Directions: Harnessing Strengths for Robust Solutions: The synergy between Elastic Weight Consolidation (EWC) and Synaptic Intelligence is evident. Researchers are actively exploring the fusion of these advanced techniques to harness their strengths for even more robust solutions to the challenges of continual learning. This integration aims to provide models with a comprehensive toolkit to tackle the complexities of retaining knowledge and adapting to new tasks.

24.3.5 Towards Human-Level Continual Learning: Adaptive and Evolving Systems: Elastic Weight Consolidation and Synaptic Intelligence represent significant strides towards achieving human-level continual learning. As research advances, these techniques pave the way for AI systems that can continually adapt to evolving tasks, closely mirroring the adaptive capabilities of the human brain. This aligns with the overarching goal of creating intelligent systems that can navigate an ever-changing landscape of information and tasks.

24.4 Building AI Systems that Continuously Improve: The journey towards building AI systems that can continuously improve and adapt to new challenges is marked by a convergence of cutting-edge techniques, innovative strategies, and a deep understanding of the intricacies of continual learning. In this section, we explore the pathways that lead to the creation of AI systems capable of not only acquiring new skills but also refining and expanding their knowledge base over time.

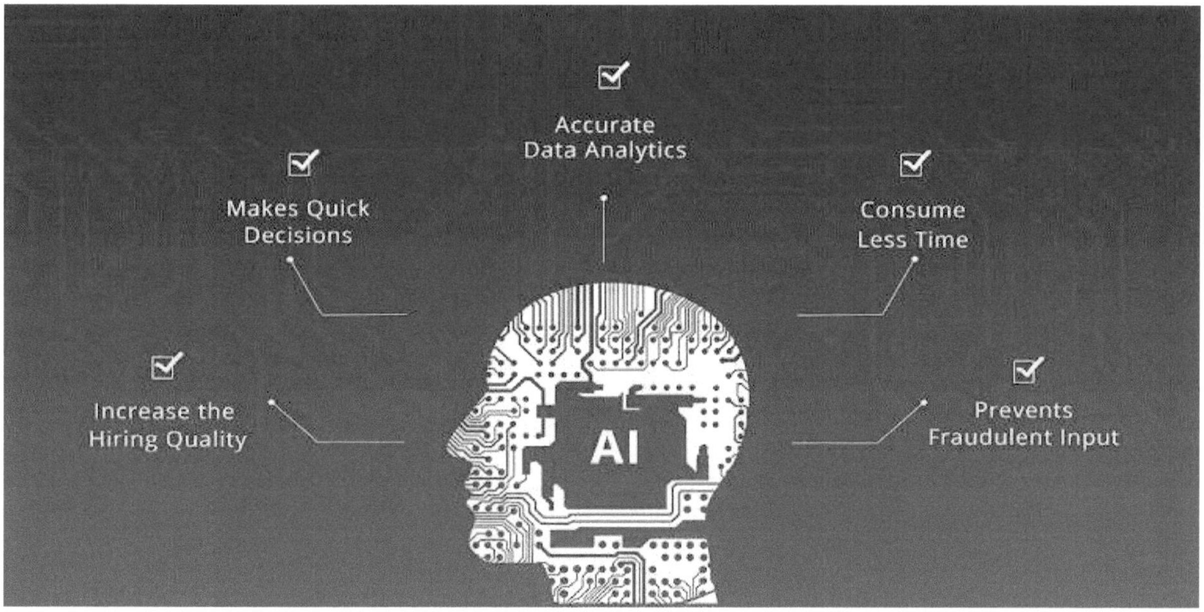

24.4.1 Harnessing the Power of Continual Learning: The aspiration to build AI systems that continually improve is deeply rooted in the concept of continual learning. This paradigm challenges the traditional assumption that a model's learning process concludes after its initial training phase. Instead, continual learning recognizes that the acquisition of knowledge is an ongoing journey that extends throughout the system's operational lifetime. By adopting this perspective, AI systems gain the capacity to evolve in synchrony with the ever-shifting landscape of tasks and information.

A Paradigm Shift: Continual learning represents a paradigm shift from the static notion of AI models as "trained and fixed" entities. It acknowledges that the world is not static, and the challenges AI systems encounter are not isolated. Instead, they exist in a dynamic environment where new tasks, data, and insights constantly emerge.

Adaptive and Agile Evolution: By embracing the notion of continual learning, AI systems become adaptive and agile. They don't merely operate as static models but evolve over time, continuously acquiring new skills and refining existing ones. This evolution aligns AI systems more closely with human learning, where knowledge is built upon and expanded throughout a person's life.

Meeting the Challenge of Complexity: As tasks become more complex and interconnected, the ability of AI systems to continuously improve becomes increasingly valuable. Such systems can navigate intricate tasks, leverage insights across domains, and seamlessly adapt to new challenges without losing their grasp on previously acquired knowledge.

24.4.2 Beyond Catastrophic Forgetting: Retaining and Expanding Knowledge: Central to the pursuit of AI systems that continually improve is overcoming the challenge of catastrophic forgetting. Catastrophic forgetting occurs when models learn new tasks, causing them to forget or overwrite valuable knowledge from previous tasks. Addressing this challenge is fundamental to creating AI systems that can build upon their knowledge over time.

Innovations: Elastic Weight Consolidation and Synaptic Intelligence: In response to catastrophic forgetting, innovative techniques like Elastic Weight Consolidation (EWC) and Synaptic Intelligence have emerged. These techniques offer a safeguard against the erosion of past knowledge during the learning of new tasks.

Elastic Weight Consolidation (EWC): Elastic Weight Consolidation introduces a penalty mechanism that discourages significant parameter changes crucial for earlier tasks. By maintaining a balance between adaptation to new tasks and retention of valuable insights, EWC ensures that AI systems do not lose their grasp on knowledge.

Synaptic Intelligence: Synaptic Intelligence takes a nuanced approach by dynamically retaining parameters that are critical for knowledge preservation. It identifies task-specific important parameters and allows other parameters to undergo more substantial changes. This method acknowledges that not all parameters require the same level of protection.

The Foundation for Continuous Improvement: The strategies of EWC and Synaptic Intelligence serve as the foundation for continuous improvement in AI systems. They empower these systems to learn new skills without compromising the knowledge they have gained from previous tasks, setting the stage for a future where AI continually evolves to tackle a diverse array of challenges.

the journey towards AI systems that continually improve is anchored in the principles of continual learning and the prevention of catastrophic forgetting. By recognizing that learning is an ongoing process and developing techniques that retain and expand knowledge, researchers and engineers pave the way for AI systems that can adapt, evolve, and excel in a world of dynamic tasks and information.

24.4.3 The Dynamic Learning Loop: The concept of a dynamic learning loop underpins the process of continuous improvement. AI systems engage in a cyclic journey of learning, adapting, and refining. This loop begins with the acquisition of new knowledge, followed by its integration into the existing knowledge base. As new tasks arise, the system adapts while ensuring the retention of past insights.

24.4.4 Incorporating Multi-Modal Learning: To truly achieve continuous improvement, AI systems must embrace the concept of multi-modal learning. This entails learning from a diverse array of data sources that encompass various modalities, such as text, images, audio, video, and more. By expanding its learning scope beyond a single data type, an AI system gains a deeper and more holistic understanding of tasks, thereby fostering a comprehensive knowledge base.

Diverse Perspectives: Multi-modal learning allows AI systems to view tasks from different perspectives. For instance, understanding spoken language involves not only analyzing the words but also recognizing tone, intonation, and emotions conveyed through audio. By combining these cues with visual information from images or videos, the AI system can achieve a more nuanced interpretation of the task at hand.

Enriching Learning Representations: Each modality carries unique information, and by fusing them, AI systems can enrich their learning representations. For instance, learning to identify objects in images becomes more robust when the system can simultaneously process textual descriptions or spoken context related to those objects.

Tackling Complex Challenges: Multi-modal learning equips AI systems to tackle complex and multifaceted challenges. Consider an AI system for medical diagnosis. By analyzing patient records (text), medical images (visual), and potentially audio data (patient history), the system gains a comprehensive view of a patient's health, leading to more accurate and holistic diagnostic decisions.

24.4.5 Active Learning and Task Selection: At the heart of the vision for AI systems that continually improve lies the concept of active learning and task selection. These strategies empower AI systems to autonomously decide which tasks to learn and when, thereby striking a balance between adapting to new challenges and preserving valuable knowledge.

Autonomous Task Selection: In the context of active learning, AI systems take on a proactive role in deciding which tasks to engage with. Rather than passively receiving tasks, the system actively evaluates its current knowledge and selects tasks that align with its learning objectives.

Balancing Adaptation and Retention: Active learning and task selection are powerful tools for balancing adaptation and retention. The system intelligently selects tasks that provide opportunities for learning new skills while also strategically revisiting tasks that reinforce previously acquired knowledge.

Adapting to Changing Contexts: By autonomously selecting tasks, AI systems demonstrate a capacity to adapt to changing contexts. Just as humans prioritize learning based on personal goals and needs, AI systems can dynamically shift their focus to tasks that align with current requirements and objectives.

Preserving Foundational Knowledge: The significance of active learning and task selection lies in their ability to preserve foundational knowledge. By strategically engaging with tasks that reinforce core concepts, the system ensures that valuable insights from the past remain intact, even as it acquires new skills.

incorporating multi-modal learning and implementing active learning and task selection strategies are pivotal steps in building AI systems that continually improve. Multi-modal learning enriches the learning process by providing diverse perspectives and tackling complex challenges, while active learning and task selection empower systems to autonomously adapt, evolve, and strike a harmonious balance between adaptation and knowledge retention. These strategies bring us closer to the realization of AI systems that can seamlessly navigate the dynamic landscape of tasks and information, continually enhancing their capabilities over time.

24.4.6 Meta-Learning: Learning to Learn: The concept of meta-learning, also known as learning to learn, represents a transformative approach in the pursuit of AI systems that continually improve. Meta-learning is based on the idea that AI models can develop a generalized learning ability by training on a diverse range of tasks. This acquired ability enables the models to rapidly adapt to new tasks while mitigating the impact of catastrophic forgetting.

Training for Generalization: In meta-learning, AI models are exposed to a multitude of tasks during their training phase. This exposure fosters a higher-level understanding of underlying patterns and relationships across different tasks. As a result, the model becomes adept at generalizing from its prior experiences, allowing it to quickly grasp the essence of new tasks.

Rapid Adaptation and Minimized Forgetting: The transformative power of meta-learning lies in its ability to enable rapid adaptation to new tasks. When faced with a novel challenge, the meta-learned model leverages the insights it has gained from diverse tasks to quickly acquire new skills. Importantly, this adaptive process minimizes the risk of catastrophic forgetting, as the model draws upon its generalized knowledge to retain key insights from previous tasks.

24.4.7 Lifelong Learning and Human-Like Adaptation: The ultimate aspiration in the pursuit of AI systems that continually improve is to attain a level of lifelong learning that mirrors human adaptability. Just as humans continually acquire, retain, and build upon knowledge throughout their lives, AI systems should possess the capacity to seamlessly integrate new skills into their existing repertoire.

Lifelong Learning Paradigm: Lifelong learning represents a paradigm shift in AI. Instead of distinct learning phases, the system undergoes a continuous process of growth and adaptation. This approach mimics the way humans accumulate knowledge over time, creating an ecosystem of learning that continually enriches the system's capabilities.

Human-Like Adaptation: The aspiration for human-like adaptation is rooted in the understanding that humans excel not only at learning new skills but also at retaining and applying their existing knowledge. AI systems that emulate this process can transcend the limitations of task-specific expertise, evolving into adaptable entities that excel in a multitude of scenarios.

24.4.8 The Road Ahead: The trajectory of AI research is firmly directed towards the goal of building systems that continuously improve. The integration of advanced techniques, active learning strategies, and meta-learning principles is driving the momentum in this direction. As the field advances, AI systems are poised to achieve levels of adaptability and proficiency that parallel human capabilities.

Refinement and Integration: The road ahead involves further refinement of these techniques and their integration into real-world applications. Researchers and engineers will continue to collaborate in crafting AI systems that seamlessly navigate the dynamic landscape of tasks and information. By harnessing the power of meta-learning, lifelong learning, and human-like adaptation, the future holds the promise of AI systems that continually evolve, learn, and excel in ways previously unimagined. meta-learning and the aspiration for lifelong learning and human-like adaptation are pivotal components in building AI systems that continuously improve? Through their ability to generalize learning, rapidly adapt, and emulate the continuous learning journey of humans, these approaches are steering AI research towards the creation of adaptable and proficient systems that thrive in dynamic and evolving environments.

24.5 Project

Unsolved Project

Suppose you're developing a project focused on adaptive learning and lifelong learning in AI systems. To ensure your project is effective, you need to understand catastrophic forgetting and its implications, continual learning strategies and techniques, methods like elastic weight consolidation and synaptic intelligence, and approaches to building AI systems that continuously improve. Before starting, research the following: the phenomenon of catastrophic forgetting and its impact on AI models, various strategies and techniques for continual learning to enable AI systems to learn incrementally, the principles behind elastic weight consolidation and synaptic intelligence, and methods for designing AI systems capable of continuous improvement. This foundational knowledge will help you create a project that explores and implements adaptive and lifelong learning in AI systems.

24.6 Lab Activity

Unsolved Lab Activity

Implement a neural network to demonstrate catastrophic forgetting using a simple task sequence (e.g., learning different patterns sequentially). Document the effects observed.

Task: Use a deep learning framework (e.g., TensorFlow or PyTorch) to implement a neural network and train it sequentially on different tasks (e.g., learning different patterns). Document the training process and observe the effects of catastrophic forgetting. Provide visualizations of the model's performance on previously learned tasks as it learns new ones.

Exercises

Exercise 1 – Multiple Choice Questions

1. What is catastrophic forgetting in neural networks?
   A. Rapid learning of new information
   B. Complete loss of previously learned information
   C. Gradual adaptation to new tasks
   D. Efficient knowledge transfer
2. Which factor contributes to catastrophic forgetting in neural networks?
   A. High model capacity
   B. Limited optimization during training
   C. Strong regularization techniques
   D. Unlimited computational resources
3. What is continual learning in deep learning?
   A. Learning from a single dataset
   B. Learning without adapting to new tasks
   C. Learning sequentially from a stream of data
   D. Learning only once and never updating the model
4. In which application domain is catastrophic forgetting particularly concerning for autonomous systems?
   A. E-commerce
   B. Healthcare
   C. Entertainment
   D. Self-driving cars
5. Which of the following is NOT an implication of catastrophic forgetting?
   A. Diminished Performance
   B. Enhanced Reliability
   C. Safety Risks
   D. Reduced Safety

Exercise 2 – True/False

1. Elastic Weight Consolidation helps in mitigating catastrophic forgetting.
2. Continual learning strategies do not involve any techniques for lifelong learning.
3. Catastrophic forgetting has no significant implications for adaptive learning systems.

Review Questions

1. What is catastrophic forgetting in the context of neural networks, and why is it a significant challenge?
2. Explain how the plasticity of neural networks contributes to catastrophic forgetting.
3. What are some implications of catastrophic forgetting in real-world applications like autonomous systems and medical diagnosis?
4. Describe the concept of continual learning and its importance in deep learning.
5. How can catastrophic forgetting impact the performance of deep learning models?
6. Name three potential risks associated with models suffering from catastrophic forgetting.
7. What are some mitigation strategies for addressing catastrophic forgetting in neural networks?
8. Explain the concept of regularization techniques and provide examples of such techniques.
9. How does Elastic Weight Consolidation (EWC) help prevent catastrophic forgetting?
10. What is Learning without Forgetting (LwF), and how does it leverage distillation to address the issue of forgetting?
11. Describe the key idea behind Progressive Neural Networks (ProgNNs) and how they mitigate catastrophic forgetting.
12. What is experience replay, and how does it contribute to mitigating catastrophic forgetting, especially in reinforcement learning contexts?
13. How does Neural Episodic Control (NEC) prevent catastrophic forgetting, and what is the role of episodic memory in this approach?
14. Explain the concept of generative replay in the context of continual learning.
15. How do hybrid methods combine different techniques to address catastrophic forgetting?
16. What is meta-learning, and how does it contribute to preventing catastrophic forgetting?
17. How do task prioritization and scheduling strategies help models manage their learning process effectively in continual learning scenarios?

Answers

Exercise 1- 1. B 2. A 3. C 4. D 5. B
Exercise 2- 1) True, 2) False, 3) False

Online Resources

Online Exam Paper:
Link: **https://forms.gle/ABJLLEY3mu11KSce8**
QR Code:

Chapter 24 Videos Playlist:
Link: **https://www.youtube.com/playlist?list=PLzlh_31VWEFofpABLMzfKtSxXzxfxy0Im**
QR Code:

Chapter 25: Beyond Deep Learning: Quantum and Neuromorphic AI

25.1 Quantum Computing's Potential Impact on AI: The intersection of quantum computing and artificial intelligence (AI) presents an intriguing frontier that has the potential to reshape the landscape of computation, problem-solving, and data analysis. Quantum computing's unique properties promise to unlock new capabilities, accelerating AI research and expanding the horizons of what AI systems can achieve.

25.1.1 Quantum Speedup: Revolutionizing Computation: Quantum computing stands poised to revolutionize the field of artificial intelligence (AI) through the profound concept of quantum speedup. At its core, quantum speedup redefines the boundaries of computation by leveraging the unique properties of quantum bits (qubits), paving the way for AI systems with unprecedented computational power.

Quantum Bits and Superposition: Unlike classical bits that can only exist in states of 0 or 1, qubits possess a remarkable property known as superposition. This means that qubits can exist in a combination of both states simultaneously. This inherent flexibility exponentially increases the computational potential of quantum systems.

Entanglement and Complex Calculations: Another fundamental attribute of qubits is entanglement. Qubits can become entangled, meaning the state of one qubit is dependent on the state of another, even if they are physically separated. This phenomenon enables qubits to perform complex calculations by exploiting intricate relationships between qubits, thereby unlocking a realm of computational possibilities.

Quantum Speedup in Problem Solving: Quantum speedup is particularly revolutionary in addressing complex problems that are difficult or practically impossible for classical computers to solve in a reasonable amount of time. Tasks that involve massive amounts of computation, like factoring large numbers or searching unsorted databases, can experience a dramatic acceleration in their solutions through quantum algorithms.

25.1.2 Accelerating Optimization and Simulation: The potential of quantum computing's speedup resonates strongly in the domains of optimization and simulation, two critical pillars of AI.

Optimization Unleashed: Optimization problems are pervasive in AI, spanning tasks such as parameter tuning, resource allocation, and model optimization. Quantum algorithms excel at tackling intricate optimization problems by exploring a multitude of solutions in parallel. This quantum-enhanced optimization promises to reshape the way AI systems refine their processes, potentially leading to faster and more effective outcomes.

Insights from Quantum Simulations: Quantum simulations hold immense promise for AI-driven advancements in understanding complex systems. Quantum computers can simulate intricate interactions within molecules, materials, and other systems at a level of detail unattainable by classical computers. This ability opens doors to unprecedented insights into the behavior of complex systems, impacting fields like drug discovery, materials science, and more.

quantum computing's impact on AI extends to its core through quantum speedup. By harnessing the power of qubits' superposition and entanglement, quantum computers transcend classical limitations, revolutionizing the speed and efficiency of problem-solving. Moreover, the potential for quantum speedup in optimization and simulation can significantly enhance AI's capabilities, enabling more efficient and accurate decision-making processes across various domains. As quantum technologies mature, their integration with AI promises to propel us into an era of computational prowess previously thought unattainable.

25.1.3 Quantum Machine Learning: The synergy between quantum computing and machine learning has given rise to a new frontier known as quantum machine learning. This intersection holds the potential to transform the landscape of AI by leveraging quantum algorithms to enhance classical machine learning tasks.

Quantum Enhancements in Machine Learning: Quantum machine learning harnesses the unique properties of quantum systems to bolster classical machine learning tasks. Quantum algorithms can accelerate processes like clustering and classification, key components of AI systems. These algorithms can explore a vast solution space in parallel, potentially outpacing classical methods in solving complex problems.

Efficient Data Processing: One of the most promising aspects of quantum machine learning is its ability to process and analyze large datasets more efficiently. Quantum computers can explore various data patterns and relationships in parallel, uncovering subtle insights that classical algorithms might miss due to their computational limitations.

Overcoming Classical Bottlenecks: While quantum machine learning is still in its infancy, it holds potential to address some of the computational bottlenecks encountered by classical machine learning. It's important to note that quantum machine learning is not a replacement for classical techniques: rather, it's an augmentation that can enhance the capabilities of AI systems.

25.1.4 Breaking Cryptographic Codes: The advent of quantum computing has triggered concerns in the field of cryptography, where classical encryption methods face a potential threat from algorithms capable of exploiting quantum speedup.

Shor's Algorithm and Cryptographic Vulnerability: Shor's algorithm, a prominent quantum algorithm, can efficiently factor large numbers, a task considered computationally infeasible for classical computers. This property undermines the security of widely used cryptographic techniques based on the difficulty of factoring large numbers, such as RSA encryption.

Quantum-Resistant Cryptography: The pursuit of quantum-resistant cryptographic techniques is a response to this challenge. Researchers are exploring cryptographic methods that remain secure even in the presence of quantum computers. These methods aim to safeguard AI systems, data, and communications in an era where quantum computing could potentially break classical cryptographic codes.

Securing AI Systems: The potential for quantum computing to break cryptographic codes underscores the importance of securing AI systems against future threats. Ensuring the confidentiality and integrity of AI-generated insights and data becomes paramount in this evolving landscape.

quantum computing's influence extends to quantum machine learning, enhancing classical AI tasks through the power of quantum algorithms. While quantum machine learning is a promising avenue, the potential of quantum computing to break cryptographic codes presents a significant challenge that prompts the exploration of quantum-resistant cryptographic techniques. As quantum computing matures, its impact on AI and cryptography will reshape the foundations of digital security and computational capabilities.

25.1.5 Quantum Data Analysis: The convergence of quantum computing and data analysis heralds a transformative era in the world of AI. Quantum data analysis has the potential to revolutionize how we handle and glean insights from massive datasets, offering an exponential speedup in tasks like database search and data pattern recognition.

Unleashing Quantum Speedup: Quantum computers have the ability to process multiple possibilities in parallel, allowing them to explore vast solution spaces with incredible efficiency. This property translates into a substantial acceleration in tasks like searching large databases, where a quantum computer can identify target items significantly faster than classical counterparts.

Tackling Complex Data Patterns: Quantum-enhanced data analysis promises to unearth intricate patterns hidden within extensive datasets. Quantum algorithms can sift through a plethora of potential patterns simultaneously, uncovering insights that would require impractical amounts of time for classical computers to discern.

Pioneering Discovery: In fields like medicine, finance, and scientific research, quantum data analysis can lead to groundbreaking discoveries by swiftly identifying correlations, anomalies, and trends that might have remained buried due to computational limitations.

25.1.6 Quantum AI Collaboration: The relationship between quantum computing and artificial intelligence (AI) is symbiotic, with each field enriching the other through collaboration.

Quantum System Control and Error Correction: AI techniques play a vital role in the development and deployment of quantum computing. AI-driven control systems optimize the behavior of quantum systems, enhancing their performance. Additionally, AI algorithms assist in error correction, a critical aspect in maintaining the integrity of quantum computations.

Quantum Acceleration for AI: Conversely, quantum computing holds potential in expediting AI processes. Quantum-enhanced optimization can accelerate training and fine-tuning of AI models, optimizing parameters with a speed and efficiency that classical optimization methods struggle to achieve.

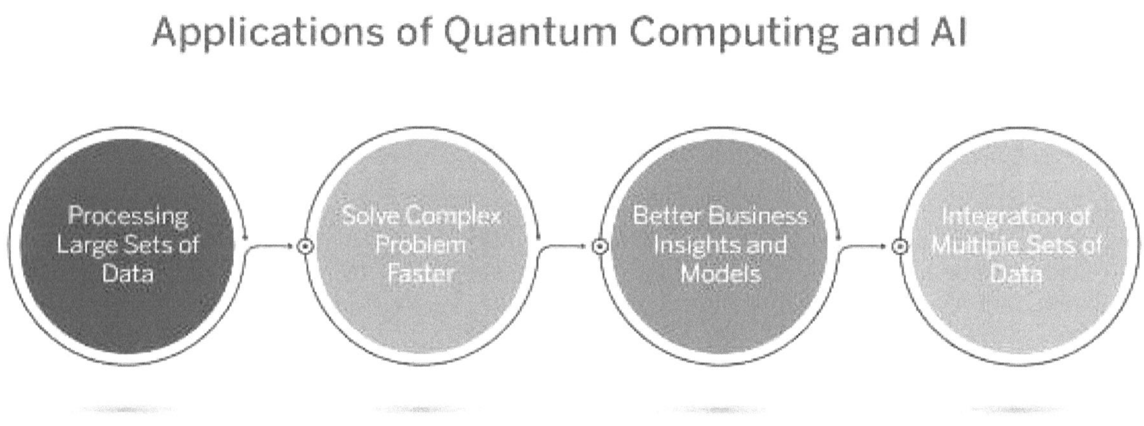

25.1.7 Challenges and Outlook: While the potential for quantum computing's impact on AI is immense, several challenges must be overcome for its realization.

The Quantum Challenge: Quantum computers are still in their infancy, and creating robust quantum algorithms is a complex endeavor. Quantum systems are sensitive to environmental factors and susceptible to errors, necessitating advanced error-correction techniques.

Hybrid Approaches: Effective integration of quantum computing with classical AI techniques poses another challenge. Hybrid approaches that leverage the strengths of both classical and quantum systems are necessary for practical implementation, requiring interdisciplinary collaboration and innovation.

The Road Ahead: Despite these challenges, the outlook remains optimistic. As quantum technologies advance, their integration with AI holds the promise of reshaping computational paradigms, enabling AI systems to tackle increasingly complex tasks and unlocking insights previously beyond reach.

quantum computing's influence on AI spans the realms of data analysis and collaborative innovation. Quantum data analysis offers unparalleled speedup in uncovering insights from vast datasets, while the synergy between quantum computing and AI empowers both fields to enrich each other's capabilities. Challenges notwithstanding, the prospects of quantum computing's impact on AI remain intriguing, holding the potential to redefine the limits of computational power and problem-solving prowess.

25.2 Neuromorphic Hardware and Brain-Inspired Computing: In the pursuit of advancing artificial intelligence (AI), researchers have turned their attention to the design and development of neuromorphic hardware—computing systems that draw inspiration from the intricate architecture and functioning of the human brain. This chapter delves into the realm of neuromorphic hardware and its potential to revolutionize AI by emulating brain-inspired computation.

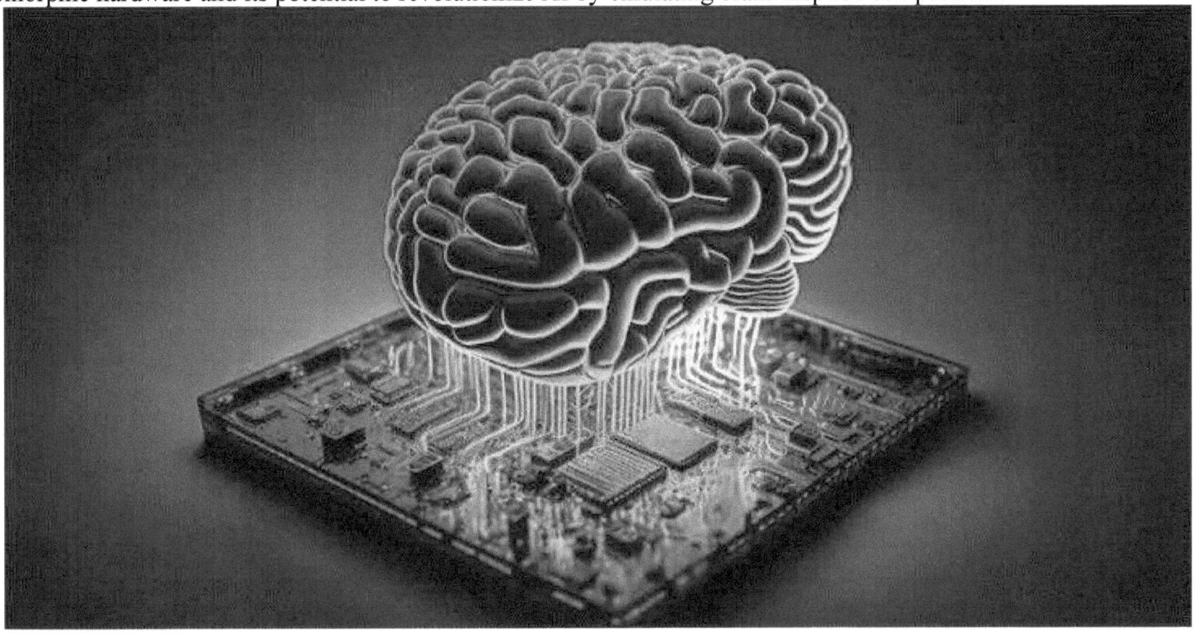

25.2.1 Mimicking Neural Networks: At the core of neuromorphic hardware lies a visionary goal: to mimic the intricate architecture and functionality of neural networks, the foundational components of the human brain's computational prowess. Neural networks are composed of interconnected neurons that communicate through electrical signals, forming intricate patterns of activation that underpin cognitive processes. The aspiration of neuromorphic hardware is to faithfully replicate this neural connectivity in order to enable efficient and highly parallelized computation.

Neural Network Architecture: Neural networks in the brain consist of neurons linked by synapses. These neurons receive and transmit electrical impulses, which collectively give rise to the brain's remarkable cognitive capabilities. The intricate interplay of interconnected neurons enables functions ranging from sensory perception to complex reasoning.

Information Processing: Information in the brain is processed through the transmission of signals between neurons. When a neuron's electrical potential surpasses a certain threshold, it fires an action potential—a brief electrical spike. This spike travels along the neuron's axon, transmitting information to connected neurons via synapses. This dynamic pattern of activation forms the basis for neural computation.

Replicating Neural Connectivity: Neuromorphic hardware endeavors to replicate the connectivity and behavior of biological neural networks. By emulating the transmission of signals and the intricate interconnections between artificial neurons, these systems aim to capture the essence of neural computation.

25.2.2 Spiking Neural Networks: A transformative innovation within the domain of neuromorphic hardware is the concept of spiking neural networks (SNNs). Diverging from the continuous activation functions of conventional artificial neural networks, SNNs mirror the firing patterns of biological neurons. This departure holds the potential for more energy-efficient computation that aligns with the brain's innate information processing mechanisms.

Emulating Biological Firing: Unlike traditional artificial neural networks, where activations are continuous, SNNs simulate the discrete and sporadic firing of biological neurons. Neurons in SNNs communicate through discrete spikes, a behavior closer to the brain's natural mode of operation.

Energy Efficiency: The adoption of spiking behavior contributes to increased energy efficiency in neuromorphic hardware. Since computations occur only when spikes are generated, power consumption is reduced compared to continuous processing. This aligns with the brain's economy of energy expenditure.

Brain-Inspired Learning: SNNs bring the prospect of brain-inspired learning to neuromorphic hardware. The spiking behavior facilitates spike-timing-dependent plasticity, a learning rule where the timing of spikes influences synaptic strength. This enables systems to adapt and learn in a manner reminiscent of biological neural networks.

the aspiration to mimic neural networks and the innovation of spiking neural networks lie at the heart of neuromorphic hardware's pursuit. By capturing the intricate connectivity and spiking behavior of biological neurons, these systems hold the potential to revolutionize computation, enable energy-efficient processing, and bring brain-inspired learning to the forefront of artificial intelligence.

25.2.3 Event-Based Processing: The paradigm of event-based processing is a distinctive hallmark of neuromorphic hardware, representing a departure from the traditional clock-driven systems that dominate conventional computing. Inspired by the brain's inherent asynchronous nature, event-based processing introduces a novel way of performing computations—only when relevant events occur. This innovation not only conserves energy but also enables systems to respond in real-time to dynamic inputs.

Asynchronous Nature of the Brain: The brain's neural networks operate in an inherently asynchronous manner. Neurons fire in response to specific stimuli or conditions, giving rise to a sequence of discrete events rather than rigid clock cycles. Event-based processing seeks to capture this natural rhythm of information flow and adapt it to computational systems.

Energy Conservation: Event-based processing significantly contributes to energy conservation. In contrast to traditional clock-driven architectures that execute instructions at fixed intervals, event-based systems only activate when an event of interest occurs. This minimizes unnecessary computations, leading to substantial power savings, particularly in scenarios where computational demands fluctuate.

Real-Time Responsiveness: The asynchronous and event-driven nature of neuromorphic hardware enhances real-time responsiveness. Systems can react immediately to relevant inputs, making them well-suited for tasks that require quick decision-making or adaptation to changing environments.

25.2.4 Neuromorphic Hardware in AI: The fusion of neuromorphic hardware with artificial intelligence (AI) presents a realm of transformative possibilities that hold the potential to reshape the landscape of AI systems.

Brain-Like Learning: One of the standout attributes of neuromorphic hardware is its facilitation of brain-like learning. These systems emulate the brain's plasticity, enabling AI to learn and adapt from data in a manner that mirrors the brain's ability to rewire itself. This intrinsic adaptability leads to continuous learning and evolution without the need for manual reprogramming.

Energy Efficiency: Neuromorphic hardware's commitment to energy efficiency extends beyond its event-based processing. By emulating the brain's energy-efficient computation—where only relevant neurons fire—these systems offer the prospect of substantial power savings compared to traditional computing architectures. This efficiency is particularly advantageous in resource-constrained environments.

Real-World Applications: The unique characteristics of neuromorphic hardware lend themselves to a myriad of real-world applications. In domains such as robotics, sensor networks, and edge computing, where real-time processing and low energy consumption are paramount, these systems shine. Their event-driven nature aligns with scenarios that demand immediate responsiveness and efficient use of resources.

the principles of event-based processing and the integration of neuromorphic hardware into AI systems herald a new era of computational efficiency and adaptability. Inspired by the brain's natural rhythms, these innovations open doors to energy-efficient, real-time AI applications with the potential to reshape diverse industries and domains.

25.2.5 Challenges and Future Prospects: The vision of neuromorphic hardware as a transformative force in artificial intelligence is not without its challenges. While the potential is undeniable, several hurdles must be surmounted to fully realize the promise of brain-inspired computation.

Scalability: Emulating Complexity: One of the most formidable challenges lies in scaling up neuromorphic hardware to match the intricate complexity of the human brain. The brain houses billions of neurons and trillions of synapses that interact in intricate ways. Replicating this level of complexity with high efficiency demands innovative engineering solutions that can accommodate the massive connectivity and computational demands of such systems.

Programming Paradigms: Adaptation and Innovation: Developing programming paradigms and tools tailored for neuromorphic hardware presents a significant challenge. Adapting AI algorithms to the event-driven, spike-based nature of these systems requires novel approaches that harness their unique characteristics. Traditional programming paradigms may need to be reimagined to fully exploit the potential of neuromorphic hardware.

25.2.6 The Road Ahead: Despite the challenges, the path forward for neuromorphic hardware is one of immense promise and potential.

Advancing Scalability: Addressing scalability challenges will be a focal point of future research and development. Innovative engineering solutions that enable the creation of larger and more complex neuromorphic systems will be crucial for achieving brain-like computational power.

Refining Programming Paradigms: The development of programming paradigms that seamlessly integrate with the event-based, spiking nature of neuromorphic hardware will be pivotal. Researchers and engineers must devise new approaches that allow AI algorithms to leverage the benefits of these systems, enabling efficient and adaptive computation.

Bridging the Gap: The integration of neuromorphic hardware with AI represents an exciting bridge between artificial and biological intelligence. As research continues to push the boundaries of what's possible, the potential to achieve AI systems that emulate the brain's sophistication and efficiency becomes increasingly tangible.

the journey of neuromorphic hardware is both promising and challenging. Overcoming scalability and programming hurdles will be key to unlocking its transformative potential. As these challenges are tackled, the integration of neuromorphic hardware with AI holds the promise of ushering in an era of brain-inspired computing that bridges the gap between the artificial and the biological.

25.3 Hybrid Approaches: Combining Deep and Quantum Learning: The convergence of deep learning and quantum computing represents a frontier in the evolution of artificial intelligence. This chapter explores the realm of hybrid approaches that leverage the strengths of both deep and quantum learning to unlock new frontiers in computation, optimization, and problem-solving.

25.3.1 Leveraging Quantum Advantage: At the core of hybrid approaches lies the concept of leveraging quantum advantage. Quantum computing possesses a unique prowess in solving certain types of problems that challenge classical computers. These problems, such as factorization and optimization, often involve complex calculations that can be extremely time-consuming for classical algorithms. Quantum computers exploit the principles of superposition and entanglement to process information in ways that classical computers cannot replicate.

Quantum Superiority: Quantum computers exhibit the potential for quantum superiority, where they can outperform classical computers in specific tasks. Notably, they excel in solving problems that require exploring a vast number of possibilities simultaneously, a feat unattainable by classical algorithms due to their sequential nature. Factorization, for instance, is a fundamental problem in cryptography that can be solved exponentially faster by quantum computers using Shor's algorithm.

Expanding Computational Horizons: By integrating quantum computation into the deep learning pipeline, hybrid models can address challenges that were once deemed computationally intractable. Complex problems that involve massive datasets or intricate optimization landscapes can be tackled more efficiently by leveraging the quantum processing capabilities. This paves the way for novel applications in various domains, from cryptography to molecular simulation.

25.3.2 Quantum-Assisted Optimization: Among the compelling applications of hybrid approaches, quantum-assisted optimization stands out as a prominent example. Optimization tasks involve finding the best solution from a vast set of possible solutions, a challenge prevalent in various fields, including logistics, finance, and machine learning.

Quantum Speedup in Optimization: Quantum computers offer a significant speedup in optimization tasks. Quantum algorithms, such as the Quantum Approximate Optimization Algorithm (QAOA), efficiently explore solution spaces and provide shortcuts to finding optimal or near-optimal solutions. This quantum advantage becomes particularly pronounced as the size and complexity of optimization problems increase.

Enhancing Efficiency: Integrating quantum algorithms into optimization tasks enhances efficiency and accelerates problem-solving. The ability of quantum computers to explore multiple solutions simultaneously allows them to navigate complex landscapes and identify optimal solutions more quickly than classical counterparts. This capability holds promise for revolutionizing industries that rely on optimization, including supply chain management and portfolio optimization.

the notion of leveraging quantum advantage and employing quantum-assisted optimization represents a significant leap in AI research. By integrating the power of quantum computation with deep learning methodologies, hybrid models enable the efficient resolution of complex problems that were previously beyond the reach of classical methods. This convergence holds the potential to reshape industries and domains by unlocking new avenues of problem-solving and optimization.

25.3.3 Quantum Neural Networks: In the realm of hybrid approaches, quantum neural networks emerge as a captivating concept that marries the expressive capabilities of classical neural networks with the quantum processing prowess of quantum computers. This fusion of technologies opens up new vistas of potential, offering to enhance the representation and handling of intricate patterns and relationships in data.

Enhancing Representation: Quantum neural networks leverage quantum states and quantum operations to encode and process information. This enables them to capture complex relationships within data that might elude classical neural networks. By exploiting quantum parallelism and superposition, these networks possess the potential to represent and manipulate data in more nuanced and sophisticated ways.

Handling Quantum Phenomena: Quantum neural networks excel in tasks that involve quantum phenomena. In domains such as quantum chemistry and materials science, where traditional simulation methods struggle due to the inherent quantum nature of the systems, quantum neural networks can provide an alternative means of analysis and prediction.

25.3.4 Quantum Data: A distinctive facet of hybrid approaches involves the leveraging of quantum data. Quantum computers possess the capacity to process and analyze quantum data, which holds immense promise in fields characterized by quantum phenomena.

Quantum Chemistry and Materials Science: Fields such as quantum chemistry and materials science deal with quantum systems that are exceedingly challenging to simulate using classical computers. Quantum data processing, powered by quantum computers, enables AI systems to glean insights from complex quantum datasets, revolutionizing our understanding of molecular structures, chemical reactions, and material properties.

Insights from Complex Quantum Datasets: Integrating quantum data processing with deep learning techniques offers a powerful synergy. Deep learning's ability to discern intricate patterns aligns well with the complexity of quantum data. This collaboration empowers AI to extract meaningful insights from vast and complex quantum datasets that hold the keys to breakthroughs in various scientific disciplines.

quantum neural networks and the integration of quantum data processing represent a novel frontier in hybrid AI research. By merging classical and quantum computational paradigms, these approaches hold the potential to elevate the capabilities of AI systems, enabling them to grapple with the complexities of quantum phenomena and glean insights from quantum datasets that were previously inscrutable.

25.3.5 Challenges and Future Directions: While hybrid approaches that combine deep learning and quantum computing hold tremendous promise, they are not without challenges. Overcoming these challenges is essential to fully realize the potential of these novel paradigms.

Quantum Noise and Error Correction: One of the significant hurdles facing hybrid approaches is quantum noise and error correction. Quantum computers are inherently susceptible to noise and errors due to their quantum nature and interactions with the environment. These errors can propagate and compromise the accuracy of quantum computations. Developing effective error correction techniques is crucial to ensuring the reliability of quantum-assisted computations in hybrid models.

Algorithm Development: The seamless integration of quantum algorithms into deep learning architectures requires innovative algorithm development. Adapting quantum algorithms to work in harmony with classical deep learning techniques demands creative algorithmic design. This involves devising algorithms that can leverage quantum computation efficiently while complementing the strengths of classical deep learning algorithms.

25.3.6 The Road Ahead: Despite the challenges, the trajectory of hybrid approaches is promising and opens up new avenues for research and innovation.

Transcending Boundaries: Hybrid models have the potential to transcend the limitations of classical computing by harnessing the strengths of both quantum and deep learning paradigms. This opens the door to tackling problems that were once deemed too complex or computationally intensive.

Collaborative Efforts: Collaboration between quantum physicists, AI researchers, and algorithm designers will be pivotal in shaping the future of hybrid approaches. Combining expertise from these diverse fields is crucial for developing robust algorithms, effective error correction techniques, and practical applications.

Revolutionizing Industries: As hybrid approaches mature, they have the potential to revolutionize industries ranging from pharmaceuticals and materials science to optimization and cryptography. The ability to solve complex problems more efficiently and accurately holds the promise of transformative impact.

the journey of hybrid approaches represents an exciting frontier in AI research. By addressing challenges related to quantum noise, error correction, and algorithm development, researchers pave the way for innovative applications that leverage the strengths of both quantum computing and deep learning. As collaborations thrive and technologies advance, hybrid models have the potential to reshape industries and push the boundaries of what is achievable in artificial intelligence.

25.4 Anticipating the Next Frontiers of AI Research: The rapid evolution of artificial intelligence (AI) has marked numerous milestones, but the journey is far from over. This chapter delves into the intriguing question of what lies ahead in AI research, exploring the frontiers that promise to shape the future of this dynamic field.

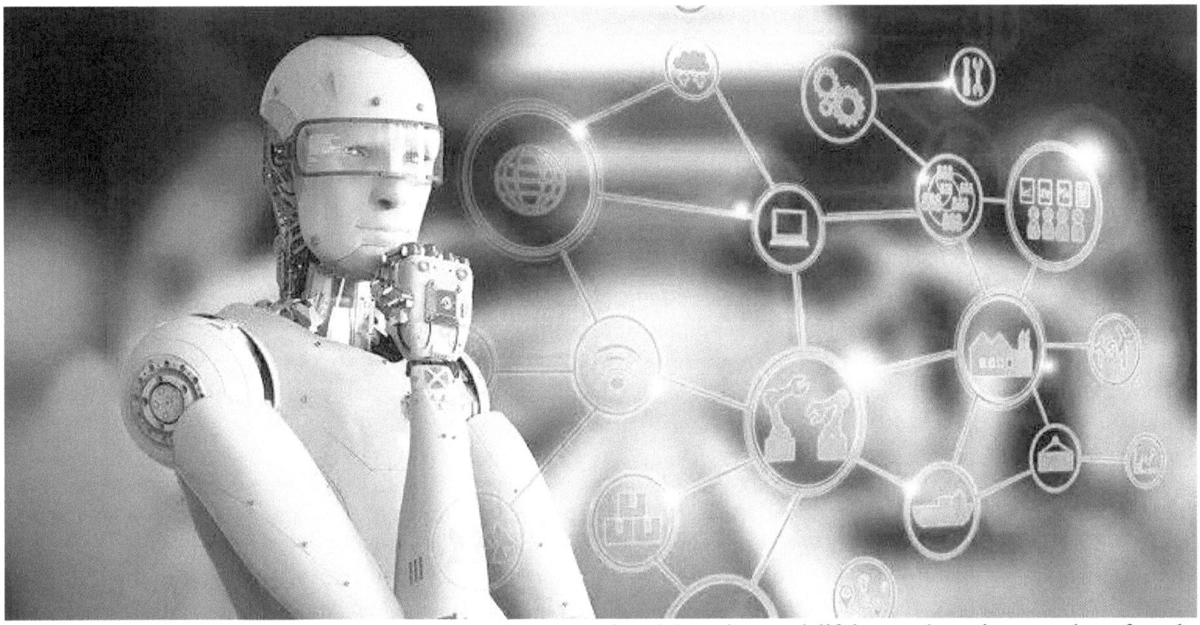

25.4.1 Continual Learning and Lifelong Adaptation: Continual learning and lifelong adaptation stand as foundational frontiers in the realm of AI research. These concepts address the challenge of developing AI systems that can evolve and improve over time, learning from new experiences while retaining valuable knowledge acquired from previous tasks.

Learning in Dynamic Environments: In dynamic real-world scenarios, AI systems encounter evolving data distributions and new tasks. Continual learning seeks to equip these systems with the ability to adapt to new information and acquire new skills as they arise. This adaptation is akin to how humans learn throughout their lives, incorporating new knowledge while building upon past experiences.

Overcoming Catastrophic Forgetting: A critical challenge in continual learning is catastrophic forgetting, where AI models forget previously learned knowledge when trained on new tasks. Overcoming this challenge involves devising techniques that allow models to retain past knowledge while adapting to new tasks. By doing so, AI systems can accumulate a diverse range of skills over time without erasing valuable expertise.

25.4.2 Explainable and Ethical AI: As AI becomes more integrated into decision-making processes across various domains, the importance of explainable and ethical AI has become increasingly evident. This frontier focuses on creating AI models that not only deliver accurate results but also offer transparent insights into how those results are achieved.

Transparency in Decision-Making: Explainable AI aims to uncover the rationale behind AI decisions. Providing clear and interpretable explanations enables users to understand the factors that influenced a particular outcome. This is particularly crucial in domains where decisions impact individuals' lives, such as healthcare, finance, and criminal justice.

Ethical Considerations: Ethical AI involves ensuring that AI systems make decisions that adhere to human-defined ethical principles. This includes mitigating biases, avoiding discriminatory outcomes, and respecting privacy. By embedding ethical considerations into the design and training of AI models, we can build systems that contribute positively to society.

Accountability and Regulation: Strides in explainable and ethical AI contribute to accountable AI development. Regulatory bodies and organizations are increasingly recognizing the need to ensure AI transparency and ethical behavior. The responsible deployment of AI requires a collaborative effort among researchers, policymakers, and industries to establish guidelines that govern AI's usage.

25.4.3 Quantum and Neuromorphic Computing Synergy: The intersection of AI with emerging technologies, such as quantum computing and neuromorphic hardware, presents an exciting frontier. Exploring the synergies between these technologies can open new horizons in computation, optimization, and data analysis. Hybrid approaches that combine quantum and neuromorphic principles with AI methodologies promise transformative breakthroughs.

Unveiling New Horizons: The synergy between quantum computing and AI opens new horizons in computation. Quantum computers possess the extraordinary ability to perform complex calculations at an exponential speedup compared to classical computers. When combined with AI methodologies, these quantum-enhanced computations can drastically accelerate tasks like optimization, machine learning, and cryptography, heralding a new era of efficiency and capability.

Harnessing Brain-Inspired Hardware: The fusion of AI with neuromorphic hardware takes inspiration from the brain's neural networks. Neuromorphic systems emulate the brain's parallelism and energy efficiency, offering potential advantages in tasks that require real-time processing and adaptability. By blending AI techniques with neuromorphic principles, researchers are unlocking novel ways to solve complex problems, design adaptive systems, and emulate human-like cognition.

25.4.4 AI for Scientific Discovery: The vast potential of AI for scientific discovery is a frontier that continues to expand with immense promise. AI's prowess in analyzing massive datasets, simulating intricate systems, and uncovering hidden patterns has the power to accelerate scientific progress across a spectrum of disciplines.

Revolutionizing Drug Discovery: In fields like drug discovery, AI algorithms can rapidly sift through colossal databases to identify potential candidates for novel therapies. Machine learning models can predict the behavior of molecules, enabling scientists to focus their efforts on compounds with the highest likelihood of success.

Advancing Materials Science: Materials science is another domain profoundly impacted by AI. Through simulations and data analysis, AI can facilitate the discovery of new materials with tailored properties, revolutionizing industries from electronics to renewable energy.

Probing Fundamental Physics: AI's potential to analyze complex data sets also extends to fundamental physics. From particle accelerators to cosmic observations, AI algorithms can assist in deciphering intricate patterns, identifying rare events, and advancing our understanding of the universe's fundamental laws.

25.4.5 AI's Impact on Creativity and Art: AI's foray into creativity and art presents a fascinating and emerging frontier that challenges traditional notions and expands the boundaries of human expression.

Transforming Content Creation: Generative models like GANs and transformer networks are at the forefront of transforming content creation. These models can generate realistic images, music, text, and more, blurring the lines between human and AI-generated content. As AI-generated art gains recognition, it prompts discussions on authenticity, authorship, and the very nature of creativity.

Unleashing New Creative Avenues: AI-powered tools are providing artists with fresh avenues for creativity. Artists can collaborate with AI algorithms to create novel visual styles, generate music compositions, and even explore uncharted artistic realms. This collaborative interplay between humans and machines is redefining how art is conceived and produced.

25.4.6 Charting the Future: the frontiers of quantum and neuromorphic computing, AI for scientific discovery, and AI's influence on creativity and art promise a future where technology advances in leaps and bounds. As researchers delve into these uncharted territories, they are shaping a landscape where AI not only accelerates our understanding of the world but also enriches human creativity and innovation in unprecedented ways.

25.4.6 Human-AI Collaboration: The emerging frontier of human-AI collaboration marks a profound shift in the relationship between humans and technology. As AI systems advance in complexity and capability, the potential for cooperative partnerships between humans and machines becomes increasingly evident. This synergy has the potential to reshape decision-making, creativity, and problem-solving in unprecedented ways.

Symbiotic Decision-Making: In complex decision-making scenarios, AI can serve as a valuable partner, providing insights derived from extensive data analysis. Human experts can leverage AI's ability to process vast amounts of information quickly, enabling more informed and efficient decisions. From medical diagnoses to financial forecasts, human-AI collaboration can enhance accuracy and confidence.

Amplifying Creativity: The fusion of human creativity and AI's generative capabilities unlocks new dimensions of artistic expression and innovation. Creative professionals can work alongside AI algorithms to explore unconventional ideas, develop novel designs, and push the boundaries of traditional artistic mediums. This cooperative creativity leads to the emergence of new artistic styles and forms.

25.4.7 Ethical Considerations and Regulation: With the integration of AI into various facets of society, ethical considerations have emerged as a central concern. The ethical implications of AI's decisions, biases, and potential consequences are pivotal for its responsible development and deployment.

Striking an Ethical Balance: The development of AI regulations, standards, and guidelines is essential to ensure that AI systems uphold human values, fairness, and accountability. Striking a balance between technological innovation and ethical safeguards is a challenge that requires collective efforts from researchers, policymakers, and industry stakeholders.

25.4.8 Beyond Supervised Learning: The expanding frontier beyond supervised learning heralds a shift towards more autonomous and human-like AI learning. Advancements in unsupervised learning and self-supervised learning are transforming how AI systems acquire knowledge and understanding from raw data.

Learning from Unlabeled Data: Unsupervised learning allows AI to identify patterns and relationships within data without explicit labels or guidance. Self-supervised learning takes this a step further, enabling AI to learn from its own predictions, mimicking the way humans learn by observing and making inferences from their environment.

25.4.9 Global Collaboration and Accessibility: The importance of global collaboration and accessibility cannot be overstated. AI research and development are most effective when researchers, policymakers, and industries from around the world collaborate to share knowledge, insights, and resources.

Equitable Access: Fostering accessibility to AI resources, tools, and education ensures that advancements are not limited to a few privileged regions. This democratization of AI empowers individuals from diverse backgrounds to contribute to and benefit from AI's potential.

25.4.10 The Uncharted Landscape: In closing, the horizon of AI research is an expansive landscape filled with potential and challenges. From continual learning and quantum computing to ethical AI and beyond, the journey toward harnessing AI's full capabilities is ongoing. Through innovation, ethical awareness, and global cooperation, AI's transformative impact on society and technology is set to shape the future in ways we are only beginning to imagine.

25.5 Project

Unsolved Project

Suppose you're working on a project that investigates the future directions of AI, focusing on quantum and neuromorphic AI. To ensure a comprehensive exploration, you need to understand the potential impact of quantum computing on AI, the role of neuromorphic hardware and brain-inspired computing, hybrid approaches that combine deep and quantum learning, and the next frontiers of AI research. Before starting, research the following: how quantum computing could transform AI by solving complex problems more efficiently, the principles and applications of neuromorphic hardware and brain-inspired computing, techniques and benefits of combining deep learning with quantum computing (hybrid approaches), and emerging trends and future directions in AI research. This foundational knowledge will help you develop a project that examines and anticipates the next significant advancements in the field of AI.

25.6 Lab Activity

Unsolved Lab Activity

Implement a spiking neural network (SNN) using a framework like NEST or Brian2. Simulate a basic task and evaluate its performance.

Task: Use a framework like NEST or Brian2 to implement a spiking neural network (SNN). Simulate a basic task, such as pattern recognition or digit classification, and evaluate the performance of the SNN. Document the implementation process, including data preprocessing, model architecture, training procedure, and performance evaluation. Provide visualizations of the spiking activity and network performance.

Exercises

Exercise 1 – Multiple Choice Questions

1. What is the fundamental property of quantum bits (qubits) that sets them apart from classical bits?
   A. Superposition
   B. Entanglement
   C. Interference
   D. Quantum speedup
2. In quantum computing, what does "entanglement" refer to?
   A. The physical proximity of qubits
   B. The ability of qubits to exist in multiple states
   C. The dependence of one qubit's state on another, even when separated
   D. The synchronization of qubits' operations
3. How does quantum speedup redefine the boundaries of computation?
   A. By utilizing classical bits more efficiently
   B. By exploiting quantum bits (qubits) to solve problems faster
   C. By introducing a new type of classical algorithm
   D. By minimizing the need for superposition
4. Which type of problems can benefit the most from quantum speedup?
   A. Simple arithmetic calculations
   B. Complex problems with massive computation requirements
   C. Image recognition tasks
   D. Text-based natural language processing
5. How does quantum computing enhance optimization tasks in AI?
   A. By speeding up quantum simulations
   B. By making AI models more complex
   C. By tackling intricate optimization problems in parallel
   D. By simplifying optimization algorithms

Exercise 2 – True/False

1. Quantum computing has no potential impact on AI.
2. Neuromorphic hardware is inspired by the structure and function of the human brain.
3. Hybrid approaches in AI combine deep learning with quantum learning.

Review Questions

1. What is catastrophic forgetting in the context of neural networks, and why is it a significant challenge?
2. Explain how the plasticity of neural networks contributes to catastrophic forgetting.
3. What are some implications of catastrophic forgetting in real-world applications like autonomous systems and medical diagnosis?
4. Describe the concept of continual learning and its importance in deep learning.
5. How can catastrophic forgetting impact the performance of deep learning models?

6. Name three potential risks associated with models suffering from catastrophic forgetting.
7. What are some mitigation strategies for addressing catastrophic forgetting in neural networks?
8. Explain the concept of regularization techniques and provide examples of such techniques.
9. How does Elastic Weight Consolidation (EWC) help prevent catastrophic forgetting?
10. What is Learning without Forgetting (LwF), and how does it leverage distillation to address the issue of forgetting?
11. Describe the key idea behind Progressive Neural Networks (ProgNNs) and how they mitigate catastrophic forgetting.
12. What is experience replay, and how does it contribute to mitigating catastrophic forgetting, especially in reinforcement learning contexts?
13. How does Neural Episodic Control (NEC) prevent catastrophic forgetting, and what is the role of episodic memory in this approach?
14. Explain the concept of generative replay in the context of continual learning.
15. How do hybrid methods combine different techniques to address catastrophic forgetting?
16. What is meta-learning, and how does it contribute to preventing catastrophic forgetting?
17. How do task prioritization and scheduling strategies help models manage their learning process effectively in continual learning scenarios?

Answers

Exercise 1- 1. B 2. A 3. C 4. D 5. B
Exercise 2- 1) False, 2) True, 3) True

Online Resources

Online Exam Paper:
Link: https://forms.gle/A4JnFsbep4jjou6i9
QR Code:

Chapter 25 Videos Playlist:
Link: https://www.youtube.com/playlist?list=PLzlh_31VWEFr6n_Pb_8RzzIEvMS6f9cBA
QR Code:

Chapter 26: Quantifying Uncertainty in Deep Learning

26.1. Sources of Uncertainty in Neural Networks: Neural networks are powerful machine learning models that have demonstrated remarkable performance in various tasks. However, they are not immune to uncertainty. Uncertainty in neural networks arises from various sources, affecting their reliability, generalization, and decision-making capabilities.

26.1.1. Data Uncertainty: Sources and Implications: Data is the foundation upon which neural networks learn and make predictions. However, the inherent nature of data introduces various sources of uncertainty that can impact the reliability and generalization capabilities of neural networks.

Data Variability

Definition: Neural networks are trained on finite datasets, which might not encompass the entire spectrum of possible variations in the real world. As a result, encountering data points that significantly deviate from the training distribution can introduce uncertainty.

Implications:

Generalization Challenges: Data variability can cause neural networks to struggle when confronted with novel, out-of-distribution data points. Their inability to handle such data points leads to decreased generalization performance.

Bias and Skew: If the training data is skewed towards certain patterns or demographics, the neural network might exhibit skewed predictions, further exacerbating uncertainties in real-world scenarios.

Noisy Data

Definition: Noisy data contains errors, inconsistencies, or random fluctuations that do not reflect true underlying patterns. Neural networks trained on noisy data might misinterpret these variations as meaningful features.

Implications:

Overfitting: Noisy data can lead to overfitting, where neural networks capture noise instead of genuine patterns. This compromises the model's ability to make accurate predictions on new, unseen data.

Reduced Confidence: Noisy data confuses neural networks, causing uncertainty in their predictions. The model may assign high confidence to incorrect predictions, impacting decision-making.

Limited Data

Definition: In complex tasks, neural networks require substantial amounts of data to uncover intricate underlying patterns. Limited data availability can lead to uncertainty as the model fails to grasp the complexities.

Implications:

Underfitting: Neural networks trained on limited data might underfit, meaning they fail to capture the nuances and details required for accurate predictions, leading to uncertainty in their outcomes.

Unreliable Estimates: With limited data, neural networks might provide uncertain predictions, as they lack sufficient information to make confident inferences about new examples.

Data uncertainty introduces challenges that affect the reliability and robustness of neural networks. Recognizing the sources of uncertainty stemming from data variability, noisy data, and limited data is crucial for developing strategies that mitigate their impact. Techniques such as data augmentation, noise reduction, and transfer learning can help neural networks become more resilient to these uncertainties, enhancing their performance in real-world applications.

26.1.2. Model Uncertainty: Balancing Complexity and Reliability: Model uncertainty arises from the characteristics and complexities of neural network architectures, as well as the parameters learned during training. This uncertainty can impact a model's generalization, robustness, and ability to represent underlying patterns accurately.

Model Complexity

Definition: Highly complex neural network architectures, especially those with numerous layers and parameters, can be susceptible to overfitting. Overfitting occurs when the model captures noise and random fluctuations in the training data rather than true underlying patterns.

Implications:

Limited Generalization: Overfitted models might perform exceedingly well on the training data but struggle to generalize to new, unseen data. This limited generalization capacity introduces uncertainty in real-world scenarios.

Sensitivity to Noise: Complex models can amplify the effects of noisy data, leading to uncertain and potentially erroneous predictions when faced with noisy inputs.

Model Parameters

Definition: Neural networks adjust their weights and biases during training to minimize prediction errors. Uncertainty arises from the specific values of these parameters, especially when the data available for training is limited.

Implications:

Parameter Estimation: Limited data can result in uncertainty about the optimal values of model parameters. The model might lack confidence in its learned weights, leading to uncertain predictions.

Parameter Initialization: The initialization of model parameters can affect convergence and learning. Variability in initialization might result in uncertainty about the final learned model.

Expressiveness Limits

Definition: Neural networks have a finite capacity to represent complex functions. In cases where the true underlying function is beyond the model's representational capabilities, uncertainty emerges.
Implications:
Inaccurate Representations: When neural networks encounter functions they cannot accurately represent, they might provide uncertain or incorrect predictions. This is particularly relevant in complex tasks requiring intricate functions.
Model Confidence: Neural networks might express uncertainty through low confidence scores when encountering functions that challenge their expressiveness limits.
Understanding the sources of uncertainty related to model complexity, parameter estimation, and expressiveness limits is essential for building neural networks that strike a balance between complexity and reliability. Techniques such as regularization, model architecture adjustments, and ensembling can help mitigate these uncertainties, ensuring that neural networks make more accurate and reliable predictions in diverse scenarios.
26.1.3. Epistemic Uncertainty: Epistemic uncertainty arises from a lack of knowledge about the true model that generated the data. It can be reduced with more data, improved architectures, and better training methods.
Model Variability: Different initializations or training runs can lead to varying model outcomes, highlighting the epistemic uncertainty present in neural networks.
Out-of-Distribution Data: Neural networks might be confident about predictions for in-distribution data, but uncertainty increases significantly when encountering data that differs significantly from the training distribution.
26.1.4. Aleatoric Uncertainty: Embracing Inherent Variability: Aleatoric uncertainty, distinct from epistemic uncertainty, arises from the intrinsic variability within the data itself. It represents the uncertainty that cannot be reduced through more data or improved models, as it originates from the inherent noise and ambiguity present in real-world observations.
Measurement Errors
Definition: In tasks such as regression or measurement-based predictions, aleatoric uncertainty accounts for errors introduced by imperfect measurement instruments or inherent noise in the data.
Implications:
Confidence Intervals: Aleatoric uncertainty results in confidence intervals around predictions. This interval reflects the range of potential outcomes due to measurement errors.
Uncertain Predictions: Neural networks might express higher uncertainty in predictions when dealing with data containing significant measurement errors.
Ambiguity
Definition: In tasks involving complex scenes or objects, such as object detection, aleatoric uncertainty captures the inherent ambiguity in identifying objects accurately.
Implications:
Uncertain Object Boundaries: In object detection, neural networks might struggle to precisely define object boundaries due to the inherent complexity of scenes, leading to uncertain localization.
Multiple Interpretations: Aleatoric uncertainty highlights the existence of multiple plausible interpretations of the same data, causing the model to express uncertainty about the true identity of objects.
Irreducible Nature
Definition: Aleatoric uncertainty is irreducible; it cannot be eliminated by obtaining more data or improving model architecture. It is a fundamental aspect of dealing with real-world data.
Implications:
Model Confidence: Neural networks inherently account for aleatoric uncertainty in their predictions. They provide not only point predictions but also a measure of confidence in those predictions.
Robust Decision-Making: Acknowledging aleatoric uncertainty encourages models to make more cautious decisions, considering the inherent variability in the data.
Aleatoric uncertainty is an integral part of dealing with real-world data, reflecting the intrinsic variability and noise in observations. While it cannot be eliminated, understanding its presence and implications can lead to more nuanced decision-making and models that provide informative confidence measures. Embracing aleatoric uncertainty ensures that neural networks offer reliable predictions even in the face of inherent variability and ambiguity in the data.
26.1.5. Decision Boundary Uncertainty: Navigating Prediction Boundaries: In the context of neural networks, decision boundaries are the lines, surfaces, or hypersurfaces that separate different classes or categories within the input data space. Decision boundary uncertainty pertains to situations where neural networks make predictions based on these boundaries, introducing uncertainty when data points lie near these boundaries.
Decision Boundaries
Definition: Neural networks classify input data by mapping them to different classes based on learned decision boundaries. These boundaries determine which data points are assigned to specific categories.
Implications:
Close-to-Boundary Uncertainty: Uncertainty arises when input data points are located in proximity to decision boundaries. Small perturbations or variations in these points might lead to different predictions.
Boundary Ambiguity: Decision boundaries might be ambiguous in regions where classes are close or overlap, contributing to uncertainty about which class a particular data point belongs to.

Sensitivity to Input
Definition: Sensitivity to input refers to how neural networks' predictions change in response to small changes in the input data. High sensitivity indicates that even slight perturbations can alter predictions.
Implications:
Uncertainty Amplification: When neural networks are sensitive to minor input variations, predictions can become highly uncertain for data points near decision boundaries.
Robustness Concerns: High sensitivity suggests that neural networks lack robustness in their decision boundaries, and small input changes can lead to unpredictable outcomes.
26.1.6. Interpretability Uncertainty: Deciphering Neural Networks: Interpretability uncertainty relates to the challenge of understanding and interpreting the decision-making process of neural networks, primarily due to their inherent complexity and opaque behavior.
Black-Box Nature
Definition: Neural networks are often referred to as black-box models due to their intricate architecture and intricate internal workings that are not easily interpretable by humans.
Implications:
Uncertain Predictive Rationale: The inability to understand the rationale behind predictions leads to uncertainty about why a neural network made a specific decision.
Trust and Accountability: Lack of interpretability can diminish trust in the model's predictions, particularly in high-stakes applications like healthcare or finance.
Feature Importance
Definition: Feature importance refers to understanding which input features or neurons play a significant role in influencing a neural network's predictions.
Implications:
Uncertainty in Attribution: In complex models, identifying the precise features driving a particular prediction can be uncertain, making it difficult to ascertain the factors leading to certain outcomes.
Limited Insights: Uncertain feature importance can hinder understanding the decision-making process, impacting the model's application in critical domains.
26.1.7. Transfer Uncertainty: Navigating Unseen Data Domains: Transfer uncertainty arises when neural networks are exposed to new data domains during deployment or adaptation, leading to uncertainty due to differences between the training and deployment distributions.
Domain Shift
Definition: Domain shift occurs when there are disparities between the distribution of data the neural network was trained on and the distribution of data in the new deployment domain.
Implications:
Uncertain Predictions: Neural networks might provide uncertain predictions when faced with data from domains that significantly differ from their training data, as the model lacks familiarity with these new variations.
Distribution Mismatch: The uncertainty stems from the inability to account for all potential variations that might exist in the new domain.
Adaptation Challenges
Definition: Adaptation challenges arise when models trained on one domain are adapted or fine-tuned for another domain, but uncertainties emerge due to discrepancies between the two data distributions.
Implications:
Uncertainty During Adaptation: Neural networks might exhibit uncertainty during the adaptation process, leading to suboptimal performance in the new domain.
Data Scarcity in New Domains: Limited data availability in the new domain can exacerbate adaptation challenges, as neural networks struggle to capture its nuances.
Decision boundary uncertainty, interpretability uncertainty, and transfer uncertainty are critical aspects that underscore the complexities and challenges of deploying and understanding neural networks in real-world scenarios. Acknowledging and addressing these uncertainties is essential for building robust and reliable AI systems that can navigate various data distributions, interpret predictions, and adapt to new environments.
26.2. Bayesian Deep Learning and Probabilistic Models: Bayesian deep learning represents a paradigm shift in the field of machine learning, moving from deterministic approaches to probabilistic ones. It introduces uncertainty estimation and enables models to quantify and manage uncertainty in predictions. This chapter explores Bayesian deep learning, probabilistic models, and their applications.
26.2.1. Bayesian Deep Learning: Embracing Uncertainty
Bayesian deep learning leverages Bayesian inference to estimate the uncertainty associated with neural network predictions. Unlike traditional neural networks that produce point estimates, Bayesian neural networks provide probability distributions over possible outcomes.
Bayesian Inference

Definition: Bayesian inference is a statistical approach that incorporates prior knowledge and evidence from observed data to update the probability distribution over model parameters.
Implications:
Uncertainty Quantification: Bayesian inference provides a principled way to quantify uncertainty in predictions. It results in predictive distributions, reflecting the model's confidence in various outcomes.
Better Decision-Making: Bayesian models can assist decision-making by offering uncertainty estimates. This is crucial in critical applications where uncertainty can impact the consequences of decisions.

Dropout as Bayesian Approximation

Definition: Dropout, a regularization technique, can be interpreted as a Bayesian approximation. It involves randomly deactivating neurons during training, effectively creating an ensemble of models.
Implications:
Uncertainty Estimation: Dropout-based Bayesian neural networks can estimate uncertainty by considering the variations in predictions across different dropout masks.
Ensemble Benefits: The ensemble nature of dropout-based models improves model performance and generalization, while providing valuable uncertainty information.

26.2.2. Probabilistic Models: Modeling Uncertainty

Probabilistic models encompass a range of techniques that allow neural networks to capture uncertainty through probabilistic distributions.

Variational Inference

Definition: Variational inference approximates complex posterior distributions with simpler distributions, enabling efficient uncertainty estimation in Bayesian models.
Implications:
Efficient Uncertainty Estimation: Variational inference offers a computationally efficient way to estimate uncertainty without requiring costly sampling methods.Balancing Complexity and Accuracy: Variational inference finds a trade-off between model complexity and accuracy, crucial for practical applications.

Gaussian Processes

Definition: Gaussian processes are non-parametric models that define distributions over functions, providing a flexible framework for capturing uncertainty.
Implications:
Flexibility in Uncertainty Modeling: Gaussian processes are well-suited for tasks where uncertainty is not constant across the input space, allowing nuanced uncertainty representation.
Small Data Settings: Gaussian processes excel in scenarios with limited data, as they can provide reliable uncertainty estimates even with sparse observations.

26.2.3. Applications of Bayesian Deep Learning: Bayesian deep learning and probabilistic models find applications across various domains due to their enhanced capability of handling uncertainty.

Medical Diagnostics: Bayesian deep learning aids in medical diagnostics by providing not only predictions but also the associated uncertainty, assisting doctors in making informed decisions.

Autonomous Systems: In autonomous systems, Bayesian models enhance decision-making by quantifying uncertainty. Self-driving cars, for instance, can navigate complex scenarios while considering the uncertainty in sensor data.

Financial Forecasting: Bayesian models contribute to financial forecasting by offering uncertainty estimates in predictions, guiding investment decisions more effectively.

Bayesian deep learning and probabilistic models revolutionize the way uncertainty is incorporated into machine learning. These approaches provide more nuanced and informative predictions, critical for domains where uncertainty management is paramount. As these techniques continue to evolve, they hold the potential to enhance the robustness, reliability, and interpretability of AI systems across a wide array of applications.

26.3. Uncertainty Estimation in Classification and Regression: Uncertainty estimation is a critical aspect of deep learning that goes beyond producing point predictions. In both classification and regression tasks, understanding and quantifying uncertainty provide valuable insights into the reliability of model predictions. This chapter delves into the techniques and methods for uncertainty estimation in both classification and regression scenarios.

26.3.1. Uncertainty in Classification: In classification tasks, the goal is to assign input data to predefined classes. Uncertainty estimation in classification involves assessing the model's confidence in its predictions and recognizing situations where predictions might be less reliable.

Softmax Outputs as Probabilities

Definition: Softmax is a commonly used activation function in the output layer of a classification neural network. It transforms raw scores into probability distributions over classes.
Implications:
Uncertainty Interpretation: The softmax probabilities reflect the model's estimated probability for each class. Lower probabilities indicate higher uncertainty.
Thresholding: Setting a threshold on softmax probabilities can help classify instances with high certainty while flagging uncertain predictions for further scrutiny.

Monte Carlo Dropout

Definition: Monte Carlo Dropout involves running multiple forward passes with dropout activated during inference and observing the variations in predictions.

Implications:

Uncertainty Estimation: Monte Carlo Dropout generates a distribution of predictions, which can be used to calculate variance and confidence intervals for each class probability.

Robust Decision-Making: Higher variance indicates uncertainty, allowing for more cautious decision-making when encountering instances with uncertain predictions.

26.3.2. Uncertainty in Regression: Regression tasks involve predicting continuous values. Uncertainty estimation in regression provides insights into the model's confidence in its predictions and helps identify scenarios where predictions might be less reliable.

Prediction Intervals

Definition: Prediction intervals are ranges that encompass the uncertainty around a predicted value. They indicate the possible range of values the true outcome might fall within.

Implications:

Quantifying Uncertainty: Prediction intervals provide a clear measure of uncertainty, allowing decision-makers to assess the range of possible outcomes.

Tailoring Risk Tolerance: Decision-makers can choose prediction intervals that align with their risk tolerance, making more informed choices based on the level of acceptable uncertainty.

Bayesian Regression

Definition: Bayesian regression combines Bayesian inference with regression models, enabling the estimation of uncertainty in the form of a posterior distribution over the predicted values.

Implications:

Probabilistic Predictions: Bayesian regression provides not only point estimates but also probability distributions over predicted values, allowing for nuanced understanding of uncertainty.

Decision Support: The posterior distribution guides decision-making by offering a comprehensive view of possible outcomes and their associated probabilities.

26.3.3. Applications of Uncertainty Estimation: The application of uncertainty estimation techniques extends to various domains, enhancing decision-making and model robustness.

Medical Diagnostics: Uncertainty estimation in medical diagnostics helps doctors assess the reliability of predictions and determine when additional tests or expert opinions are necessary.

Financial Forecasting: In financial forecasting, uncertainty estimates provide a clearer picture of potential risks and guide investment decisions with a better understanding of potential outcomes.

Autonomous Systems: Uncertainty estimation is crucial in autonomous systems, such as self-driving cars, enabling them to navigate complex scenarios with awareness of prediction reliability.

Uncertainty estimation in classification and regression tasks empowers deep learning models to provide more informative and reliable predictions. Whether in medical diagnosis, financial forecasting, or autonomous systems, these techniques enhance decision-making, mitigate risks, and ensure the responsible deployment of AI in real-world applications.

26.4. Practical Applications of Uncertainty Quantification: Uncertainty quantification is a critical aspect of deep learning that provides valuable insights into the reliability of predictions. In real-world applications, understanding and managing uncertainty are crucial for making informed decisions, enhancing model robustness, and ensuring responsible AI deployment. This chapter explores the practical applications of uncertainty quantification across various domains.

26.4.1. Autonomous Systems

Path Planning: In the realm of autonomous systems, like self-driving cars, navigating real-world environments involves numerous uncertainties. Path planning requires considering dynamic factors such as changing traffic conditions, pedestrians, and road obstructions. Uncertainty quantification plays a pivotal role in ensuring the safety of these systems.

Scenario: Imagine a self-driving car navigating through a busy urban area. The system must decide whether to proceed through an intersection where visibility is limited due to heavy rain.

Role of Uncertainty Quantification:

Safe Navigation: Uncertainty quantification allows the self-driving car to assess the uncertainty of its sensor readings and predictions about the movement of other vehicles and pedestrians. In uncertain scenarios, the car might proceed cautiously or even stop to avoid potential collisions.

Risk Management: By incorporating uncertainty estimates, the autonomous system can weigh the risks associated with different paths and prioritize routes that have lower uncertainty levels. This proactive approach minimizes the chances of accidents and enhances road safety.

26.4.2. Healthcare and Medical Diagnosis

Disease Diagnosis: In the medical field, diagnosing diseases accurately is of utmost importance for patient care. Uncertainty quantification assists medical professionals in making well-informed decisions by providing insights into the reliability of diagnostic predictions.

Scenario: Consider a radiologist examining a medical image to detect early signs of a specific type of cancer.

Role of Uncertainty Quantification:
Confidence in Diagnosis: Uncertainty quantification accompanies diagnostic predictions with a measure of certainty. For example, when identifying a potential tumor, the system might provide an uncertainty estimate that communicates the level of confidence in the diagnosis.
Prioritizing Cases: Higher uncertainty estimates can prompt medical practitioners to recommend further tests, consultations, or screenings to confirm the diagnosis. This reduces the chances of misdiagnosis and ensures patient well-being.

26.4.3. Financial Decision-Making

Stock Price Prediction: Financial markets are inherently uncertain, making accurate predictions of stock prices challenging. Uncertainty quantification plays a significant role in supporting financial analysts' decision-making processes.
Scenario: Imagine a financial analyst predicting the future price of a tech company's stock.
Role of Uncertainty Quantification:
Risk Assessment: Financial analysts use uncertainty estimates to assess the potential risk associated with investment decisions. A higher uncertainty indicates a wider range of possible price outcomes, enabling analysts to make risk-adjusted choices.
Portfolio Diversification: Incorporating uncertainty in stock price predictions allows investors to create diversified portfolios that account for potential market fluctuations. Diversification helps manage risk and enhance the overall stability of an investment portfolio.

26.4.4. Natural Language Processing (NLP)

Sentiment Analysis: In the field of NLP, understanding the sentiment expressed in text is essential for applications ranging from social media analysis to customer feedback assessment.
Scenario: Consider a sentiment analysis model assessing customer reviews for a product.
Role of Uncertainty Quantification:
Refined Insights: Uncertainty quantification adds depth to sentiment analysis by indicating the level of confidence in the predicted sentiment. For instance, if a review is classified as "positive" with high uncertainty, it suggests that the sentiment might not be strongly expressed in the text.
Decision-Specific Sentiment: In situations where sentiment analysis guides critical decisions, such as product launches or public relations strategies, knowing the uncertainty associated with sentiment predictions helps stakeholders make well-grounded choices.

26.4.5. Environmental Monitoring

Disaster Prediction: Predicting natural disasters, such as earthquakes or hurricanes, is crucial for minimizing damage and ensuring the safety of populations in affected areas.
Scenario: Imagine an earthquake prediction system monitoring seismic activities in a region prone to earthquakes.
Role of Uncertainty Quantification:
Reliable Warnings: Uncertainty quantification improves the accuracy of disaster predictions by providing estimates of prediction reliability. Authorities can issue warnings based on not only the predicted event but also the level of confidence in the prediction.
Resource Allocation: When disaster strikes, the uncertainty of predictions can guide resource allocation and emergency response efforts. A more certain prediction might trigger a faster and more comprehensive response, while predictions with higher uncertainty might lead to more cautious planning.and improving the robustness of AI systems. By addressing uncertainty in autonomous systems, healthcare, finance, NLP, and environmental monitoring, we ensure the responsible and effective use of AI technologies in a wide range of real-world scenarios.

26.5 Project

Unsolved Project

Suppose you're developing a project focused on quantifying uncertainty in deep learning models. To create a comprehensive and effective project, you need to understand the sources of uncertainty in neural networks, Bayesian deep learning and probabilistic models, uncertainty estimation techniques in classification and regression tasks, and the practical applications of uncertainty quantification. Before starting, research the following: the different sources of uncertainty in neural networks, including aleatoric and epistemic uncertainty, the principles of Bayesian deep learning and how probabilistic models can be used to quantify uncertainty, methods for estimating uncertainty in both classification and regression tasks, and various practical applications where uncertainty quantification is crucial, such as in medical diagnosis, autonomous driving, and financial forecasting. This foundational knowledge will help you develop a project that effectively incorporates uncertainty quantification in deep learning models.

26.6 Lab Activity

Unsolved Lab Activity

Implement a practical application of uncertainty quantification in a chosen field (e.g., predicting patient outcomes in healthcare). Evaluate the impact of uncertainty estimation on the decision-making process.

Task: Choose a practical application of uncertainty quantification (e.g., predicting patient outcomes in healthcare) and implement a deep learning model with uncertainty estimation. Evaluate the impact of uncertainty estimation on the decision-making process. Document the implementation process, including data preprocessing, model architecture, training procedure, and evaluation. Provide visualizations and analysis of how uncertainty estimation influences decisions and outcomes.

Exercises

Exercise 1 – Multiple Choice Questions

1. What is one of the key challenges introduced by data variability in neural networks?
   A. Overfitting
   B. Robust predictions
   C. Increased generalization
   D. Improved reliability
2. What is the definition of noisy data in neural networks?
   A. Data with high variability
   B. Data with low variance
   C. Data with errors and inconsistencies
   D. Data with clear patterns
3. What does limited data availability lead to in neural networks?
   A. Overfitting
   B. Underfitting
   C. Enhanced generalization
   D. Increased reliability
4. What is the primary implication of model complexity in neural networks?
   A. Improved generalization
   B. Reduced sensitivity to noise
   C. Limited decision-making
   D. Increased risk of overfitting
5. How can Bayesian inference assist in decision-making with Bayesian deep learning models?
   A. By providing certainty in predictions
   B. By offering point estimates
   C. By offering probability distributions
   D. By reducing model complexity

Exercise 2 – True/False

1. Bayesian Deep Learning utilizes probabilistic models to quantify uncertainty.
2. Uncertainty estimation is only applicable to classification tasks, not regression.
3. Practical applications of uncertainty quantification include fields such as healthcare and autonomous driving.

Review Questions

1. What are some sources of uncertainty in neural networks, and how do they affect reliability and generalization?
2. Explain the concept of data variability and its implications for neural networks.
3. How does noisy data impact the training and predictions of neural networks?
4. Describe the challenges posed by limited data availability in neural network training.
5. What is overfitting, and how is it related to data variability and noisy data?
6. How can neural networks mitigate uncertainties related to data variability?
7. What is epistemic uncertainty, and how is it different from aleatoric uncertainty?
8. How does model complexity affect the generalization of neural networks, and what are its implications?
9. Explain the role of model parameters in introducing uncertainty in neural networks.
10. What is expressiveness limits, and how does it relate to model uncertainty?

11. How can techniques like regularization and assembling help mitigate model uncertainty?
12. Describe Bayesian deep learning and its approach to handling uncertainty in neural networks.
13. What is the significance of Bayesian inference in Bayesian deep learning?
14. How does dropout act as a Bayesian approximation in neural networks?
15. What are probabilistic models, and how do they capture uncertainty?
16. Explain the concept of variational inference and its role in uncertainty estimation.
17. What are Gaussian Processes, and in what scenarios are they particularly useful for uncertainty modeling?
18. Provide examples of applications for Bayesian deep learning in real-world domains.
19. How can uncertainty estimation be beneficial in medical diagnostics?
20. In what ways does uncertainty quantification support financial forecasting?
21. How can uncertainty quantification enhance sentiment analysis in natural language processing?
22. Describe a scenario where uncertainty quantification is crucial in environmental monitoring.
23. What role does uncertainty quantification play in path planning for autonomous systems?
24. How does uncertainty quantification help in decision-making for autonomous vehicles?
25. What are prediction intervals, and how do they provide insights into regression tasks?

Answers

Exercise 1- 1.A 2.C 3.B 4.D 5.C
Exercise 2- 1) True, 2) False, 3) True

Online Resources

Online Exam Paper:
Link: **https://forms.gle/Z9ZSB5BFzV5fSNQj7**
QR Code:

Chapter 26 Videos Playlist:
Link: **https://www.youtube.com/playlist?list=PLzlh_31VWEFopNzE_ZcVrytKhqOZ-kSvH**
QR Code:

Chapter 27: Neural Style Transfer and Creative Applications

27.1 Understanding Neural Style Transfer:

27.1.1 Introduction to Neural Style Transfer: Neural Style Transfer (NST) is a captivating convergence of deep learning and artistic expression. It merges the content of one image with the artistic style of another, producing visually captivating compositions that incorporate content and style features from the input images.

27.1.2 Content and Style Representation: NST centers around two fundamental aspects: content and style. Content pertains to an image's high-level features, including objects and structures. Style encompasses textures, colors, and artistic patterns that define an image's stylistic character. NST's objective is to untangle and recombine these elements, generating novel visuals that blend content and style.

27.1.3 Working Principle of NST: Neural Style Transfer (NST) harnesses pre-trained deep neural networks, notably convolutional neural networks (CNNs), to extract content and style features from input images. Deeper layers of the network provide content features, capturing semantic information, while intermediate layers supply style features, encoding textures and patterns.

27.1.4 Loss Functions for Style Transfer: NST relies on loss functions to steer the transformation process. The content loss quantifies the divergence between content features of the input and generated images. Meanwhile, the style loss measures discrepancies in the Gram matrices of style features, capturing their interrelations.

27.1.5 Optimization Process: The optimization process within Neural Style Transfer (NST) involves a series of iterations that refine the generated image. The goal is to minimize both content and style losses simultaneously. This iterative approach seeks to achieve a delicate equilibrium: preserving the original content details of the input image while incorporating the desired stylistic elements from the reference style image. The optimization process gradually transforms the generated image to strike a balance that encapsulates both content and style in the final composition.

27.1.6 Applications of Neural Style Transfer: Neural Style Transfer finds a multitude of applications across various domains, showcasing its versatility and creative potential. One prominent application is in artistic creation, allowing artists, designers, and enthusiasts to experiment with blending different styles and generating entirely new visual aesthetics. It serves as a powerful tool for image enhancement, offering ways to imbue images with distinct artistic qualities. Moreover, NST plays a role in storytelling, enabling unique visual representations that evoke specific moods or convey narratives. By emulating the styles of renowned artists, NST can transform ordinary images into mesmerizing pieces that bear the unmistakable signature of art history's great masters.

27.1.7 Challenges and Future Directions: While Neural Style Transfer (NST) offers a captivating realm of creative possibilities, it is not without challenges and avenues for future exploration.

Precision and Control: One challenge lies in achieving precise control over the generated images. Fine-tuning the balance between content and style can be intricate, and enhancing the ability to steer the artistic output according to specific preferences remains an ongoing pursuit.

Real-Time Style Transfer: Enabling real-time style transfer is another challenge. The optimization process in NST can be computationally intensive, hindering its seamless application in interactive scenarios. Future directions involve developing more efficient algorithms and architectures to achieve real-time or near-real-time style transformations.

Advanced Architectures and Algorithms: Researchers are actively delving into more advanced neural network architectures and optimization algorithms for NST. Exploring novel architectures, such as generative adversarial networks (GANs) and transformer-based models, can further enhance the quality and diversity of generated images.

Cross-Domain Style Transfer: Extending NST to handle cross-domain style transfer is an exciting direction. Enabling the transfer of styles from vastly different domains, such as transferring artistic styles to photographs of real-world scenes, presents intriguing challenges in capturing and preserving distinctive stylistic features.

Semi-Supervised and Unsupervised NST: While current NST methods often require a separate style reference image, future directions involve exploring semi-supervised or unsupervised NST. This would allow the model to learn and adapt styles from a broader range of images without the need for explicit reference.

Hybrid Approaches: Combining NST with other techniques, such as generative models, can lead to hybrid approaches that offer enhanced creative control and stylistic diversity.

Neural Style Transfer is an evolving field with exciting prospects. Overcoming current challenges and exploring these future directions will contribute to making NST an even more powerful tool for artistic expression, image manipulation, and visual storytelling.

27.2 Art Generation and Style Transfer Techniques:

27.2.1 Neural Style Transfer Variants: Neural Style Transfer (NST) has evolved beyond its original form to inspire a range of creative variants, each with its own distinctive approach to merging content and style. These variants have expanded the possibilities of artistic expression and pushed the boundaries of style transfer techniques. One such notable variant is Style Interpolation.

Style Interpolation introduces a fascinating twist to traditional style transfer by allowing the creation of images that seamlessly blend two distinct artistic styles. This technique enables artists and creators to explore the synthesis of contrasting aesthetics, resulting in visually captivating compositions that showcase the fusion of different artistic identities.

The core idea behind Style Interpolation is to find a harmonious balance between two separate style images. Instead of choosing a single style image to apply to the content, this variant involves computing intermediate style representations between two chosen style images. These intermediate style representations serve as transition points, gradually shifting from the characteristics of one style to the other.

The process of Style Interpolation begins by selecting two style images with distinct artistic qualities. The algorithm then calculates intermediary style representations, effectively creating a trajectory of style transformation between the two chosen styles. These intermediary styles are applied to the content image, which retains its original content features. The resulting image captures the essence of both styles, gradually transitioning from one to the other in a visually coherent manner.

The impact of Style Interpolation is particularly pronounced in artworks that exhibit strong stylistic contrasts. For instance, it could blend the brushstroke patterns of a Van Gogh painting with the minimalist geometry of a Mondrian artwork. The final image reflects an aesthetic fusion that balances the intricate textures of one style with the structured simplicity of the other.

In summary, Style Interpolation within Neural Style Transfer offers a novel and compelling way to explore the intersection of different artistic styles. By creating a seamless transition between two distinct aesthetics, it unlocks the potential for generating artwork that harmoniously combines the best of both worlds. This approach not only showcases the versatility of style transfer techniques but also opens up new avenues for creative expression and artistic exploration.

27.2.1.2 Instance Normalization: Instance normalization is a technique that enhances the process of neural style transfer by addressing a common issue known as style bias. In traditional style transfer, the generated image can sometimes overly emphasize the style features, leading to results that might not be visually balanced or harmonious. Instance normalization aims to mitigate this bias and achieve more coherent outcomes. The central idea behind instance normalization is to normalize the style features of the generated image to align them with the statistical characteristics of the content image. Unlike traditional normalization techniques that consider the entire batch of images, instance normalization operates on a per-image basis. It normalizes the style features of each pixel or instance within the generated image with respect to the corresponding instance in the content image. By performing normalization at the instance level, instance normalization reduces the discrepancy between the style features and the content features. This helps in preventing the style features from dominating the image while still retaining the desired stylistic effects. As a result, the generated image achieves a better balance between content and style, leading to more visually pleasing and coherent outcomes.

Instance normalization is particularly effective in scenarios where the style image has a strong influence, and achieving an appropriate balance is challenging. By ensuring that the style influence is aligned with the content's visual characteristics, instance normalization contributes to the refinement of neural style transfer results.

In summary, instance normalization is a valuable addition to the toolkit of neural style transfer techniques. By addressing the style bias issue and promoting a better balance between content and style, it enhances the quality and visual coherence of the generated images, leading to more satisfying artistic outcomes.

27.2.2 Arbitrary Style Transfer: Arbitrary style transfer widens the scope of style sources beyond predefined artistic styles. This technique allows users to input arbitrary images as style references, enabling the application of various textures and patterns to the content image. It empowers users to experiment with unconventional artistic inspirations.

27.2.3 Progressive Neural Style Transfer: Progressive Neural Style Transfer refines the optimization process by gradually introducing style features to the generated image. It begins with the content image and progressively incorporates style characteristics at different stages. This approach results in smoother stylistic transitions and improved convergence.

27.2.4 Neural Style Transfer for Videos: Expanding NST to videos involves applying style transfer techniques frame by frame. This creates dynamic visual experiences where each frame inherits the style of choice. Video-based NST opens up possibilities for creating artistic videos, interactive multimedia, and immersive visual content.

27.2.5 Deep Generative Models for Art: Deep Generative Models, like Generative Adversarial Networks (GANs), extend artistic creation beyond style transfer. GANs generate entirely new images that adhere to a specific style. By training the generator to replicate artistic features, GANs contribute to the generation of unique and novel artworks.

27.2.6 Future Innovations and Cross-Domain Exploration: The realm of art generation and style transfer is poised for captivating advancements and cross-domain exploration, offering a glimpse into a creative landscape that extends beyond traditional boundaries. As the field of neural style transfer (NST) continues to evolve, it holds the potential to transcend its current boundaries and influence a diverse range of domains, fostering innovation and inspiration.

One of the most promising directions lies in the intersection of NST with various industries such as fashion, architecture, and product design. The ability of NST techniques to seamlessly blend content and style opens doors for novel applications. For instance, in fashion, NST could facilitate the creation of unique and personalized clothing designs by combining individual preferences with artistic styles. In architecture, it could aid in envisioning imaginative building designs that merge distinct aesthetics. In product design, NST might enable the generation of captivating visual representations of items with specific stylistic influences.

As deep learning methods continue to advance, the creative algorithms underpinning NST are likely to become more sophisticated. This evolution could lead to the emergence of entirely new artistic styles, pushing the boundaries of artistic expression. Artists, designers, and creators may harness these algorithms to explore uncharted territories, resulting in awe-inspiring and thought-provoking creations.

Cross-domain exploration also paves the way for collaborations between artists and AI systems. Artists could provide their unique perspectives, while AI algorithms contribute novel stylistic elements. This synergistic interaction between human creativity and AI-driven innovation could spark entirely new artistic movements and redefine the boundaries of what is possible in the realm of visual art.

the future of art generation and style transfer is marked by the convergence of AI techniques and artistic imagination. As NST techniques evolve and extend their influence into various industries, we can anticipate a dynamic landscape where creativity knows no limits. Through innovative algorithms, cross-domain exploration, and collaborations between humans and machines, the art world is poised to experience a renaissance of inspiration and innovation.

27.3 Deep Learning in Music Composition and Generation: The integration of deep learning techniques into the domain of music composition and generation has ushered in a new era of creative possibilities. Deep learning algorithms, known for their ability to learn patterns and representations from data, are being harnessed to create, enhance, and transform musical compositions in ways that were previously unimaginable.

27.3.1 Music Generation with Recurrent Neural Networks (RNNs): In the realm of music composition, the utilization of Recurrent Neural Networks (RNNs) stands out as a powerful technique for generating new musical compositions. RNNs are a class of deep learning models that excel at handling sequences of data, making them particularly well-suited for capturing the temporal dependencies inherent in music.

Temporal Dependencies in Music: Music is inherently structured in time, with notes, melodies, and harmonies unfolding over time intervals. This temporal structure is crucial for creating musical pieces that sound coherent and expressive. Traditional computer-generated music often struggled to capture these temporal patterns convincingly. However, RNNs, and their more advanced variant Long Short-Term Memory (LSTM) networks, address this challenge by recognizing and learning the sequential relationships between musical elements.

Function of RNNs in Music Generation: When used for music generation, an RNN, or more often an LSTM, is trained on a dataset of existing musical compositions. The model learns to predict the next note or event in a sequence based on the preceding ones. This learned knowledge of musical patterns, such as melodies, harmonies, and rhythms, allows the RNN to generate new sequences of notes that exhibit similar patterns to those in the training data.

Generating Novel Compositions: Once trained, the RNN can be used to compose new music. Starting with a seed sequence or even a single note, the model generates subsequent notes by predicting what note should follow based on the patterns it has learned. This iterative process continues, gradually building a new musical composition that inherits the stylistic characteristics of the training data. The generated composition can be as short as a few bars or as long as a complete piece, such as a symphony.

Limitations and Creative Exploration: While RNNs and LSTMs have shown remarkable capabilities in capturing temporal dependencies and generating coherent music, they also have limitations. They tend to replicate existing musical patterns and structures, which can result in compositions that sound too familiar or imitative. However, these limitations can also be turned into opportunities for creative exploration. Musicians and composers often use the output of RNN-generated compositions as starting points, tweaking and transforming the generated music to create unique and novel pieces.

In summary, the application of RNNs and LSTMs in music generation represents a significant advancement in AI-driven artistic expression. These models leverage their ability to comprehend and replicate temporal patterns to create new musical compositions that draw inspiration from existing music while also opening doors to innovative sonic landscapes.

27.3.2 Style Transfer and Fusion: In the realm of music composition and generation, deep learning techniques are not limited to generating new compositions: they also enable the fusion and transformation of musical styles. Much like the concept of visual style transfer, where artistic styles are applied to images, music style transfer involves imbuing the characteristics of one musical genre, artist, or piece onto another, resulting in a captivating blend of musical elements and styles.

Adapting Visual Style Transfer to Music: The idea behind music style transfer draws parallels with its visual counterpart. In visual style transfer, the content of one image is combined with the artistic style of another, resulting in a novel image that retains the content while adopting the stylistic features of a different artwork. In a similar manner, music style transfer aims to retain the melodic and structural elements of a piece while infusing it with the sonic characteristics and stylistic nuances of another musical genre, artist, or composition.

Fusion of Diverse Musical Elements: Music style transfer allows for the fusion of diverse musical elements. Imagine taking the rhythmic complexity of jazz and blending it with the harmonic richness of classical music. Alternatively, one could experiment with applying the characteristics of a renowned composer, like Mozart, onto a contemporary pop song. These experiments result in compositions that transcend traditional genre boundaries, offering listeners and creators a novel auditory experience that is both innovative and expressive.

Challenges and Opportunities: While the concept of music style transfer is exciting, it also presents challenges. Transferring styles seamlessly while preserving the coherence of the composition requires careful balancing of musical elements. Just as in visual style transfer, the challenge lies in finding the right balance between content retention and style integration to produce compositions that are both coherent and artistically interesting.

Creative Exploration and Musical Diversity: Music style transfer opens doors to creative exploration and musical diversity. Musicians and composers can draw inspiration from a wide array of genres and influences, leading to the creation of compositions that challenge traditional musical norms and conventions. This fusion of styles not only encourages artistic experimentation but also enriches the musical landscape by introducing fresh sounds and innovative combinations.

In essence, music style transfer using deep learning techniques embodies the spirit of musical experimentation and cross-genre exploration. By allowing musicians to blend and fuse diverse musical elements, this approach contributes to the evolution of music and the creation of compositions that are as unique as they are harmoniously multifaceted. **27.3.3 Enhancing Creativity**

and Composition: Deep learning models are not only tools for generating music: they can also function as creative assistants that enhance the creative process for composers. This interaction between human composers and AI-driven assistance offers a dynamic and collaborative approach to music composition, leading to the emergence of innovative and unexpected musical creations.

Composer's Style and AI Analysis: One of the key ways in which deep learning models can aid composers is by analyzing a composer's existing body of work. By training on the composer's compositions, these models can learn the nuances, patterns, and characteristics that define the composer's unique style. This understanding enables the model to generate new musical elements that seamlessly align with the composer's established artistic identity.

Suggesting Melodies, Harmonies, and Arrangements: With this knowledge of the composer's style, deep learning models can suggest new melodies, harmonies, chord progressions, and arrangements that resonate with the composer's musical preferences. These suggestions serve as creative prompts, sparking inspiration and offering alternative directions for the composition. Composers can explore these AI-generated ideas and adapt them to their artistic vision.

Collaborative Exploration and Innovation: The collaboration between composers and AI-driven creative assistants leads to a symbiotic relationship. Composers bring their artistic intuition, emotion, and vision to the table, while AI models provide an expansive database of musical possibilities based on learned patterns. This interplay encourages composers to venture beyond their usual comfort zones, exploring new melodic paths, harmonic relationships, and structural approaches.

Unlocking Unanticipated Musical Directions: The true beauty of this collaborative approach is its capacity to unlock unanticipated musical directions. AI-driven suggestions might introduce composers to novel chord progressions, unconventional rhythms, or unexpected instrumentations that they might not have considered otherwise. This process of creative cross-pollination can lead to compositions that defy genre boundaries and embrace a rich blend of influences.

Fostering Innovation and Growth: Enhancing creativity through AI-driven assistance fosters innovation and growth in music composition. Composers are not limited to their own experiences and musical instincts: they have a partner that offers a fresh perspective and a wellspring of ideas. This augmentation of the creative process can lead to the creation of pieces that push the boundaries of musical expression and offer unique sonic experiences to audiences.

27.3.4 Music Analysis and Understanding: Deep learning techniques play a pivotal role in enhancing the analysis and understanding of music. These techniques leverage the power of neural networks to automatically decipher complex musical patterns and structures, contributing to various aspects of music scholarship, recommendation systems, and genre classification.

Automated Musical Note Transcription: One significant application of deep learning in music analysis is automated musical note transcription. Neural networks can process audio recordings and accurately extract the musical notes and their timings. This transcription process, which was traditionally labor-intensive and required human expertise, is now expedited by deep learning models. This capability is invaluable for musicologists, composers, and performers, enabling them to quickly obtain notated representations of audio recordings.

Pattern Recognition and Musicology: Deep learning models excel at recognizing intricate patterns within music. They can identify recurring motifs, chord progressions, melodic sequences, and rhythmic patterns across large datasets of musical compositions. Musicologists and researchers can utilize these pattern recognition capabilities to uncover trends, influences, and evolutionary trajectories within different musical genres and historical periods.

Music Genre Classification: Another area where deep learning shines is music genre classification. Neural networks can be trained on vast collections of audio tracks, learning the distinctive features that characterize different musical genres. This enables models to accurately classify music based on its sonic attributes, such as tempo, instrumentation, harmony, and rhythm. Such genre classification has practical applications in music recommendation systems, where songs are suggested to listeners based on their preferred genres.

Enhancing Music Recommendation Systems: Deep learning's ability to understand the intricacies of musical compositions enhances the capabilities of music recommendation systems. By analyzing the content and style of songs, these systems can offer personalized recommendations to users. For instance, if a user enjoys songs with specific harmonic progressions or rhythmic characteristics, the recommendation system can suggest similar tracks that align with the user's musical preferences.

Deeper Insights into Music Structures: The application of deep learning in music analysis provides a means to delve deeper into the underlying structures of different musical genres. By automatically identifying motifs, themes, and variations, researchers gain a more comprehensive understanding of how music is constructed. This knowledge can illuminate the historical evolution of musical genres, shed light on cultural influences, and offer insights into the creative processes of composers and musicians.

deep learning techniques contribute significantly to the field of music analysis and understanding. By automating tasks like musical note transcription, recognizing patterns, classifying genres, and enhancing recommendation systems, these techniques empower musicologists, scholars, artists, and enthusiasts with new tools to explore the intricate world of music in unprecedented ways.

27.3.5 Challenges and Future Directions: As deep learning continues to reshape music composition and generation, several challenges and exciting future directions emerge, shaping the trajectory of this field.

Coherent and Expressive Compositions: One ongoing challenge is the creation of coherent and emotionally expressive compositions. While deep learning models can generate musical sequences, ensuring that these sequences form cohesive musical pieces with emotional resonance remains complex. Current models might produce fragments that lack logical progression or fail to convey the intended emotions, indicating the need for improved coherence and expressiveness.

Handling Long-Term Dependencies: Music often involves long-term dependencies, where musical motifs and themes evolve over extended periods. Existing deep learning architectures, like recurrent neural networks (RNNs), can struggle with capturing such long-range relationships effectively. Future directions may involve exploring novel architectures or combining multiple neural network layers to better capture intricate musical structures that span across measures or phrases.

Balance between Creativity and Imitation: Deep learning models can sometimes become excessively imitative, replicating existing compositions without introducing innovative elements. Striking a balance between drawing inspiration from existing music and generating novel, creative content is an ongoing challenge. Researchers are working towards developing techniques that encourage models to explore uncharted musical territories while respecting stylistic conventions.

Addressing Copyright and Intellectual Property: As AI-generated music becomes more sophisticated, ethical considerations related to copyright and intellectual property become paramount. Ensuring that AI models respect copyright laws and generate content that is original and doesn't infringe upon existing compositions is crucial. Striking a balance between learning from existing music and producing content that is uniquely creative is a challenge that requires legal and technical solutions.

Human-AI Collaboration: Future directions in this field involve fostering collaboration between human composers and AI models. Rather than replacing human creativity, AI can serve as a creative assistant, sparking new ideas and providing composers with fresh perspectives. This symbiotic relationship could lead to the emergence of entirely new musical genres or hybrid compositions that seamlessly blend human intuition with AI's computational prowess.

Exploration of Multimodal Music Generation: The incorporation of multimodal inputs, such as visual stimuli or textual descriptions, could open new frontiers in music composition. Models that generate music in response to visual art, poetry, or emotional cues could yield innovative and diverse musical outputs, expanding the possibilities of creative expression.

Ethical and Cultural Considerations: As AI-generated music gains prominence, considerations regarding cultural sensitivity and the potential impact on musical diversity come to the forefront. Ensuring that AI systems understand and respect the nuances of various musical traditions while fostering cross-cultural collaborations is a vital aspect of responsible AI-driven music generation.

while deep learning has already transformed music composition and generation, challenges persist in achieving coherence, handling long-term dependencies, and navigating ethical considerations. As researchers and musicians work collaboratively to overcome these challenges, the future holds exciting possibilities for the integration of AI and human creativity in the realm of music.

27.4 Creative AI: Challenges and Opportunities: The dynamic realm of AI and creativity presents a dichotomy of challenges and opportunities, reshaping the landscapes of innovation and artistic expression. The evolution of AI technologies promises to elevate creative potential in diverse domains, but concurrently introduces intricate obstacles that demand nuanced examination.

Challenges:

Originality vs. Imitation: The juxtaposition of AI-generated content with originality raises inquiries into authenticity. Finding equilibrium between AI-driven inspiration and outright replication is an ongoing challenge. Ensuring that AI-generated works contribute to artistic expansion rather than mimicry is paramount.

Bias and Diversity: AI models learn from existing data, potentially inheriting biases present within. Particularly pertinent in creative fields, such biases may perpetuate stereotypes and hinder diversity. The challenge lies in cultivating fair, inclusive, and culturally sensitive approaches that transcend these limitations.

Human-AI Synergy: Harmonizing human creativity with AI assistance demands careful orchestration. Integrating AI as a creative collaborator, amplifying rather than overshadowing human creativity, necessitates finely tuned models. Crafting interfaces for seamless interaction between human artists and AI tools poses ongoing complexity.

Ethical Contemplations: The ethical fabric of AI-generated content prompts contemplation over ownership, copyright, and misinformation. Defining ownership of AI-fostered artworks, safeguarding intellectual property rights, and establishing transparent disclosure protocols remain essential for ethical conduct.

Preserving the Human Essence: While AI augments creative processes, the intangible facets of human emotion, intuition, and interpretation remain invaluable. Safeguarding these human nuances amidst AI integration demands delicate handling, ensuring that artworks resonate with genuine human sentiment.

Opportunities:

Creative Amplification: AI has the potential to magnify human creativity by introducing novel tools, perspectives, and inspirations. Creative practitioners can leverage AI algorithms to explore uncharted territories, experiment with unconventional ideas, and extend the limits of traditional artistic norms.

Interdisciplinary Fusion: The realm of creative AI serves as a nexus for interdisciplinary collaboration, fostering interactions among artists, scientists, engineers, and scholars. Converging diverse viewpoints can drive innovation and give birth to entirely new art forms that span multiple domains.

Democratizing Access: AI democratises creativity by rendering artistic tools and experiences accessible to a wider populace. AI-generated music, visual art, and literature enable individuals lacking formal training to engage in creative expression, thus democratizing the process of artistic creation.

Personalization and Expression: AI-powered personalization tailors content to individual preferences, intensifying user engagement and immersion. In music, literature, and visual arts, AI crafts experiences that resonate on a deeply personal level, furnishing distinctive and profound creative interactions.

Unveiling New Aesthetics: AI transcends human confines and explores aesthetics that challenge traditional norms. It synthesizes novel amalgamations of styles, genres, and techniques, culminating in art forms that stretch the limits of established artistic conventions.

Conclusion: As AI converges with creative endeavors, the pursuit of harnessing its potential while maneuvering complexities becomes collective. Seizing the prospects of AI's contributions while grappling with ethical, cultural, and creative considerations is pivotal for forging a future wherein AI amplifies human creativity, enriches artistic expression, and weaves itself into the vibrant fabric of human culture.

27.5 Project

Unsolved Project

Suppose you're developing a project that explores creative applications of deep learning, focusing on neural style transfer and other artistic domains. To create a comprehensive project, you need to understand neural style transfer, techniques for art generation and style transfer, deep learning applications in music composition and generation, and the challenges and opportunities in creative AI. Before starting, research the following: the principles and mechanisms behind neural style transfer, various techniques used for generating and transferring artistic styles, the use of deep learning in composing and generating music, and the broader challenges and opportunities associated with creative AI applications, including ethical considerations, originality, and the potential for enhancing human creativity. This foundational knowledge will help you develop a project that effectively utilizes deep learning for creative purposes.

27.6 Lab Activity

Unsolved Lab Activity

Implement a deep learning model for music composition using an RNN or LSTM. Train the model on a dataset of music sequences and generate new compositions.

Task: Use a deep learning framework to implement an RNN or LSTM model for music composition. Train the model on a dataset of music sequences and use it to generate new compositions. Document the implementation process, including data preprocessing, model architecture, training procedure, and examples of the generated music.

Exercises

Exercise 1 – Multiple Choice Questions

1. What is Neural Style Transfer (NST)?
   a. A technique for text summarization
   b. A method for image compression
   c. A convergence of deep learning and artistic expression
   d. A way to enhance audio quality
2. In NST, what does "content" refer to?
   a. Textures and colors
   b. High-level features like objects and structures
   c. Artistic patterns
   d. The artistic signature of an image
3. Which type of neural networks are commonly used in NST for extracting content and style features?
   a. Recurrent Neural Networks (RNNs)
   b. Convolutional Neural Networks (CNNs)
   c. Generative Adversarial Networks (GANs)
   d. Long Short-Term Memory (LSTM) networks
4. What is the primary purpose of the content loss in NST?
   a. Quantify the divergence between content features of the input and generated images
   b. Measure discrepancies in the Gram matrices of style features
   c. Enhance the artistic style of the image
   d. Reduce computational intensity during optimization
5. What is the goal of the optimization process in NST?
   a. To maximize content loss
   b. To minimize both content and style losses simultaneously
   c. To generate entirely new images from scratch
   d. To prioritize style over content

Exercise 2 – True/False

1. Neural Style Transfer can only be applied to images, not music.

2. One of the applications of Neural Style Transfer is in generating art by applying the style of one image to another.
3. Deep Learning is used in music composition and generation.

Review Questions

1. What is the core concept of Neural Style Transfer (NST)?
2. Describe the difference between content and style in NST.
3. Which types of features do deeper layers of neural networks provide in NST?
4. How are content and style losses used in NST?
5. Explain the optimization process in Neural Style Transfer.
6. What are some applications of Neural Style Transfer mentioned in the chapter?
7. What are the challenges in achieving precise control over generated images in NST?
8. What is the challenge associated with real-time style transfer in NST?
9. How does instance normalization address the style bias issue in style transfer?
10. What is arbitrary style transfer, and what does it enable users to do?

Answers

Exercise 1- 1. c 2. b 3. b 4. a 5. b
Exercise 2- 1) False, 2) True, 3) True

Online Resources

Online Exam Paper:
Link: https://forms.gle/dE9ktaqzXbxcgSwYA
QR Code:

Chapter 27 Videos Playlist:
Link: https://www.youtube.com/playlist?list=PLzlh_31VWEFqEU7thYi0XoexALnwzlHFV
QR Code:

Chapter 28: Deep Learning for Social Good

28.1. The Role of Artificial Intelligence in Tackling Societal Challenges: In recent years, artificial intelligence (AI) has emerged as a powerful tool with the potential to address some of the most pressing societal challenges that our world faces today. As AI technologies continue to advance, they offer innovative solutions and insights across various domains, from healthcare to environmental conservation. This chapter explores the transformative impact of AI in tackling complex societal issues.

28.1.1. Understanding Societal Challenges: In order to comprehend the profound impact of artificial intelligence (AI) in addressing societal challenges, it's crucial to first gain a comprehensive understanding of the nature and complexity of these challenges. Societal challenges encompass a wide array of issues that affect communities, regions, and the world at large. These challenges often transcend individual boundaries and require collaborative efforts to find effective solutions. Some of the prominent societal challenges include healthcare disparities, climate change, poverty, and urbanization.

Healthcare Disparities: One of the critical issues in society is the uneven distribution of healthcare resources and services. This leads to disparities in health outcomes among different socioeconomic groups. Marginalized communities often lack access to quality healthcare, resulting in higher rates of preventable diseases and reduced life expectancy. Addressing healthcare disparities involves not only improving access to medical services but also understanding the underlying socioeconomic factors contributing to these disparities.

Climate Change: The global climate crisis poses a significant threat to the planet's ecosystems and human societies. Rising temperatures, extreme weather events, and environmental degradation have far-reaching consequences, impacting everything from agriculture and water resources to public health. Addressing climate change requires coordinated efforts to reduce greenhouse gas emissions, develop sustainable energy sources, and implement resilient infrastructure.

Poverty: Poverty remains a persistent challenge in many parts of the world. It hinders access to education, healthcare, and economic opportunities, trapping individuals and communities in cycles of deprivation. Poverty eradication involves strategies that promote inclusive economic growth, social safety nets, and equitable distribution of resources.

Urbanization: As the world's population becomes increasingly urbanized, cities face unique challenges related to infrastructure, housing, transportation, and resource management. Rapid urbanization can lead to overcrowding, inadequate living conditions, and strain on essential services. Sustainable urban planning and smart city initiatives are essential to create livable and efficient urban environments.

Addressing these multifaceted challenges necessitates approaches that go beyond the boundaries of traditional disciplines. Multidisciplinary collaboration is essential to tackle the root causes and interconnected nature of these problems. Furthermore, effective solutions often require a combination of data-driven insights, technological innovations, and human expertise.

28.1.2. Leveraging Data for Insights: At the heart of AI's transformative potential lies its ability to process and analyze vast volumes of data to extract valuable insights. Data is the fuel that powers AI algorithms, enabling them to discern patterns, correlations, and trends that might be imperceptible to human analysis. This capability holds immense promise for addressing societal challenges.

Diverse Data Sources: AI can leverage data from a wide range of sources, including sensors, social media platforms, satellite imagery, and healthcare records. This diverse array of data provides a holistic view of complex issues, allowing for a more comprehensive understanding of the challenges at hand.

Pattern Recognition: AI algorithms excel at recognizing intricate patterns within datasets. For instance, in healthcare, AI can analyze medical images to identify early signs of diseases such as cancer, facilitating timely intervention and treatment.

Predictive Modeling: Machine learning algorithms can develop predictive models based on historical data. These models can forecast trends and outcomes, aiding decision-making and policy formulation. For instance, in climate science, AI models can predict the trajectory of temperature changes and sea level rise.

Data-Driven Decision-Making: The insights derived from data analysis enable informed decision-making. Governments, organizations, and policymakers can use AI-generated insights to develop strategies that address societal challenges more effectively.

Uncovering Hidden Correlations: AI can reveal hidden correlations and causal relationships within complex datasets. This is particularly valuable when dealing with challenges that involve a multitude of interrelated factors, such as poverty and urbanization.

By leveraging AI-powered data analysis, we can make better-informed decisions and design targeted interventions that have the potential to create lasting positive impacts on society. However, it's important to approach data usage ethically and responsibly, ensuring privacy, transparency, and fairness in AI applications.

28.1.3. Enhancing Healthcare and Medicine: In recent years, the integration of artificial intelligence (AI) into the field of healthcare has ushered in a new era of diagnostics, treatment, and patient care. AI's ability to process and analyze vast amounts of medical data has led to significant advancements, enhancing the accuracy, efficiency, and personalization of healthcare practices.

Medical Imaging and Diagnostics: One of the most prominent areas where AI has demonstrated its capabilities is in medical imaging. AI-powered algorithms can analyze medical images, such as X-rays, MRIs, and CT scans, to identify abnormalities and assist radiologists in diagnosing diseases like cancer and neurological disorders. This not only speeds up the diagnostic process but also improves accuracy by reducing human errors.

Predictive Analytics for Patient Outcomes: AI is increasingly being used to predict patient outcomes based on historical data and current health conditions. By analyzing patient data, AI algorithms can identify patterns that contribute to certain health outcomes, allowing medical professionals to intervene proactively and tailor treatment plans to individual patients.

Precision Medicine: The concept of precision medicine involves tailoring medical treatments and interventions to individual patients based on their genetic makeup, lifestyle, and medical history. AI plays a pivotal role in analyzing genetic data, identifying genetic markers, and suggesting personalized treatment approaches. This approach has the potential to revolutionize how we treat diseases, moving away from a one-size-fits-all approach to more targeted and effective treatments.

Drug Discovery and Development: AI is accelerating the drug discovery process by analyzing vast databases of molecular information and predicting potential drug candidates. This not only reduces the time and cost associated with drug development but also increases the likelihood of identifying novel treatments for various diseases.

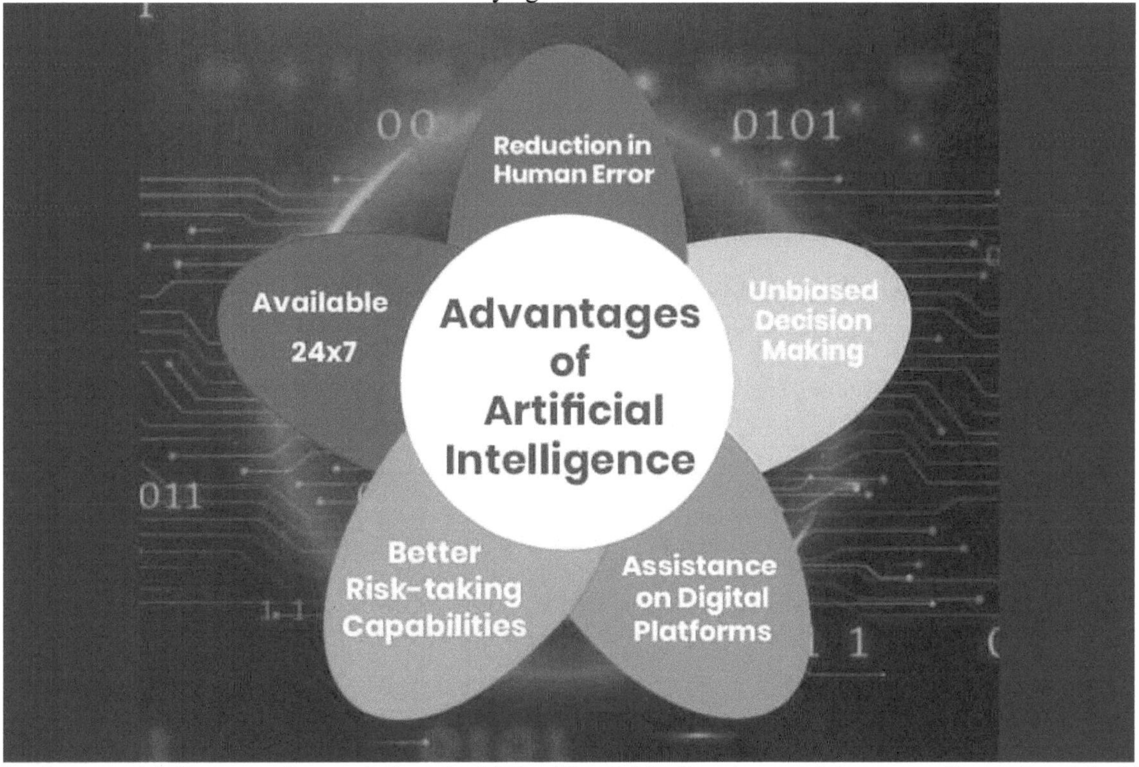

28.1.4. Environmental Conservation and Sustainability: The field of environmental conservation and sustainability has found a powerful ally in artificial intelligence. AI's capacity to process and analyze large-scale environmental data has opened up new avenues for monitoring, predicting, and managing our planet's ecosystems.

Environmental Monitoring: AI-powered analytics can process data from satellite imagery, sensors, and other sources to monitor changes in the environment. This includes tracking deforestation, land use changes, ocean health, and air quality. Such monitoring provides valuable insights into the state of the environment and aids in timely interventions to prevent degradation.

Wildlife Conservation: AI is being employed to track and monitor wildlife populations, particularly endangered species. Camera traps and sensors can collect data on animal behaviors and movement patterns, enabling conservationists to make informed decisions about habitat preservation and protection.

Disaster Preparedness and Response: AI's predictive capabilities extend to natural disasters. By analyzing historical and real-time data, AI algorithms can predict the occurrence of natural disasters such as hurricanes, floods, and wildfires. This allows authorities to implement proactive measures and allocate resources for disaster response and recovery.

Energy Efficiency: AI is also being used to optimize energy consumption and improve energy efficiency. Smart grids, powered by AI algorithms, can balance energy supply and demand, reducing waste and promoting the use of renewable energy sources.

Sustainable Agriculture: AI can assist in optimizing agricultural practices by analyzing data related to soil quality, weather conditions, and crop health. This leads to improved yields, reduced resource waste, and more environmentally friendly farming methods.

In both healthcare and environmental conservation, AI showcases its potential to address some of the most pressing challenges of our time. Through accurate diagnostics, personalized treatments, environmental monitoring, and predictive modeling, AI contributes to building a healthier and more sustainable future for humanity and the planet.

28.1.5. Social Equality and Inclusion: Artificial intelligence (AI) holds significant promise as a tool to promote social equality and inclusivity by identifying and addressing disparities across various domains. Through data analysis and targeted interventions, AI has the potential to bridge gaps and create a more equitable society.

Data-Driven Insights: AI's ability to process vast amounts of data enables it to identify patterns of inequality and discrimination. By analyzing demographic and socioeconomic data, AI can uncover disparities in areas such as education, employment, healthcare, and criminal justice.

Highlighting Inequalities: AI can shed light on systemic biases and discriminatory practices that perpetuate inequality. For example, AI algorithms can analyze hiring practices to identify biases in recruitment and recommend changes to promote diversity in the workplace.

Policy Recommendations: AI can provide data-backed recommendations for policy changes that address social inequalities. By identifying root causes and suggesting evidence-based solutions, AI can assist policymakers in developing more effective and targeted interventions.

Educational Tools: AI-powered educational tools have the potential to democratize access to quality learning resources. These tools can adapt to individual learning styles, making education more inclusive for diverse groups of learners, including those with disabilities.

Reducing the Digital Divide: AI can play a role in narrowing the digital divide by providing technology and internet access to underserved communities. Chatbots and AI-driven educational platforms can offer learning opportunities even in regions with limited access to traditional educational resources.

28.1.6. Ethical Considerations and Responsible AI: While AI presents transformative possibilities for addressing societal challenges, it also introduces ethical complexities that demand careful consideration. Ensuring that AI technologies are developed, deployed, and used responsibly is paramount to prevent unintended negative consequences.

Bias and Fairness: AI systems can inadvertently inherit biases present in training data, which may lead to discriminatory outcomes. It's essential to implement mechanisms that detect and mitigate bias to ensure fair treatment for all individuals, regardless of their background.

Transparency: Transparent AI systems are essential for building trust. Users and stakeholders should understand how AI arrives at its decisions. Explainable AI (XAI) techniques aim to make AI's decision-making processes understandable to humans.

Accountability: As AI systems make decisions that impact individuals and society, accountability mechanisms must be in place. Establishing clear lines of responsibility for AI-generated outcomes is crucial, especially in critical domains like healthcare, law enforcement, and finance.

Privacy: AI often requires access to sensitive data to function effectively. Privacy-preserving techniques, such as differential privacy and secure multi-party computation, can help protect individuals' privacy while still enabling meaningful analysis.

Human-Centric Design: AI systems should prioritize human well-being and empowerment. Designing AI interfaces that are user-friendly and intuitive enhances the technology's positive impact on society.

Regulation and Governance: Governments and organizations should collaborate to establish regulations that guide the development and deployment of AI. Ethical frameworks, industry standards, and oversight mechanisms are essential for ensuring responsible AI use.

Striking a balance between innovation and ethical considerations is essential for realizing the full potential of AI in addressing societal challenges. By proactively addressing ethical concerns and prioritizing the well-being of individuals and communities, we can harness AI's capabilities to create a more just and equitable world. Certainly, let's explore the topic of "Disaster Response and Humanitarian Aid."

28.2. Disaster Response and Humanitarian Aid:

28.2.1. The Role of Technology in Disaster Response: In the face of natural disasters and humanitarian crises, timely and efficient disaster response is of paramount importance. Technological advancements, including artificial intelligence (AI), have transformed disaster response and humanitarian aid by enabling faster assessments, better resource allocation, and improved coordination among relief organizations.

Early Warning Systems: AI-powered early warning systems play a pivotal role in disaster preparedness. These systems analyze data from various sources, such as weather forecasts, seismic activity, and sensor networks, to predict the occurrence of disasters such as hurricanes, earthquakes, and floods. By providing advance notice, these systems allow communities to evacuate and authorities to allocate resources for response and recovery.

Remote Sensing and Data Collection: AI-driven remote sensing technologies, such as satellite imagery and drones, provide critical data in the aftermath of disasters. These technologies can quickly assess the extent of damage, identify areas in need of assistance, and map out access routes for relief efforts. Drones equipped with cameras and sensors can survey disaster-stricken areas, enabling responders to make informed decisions without risking additional lives.

Predictive Analytics: AI's predictive capabilities extend to disaster response by analyzing historical and real-time data to forecast the impact of disasters. Predictive models can estimate the number of casualties, identify vulnerable populations, and anticipate the needs of affected communities. This information helps humanitarian organizations preposition resources and plan their response strategies more effectively.

28.2.2. AI in Humanitarian Aid Operations: AI is reshaping how humanitarian organizations operate during crises, streamlining processes and enhancing the impact of their efforts.

Resource Allocation: During a disaster, resources are often limited and need to be allocated strategically. AI algorithms can analyze data from various sources, including population density, infrastructure, and severity of damage, to optimize the distribution of aid. This ensures that help reaches those who need it the most, reducing waste and improving overall efficiency.

Natural Language Processing for Communication: In the aftermath of a disaster, effective communication is crucial for coordination among responders and affected communities. AI-powered natural language processing (NLP) tools can process and translate messages in real-time, enabling responders to understand the needs of diverse language speakers and respond accordingly.

Data-driven Decision-making: Humanitarian aid organizations gather vast amounts of data during response operations. AI analytics can process this data to extract actionable insights, helping organizations adapt their strategies based on changing conditions and emerging needs.

28.2.3. Challenges and Considerations: While AI holds immense potential in disaster response and humanitarian aid, there are challenges that must be addressed:

Accessibility: AI technologies may not be accessible in all disaster-affected areas due to limitations in infrastructure and resources. Efforts should be made to ensure that the benefits of AI are extended to even the most remote and underserved regions.

Ethical Considerations: The ethical use of AI in disaster response is crucial. Data privacy, consent, and the potential for bias in AI algorithms need to be carefully considered to prevent unintended negative consequences.

Interoperability: Coordination among various responders and organizations is essential in disaster situations. Ensuring that AI systems and data-sharing platforms are interoperable facilitates seamless collaboration and information exchange.

Conclusion: The integration of AI into disaster response and humanitarian aid has the potential to save lives, enhance efficiency, and improve the effectiveness of relief efforts. By harnessing AI's capabilities for early warning, data analysis, and resource allocation, humanitarian organizations can respond more effectively to crises and provide timely assistance to those in need. However, ethical considerations, accessibility, and interoperability remain important factors in maximizing the positive impact of AI in this critical domain.

28.3. Education, Healthcare, and Accessibility:

28.3.1. Revolutionizing Education through Technology: The integration of technology, particularly artificial intelligence (AI), has ushered in a new era of education. From personalized learning experiences to innovative teaching methods, AI is reshaping how students learn and educators teach.
Personalized Learning Paths: AI-powered educational platforms analyze individual student performance and learning styles to tailor lessons and assignments. This personalized approach helps students learn at their own pace, ensuring that they grasp concepts fully before moving on.
Adaptive Assessment and Feedback: AI algorithms evaluate student responses in real-time, adapting the difficulty of questions based on their performance. This dynamic assessment provides more accurate insights into a student's knowledge and helps educators offer timely feedback.
Virtual Classrooms and Remote Learning: AI enables the creation of immersive virtual classrooms, connecting students and educators worldwide. This technology becomes even more critical during unforeseen events, such as pandemics, where remote learning ensures continuity of education.
28.3.2. Transforming Healthcare with AI: AI's potential in healthcare is vast, ranging from early disease detection to drug discovery and patient care enhancement. By processing complex medical data, AI offers innovative solutions to long-standing challenges.
Medical Imaging and Diagnostics: AI algorithms analyze medical images with remarkable accuracy, assisting radiologists in identifying anomalies and diseases. This technology expedites diagnosis and treatment planning.
Drug Discovery and Development: AI accelerates drug discovery by predicting potential drug candidates and simulating their interactions with biological systems. This expedites the identification of novel treatments for various diseases.
Predictive Analytics and Early Intervention: AI's predictive capabilities extend to healthcare, forecasting disease outbreaks and identifying individuals at risk. This enables timely interventions and more effective resource allocation.
28.3.3. Advancing Accessibility through AI: AI has the potential to break down barriers and enhance accessibility for individuals with disabilities, ensuring that they can participate fully in education, healthcare, and various aspects of life.
Assistive Technologies: AI-powered assistive technologies, such as speech recognition and text-to-speech tools, empower individuals with disabilities to interact with digital platforms and communicate effectively.
Language Translation and Communication: AI-driven translation tools facilitate communication between individuals who speak different languages, fostering inclusivity in education and healthcare settings.
Accessibility in Design: AI assists in designing accessible user interfaces and environments, making digital content and physical spaces more navigable for individuals with disabilities.
28.3.4. Ethical Considerations and Equitable Access: As AI transforms education and healthcare, ethical considerations must guide its implementation to ensure equitable access, data privacy, and unbiased decision-making.
Equity in Access: Efforts should be made to ensure that AI-enhanced education and healthcare are accessible to all, regardless of socioeconomic background or geographic location.
Data Privacy: AI applications must adhere to robust data privacy standards to safeguard sensitive medical and educational information.
Bias Mitigation: AI algorithms should be designed to mitigate biases and avoid perpetuating existing disparities in education and healthcare.
the integration of AI in education, healthcare, and accessibility holds transformative potential. From personalized learning to early disease detection, AI contributes to more efficient and effective systems that benefit individuals and society as a whole. However, ethical considerations and equitable access must remain central to these developments to ensure a positive and inclusive impact.

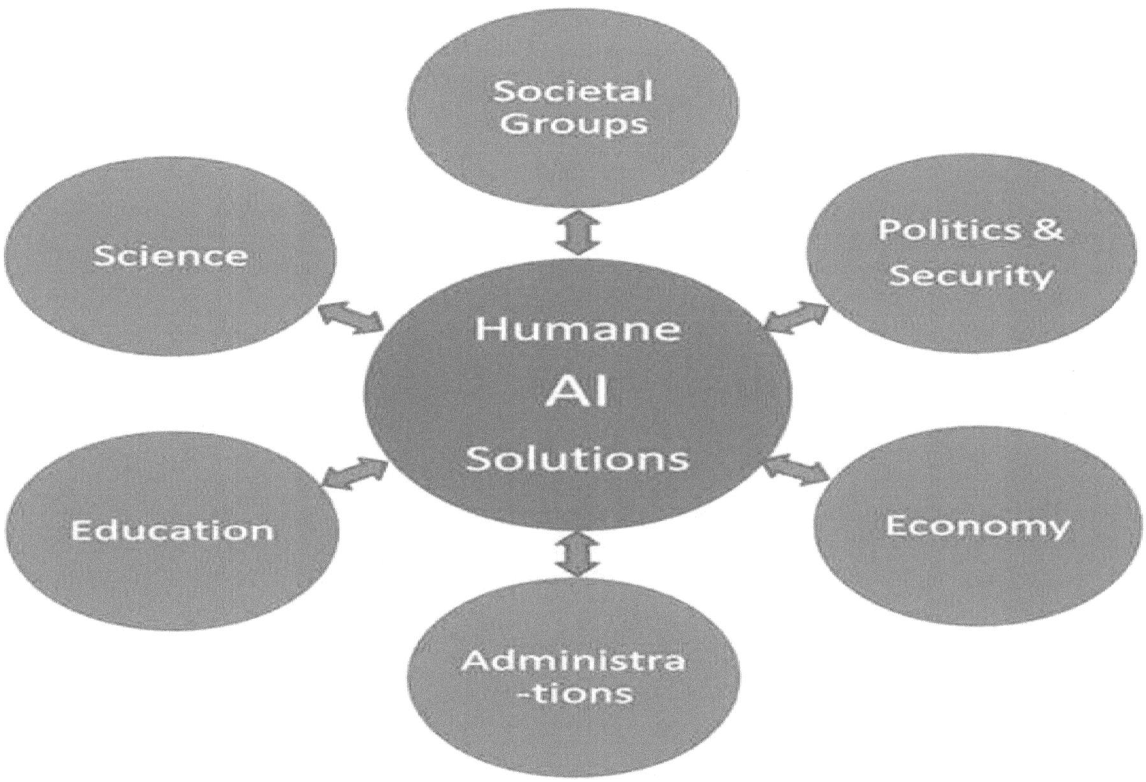

28.4. Promoting Ethical AI for Positive Impact:

28.4.1. The Importance of Ethical AI: As artificial intelligence (AI) technologies continue to advance and permeate various aspects of our lives, ensuring their ethical development and deployment is paramount. Ethical AI refers to the responsible and conscientious design, implementation, and use of AI systems that prioritize human well-being, fairness, transparency, and accountability.

Human-Centric Approach: Ethical AI places humans at the center of its design and operation. It prioritizes creating systems that enhance human capabilities, protect human rights, and align with human values and needs.

Addressing Bias and Fairness: AI systems can inadvertently perpetuate biases present in training data, leading to discriminatory outcomes. Ethical AI mandates the identification and mitigation of bias to ensure fair and equitable treatment for all individuals, regardless of their background.

Transparency and Explainability: Transparent AI systems are crucial for building trust and understanding. Ethical AI emphasizes the development of algorithms and models that provide clear explanations for their decisions, making the decision-making process understandable to humans.

28.4.2. Ethical Principles for AI: Promoting ethical AI involves adhering to a set of principles that guide its development and deployment.

Beneficence and Non-Maleficence: AI systems should be designed to do good and avoid harm. Their impact on individuals, society, and the environment should be positive and should not cause unnecessary harm.

Autonomy and Privacy: Ethical AI respects individuals' autonomy by ensuring that AI systems provide choices and respect personal privacy. Consent and data privacy should be upheld.

Justice and Fairness: AI should be developed and deployed in ways that ensure fairness, prevent discrimination, and reduce disparities among different groups.

Transparency and Accountability: AI developers and operators should be transparent about the capabilities and limitations of AI systems. Clear lines of accountability should be established for the outcomes of AI-generated decisions.

28.4.3. Implementing Ethical AI: Ensuring ethical AI requires collaboration across various stakeholders and the integration of ethical considerations at every stage of AI development and deployment.

Ethical Design: AI systems should be designed with ethical principles in mind from the outset. This involves considering potential biases, transparency, and fairness during the algorithm's development.

Data Ethics: Data used to train AI models should be diverse, representative, and unbiased. Ethical data collection practices, including obtaining informed consent, are essential.

Continuous Monitoring and Auditing: Regular monitoring and auditing of AI systems are necessary to detect and rectify biases, errors, and unintended consequences that may arise during their operation.

Collaboration and Governance: Ethical AI requires collaboration among governments, organizations, researchers, and the public. Establishing clear governance frameworks and ethical guidelines helps ensure responsible AI use.

28.4.4. Beyond Compliance: A Cultural Shift: Ethical AI is not just about complying with regulations but fostering a cultural shift that prioritizes ethical considerations in AI development and use. Promoting ethical AI is crucial for harnessing the potential of artificial intelligence to bring positive and transformative changes to various domains. By adhering to ethical principles, prioritizing transparency, and ensuring accountability, we can create AI systems that not only deliver technological advancements but also contribute to a more just, fair, and inclusive future for all.

Education and Awareness: Building a Responsible AI Community: Promoting ethical AI goes hand in hand with raising awareness and educating various stakeholders about the significance of responsible AI development and deployment.

AI Practitioners: Educating AI practitioners, including data scientists, machine learning engineers, and AI researchers, is essential to instill a deep understanding of ethical considerations. Workshops, training programs, and certifications can equip professionals with the knowledge and tools to implement AI solutions that prioritize fairness, transparency, and accountability.

Policymakers: Policymakers play a pivotal role in shaping the regulatory landscape surrounding AI technologies. They need to be well-informed about the ethical implications of AI, enabling them to craft legislation and regulations that ensure responsible AI development and protect the rights of individuals.

General Public: Raising awareness among the general public fosters a more informed and discerning attitude towards AI technologies. Public education campaigns, workshops, and online resources can help individuals understand how AI works, its potential benefits, and the importance of questioning its ethical implications.

Research and Innovation: Advancing Ethical AI Practices: Ethical AI encourages ongoing research and innovation to create AI systems that align with ethical principles and address potential biases and challenges.

Bias Mitigation: Researchers are tasked with developing algorithms and techniques that mitigate bias in AI systems. This involves identifying sources of bias, developing bias detection tools, and implementing corrective measures to ensure fair and equitable outcomes.

Transparency Tools: Innovation in transparent AI is crucial. Research should focus on developing tools and methodologies that provide clear explanations for AI-generated decisions, enhancing accountability and user trust.

Accountability Mechanisms: Incorporating mechanisms for tracking and auditing AI decisions can enhance accountability. Researchers can innovate by developing systems that provide an audit trail of AI processes, ensuring that outcomes are traceable and explainable.

Social Responsibility: Ethical Tech for Positive Impact: Ethical AI encourages organizations and developers to recognize their social responsibility and contribute to the betterment of society.

Human-Centered Design: Developers should prioritize human well-being when designing AI systems. This involves considering the potential impact on individuals, communities, and society as a whole.

Proactive Problem Solving: Organizations should actively seek solutions to societal challenges using AI. For example, they can create AI-driven initiatives that address issues like environmental conservation, healthcare disparities, and educational inequities.

Ethical Business Practices: Companies should integrate ethical considerations into their business models. This includes transparent communication about AI use, data handling practices, and the steps taken to ensure ethical AI deployment.

Promoting ethical AI requires a multi-faceted approach involving education, research, and social responsibility. By educating practitioners and the public, advancing research to address biases and enhance transparency, and fostering a sense of social responsibility, we can create an AI ecosystem that serves the best interests of individuals, communities, and society at large. This approach not only advances technology but also ensures that AI contributes positively to our world's most pressing challenges.

28.5 Project

Unsolved Project

Suppose you're developing a project that leverages deep learning for social good, focusing on addressing societal challenges. To create an impactful project, you need to understand how AI can be used to tackle societal issues, aid in disaster response and humanitarian efforts, improve education, healthcare, and accessibility, and promote ethical AI for positive impact. Before starting, research the following: various ways AI can be applied to solve societal challenges, the role of deep learning in enhancing disaster response and providing humanitarian aid, applications of AI in improving education systems, healthcare services, and accessibility for individuals with disabilities, and strategies for promoting ethical AI practices to ensure a positive impact on society. This foundational knowledge will enable you to develop a project that harnesses deep learning for the betterment of society.

28.6 Lab Activity

Unsolved Lab Activity

Implement a deep learning model to tackle a specific societal challenge (e.g., predicting air quality levels). Document the implementation process and evaluate the model's effectiveness.

Task: Use a deep learning framework (e.g., TensorFlow or PyTorch) to implement a model designed to tackle a specific societal challenge, such as predicting air quality levels. Document the implementation process, including data collection, preprocessing, model architecture, training procedure, and performance evaluation. Provide visualizations of the model's predictions and assess its effectiveness in addressing the challenge.

Exercises

Exercise 1 – Multiple Choice Questions

1. What is the main focus of this chapter?
   A. The history of artificial intelligence
   B. The ethics of AI
   C. The impact of AI on societal challenges
   D. AI in education
2. Which of the following is NOT mentioned as one of the societal challenges addressed by AI?
   A. Healthcare disparities
   B. Climate change
   C. Cybersecurity
   D. Poverty
3. What is one of the key aspects of addressing healthcare disparities using AI?
   A. Developing more expensive medical equipment
   B. Reducing access to healthcare services
   C. Understanding socioeconomic factors
   D. Focusing only on marginalized communities
4. What is the global climate crisis primarily driven by?
   A. AI technology
   B. Rising temperatures
   C. Urbanization
   D. Environmental degradation
5. What does sustainable urban planning aim to achieve?
   A. Overcrowding in cities
   B. Inadequate living conditions
   C. Efficient urban environments
   D. Increased resource waste

Exercise 2 – True/False

1. AI cannot be used to improve accessibility in education and healthcare.
2. Promoting ethical AI is crucial for ensuring its positive impact on society.
3. Deep learning has no role in disaster response and humanitarian aid.

Review Questions

1. What are some of the key societal challenges that AI is capable of addressing?
2. Why is it important to understand the nature and complexity of societal challenges before applying AI?
3. Describe the concept of healthcare disparities and how AI can contribute to addressing them.
4. How can AI be leveraged to tackle the challenges posed by climate change?
5. What strategies can be employed to address poverty, and how can AI play a role in these efforts?
6. Explain the challenges associated with rapid urbanization and how AI can contribute to sustainable urban planning.
7. Why is multidisciplinary collaboration essential in addressing societal challenges with AI?
8. What is the significance of data in AI's ability to address complex issues, and what are some diverse data sources mentioned in the chapter?
9. How do AI algorithms excel at pattern recognition, and what real-world applications does this have, particularly in healthcare?
10. In what ways can AI contribute to predictive modeling, and how is this applied in climate science?
11. How does data-driven decision-making benefit governments, organizations, and policymakers when addressing societal challenges?
12. What is the role of AI in uncovering hidden correlations within complex datasets, and why is this valuable?
13. How can AI enhance healthcare and medicine, and what are some specific applications mentioned in the chapter?
14. What is precision medicine, and how does AI play a pivotal role in its implementation?
15. How does AI contribute to drug discovery and development, and what benefits does this offer in the healthcare domain?

16. How is AI being applied in environmental conservation and sustainability, and what specific areas within this field does it impact?
17. In what ways does AI promote social equality and inclusion, and what role does data analysis play in achieving these goals?

Answers

Exercise 1- 1. C 2. C 3. C 4. D 5. C
Exercise 2- 1) False, 2) True, 3) False

Online Resources

Online Exam Paper:
Link: https://forms.gle/jbdGrM9u1GvrCXcU6
QR Code:

Chapter 28 Videos Playlist:
Link: https://www.youtube.com/playlist?list=PLzlh_31VWEFp1ElAdAfYZnQ9DyNr_dCOI
QR Code:

Chapter 29: Neural Network Interpretability and Explainability

29.1 Importance of Model Explainability: In the realm of deep learning, where complex neural networks and algorithms are used to tackle intricate tasks, the concept of model explainability has emerged as a critical aspect. Model explainability refers to the ability to understand and interpret the inner workings of a machine learning model, particularly deep learning models, in a human-readable and intuitive manner. It is essential for various reasons, ranging from building trust in AI systems to aiding in regulatory compliance and facilitating model improvement.

29.1.1 The Black Box Conundrum: Deep learning models, particularly deep neural networks, are often referred to as "black boxes" due to their inherent complexity. These models have numerous layers and millions of parameters, making it challenging to comprehend how they arrive at their decisions. This lack of transparency is a major concern, especially in high-stakes applications such as healthcare, finance, and autonomous vehicles, where understanding the rationale behind a decision is crucial. Model explainability aims to shed light on this black box and provide insights into why a particular prediction or classification was made.

29.1.2 Building Trust and Adoption: Explainable models are more likely to gain the trust of users and stakeholders. When the inner workings of a model are transparent and interpretable, users can better understand the basis of predictions and decisions. This understanding, in turn, fosters confidence in the system's reliability and encourages its adoption. In scenarios like medical diagnoses, where lives are at stake, explainable models can help doctors and healthcare professionals make informed decisions and provide justifications for their actions.

29.1.3 Regulatory and Ethical Considerations: In the dynamic landscape of artificial intelligence (AI) and deep learning, the significance of model explainability is greatly amplified by regulatory mandates and ethical considerations. As AI systems play an increasingly influential role in decision-making across various sectors, it becomes imperative to strike a balance between innovation and accountability. Regulatory frameworks, exemplified by the General Data Protection Regulation (GDPR) in Europe, underscore the right of individuals to receive transparent explanations for decisions made by automated systems. This emphasis on transparency aligns with the broader ethical imperative to mitigate bias, discrimination, and opacity in AI applications.

GDPR and the Right to Explanation: The General Data Protection Regulation (GDPR), enacted in 2018, serves as a landmark piece of legislation that shapes how personal data is collected, processed, and utilized. One of the central tenets of GDPR is the right to explanation, which empowers individuals to seek clear and intelligible explanations for decisions that affect them. This right becomes particularly relevant when such decisions are made by automated systems, including deep learning models. In cases where an individual's personal data is utilized to make decisions about their creditworthiness, job applications, or other significant aspects of their lives, the GDPR mandates that they should have the ability to understand the rationale behind those decisions.

Bias Mitigation and Fairness: An ethically responsible deployment of AI systems requires addressing the potential biases that can inadvertently be ingrained within these models. Machine learning algorithms, including deep learning, learn patterns from training data, which can inadvertently contain societal biases present in the data. When these biases find their way into model predictions, they can perpetuate and even exacerbate societal inequalities. Model explainability becomes a vital tool for detecting and addressing these biases. By providing insights into the factors influencing a model's output, explainability aids in identifying discriminatory patterns and supports the development of strategies to mitigate bias.

Accountability and Transparency: As AI systems become more sophisticated and autonomous, the question of accountability arises. When an AI system makes a decision with significant consequences, who should be held responsible? Model explainability offers a means to establish accountability by enabling organizations to trace the decision-making process. With transparent explanations, it becomes feasible to determine whether a decision was made in accordance with ethical guidelines and regulatory requirements. This traceability promotes responsible AI development and discourages the deployment of "black box" models that lack transparency.

Public Trust and Acceptance: Public perception and acceptance of AI systems are pivotal to their widespread adoption. Model explainability plays a crucial role in building and maintaining public trust. When individuals can comprehend how AI systems arrive at their decisions, they are more likely to trust these systems and accept their outcomes. This trust is essential in contexts such as healthcare diagnostics, where individuals rely on AI for critical decisions that affect their well-being. By fostering trust, explainable AI contributes to the responsible integration of technology into society.

Conclusion: The significance of model explainability reverberates throughout the intersection of technology, regulation, and ethics. Regulatory frameworks like GDPR underscore the individual's right to understand and contest automated decisions. Furthermore, ethical considerations mandate the detection and mitigation of biases, as well as the establishment of accountability in AI systems. The nexus of regulatory compliance and ethical responsibility finds resonance in the practice of model explainability, ensuring that AI and deep learning technologies contribute positively to society while maintaining transparency and fairness.

29.1.4 Debugging and Model Improvement: In the intricate landscape of deep learning, where the performance of models often hinges on countless parameters and complex architectures, the role of explainability tools in debugging and model improvement cannot be overstated. These tools provide a powerful diagnostic mechanism that allows developers to understand the inner workings of their models. When a deep learning model generates unexpected or erroneous results, the ability to decipher the rationale behind these outputs is instrumental in uncovering underlying issues within the model architecture or the training data. This diagnostic capability not only streamlines the debugging process but also serves as a springboard for refining models, enhancing their performance, and optimizing their effectiveness.

Uncovering Model Behavior: Deep learning models can sometimes exhibit behaviors that defy conventional expectations, leading to puzzling outputs. These behaviors can stem from various sources, such as incorrect weight initialization, vanishing or exploding gradients, or overfitting to the training data. Explainability tools offer a window into the inner workings of the model, shedding light on how different layers, neurons, and features contribute to the final predictions. By visualizing the patterns and activations in the model, developers can gain insights into why certain inputs lead to unexpected outputs.

Identifying Data Discrepancies: In many cases, issues with model performance can be attributed to problems within the training data. These problems might include mislabeled samples, insufficient data diversity, or data that does not adequately represent the real-world scenarios the model is intended to handle. Explainability tools can be leveraged to analyze which parts of the input data the model is focusing on during prediction. This can reveal if the model is overly sensitive to certain features or if it's making predictions based on irrelevant information. Such insights help developers identify data discrepancies that need to be addressed to improve model accuracy.

Refining Model Architecture: Model architecture plays a pivotal role in determining a deep learning model's capacity to learn and generalize. However, selecting the optimal architecture can be a daunting task, especially given the myriad of available options. Explainability tools aid in this process by showing the contribution of each layer and neuron to the overall model prediction. If certain components of the model appear to have negligible impact or are causing instability, developers can make informed decisions about modifying or removing them.

Fine-tuning Hyperparameters: Hyperparameters, such as learning rate, batch size, and regularization strength, significantly influence a model's learning dynamics and convergence. Tweaking these hyperparameters can lead to vastly different outcomes in terms of training speed, convergence, and generalization. Explainability tools can help developers understand how changes in hyperparameters affect the model's behavior and performance. This insight enables a more systematic approach to hyperparameter tuning, resulting in improved model convergence and accuracy.

Conclusion: In the intricate and often unpredictable world of deep learning, explainability tools offer a valuable lens through which developers can understand their models. The ability to diagnose issues, uncover unexpected behaviors, identify data-related problems, refine model architecture, and fine-tune hyperparameters enhances the model development process. By streamlining the debugging process and facilitating iterative model improvement, these tools empower developers to create deep learning models that are more accurate, robust, and effective in addressing real-world challenges.

29.1.5 Techniques for Model Explainability: In the intricate landscape of deep learning, where complex neural networks and algorithms often operate as "black boxes," techniques for model explainability have emerged as indispensable tools. These techniques provide insights into the decision-making processes of these models, making it possible to understand why specific predictions are made. Here are several notable techniques designed to enhance model explainability in the context of deep learning:

Feature Importance Analysis: Feature importance analysis is a foundational technique that aims to quantify the impact of individual features or inputs on a model's predictions. By evaluating how changes in each feature affect the model's output, developers can identify which features have the most significant influence. Common approaches include calculating feature gradients with respect to the model's predictions or employing techniques like permutation feature importance. This analysis not only provides insights into which features drive decisions but also aids in identifying irrelevant or redundant features that can be omitted to simplify the model.

LIME (Local Interpretable Model-agnostic Explanations): LIME is a technique that bridges the gap between complex deep learning models and human understanding by creating interpretable surrogate models. It works by selecting a specific instance for which an explanation is required and generating a dataset of perturbed instances around it. These instances are then labeled by the original black-box model. A simple, interpretable model is trained on this dataset to approximate the behavior of the original model for that instance. This surrogate model can provide insight into the decision rationale for that specific case, effectively translating the black-box model's prediction into a human-readable explanation.

SHAP (SHapley Additive exPlanations): SHAP is a technique grounded in cooperative game theory that provides a comprehensive view of feature importance by attributing contributions of each feature to a prediction. It calculates Shapley values, which represent the average marginal contribution of a feature across all possible coalitions of features. These values ensure that contributions are fairly allocated among features. SHAP values offer a unified way to quantify the impact of each feature on a prediction and help uncover interactions between features that influence the model's output.

Attention Mechanisms: Attention mechanisms have gained significant traction, particularly in natural language processing tasks. They provide insight into which parts of an input the model is focusing on while making predictions. In text-based applications, attention mechanisms visualize the importance or relevance of individual words or phrases within a sentence. This visualization enables understanding not only the final prediction but also the context that led to it. Attention maps can highlight specific words or segments that the model deems crucial, offering transparency into the decision-making process.

The techniques outlined above stand as beacons of understanding in the often complex and opaque world of deep learning. By enabling feature importance analysis, creating interpretable surrogate models, utilizing cooperative game theory, and visualizing attention mechanisms, these techniques empower developers and stakeholders to grasp the inner workings of their models. As the pursuit of model explainability gains momentum, these techniques continue to illuminate the path towards transparency, accountability, and responsible deployment of deep learning systems.

29.2 Interpretable Neural Network Architectures: Interpretable neural network architectures represent a concerted effort to demystify the intricate decision-making processes of deep learning models. By incorporating design principles that prioritize transparency, these architectures offer insights into model behavior, decision rationales, and the significance of different inputs. As the demand for responsible AI continues to grow, interpretable neural network architectures stand as powerful tools that enable practitioners to harness the capabilities of deep learning while maintaining a clear understanding of the models they develop and deploy.

29.2.1 Convolutional Neural Networks (CNNs) with Global Average Pooling: Convolutional Neural Networks (CNNs) are a cornerstone of image analysis and recognition tasks. To enhance interpretability, the combination of CNNs with Global Average Pooling (GAP) has gained prominence. Instead of flattening the spatial features extracted by the convolutional layers, GAP computes the average value for each feature map, resulting in a compact representation. This spatial aggregation provides a form of object localization, indicating which regions of the input image contribute most to specific predictions. By visualizing these weighted feature maps, practitioners can understand the model's focus and decision rationale.

29.2.2 Interpretable Recurrent Neural Networks (RNNs): Recurrent Neural Networks (RNNs) are adept at processing sequential data, making them valuable for tasks like natural language processing and time series analysis. To enhance interpretability, various modifications have been introduced. One approach involves using attention mechanisms to visualize which parts of the input sequence the model is emphasizing during prediction. Another method employs techniques like gradient-based saliency maps to highlight the input elements that most strongly influence the model's decision. These modifications enable practitioners to understand the context and reasoning behind RNN predictions.

29.2.3 Decision Trees and Rule-based Neural Networks: Decision trees are classical models known for their transparency and simplicity. Combining decision trees with neural networks offers an intriguing solution for interpretable deep learning. In these hybrid models, decision trees are often used to make initial high-level predictions, while neural networks refine these predictions. This approach provides a hierarchical structure that is easy to interpret, as decisions are made based on transparent rules. By visualizing the decision paths and rules, practitioners can gain insights into how the model arrives at its predictions.

29.2.4 Capsule Networks (Caps Nets): In the realm of neural network architectures, Capsule Networks (Caps Nets) have emerged as a pioneering approach designed to overcome the limitations of traditional Convolutional Neural Networks (CNNs) in capturing complex spatial hierarchies and handling variations in viewpoint. Caps Nets introduce the concept of capsules, which are groups of neurons that collaborate to represent specific features or components of an object. This innovative architecture revolutionizes the understanding of object structures and offers a fresh perspective on model interpretability.

Addressing CNN Limitations: While CNNs have been incredibly successful in image classification tasks, they exhibit shortcomings when it comes to understanding spatial relationships between components within an object. Traditional CNNs rely on pooling layers to capture features, leading to a loss of information about the precise spatial arrangement of features. Additionally, CNNs struggle with variations in viewpoint, making them less robust to changes in object orientation.

Introducing Capsules: Capsule Networks propose a new paradigm by introducing capsules as the fundamental building blocks. A capsule consists of a group of neurons that collaborate to encode different properties of a feature or object component. Each capsule aims to encapsulate the instantiation parameters of a specific feature, such as its presence, orientation, size, and pose. By encoding these parameters as vectors, capsules inherently account for spatial relationships and hierarchies between features.

Enabling Spatial Hierarchies: The power of Caps Nets lies in their ability to capture spatial hierarchies in a more holistic manner than traditional CNNs. Capsules are organized in layers, with higher-level capsules aiming to represent more complex object components. The capsules' vectors inherently encode the spatial relationship between the object components they represent. This organization allows Caps Nets to understand the hierarchical structure of objects, ensuring that the model can recognize the arrangement and orientation of parts within an object.

Improving Interpretability: One of the compelling features of Caps Nets is their enhanced interpretability. Traditional CNNs often appear as "black boxes," making it challenging to discern how a particular prediction was reached. In contrast, the capsule structure in Caps Nets provides insights into how the model recognizes different components of an object. By understanding the activations of capsules at different levels, practitioners can visualize how the model perceives object parts and the relationships between them. This transparency fosters greater trust and comprehension of the model's decision-making process.

Handling Variations and Occlusions: Caps Nets exhibit robustness to variations in object pose and viewpoint, a characteristic attributed to their ability to capture spatial relationships through capsules. Because capsules encode orientation and pose, they can handle changes in viewpoint more effectively than traditional CNNs. Additionally, Caps Nets have shown promise in dealing with occlusions, as the model can infer the presence of occluded components based on the activation of relevant capsules.

Conclusion: Capsule Networks (Caps Nets) represent a remarkable advancement in neural network architecture, addressing limitations in capturing spatial hierarchies and handling viewpoint variations. By introducing capsules that encode specific features or components of an object and inherently capture spatial relationships, Caps Nets enable the model to understand object structures in a more holistic manner. This architecture not only enhances model performance but also promotes transparency and interpretability by offering insights into the model's perception of object parts and relationships. As the field of deep learning continues to evolve, Caps Nets stand as a testament to the innovative spirit driving interpretability and understanding in complex neural networks.

29.2.5 Sparse Neural Networks: In the pursuit of model interpretability and efficiency, the concept of Sparse Neural Networks has emerged as a powerful technique. Sparse Neural Networks intentionally restrict the connectivity between neurons, resulting in models that rely on a subset of neurons for making predictions. This deliberate sparsity enhances not only the interpretability of the model but also its computational efficiency and memory requirements. Techniques like neuron pruning, group sparsity, and attention mechanisms are employed to induce sparsity and foster a new era of neural network architectures.

The Motivation for Sparsity: Traditional neural networks often comprise densely connected layers, where each neuron is connected to every neuron in the subsequent layer. While this architecture can capture intricate relationships within the data, it can also lead to model complexity and increased computational demands. Sparse Neural Networks introduce controlled sparsity to mitigate these challenges. By allowing only a subset of neurons to be active, the model is encouraged to focus on the most relevant features or inputs, thereby improving the model's transparency and efficiency.

Neuron Pruning: Neuron pruning involves selectively removing neurons and connections from the network while maintaining performance. This process is guided by metrics such as the importance of neurons in terms of their impact on model predictions. Neurons that contribute less to the network's performance are pruned, leading to a sparse architecture. Neuron pruning not only enhances interpretability by simplifying the model's structure but also reduces the model's computational burden, resulting in faster inference times and lower memory requirements.

Group Sparsity: Group sparsity takes sparsity a step further by enforcing structured patterns of connectivity. Instead of pruning individual neurons, entire groups of neurons are pruned together. This approach is particularly useful in scenarios where certain groups of features are related or represent specific concepts. Group sparsity enhances the interpretability of the model by promoting feature selection at a higher level, making it easier to discern which groups of features contribute to specific predictions.

Attention Mechanisms for Sparsity: Attention mechanisms, which were initially designed to focus on specific parts of input data, can also be employed to induce sparsity in neural networks. By assigning attention weights to different neurons or connections, the model can effectively prioritize the most informative components. This attention-based sparsity not only enhances interpretability by highlighting key features but also reduces computational complexity by directing resources only to the most relevant parts of the network.

Benefits and Trade-offs: Sparse Neural Networks offer a balance between accuracy, interpretability, and efficiency. While they may experience a slight drop in performance compared to their fully connected counterparts, the gained benefits in terms of model interpretability, computational speed, and memory savings often outweigh this trade-off. Sparse architectures are particularly valuable in scenarios where understanding the model's decision rationale is crucial or where resource constraints demand efficient models.

Conclusion: Sparse Neural Networks stand as a transformative approach in the landscape of neural network architectures, strategically trading off model complexity for interpretability and efficiency. By intentionally limiting connectivity, these architectures enable practitioners to better understand the features or inputs driving predictions. Techniques like neuron pruning, group sparsity, and attention mechanisms facilitate the induction of sparsity, enhancing the transparency and efficiency of models. In a world that values both interpretability and performance, Sparse Neural Networks pave the way for a new generation of neural architectures that strike the optimal balance between these essential attributes.

29.3 Local and Global Explanation Techniques: In the quest to make sense of the decisions made by complex machine learning models, the field of interpretability has given rise to a diverse array of explanation techniques. These techniques can be broadly categorized into local and global explanations, each serving a distinct purpose in unraveling the inner workings of models. This chapter delves into the nuances of local and global explanation techniques, exploring how they contribute to understanding model behavior, boosting user trust, and promoting responsible AI deployment.

29.3.1 Local Explanation Techniques:

LIME (Local Interpretable Model-agnostic Explanations): LIME is a prominent local explanation technique that bridges the gap between complex models and human understanding. It operates on the premise of creating interpretable surrogate models for specific instances. LIME selects a data point of interest and generates a perturbed dataset around it. The surrogate model is trained on this dataset to approximate the behavior of the original model for that instance. By interpreting the surrogate model's predictions, practitioners gain insight into the factors influencing the original model's decision locally. LIME's strength lies in its model-agnostic nature, enabling it to be applied to a wide range of models.

SHAP (SHapley Additive exPlanations): SHAP is another local explanation technique rooted in cooperative game theory. It provides a comprehensive understanding of feature importance by attributing contributions of each feature to a prediction. SHAP values ensure a fair allocation of contributions among features, revealing their individual impact while considering interactions with other features. This technique offers a granular view of how each feature influences a prediction on a local level, empowering practitioners to discern the driving forces behind specific model outputs.

29.3.2 Global Explanation Techniques:

Feature Importance Analysis: Global explanation techniques often start with feature importance analysis, which assesses the significance of different features across the entire dataset. This analysis provides a holistic view of the model's behavior by identifying which features have the most substantial impact on predictions on a global scale. Techniques such as permutation feature importance, random forests, and gradient-based methods contribute to unraveling the broader landscape of feature contributions.

Partial Dependence Plots: Partial Dependence Plots (PDPs) visualize the relationship between a specific feature and the model's predictions while averaging out the effects of other features. PDPs offer a global perspective by illustrating how changes in a feature's value influence the model's output across a range of values. These plots enable practitioners to observe trends and understand how the model responds to variations in individual features while holding others constant.

Global Surrogate Models: Global surrogate models aim to approximate the decision boundary of a complex model using a simpler, interpretable model. These surrogate models, often decision trees or linear models, mimic the behavior of the original model across the entire dataset. By studying the surrogate model, practitioners gain a global understanding of how different features contribute to predictions. These models offer transparency and insights into the underlying decision logic of complex models.

29.4 Using Interpretable AI for Trusted Decision-Making: In an era marked by the rapid integration of AI into critical decision-making processes, ensuring transparency, accountability, and trustworthiness has become paramount. Interpretable AI stands as a pivotal solution to this challenge, enabling practitioners to comprehend the reasoning behind AI-driven decisions and fostering user trust. This chapter delves into the role of interpretable AI in cultivating trusted decision-making, exploring how transparency, fairness, and ethical considerations intertwine with the deployment of interpretable AI systems.

29.4.1 Ensuring Transparency through Interpretability:

Regulatory Compliance and Accountability: Interpretable AI aligns with regulatory mandates that emphasize transparency in automated decision-making. Regulations like the General Data Protection Regulation (GDPR) empower individuals to seek explanations for decisions that impact their lives. Interpretable models provide the means to deliver these explanations, ensuring compliance with legal requirements and facilitating accountability.

Mitigating the "Black Box" Phenomenon: The "black box" nature of complex AI models has been a stumbling block in fostering user trust. Interpretable AI dismantles this barrier by enabling practitioners to reveal the inner workings of models. By understanding how inputs are translated into outputs, users gain insight into the decision-making process, enhancing their confidence in AI-driven outcomes.

29.4.2 Fostering Fairness and Ethical Decision-Making:

Bias Detection and Mitigation: Interpretable AI plays a pivotal role in identifying and addressing biases ingrained in training data or model predictions. By visualizing feature importance, practitioners can discern discriminatory patterns. This transparency empowers developers to mitigate biases and cultivate fairness in AI systems, which is essential for ethical decision-making.

Ethical Accountability: Interpretable AI facilitates the detection of unethical behavior by providing visibility into the factors driving predictions. In cases where AI systems are involved in sensitive decisions, such as healthcare diagnoses or loan approvals, the ability to trace the decision rationale becomes crucial. Interpretable AI promotes ethical accountability by enabling users to challenge and rectify decisions that may have adverse consequences.

29.4.3 Navigating Complex Decision Landscapes:

Healthcare and Medical Diagnoses: Interpretable AI in healthcare aids medical professionals in understanding the reasoning behind AI-generated diagnoses. By revealing the features that contribute to a particular diagnosis, practitioners can make informed decisions while retaining their clinical judgment. This collaboration between AI and human experts enhances patient care.

Financial Services and Risk Assessment: In the financial domain, interpretable AI assists in risk assessment and credit scoring. By elucidating the factors that influence credit decisions, financial institutions can ensure transparency and accountability. This transparency not only empowers applicants but also safeguards against discriminatory practices.

29.4.4 Strengthening User Trust and Adoption:

Acceptance of AI Technology: User trust is paramount for the widespread adoption of AI systems. Interpretable AI bridges the gap by providing users with insights into how decisions are reached. When individuals can comprehend the decision process, they are more likely to embrace AI technology in various domains, from autonomous vehicles to recommendation systems.

Human-Machine Collaboration: Interpretable AI promotes human-machine collaboration by making AI systems more approachable. By enhancing transparency, these systems empower users to work alongside AI models, leveraging their capabilities while maintaining human oversight and control.

Conclusion: Interpretable AI emerges as a linchpin in the pursuit of trusted decision-making in an AI-driven world. By ensuring transparency, addressing biases, promoting ethical accountability, and enhancing user trust, interpretable AI transforms the landscape of automated decision-making. The symbiotic relationship between AI and human understanding, facilitated by interpretable models, paves the way for responsible and ethical AI deployment, ultimately shaping a future where AI augments human judgment while remaining accountable and transparent.

29.5 Project

Unsolved Project

Suppose you're developing a project that focuses on enhancing the interpretability and explainability of neural networks to ensure trusted decision-making. To create a comprehensive project, you need to understand the importance of model explainability, interpretable neural network architectures, local and global explanation techniques, and the application of interpretable AI in making trusted decisions. Before starting, research the following: the significance of having interpretable models and why explainability is crucial in various applications, different neural network architectures designed for interpretability, techniques for providing local explanations (e.g., LIME, SHAP) and global explanations (e.g., feature importance, model-agnostic methods), and how interpretable AI can be used to build trust and reliability in decision-making processes across different domains such as finance, healthcare, and legal systems. This foundational knowledge will help you develop a project that effectively integrates interpretability and explainability into neural networks for reliable and transparent AI systems.

29.6 Lab Activity

Unsolved Lab Activity

Implement a local explanation technique (e.g., LIME or SHAP) and a global explanation technique (e.g., feature importance) on a neural network model. Compare their effectiveness in explaining model predictions.

Task: Use a deep learning framework to implement a neural network model for a classification or regression task. Apply a local explanation technique (e.g., LIME or SHAP) and a global explanation technique (e.g., feature importance) to explain the model's predictions. Document the implementation process, including data preprocessing, model architecture, training procedure, and explanation generation. Compare the effectiveness of the local and global explanation techniques and provide visualizations to illustrate their differences.

Exercises

Exercise 1 – Multiple Choice Questions

1. What does model explainability refer to in the context of deep learning?
   A. Understanding the color of neural networks
   B. Understanding the inner workings of a machine learning model
   C. Understanding the complexity of algorithms
   D. Understanding the speed of AI systems
2. Why are deep learning models often referred to as "black boxes"?
   A. Because they are painted black
   B. Because they are simple to understand
   C. Because they have a clear decision-making process
   D. Because they have many layers and parameters that are hard to interpret
3. How does model explainability contribute to building trust in AI systems?
   A. By making models more complex
   B. By making models less accurate
   C. By providing insights into model decisions
   D. By hiding model decisions
4. Which regulatory framework emphasizes the right to receive transparent explanations for automated decisions?
   A. GDPR
   B. AI Ethics Code
   C. Model Accountability Act
   D. AI Transparency Regulation
5. What is one of the key reasons for using model explainability in AI applications?
   A. To increase opacity in AI systems
   B. To perpetuate societal biases
   C. To detect and mitigate biases
   D. To discourage transparency

Exercise 2 – True/False

1. Interpretable AI can enhance trusted decision-making in critical applications.
2. Local explanation techniques provide insights into the overall behavior of a neural network.
3. Model explainability is not important for building trust in AI systems.

Review Questions

1. What is the significance of model explainability in the realm of deep learning?
2. Why are deep learning models often referred to as "black boxes"?
3. How does model explainability contribute to building trust in AI systems?
4. Provide an example of a high-stakes application where understanding the rationale behind a decision is crucial.
5. How does model explainability relate to regulatory compliance and ethical considerations in AI?
6. What is the "right to explanation" in the context of GDPR, and why is it important?
7. How can model explainability help mitigate bias and promote fairness in AI applications?

8. Why is accountability a growing concern as AI systems become more autonomous?
9. Explain how model explainability can impact public trust and acceptance of AI systems.
10. Summarize the key challenges associated with deep learning model debugging and improvement.
11. What role do explainability tools play in uncovering unexpected behaviors in deep learning models?
12. How can interpretable AI help identify data discrepancies and improve model accuracy?
13. What is the significance of refining model architecture, and how does explainability aid in this process?
14. How can fine-tuning hyperparameters improve deep learning model convergence and accuracy?
15. Describe the role of Capsule Networks (Caps Nets) in addressing the limitations of traditional Convolutional Neural Networks (CNNs).
16. What is the primary advantage of Caps Nets in handling variations in object viewpoint?
17. How does Capsule Networks enhance model interpretability compared to traditional CNNs?
18. Explain the concept of neuron pruning in Sparse Neural Networks and its benefits.
19. What role does group sparsity play in inducing sparsity in neural networks?
20. How can attention mechanisms be used to induce sparsity in neural networks?
21. What are the potential benefits and trade-offs of using Sparse Neural Networks?
22. Differentiate between local and global explanation techniques in the context of model interpretability.
23. How does LIME (Local Interpretable Model-agnostic Explanations) work, and when is it typically used?
24. What are SHAP (SHapley Additive exPlanations) values, and how do they contribute to local explanations?
25. What is feature importance analysis, and how does it contribute to global explanations?
26. Describe the purpose and functionality of Partial Dependence Plots (PDPs) in global model interpretation.
27. How do global surrogate models help in understanding complex model behavior?
28. Explain how interpretable AI can ensure transparency, fairness, and ethical considerations in decision-making.
29. In what scenarios can interpretable AI play a crucial role in fostering trust and user acceptance?

Answers

Exercise 1- 1.B 2. D 3.C 4.A 5.C
Exercise 2- 1) True, 2) False, 3) False

Online Resources

Online Exam Paper:
Link: https://forms.gle/Gcwk3KRxCqoEFKn37
QR Code:

Chapter 29 Videos Playlist:
Link: https://www.youtube.com/playlist?list=PLzlh_31VWEFqSMtOV5WGF5q3Rqzram25h
QR Code:

Chapter 30: Ethics in Deep Learning and AI

30.1 Bias, Fairness, and Discrimination in AI Systems: As artificial intelligence (AI) systems become increasingly integrated into various aspects of society, concerns regarding bias, fairness, and discrimination have come to the forefront. While AI holds the potential to transform industries and improve efficiency, it also inherits biases present in training data and can perpetuate discriminatory outcomes. This chapter delves into the complexities of bias and discrimination in AI systems, exploring their origins, implications, and strategies to mitigate these issues for a fair and equitable AI-driven future.

30.1.1 Understanding Bias in AI:

Bias in Data Collection: AI models are only as unbiased as the data they are trained on. Bias in AI often stems from biased training data, which might reflect historical prejudices or systemic inequalities. Data collected from biased sources can introduce unwanted stereotypes and skew model predictions, leading to unfair outcomes.

Amplification of Social Biases: AI models can inadvertently magnify societal biases present in data. Historical imbalances in opportunities or representations can manifest as biased predictions. For instance, biased hiring practices might lead to AI systems that disproportionately favor certain demographics.

30.1.2 Fairness and Discrimination in AI:

Algorithmic Discrimination: AI algorithms can result in discriminatory decisions that impact individuals or groups based on characteristics such as race, gender, or socioeconomic status. This is often unintentional and arises from biases learned during training.

Fairness Metrics: Various fairness metrics have been developed to measure and quantify bias in AI systems. These metrics assess disparate impact, equal opportunity, and other dimensions to gauge if models treat different groups fairly.

30.1.3 Consequences of Bias and Discrimination:

Social and Economic Inequity: Biased AI systems can exacerbate existing societal disparities. Discriminatory outcomes in areas like hiring, lending, and criminal justice can perpetuate inequalities, leading to negative consequences for marginalized groups.

Loss of Trust and Accountability: Unfair AI decisions erode public trust and can result in legal, ethical, and reputational issues for organizations responsible for their deployment. Without accountability, AI can further alienate users and communities.

30.1.4 Strategies for Mitigation:

Diverse and Representative Data: Addressing bias starts at the data level. Ensuring that training data is diverse and representative is a foundational step toward mitigating bias in AI systems. Efforts to collect data that includes a wide range of demographics, backgrounds, and perspectives can counteract existing imbalances and biases. Inclusion of underrepresented groups helps create a more accurate reflection of the real world, reducing the risk of perpetuating discriminatory outcomes.

Bias Detection and Measurement: AI developers play a crucial role in detecting and measuring bias within models. Employing a combination of tools and techniques to audit model behavior and evaluate fairness metrics can unveil hidden discriminatory patterns. By systematically analyzing model predictions across different demographic groups, developers can identify instances where bias emerges and take corrective measures.

Algorithmic Fairness: Researchers and practitioners are actively engaged in developing algorithmic techniques to enhance fairness in AI systems. These techniques aim to recalibrate models to reduce bias and promote equitable outcomes. Re-sampling involves adjusting the dataset to balance underrepresented groups, while re-weighting assigns different weights to different groups to achieve fairness. Adversarial training introduces a separate component to counteract bias during training, helping the model learn to mitigate its own biases.

Transparency and Explainability: Transparency is a cornerstone of addressing bias and ensuring accountability. Openly sharing information about model architectures, training data sources, and decision-making processes provides stakeholders with insights into the inner workings of AI systems. Explainable AI techniques, such as generating feature importance scores or producing human-readable decision rules, shed light on how models arrive at predictions. These techniques empower practitioners, regulators, and users to understand the factors influencing outcomes and challenge biased decisions.

Conclusion: Mitigating bias, promoting fairness, and combating discrimination in AI systems demand a multi-faceted approach that spans data collection, model development, and transparency efforts. By striving for diverse and representative data, deploying bias detection mechanisms, adopting algorithmic fairness techniques, and prioritizing transparency and explainability, the AI community can collectively work towards reducing bias and fostering equitable outcomes. These strategies underscore the ethical responsibility to harness AI's potential while ensuring that its impact remains unbiased, fair, and beneficial to all individuals and communities.

30.2 Addressing Bias in Data and Algorithms:

Addressing bias in AI systems requires a multi-pronged approach that encompasses both data and algorithms. By rectifying biased training data through preprocessing, data augmentation, and generative techniques, practitioners can foster a more representative dataset. Simultaneously, by leveraging techniques like fair representation learning, adversarial debiasing, and algorithmic auditing, algorithmic biases can be identified and mitigated. As AI systems continue to shape various sectors of society, the commitment to addressing bias stands as an ethical and technical obligation, ensuring that the impact of AI is fair, just, and unbiased for all individuals and communities.

30.2.1 Rectifying Bias in Training Data:

Data Preprocessing: Preprocessing data is a pivotal step in mitigating bias. Techniques like re-sampling and re-weighting can balance the representation of underrepresented groups, reducing the risk of bias stemming from skewed data distributions. Additionally, data augmentation can enrich the dataset with diverse samples, ensuring a more comprehensive and unbiased representation.

Data Augmentation: Data augmentation involves creating new data instances by introducing variations to existing samples. This technique is particularly beneficial when dealing with limited data for certain groups. Augmenting data with varying attributes ensures that the AI model learns from diverse examples, lessening the potential for bias.

Generative Adversarial Networks (GANs): GANs can generate synthetic data that captures the characteristics of the training data. They can be used to create diverse samples that represent underrepresented groups, helping to rectify bias. GANs offer a data-driven approach to mitigate bias by expanding the range of available data.

30.2.2 Mitigating Algorithmic Bias: Addressing algorithmic bias is a paramount concern in the development of fair and equitable AI systems. Mitigation strategies encompass a range of innovative techniques designed to rectify bias in decision-making processes. This section explores some of the key approaches in mitigating algorithmic bias.

Fair Representation Learning: Fair representation learning seeks to transform input data into a space where discriminatory information is minimized. This involves disentangling sensitive attributes, such as race or gender, from relevant features that impact the decision-making process. By creating a representation that minimizes the correlation between these attributes and outcomes, models can make predictions based on non-biased information. Fair representation learning enables AI systems to focus on factors that are genuinely influential while disregarding sensitive attributes that might lead to biased decisions.

Adversarial Debiasing: Adversarial debiasing is a strategy that simultaneously trains a model and an adversary, often a separate neural network, to predict protected attributes such as race or gender. The model learns to make accurate predictions while the adversary aims to predict the protected attribute. Through this adversarial process, the model is encouraged to make decisions independently of sensitive attributes. The goal is to create a model that becomes resilient to the influence of such attributes, effectively reducing the potential for biased decision-making.

Algorithmic Auditing and Bias Metrics: Algorithmic auditing and the development of fairness metrics are essential components of continuous bias mitigation. These tools enable the ongoing monitoring of model behavior to identify instances of bias in real-world scenarios. Fairness metrics quantify bias and assess disparate impacts across different demographic groups. Auditing tools help developers gain insights into how bias manifests and enable them to take corrective actions. By providing a feedback loop for improving model fairness, these tools contribute to the iterative refinement of AI systems.

Regularization Techniques: Regularization techniques offer a way to explicitly incorporate fairness into the training process. By modifying the model's loss function, regularization methods penalize biased predictions. For example, a fairness term can be added to the loss function that increases the penalty for predictions that exhibit bias towards certain groups. This incentivizes the model to make fairer predictions throughout the training process, effectively aligning model behavior with fairness objectives.

Conclusion: Mitigating algorithmic bias is an essential endeavor in ensuring that AI systems are fair, ethical, and accountable. Through approaches like fair representation learning, adversarial debiasing, algorithmic auditing, and regularization techniques, developers can systematically tackle bias and enhance the fairness of AI decision-making. By combining technical innovation with ethical considerations, the AI community can contribute to a future where AI systems reflect the diverse and equitable world we aspire to create.

30.3 Ethical Considerations in AI Research and Deployment: As artificial intelligence (AI) systems become increasingly integrated into our daily lives, the ethical implications of their development and deployment have garnered significant attention. The choices made during AI research and deployment can have profound impacts on individuals, society, and our future. This chapter delves into the ethical considerations that guide AI innovation, exploring issues such as transparency, accountability, bias, and the broader societal implications of AI technologies.

30.3.1 Transparency and Accountability:

Transparent Model Design: Ethical AI development demands transparency in model design. AI models should be comprehensible, allowing stakeholders to understand how decisions are made. Transparent design fosters accountability, as it enables scrutiny and minimizes the "black box" phenomenon, where AI decisions are difficult to interpret.

Responsible Data Collection: Data forms the foundation of AI systems, and ethical data collection is paramount. Ensuring data is gathered responsibly, with respect for privacy and consent, helps prevent the inadvertent reinforcement of biases. Ethical data practices contribute to building more trustworthy and unbiased AI models.

30.3.2 Mitigating Bias and Discrimination:

Bias Detection and Correction: Ethical AI mandates the detection and rectification of biases within models and data. Tools and techniques that identify biased patterns ensure that AI systems do not perpetuate discriminatory outcomes. Addressing bias is a crucial step towards building fair and just AI technologies.

Fairness Metrics and Impact Assessment: Developing fairness metrics and assessing the impact of AI decisions across diverse demographic groups are ethical imperatives. Ensuring that AI does not disproportionately harm certain groups, and promoting fairness, underscores the ethical commitment to equitable outcomes.

30.3.3 Societal Impact and Beneficence:

Anticipating Societal Impact: Ethical AI research involves considering the broader societal implications of technology deployment. By anticipating potential effects such as job displacement, economic shifts, and social inequalities, researchers and developers can take proactive measures to mitigate negative impacts.

Beneficence and Positive Impact: An ethical approach to AI prioritizes beneficence, aiming to maximize the positive impact on individuals and society. AI technologies should be designed to enhance human well-being, solve critical challenges, and contribute to the betterment of society as a whole.

30.3.4 Human Oversight and Decision-Making:

Human-AI Collaboration: Ethical AI recognizes the importance of maintaining a collaborative relationship between humans and AI systems. AI should serve as a tool to augment human capabilities, providing assistance while ensuring human judgment and oversight in decision-making.

Avoiding Unintended Consequences: Responsible AI deployment entails considering potential unintended consequences. AI systems should be developed with a deep understanding of their potential impact, and mechanisms should be in place to address unexpected outcomes that could have negative societal repercussions.

Conclusion: Ethical considerations are at the heart of AI research and deployment. By fostering transparency, mitigating bias, assessing societal impact, and promoting human oversight, the AI community can navigate the challenges of AI innovation responsibly. Ethical AI not only ensures the trustworthy and fair development of technology but also shapes a future where AI aligns with human values and contributes positively to society's progress.

30.4 Towards Responsible and Inclusive AI Development: As the potential of artificial intelligence (AI) continues to unfold, the imperative for responsible and inclusive AI development becomes increasingly evident. This chapter delves into the principles and practices that guide the journey toward creating AI technologies that are not only innovative and efficient but also uphold ethical standards and foster inclusivity.

30.4.1 Ethical Frameworks for AI Development:

Value-Centered Design: Value-centered design places ethical considerations at the forefront of AI development. It involves aligning AI systems with human values, societal norms, and cultural contexts. By prioritizing ethical principles, developers can create AI that respects individual rights and societal well-being.

Human-Centric AI: Human-centric AI puts people at the center of technology. This approach ensures that AI systems are designed to enhance human capabilities, understanding their needs, and augmenting their decision-making processes. By focusing on human benefit, AI becomes a tool for positive transformation.

30.4.2 Diversity and Inclusion in AI:

Inclusive Data Collection: Inclusive AI development starts with diverse and representative data. Collecting data from a wide range of sources and demographics ensures that AI models are not skewed towards particular groups, promoting fairness and unbiased outcomes.

Multidisciplinary Collaboration: AI development benefits from multidisciplinary collaboration involving experts from various fields. Diverse perspectives contribute to well-rounded AI solutions that consider a broad range of societal impacts and ethical considerations.

30.4.3 Public Engagement and Accountability

Public Involvement: Inclusive AI development involves engaging the public in decision-making processes. Soliciting feedback, addressing concerns, and involving communities in AI development help ensure that technology aligns with societal values.

Ethical Oversight and Accountability: Ethical oversight and accountability mechanisms are crucial. Governments, organizations, and AI developers should adhere to ethical guidelines, codes of conduct, and transparent practices to ensure that AI technologies are deployed responsibly.

30.4.4 Continuous Learning and Improvement:

Ethical Training for AI Developers: Continuous learning is essential for ethical AI development. Providing AI developers with training on bias mitigation, fairness, and ethical considerations equips them to create responsible AI systems.

Feedback Loops and Iteration: AI systems should be designed with feedback loops that facilitate ongoing assessment and improvement. As AI technologies interact with users, feedback informs iterative refinements, ensuring that AI evolves in response to real-world needs.

30.5 Project

Unsolved Project

Suppose you're developing a project that focuses on the ethical considerations in deep learning and AI to promote responsible and inclusive AI development. To ensure your project addresses key ethical concerns, you need to understand bias, fairness, and discrimination in AI systems, strategies for addressing bias in data and algorithms, ethical considerations in AI research and deployment, and the principles of responsible and inclusive AI development. Before starting, research the following: the various forms of bias, fairness, and discrimination that can arise in AI systems, techniques for identifying and mitigating bias in both data and algorithms, the ethical challenges and considerations involved in AI research and deployment, and frameworks and best practices for fostering responsible and inclusive AI development. This foundational knowledge will help you develop a project that prioritizes ethical considerations in the design and implementation of AI systems.

30.6 Lab Activity

Unsolved Lab Activity

Implement an AI model designed to address a specific social issue (e.g., accessibility for people with disabilities). Evaluate its impact and discuss the challenges and opportunities for responsible AI development.

Task: Use a deep learning framework to implement an AI model designed to address a specific social issue, such as improving accessibility for people with disabilities. Train and evaluate the model on a relevant dataset. Document the implementation process, including data preprocessing, model architecture, training procedure, and impact evaluation. Provide visualizations of the model's performance and discuss the challenges and opportunities for responsible AI development in this context.

Exercises

Exercise 1 – Multiple Choice Questions

1. What are the main concerns addressed In this section regarding AI systems?
   A. Efficiency and productivity
   B. Bias, fairness, and discrimination
   C. Technical complexities
   D. Algorithmic accuracy
2. Why can AI systems inherit biases?
   A. They create their biases during training.
   B. They are inherently biased.
   C. Bias can be introduced from biased training data.
   D. Bias is a result of intentional design.
3. What is one consequence of biased AI systems in areas like hiring and lending?
   A. Improved economic opportunities
   B. Social and economic inequity
   C. Enhanced diversity
   D. Trust and accountability
4. What is the primary goal of fairness metrics in AI?
   A. To enforce bias
   B. To measure and quantify bias
   C. To improve model efficiency
   D. To increase data diversity
5. What is adversarial training in AI aimed at?
   A. Creating adversarial models
   B. Training models to be adversarial
   C. Reducing bias during training
   D. Promoting biased decision-making

Exercise 2 – True/False

1. Addressing bias in data and algorithms is not necessary for ensuring fairness in AI systems.
2. Ethical considerations are only important during the research phase of AI development.
3. Responsible and inclusive AI development involves making sure that AI systems do not discriminate against any group.

Review Questions

1. How does a focus on ethical considerations contribute to addressing algorithmic bias in AI?
2. How can biased training data lead to biased AI models?
3. Give an example of how historical biases can manifest in AI predictions.
4. What is the significance of data collection practices in addressing bias in AI?
5. How can AI models inadvertently amplify societal biases?
6. What is algorithmic discrimination in AI, and how does it occur?
7. Why is it important to develop fairness metrics in AI systems?
8. Explain the concept of "equal opportunity" as it relates to fairness in AI.
9. Provide an example of a situation where AI might unintentionally discriminate based on sensitive attributes.
10. How can addressing bias in AI lead to more equitable outcomes in society?
11. What are the potential social and economic consequences of biased AI systems?
12. How does unfair AI decision-making affect public trust and accountability?
13. Give examples of industries or domains where biased AI decisions could have negative consequences.
14. Why is it important to consider the impact of AI on marginalized groups?
15. How can addressing bias in AI contribute to a fairer society?
16. Explain the importance of diverse and representative data in mitigating bias.
17. What role do AI developers play in detecting and measuring bias within models?
18. Describe the concept of algorithmic fairness and how it can be achieved.
19. What are some techniques mentioned for addressing bias during the training of AI models?
20. Why is transparency and explainability crucial for mitigating bias in AI?

21. What is the multi-pronged approach suggested for addressing bias in AI systems?
22. How can data preprocessing techniques help mitigate bias in training data?
23. Describe the concept of data augmentation and its role in addressing bias.
24. What is the purpose of Generative Adversarial Networks (GANs) in mitigating bias?
25. How do fair representation learning techniques work in reducing bias?
26. Explain the concept of adversarial debiasing in AI.
27. How do algorithmic auditing and bias metrics contribute to bias mitigation?
28. What role do regularization techniques play in addressing bias during AI model training?
29. Why is it crucial to continuously assess and improve AI systems for bias?

Answers

Exercise 1- 1. B 2. C 3. B 4. B 5. C
Exercise 2- 1) False, 2) False, 3) True

Online Resources

Online Exam Paper:
Link: https://forms.gle/pqjwc7mummhn3UWH6
QR Code:

Chapter 30 Videos Playlist:
Link: https://www.youtube.com/playlist?list=PLzlh_31VWEFoiZvr62_D67cYCU3-_WsaQ
QR Code:

Chapter 31: Deep Learning for Autonomous Vehicles

32.1 Perception and Sensor Fusion in Self-Driving Cars:

31.1.1 Perception: The Eyes and Ears of Self-Driving Cars: The combination of computer vision, LiDAR, and radar allows self-driving cars to perceive the world with remarkable accuracy. These sensors work in synergy, providing a comprehensive understanding of the environment's visual and spatial aspects. As self-driving technology advances, the continued refinement of these perception technologies will be pivotal in ensuring safe and reliable autonomous navigation, bringing us closer to a future where self-driving cars share the road with humans seamlessly.

Computer Vision: Computer vision serves as the "eyes" of self-driving cars, enabling them to interpret visual data captured by cameras. Cameras strategically placed on the vehicle capture images of the road, surrounding vehicles, pedestrians, traffic signs, and lane markings. Through sophisticated image processing techniques, these images are transformed into actionable insights. Advanced computer vision methods, including deep learning algorithms, allow vehicles to not only identify objects but also understand complex scenes and make informed decisions. For instance, deep learning networks can recognize different vehicle types, determine the speed of surrounding traffic, and even predict the behavior of pedestrians.

LiDAR (Light Detection and Ranging): LiDAR acts as the vehicle's "laser-based eyes," emitting laser pulses that bounce off objects and return as data points. By measuring the time it takes for these pulses to return, LiDAR systems create detailed 3D maps of the environment. These maps offer accurate depth information, allowing self-driving cars to accurately perceive the distance to surrounding objects and obstacles. This technology is particularly beneficial in scenarios where precise object localization is critical, such as navigating through complex urban environments or detecting small objects on the road. LiDAR's ability to function effectively in various lighting conditions, including darkness, further enhances the vehicle's perception capabilities.

Radar: Radar systems provide the vehicle with a form of "echolocation," emitting radio waves that bounce off objects and return as radar echoes. By analyzing the time it takes for these echoes to return, radar systems can determine the distance, speed, and even the size of detected objects. Radar's strength lies in its ability to function reliably in adverse weather conditions, such as rain, fog, or snow, where other sensors might face limitations. This makes radar a valuable addition to the sensor suite, providing crucial information to the vehicle about the movement of vehicles and objects around it.

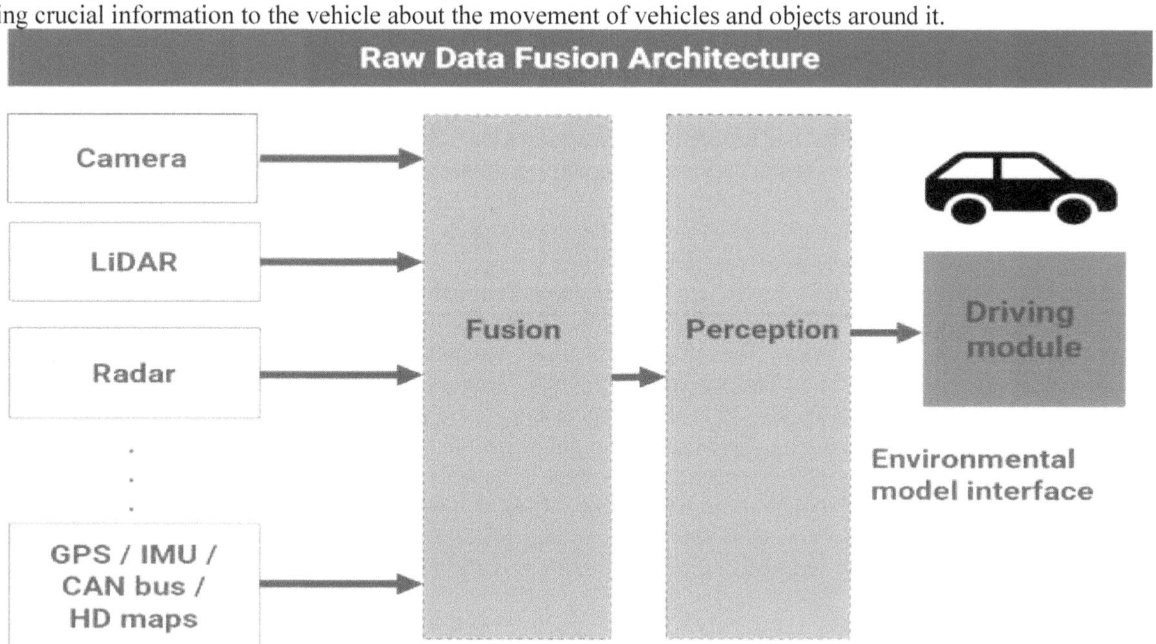

31.1.2 Sensor Fusion: Creating a Comprehensive Picture: Sensor fusion plays a pivotal role in elevating the perception capabilities of self-driving cars. By integrating data from various sensors, autonomous vehicles create a holistic and nuanced understanding of their environment, enabling safer and more reliable navigation.

Multi-Sensor Integration: Multi-sensor integration is at the heart of sensor fusion. Different sensors, such as cameras, LiDAR, and radar, each offer unique insights into the surroundings. By combining the strengths of these sensors, self-driving cars construct a unified perception that accounts for diverse aspects of the environment. This redundancy ensures robustness by reducing the risk of erroneous decisions caused by a single sensor's limitations. For instance, while cameras excel in recognizing objects, LiDAR's depth information and radar's ability to function in adverse weather conditions enhance the vehicle's perception accuracy.

Kalman Filters and Particle Filters: Filters like Kalman filters and particle filters refine sensor data by estimating the true state of objects. These filters address inaccuracies and noise present in individual sensor readings. Kalman filters, based on probabilistic models, combine sensor measurements with predictions to produce a more accurate estimation of an object's position and velocity. Particle filters, on the other hand, use a particle-based approach to iteratively converge on the actual state of an object. These filters contribute to more reliable sensor fusion, enhancing the accuracy of the perception system and facilitating informed decision-making.

Deep Sensor Fusion: Deep learning techniques are being harnessed to take sensor fusion to the next level. Neural networks can process and integrate data from different sensors, learning intricate relationships between sensor inputs and environmental cues. Deep sensor fusion enables vehicles to understand complex patterns and interactions in the environment, even when individual sensors might provide incomplete or ambiguous information. This approach leverages the power of deep learning to generate a comprehensive and accurate representation of the surroundings, ultimately aiding in making safer driving decisions.

31.1.3 Challenges and Future Directions: Despite significant advancements, the field of perception and sensor fusion in self-driving cars is not without its challenges. Looking ahead, addressing these challenges will be pivotal in advancing the capabilities of autonomous vehicles and ensuring their safe integration into our roadways.

Sensor Redundancy and Reliability: Ensuring the reliability of sensors and managing sensor redundancy is a critical challenge. Self-driving cars heavily depend on accurate and consistent sensor data for decision-making. Failures, discrepancies, or even minor malfunctions in sensors can lead to inaccurate perceptions and potentially dangerous decisions. Developing fault-tolerant systems that can detect sensor failures, switch to reliable sensors, and maintain safe operation is crucial to prevent catastrophic consequences.

Handling Complex Environments: Navigating through complex and dynamic environments is an ongoing challenge. Autonomous vehicles encounter a myriad of scenarios, from navigating crowded intersections to maneuvering through construction zones. These situations require perception algorithms that can process a vast amount of information in real-time, accurately interpreting dynamic changes and making split-second decisions. Developing algorithms that can handle such complex scenarios safely and efficiently remains an active research area.

Semantic Understanding: While self-driving cars have made impressive strides in object detection, the next frontier is achieving semantic understanding. This involves going beyond mere object recognition and understanding the context and intentions of different road users. For example, a self-driving car must not only detect a pedestrian but also predict their behavior and anticipate their next move. Similarly, interpreting complex traffic interactions, such as yielding to emergency vehicles or negotiating with human drivers, requires advanced algorithms that can comprehend the nuances of human driving behavior and intent.

31.2 Object Detection, Tracking, and Scene Understanding: Object detection, tracking, and scene understanding collectively create a comprehensive canvas upon which self-driving cars perceive and interact with their surroundings. Through these interconnected technologies, autonomous vehicles gain the ability to not only recognize individual objects but also understand their dynamics, relationships, and broader implications. As the field continues to evolve, the fusion of these elements brings us closer to a future where self-driving cars navigate complex scenarios seamlessly and safely.

31.2.1 Object Detection: Recognizing the Elements: Object detection serves as the foundational pillar of scene perception within the realm of self-driving cars. This section unveils the significance of object detection, its techniques, and its role in facilitating safe and informed autonomous driving decisions.

Importance of Object Detection: Object detection is the bedrock upon which self-driving cars build their understanding of the environment. It involves the identification and localization of various entities such as vehicles, pedestrians, cyclists, and obstacles within the vehicle's field of view. The accuracy of object detection lays the groundwork for a spectrum of driving decisions, encompassing everything from calculating safe following distances to predicting the behavior of neighboring entities.

Techniques in Object Detection: Modern object detection techniques marry the strengths of traditional computer vision methods with the prowess of deep learning. Traditional techniques include Haar cascades, Histogram of Oriented Gradients (HOG), and support vector machines (SVM), which form a robust basis for initial object recognition. However, it is the advent of deep learning, particularly convolutional neural networks (CNNs), that has revolutionized object detection. Deep learning models like Faster R-CNN, YOLO (You Only Look Once), and SSD (Single Shot MultiBox Detector) have showcased remarkable accuracy and adaptability, enabling vehicles to swiftly and accurately identify objects of diverse sizes and shapes.

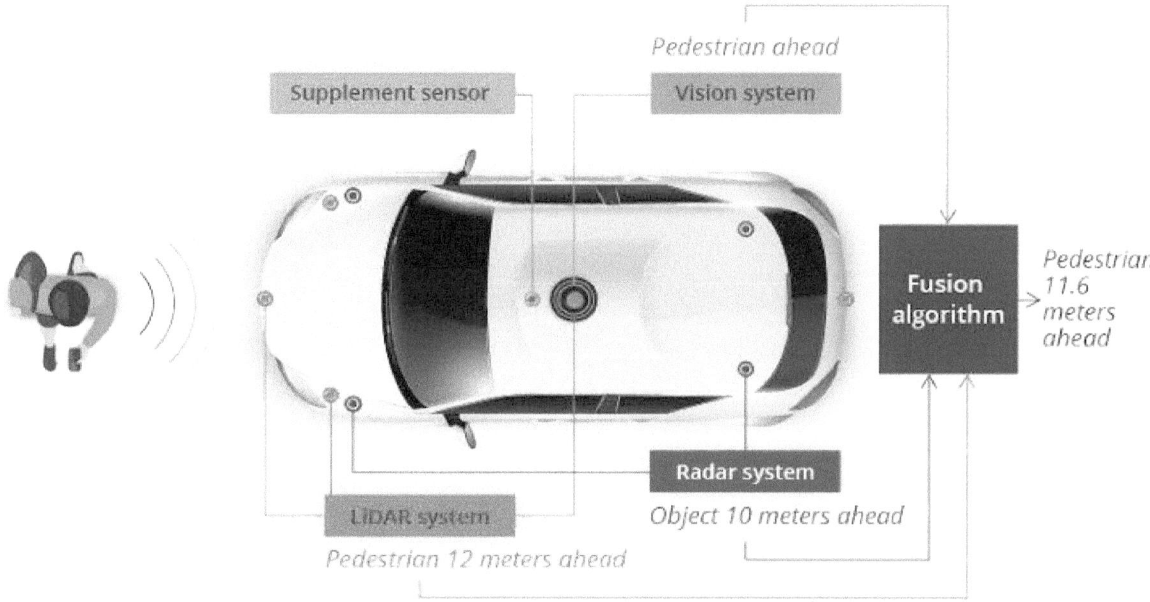

31.2.2 Object Tracking: Maintaining Continuity:

Need for Object Tracking: Object tracking takes the baton from detection and ensures the seamless continuation of an object's identity across frames. While detection provides an initial glimpse of an object's presence, tracking ensures that the object's identity is sustained as it navigates through the scene. This persistent tracking enhances the vehicle's understanding of object trajectories and behaviors.

Tracking Techniques: Object tracking techniques span a gamut from traditional to cutting-edge. Simple methods such as Kalman filters and particle filters combine motion models with sensor measurements to estimate an object's position across frames. More advanced algorithms leverage deep learning architectures, fusing spatial and temporal information to track objects even when they undergo transformations or occlusions. These methods collectively enable self-driving cars to maintain a coherent perception of object movements, a critical element for informed decision-making.

31.2.3 Scene Understanding: Beyond Objects:

Contextual Understanding: Scene understanding takes the comprehension of objects a step further, encompassing the broader context in which these objects exist. It involves deciphering the relationships between objects, interpreting the geometry of the environment, and recognizing the dynamics of complex scenes. This contextual awareness contributes to a more holistic perception of the surroundings.

Semantic Segmentation: Semantic segmentation is a refinement of scene understanding that assigns specific labels to each pixel in an image, effectively categorizing it into object classes. This granular level of understanding enables self-driving cars to differentiate between various road elements such as lanes, sidewalks, vehicles, pedestrians, and more. Semantic segmentation enhances the vehicle's capability to make nuanced driving decisions based on the nature and role of each pixel.

Holistic Decision-Making: A holistic scene understanding empowers self-driving cars to make decisions that resonate with a profound grasp of the environment. This involves predicting the intentions of pedestrians, comprehending the flow of traffic, and anticipating potential hazards or opportunities. By incorporating semantic understanding and contextual insights, self-driving cars are primed to contribute to safer, more efficient, and adaptive driving behaviors.

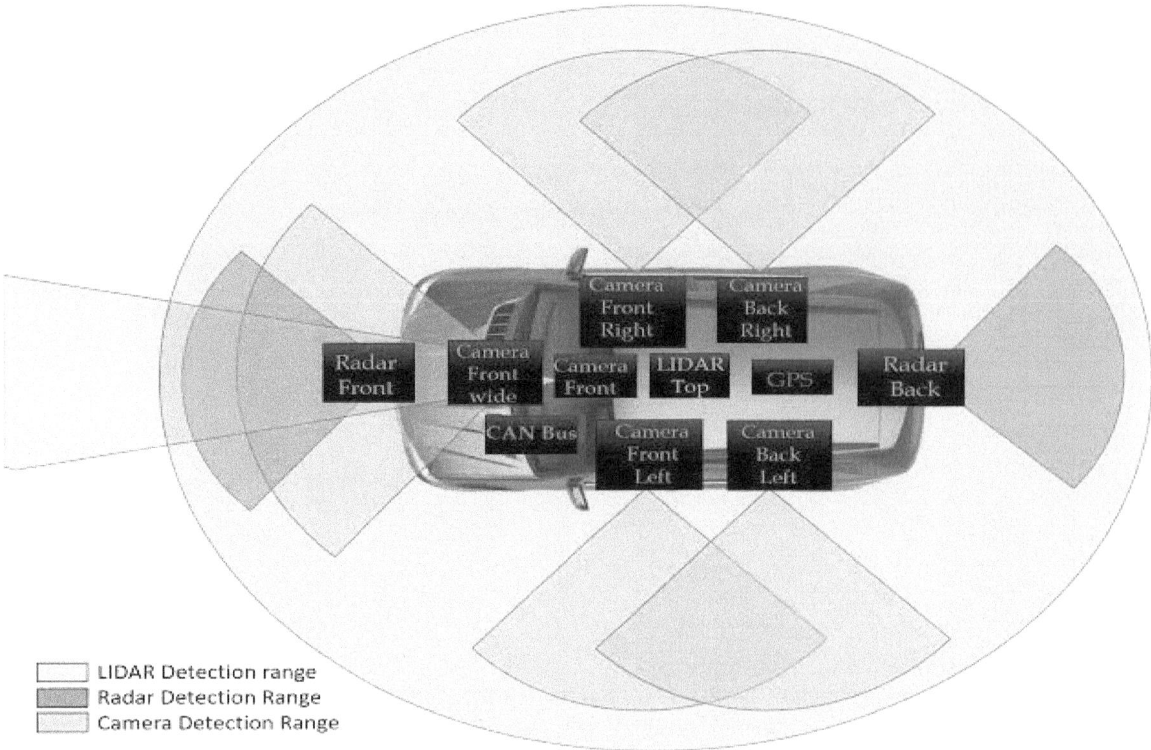

31.3 Path Planning and Decision-Making with Deep Learning: Path planning stands as the intellectual compass guiding self-driving vehicles through the intricate tapestry of our roadways. With the advent of deep reinforcement learning, vehicles evolve beyond mere rule-followers to intelligent agents capable of making contextually aware decisions. By striking a harmonious balance between safety, efficiency, and adherence to regulations, autonomous vehicles are poised to navigate the roads seamlessly, bringing us one step closer to a future of safe, autonomous transportation.

31.3.1 Path Planning: Navigating the Terrain: Navigating the intricate landscapes of the world requires more than just perceiving the environment: it necessitates intelligent and dynamic path planning. This section unveils the significance of path planning, its role in guiding autonomous vehicles, and how deep reinforcement learning is shaping this critical aspect of self-driving technology.

Importance of Path Planning: Path planning stands as a pivotal art in the realm of autonomous driving, representing the process of devising a trajectory for a vehicle through its ever-changing environment. This trajectory must strike a delicate balance between safety, adherence to traffic rules, and efficiency. It involves an intricate interplay of factors that encompass avoiding obstacles, navigating complex intersections, maintaining lane discipline, and ultimately, minimizing travel time.

Deep Reinforcement Learning for Path Planning: Deep reinforcement learning has emerged as a potent approach for enhancing path planning capabilities in autonomous vehicles. In this paradigm, self-driving agents—often represented as neural networks—interact with either simulated or real-world environments. They learn through reinforcement, where they receive rewards for making choices that lead to safe and efficient navigation. By iterating through these interactions, the agents grasp the complexities of the environment and develop a keen understanding of optimal trajectories.This approach leverages the sequential decision-making prowess of neural networks, allowing them to analyze the environment, anticipate outcomes, and select actions that result in the most favorable paths. These networks take into account both the immediate rewards and the long-term consequences of their choices, honing their path planning strategies over time.

31.3.2 Decision-Making: Navigating Choices: Decision-making is the cognitive backbone that elevates self-driving cars beyond mere mechanical operations. By integrating the foresight of deep learning, these vehicles evolve into intuitive and predictive entities that navigate choices with intelligence and precision. The union of decision-making and deep learning unlocks a new era of autonomous driving, where vehicles traverse complex traffic scenarios with a blend of anticipatory insight and unwavering adherence to safety.

Role of Decision-Making: Decision-making endows self-driving cars with the cognitive ability to interpret their surroundings, anticipate the intentions of other road users, and execute informed choices. This dynamic process encompasses a range of tasks, from seemingly simple maneuvers like lane changing and yielding to the complexity of overtaking and navigating intricate traffic scenarios. Every choice the vehicle makes reflects a well-balanced blend of situational awareness, adherence to traffic norms, and the overarching goal of reaching the destination safely and efficiently.

Deep Learning for Decision-Making: Deep learning has revolutionized decision-making in self-driving cars, particularly through the employment of recurrent neural networks (RNNs) and Long Short-Term Memory (LSTM) networks. These neural architectures excel in capturing temporal dependencies, making them adept at understanding the evolving context of the scene over time.

Through a cascade of sequential layers, RNNs and LSTMs process past observations, current conditions, and predicted future states to forecast the likely actions of other road users. This enables autonomous vehicles to anticipate potential scenarios, enabling proactive decision-making that prioritizes safety and efficiency. For instance, the network might infer that a nearby vehicle's slight drift towards the lane boundary indicates an intention to change lanes, prompting the self-driving car to adjust its trajectory accordingly.

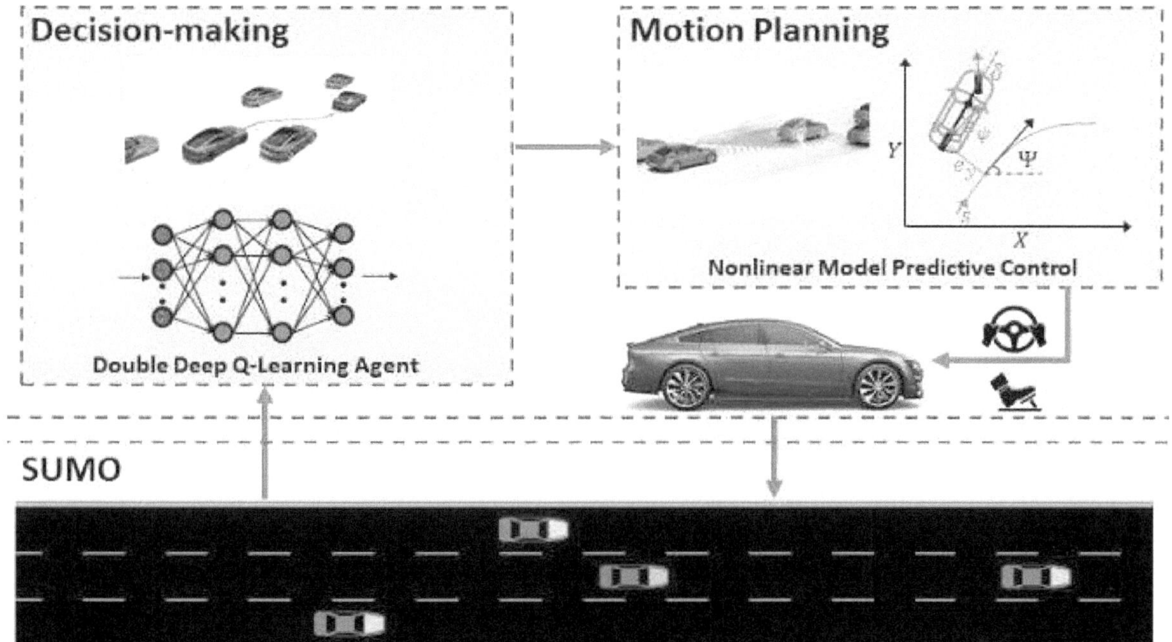

31.3.3 Challenges and Future Directions: While the journey of incorporating deep learning into path planning and decision-making is promising, As deep learning continues to reshape path planning and decision-making in autonomous vehicles, these challenges stand as signposts guiding the evolution of the technology. Overcoming these hurdles is not only a technical endeavor but a societal one, influencing how we entrust autonomous systems with the lives and well-being of passengers and other road users. The path ahead involves refining the technology to ensure that it adapts effectively to the dynamic real-world context and embodies ethical values, resulting in a safer and more responsible autonomous driving future.

these challenges will shape the trajectory of autonomous driving technology and its integration into our daily lives.

Real-World Generalization: One of the foremost challenges is translating deep learning models, which are often trained in controlled simulations, to real-world scenarios. Simulations provide a controlled environment where the models can learn from a plethora of scenarios quickly. However, real-world conditions are complex, dynamic, and sometimes unpredictable. Ensuring that the learned behaviors in simulations generalize effectively to the real world is a formidable task. Vehicles must adapt to a myriad of real-world factors, from weather conditions and road infrastructure variations to the unpredictability of human drivers and pedestrians.

Ethical Decision-Making: Autonomous vehicles must grapple with ethical dilemmas in scenarios where human safety is in tension with potential harm. These dilemmas arise when the vehicle is required to make decisions that might involve trade-offs between minimizing harm to its occupants and avoiding harm to pedestrians or other road users. Deep learning algorithms, while proficient at recognizing patterns and making decisions, lack the intrinsic ethical reasoning that humans possess. Ensuring that autonomous vehicles make ethically sound decisions demands a careful consideration of the moral principles that should guide their actions. The challenge lies in embedding ethical guidelines into the algorithms to navigate these complex moral trade-offs.

31.4 Safety, Regulations, and Future of Autonomous Vehicles: As autonomous vehicles inch closer to becoming an integral part of our daily lives, the regulatory and policy frameworks that shape their deployment are pivotal. These frameworks must navigate the intricate balance between innovation and safety, while also addressing the evolving technological landscape. As governments adapt to this transformational era, the regulatory approaches they adopt will play a critical role in determining the trajectory of autonomous vehicles and their impact on society.

Safety in Autonomous Vehicles: A Non-Negotiable Imperative:

Safety as the Central Pillar: Safety takes center stage in the realm of autonomous vehicles. Ensuring the safety of passengers, pedestrians, and other road users is a non-negotiable imperative that underpins the entire development and deployment process.

Safety Challenges and Solutions: Safety challenges in autonomous vehicles span a spectrum, from technical glitches and sensor failures to unexpected interactions with human drivers and pedestrians. To mitigate these challenges, vehicles employ redundancies, fail-safe mechanisms, and continuous testing in various scenarios, replicating real-world conditions to refine safety protocols.

31.4.2 Regulations and Policy Frameworks: The integration of autonomous vehicles into our transportation fabric brings forth a complex interplay of safety, innovation, and societal harmony.

An Evolving Regulatory Landscape: The advent of autonomous vehicles has ushered in a wave of regulatory considerations that bridge the chasm between innovation and public safety. Governments across the globe are tasked with crafting regulations that ensure the ethical, safe, and lawful integration of autonomous technology into our daily lives. The regulatory landscape is inherently dynamic, reflecting the continuous evolution of both technology and societal expectations. Policymakers grapple with the challenge of striking a harmonious balance between fostering innovation and safeguarding the well-being of citizens. As the technology matures and autonomous vehicles become more commonplace, the regulatory framework must adapt to accommodate new use cases, address unforeseen challenges, and foster an environment of trust.

Regulatory Approaches: Different regions embark on diverse regulatory pathways to navigate the autonomous vehicle revolution. These approaches reflect the unique socio-cultural, economic, and infrastructural contexts of each jurisdiction. Some regions opt for performance-based regulations, focusing on the outcomes and performance metrics that vehicles must meet. This approach offers flexibility, allowing innovators to explore various technical solutions as long as they adhere to predefined safety benchmarks. In contrast, other regions adopt prescriptive regulations, detailing specific technical requirements that autonomous vehicles must fulfill. This approach provides clarity and uniformity in the technological specifications expected from self-driving cars. Ultimately, the choice between performance-based and prescriptive regulations hinges on the regulatory philosophy of each jurisdiction and its stance on fostering innovation while ensuring public safety. The evolution of autonomous vehicle regulations is an ongoing journey, marked by collaboration among governments, industry stakeholders, and researchers to create a regulatory framework that harmonizes progress with safety.

31.4.3 The Future of Autonomous Vehicles: The future of autonomous vehicles is a tapestry woven with technological innovation, societal transformation, and ethical reflection. Gradually integrating autonomy into vehicles, revolutionizing urban mobility, and navigating ethical quandaries will define the evolution of autonomous technology. As this evolution unfolds, the collective effort of researchers, policymakers, industries, and society at large will determine how autonomous vehicles harmonize with human life, enhance transportation, and reshape the fabric of our cities.

Gradual Integration: The journey towards fully autonomous vehicles is an evolutionary voyage characterized by gradual integration. This progression encompasses a spectrum of autonomy levels, spanning from vehicles with semi-autonomous features that aid drivers to those that operate with minimal human intervention. Technological advancements in sensors, AI, and connectivity will play a pivotal role in shaping this transition. Simultaneously, societal acceptance will play a vital role, as individuals embrace the idea of sharing control with machines and entrusting autonomous systems with their safety. As vehicles advance along this continuum, regulatory frameworks will evolve to delineate responsibilities between humans and machines, defining the boundaries within which autonomy can operate. The convergence of technology, acceptance, and regulations will eventually culminate in the deployment of fully autonomous vehicles that navigate the roads with precision and reliability.

Societal Transformation: The proliferation of autonomous vehicles holds the potential to redefine urban landscapes and reshape the fabric of transportation. By minimizing traffic congestion, optimizing routes, and improving road safety through advanced perception systems, these vehicles can revolutionize the way people move within cities. Moreover, autonomous vehicles can introduce new paradigms of mobility, enabling shared autonomous fleets that transcend traditional car ownership models. This shift towards shared mobility solutions not only optimizes resource utilization but also reduces the environmental footprint of transportation.

Ethical Considerations: The road to a future of autonomous driving is paved with ethical dilemmas. The algorithms powering autonomous vehicles must grapple with complex decisions, such as choosing between preserving the safety of vehicle occupants and preventing harm to pedestrians. Developing ethical frameworks that guide these decisions is paramount, ensuring that the technology aligns with societal values and prioritizes human safety. As the capabilities of AI algorithms grow, their ethical considerations become more pronounced. Ethical considerations extend beyond immediate safety concerns to broader societal implications, including the impact on jobs, urban planning, and transportation dynamics. Crafting robust ethical guidelines and embedding them into AI systems is a fundamental step towards ensuring that the autonomous future is a responsible and just one.

31.5 Project

Unsolved Project

Suppose you're developing a project focused on the application of deep learning in autonomous vehicles. To create a comprehensive and effective project, you need to understand perception and sensor fusion, object detection, tracking, and scene understanding, path planning and decision-making, and the safety, regulatory, and future aspects of autonomous vehicles. Before starting, research the following: techniques for perception and sensor fusion to enable self-driving cars to interpret their environment, methods for object detection, tracking, and scene understanding to ensure accurate and real-time situational awareness, deep learning approaches for path planning and decision-making to navigate complex driving scenarios, and the current safety standards, regulations, and future trends in the development of autonomous vehicles. This foundational knowledge will help you develop a project that addresses the critical aspects of deep learning in the context of autonomous driving technology.

31.6 Lab Activity

Unsolved Lab Activity

Implement a deep learning-based path planning and decision-making algorithm for a simulated self-driving car. Evaluate its performance in different driving scenarios.

Task: Use a deep learning framework to implement a path planning and decision-making algorithm for a simulated self-driving car. Train the model using reinforcement learning or another suitable approach and evaluate its performance in different driving scenarios. Document the implementation process, including environment setup, model architecture, training procedure, and performance evaluation. Provide visualizations of the planned paths and decision-making outcomes in various scenarios.

Exercises

Exercise 1 – Multiple Choice Questions

1. What role does computer vision play in self-driving cars?
   a. Processing LiDAR data
   b. Detecting radar echoes
   c. Interpreting visual data from cameras
   d. Analyzing deep sensor fusion
2. How does LiDAR create detailed 3D maps of the environment?
   a. By emitting radio waves
   b. By measuring the speed of light
   c. By analyzing radar echoes
   d. By measuring the time it takes for laser pulses to return
3. Which sensor is known for its reliability in adverse weather conditions?
   a. Computer vision
   b. LiDAR
   c. Radar
   d. Infrared sensors
4. What is the primary purpose of sensor fusion in self-driving cars?
   a. To reduce the number of sensors
   b. To create redundancy
   c. To improve perception accuracy
   d. To decrease computational load
5. Which filter is used to estimate the true state of objects by combining sensor measurements with predictions?
   a. Kalman filter
   b. Particle filter
   c. Deep learning filter
   d. Radar filter

Exercise 2 – True/False

1. Perception and sensor fusion are crucial for object detection in self-driving cars.
2. Path planning in autonomous vehicles does not involve deep learning algorithms.
3. Scene understanding in self-driving cars includes detecting and tracking objects.

Review Question

1. What are the three main types of sensors used in self-driving cars for perception?
2. How does computer vision contribute to the perception capabilities of self-driving cars?
3. Explain the role of LiDAR in creating 3D maps of the environment.
4. What advantage does radar offer in adverse weather conditions?
5. What is sensor fusion, and why is it essential in autonomous vehicles?

Answers

Exercise 1- 1. c 2. d 3. c 4. c 5. a
Exercise 2- 1) True, 2) False, 3) True

Online Resources

Online Exam Paper:
Link: https://forms.gle/u7xqpwp22TbA3GiL7
QR Code:

Chapter 31 Videos Playlist:
Link: https://www.youtube.com/playlist?list=PLzlh_31VWEFr8VsB3NDJcqzlFPJNPczks
QR Code:

Chapter 32: Federated Learning and Privacy-Preserving AI

32.1.1 Introduction: Federated Learning represents a groundbreaking shift within the realm of machine learning. In stark contrast to conventional centralized methodologies, it ushers in a novel paradigm that revolves around the collaborative training of models across a geographically dispersed network of devices. What sets federated learning apart is its unwavering commitment to preserving the paramount principles of data privacy and security.

Traditionally, centralized approaches entail the aggregation of all data onto a central server for model training. However, this practice has raised concerns about data exposure, especially when dealing with sensitive or personal information. Federated Learning, on the other hand, seeks to tackle this challenge head-on by distributing the learning process while ensuring that raw data remains localized on individual devices.

32.1.2 Decentralized Model Training: The operation of Federated Learning is ingeniously simple yet profoundly transformative. At its core, it entails the decentralization of model training by performing it directly on individual user devices. These devices encompass a wide spectrum, ranging from ubiquitous smartphones to specialized IoT devices. Each device acts as a training node, autonomously participating in the learning process by training a local model using the data it holds.

The beauty of this approach lies in its ability to sidestep the necessity of transmitting raw data to a central server. Instead, the crux of the learning process unfolds within the confines of each device, where data is processed locally. This decentralized training not only adheres to stringent data privacy standards but also minimizes concerns related to data transfer, bandwidth usage, and potential security breaches.

By allowing devices to independently train their local models, Federated Learning fosters a collaborative ecosystem in which the power of machine learning is harnessed without sacrificing the sanctity of user data. This decentralized model training, underpinned by a commitment to privacy, serves as the foundation for the entire federated learning paradigm.

32.1.3 Collaborative Model Aggregation: Following the decentralized model training phase, Federated Learning proceeds to the crucial step of collaborative model aggregation. This phase orchestrates the amalgamation of the locally trained models from individual devices to form a unified, global model. While the actual aggregation process may transpire on a central server, it's important to underscore that the raw data, which embodies the essence of user privacy, remains securely localized on the respective devices.

The collaborative model aggregation serves as the bridge that connects the power of distributed learning with the creation of a comprehensive and informed global model. During this aggregation, the aggregated knowledge and insights gleaned from each device's training are harmoniously integrated. The result is a global model that benefits from the diverse perspectives and contexts present across the myriad devices, thereby enhancing its overall proficiency and adaptability.

What's particularly noteworthy is that the collaborative model aggregation is designed to be seamless and efficient. It does not necessitate the exchange of raw data, which would potentially compromise user privacy. Instead, only model updates and information essential for enhancing the global model's accuracy are shared. This nuanced approach underscores the commitment of Federated Learning to safeguarding user data while still enabling the creation of models that are both powerful and privacy-respecting.

32.1.4 Advantages: The adoption of Federated Learning confers several substantial advantages that collectively redefine the landscape of machine learning:

Privacy Preservation: By preserving raw data on user devices, Federated Learning mitigates the risk of sensitive information being exposed to external entities. This privacy-centric approach aligns with evolving data protection regulations.

Reduced Communication Costs: Federated Learning minimizes the need for extensive data transmission between devices and central servers. This results in reduced communication overhead and more efficient utilization of network resources.

Edge Intelligence: Localized model training on edge devices nurtures the concept of edge intelligence. Devices themselves become capable of making informed decisions autonomously, without the constant requirement for central server interaction.

Data Diversity: The federated approach inherently accounts for the diversity of data present across devices. This translates to a global model that is well-versed in an array of scenarios and contexts, ultimately bolstering its robustness and adaptability.

Scalability: Federated Learning exhibits a remarkable ability to scale gracefully, even in the presence of a substantial number of devices. The approach avoids overwhelming the central server and ensures efficient, large-scale participation.

In essence, Federated Learning presents a dynamic blend of privacy-consciousness, efficiency, and enhanced model capabilities. This amalgamation of advantages holds the potential to reshape the trajectory of machine learning applications across industries and domains.

32.1.5 Use Cases: Federated Learning finds application in various sectors:

Healthcare: Collaborative model training aids disease prediction and treatment without sharing patient data.

Smart Devices: IoT devices improve functionality collectively while preserving user privacy.

Natural Language Processing: Language models benefit from diverse linguistic insights without compromising data.

Autonomous Vehicles: Vehicles share road insights without compromising vehicle-to-vehicle privacy.

32.1.6 Conclusion: Federated Learning presents a novel solution by combining data privacy, communication efficiency, and model enhancement. This approach unlocks versatile machine learning applications while prioritizing user privacy and data security.

32.2 Secure Aggregation and Differential Privacy: In the realm of modern data-driven technologies, maintaining the sanctity of data privacy has emerged as a paramount concern. Secure Aggregation and Differential Privacy stand as pioneering approaches that address this concern within the context of machine learning and data analysis. These concepts offer innovative mechanisms to safeguard sensitive information while still allowing the extraction of valuable insights.

32.2.1 Secure Aggregation: Secure Aggregation is a groundbreaking technique aimed at preserving the confidentiality of individual contributions while performing global computations on aggregated data. In Federated Learning scenarios, where decentralized devices contribute to a central model, secure aggregation ensures that each device's input remains encrypted during the aggregation process. This obfuscation prevents any single device's data from being revealed, thereby fortifying user privacy.

The essence of secure aggregation lies in cryptographic protocols that enable computations on encrypted data. Homomorphic encryption, in particular, plays a pivotal role. Through a series of mathematical operations performed on encrypted data, secure aggregation permits the extraction of meaningful aggregate insights without exposing the raw individual data points. This cryptographic choreography ensures that the privacy of participants is upheld, making secure aggregation an indispensable tool for Federated Learning and collaborative analytics.

32.2.2 Differential Privacy: Differential Privacy is a profound concept that tackles the delicate equilibrium between data utility and privacy. It seeks to enable data analysis while safeguarding individual privacy, even in the presence of powerful adversaries. The core principle is to inject a controlled amount of noise into the data to obscure individual contributions while still yielding accurate aggregate results.

In the context of Federated Learning, differential privacy is employed to add carefully calibrated noise to gradients or model updates shared by devices. This noise addition ensures that any singular device's contribution cannot be accurately isolated, thereby thwarting potential attempts to reverse-engineer sensitive data. This ensures that the model's training process doesn't inadvertently reveal private information about any specific participant.

32.2.3 Advantages: The synergy between Secure Aggregation and Differential Privacy offers a range of substantial advantages that are pivotal in the realm of modern data-driven technologies:

Data Confidentiality: Secure Aggregation serves as a fortress for individual data points, preserving their confidentiality throughout the aggregation process. By employing cryptographic techniques, sensitive information remains concealed from prying eyes. This impenetrable shield ensures that participants' personal data remains cryptographically hidden, mitigating the risks associated with unauthorized data exposure.

Privacy-Preserving Insights: Through the orchestrated marriage of Secure Aggregation, the encrypted nature of data persists, allowing for the derivation of insightful patterns and trends without compromising individual privacy. This attribute permits the extraction of meaningful information while respecting the sanctity of users' sensitive data. As a result, organizations and researchers can glean valuable insights without transgressing ethical boundaries.

Mitigated Re-Identification Risk: Differential Privacy introduces a unique mechanism to mitigate the risk of re-identifying participants based on their contributions. By injecting calibrated noise into aggregated data, the distinctiveness of individual inputs is blurred, making it exceedingly challenging to isolate specific individuals. This prophylactic measure thwarts adversarial attempts to reverse-engineer private information from the aggregated data, safeguarding the identities of participants.

Responsible Collaboration: The amalgamation of Secure Aggregation and Differential Privacy underpins a collaborative ecosystem characterized by responsible data sharing. As multiple parties collaborate on model training or analysis, the assurance of data confidentiality and privacy-preserving techniques fosters an environment of trust and ethical collaboration. This allows organizations to pool their resources without compromising the sensitive information of individuals.

Trust Building: In the era of data breaches and privacy concerns, the utilization of Secure Aggregation and Differential Privacy instills a sense of trust among users. Participants can have confidence that their data is subject to robust security measures, thus elevating their comfort levels in engaging with AI systems. This trust-building factor is pivotal in forging positive relationships between organizations and their users.

The cumulative advantages of Secure Aggregation and Differential Privacy represent a paradigm shift in data-driven methodologies. Their integration ensures that data-driven insights can be harnessed while maintaining the highest standards of privacy, ethics, and responsible collaboration. As these approaches continue to evolve, they cement themselves as cornerstones in the ethical and secure advancement of AI and machine learning technologies.

32.2.4 Challenges and Future Directions: The convergence of Secure Aggregation and Differential Privacy presents a robust framework for privacy-preserving data analysis. However, this convergence is not without its challenges and considerations. Navigating these challenges is essential to fully harness the potential of these techniques and ensure their seamless integration into the landscape of AI and machine learning.

Balancing Noise and Utility: A critical challenge lies in striking the delicate balance between noise addition for privacy preservation and retaining data utility. Injecting noise is fundamental to safeguarding individual contributions, but excessive noise can lead to distorted results. Innovations that optimize noise levels while preserving the accuracy and usefulness of aggregated insights are pivotal to the success of these approaches.

Scalable Cryptographic Protocols: The development of scalable cryptographic protocols is paramount. Cryptographic techniques play a central role in Secure Aggregation and Differential Privacy, but their applicability at scale can be complex.

Overcoming cryptographic bottlenecks and exploring advanced cryptographic methods that accommodate the demands of large-scale data aggregation are imperative for real-world adoption.

User Education and Transparency: Educating users about the intricacies of Secure Aggregation and Differential Privacy is vital. Users need to understand the mechanisms in place to protect their privacy and how these techniques contribute to responsible data sharing. Transparent communication can help build trust and ensure that users are confident in participating in data-driven collaborations.

Real-World Implementation: Translating theoretical concepts into practical, real-world implementations is a challenge that requires interdisciplinary collaboration. Researchers, cryptographers, data scientists, and policymakers need to collaborate to design systems that seamlessly integrate Secure Aggregation and Differential Privacy into existing frameworks, software, and hardware.

Ethical Considerations: As these techniques gain traction, addressing ethical considerations becomes paramount. Decisions about how much noise to add, the level of data aggregation, and the balance between utility and privacy require careful ethical deliberation. Ensuring that these methods align with ethical principles and do not inadvertently introduce new biases or risks is crucial.

Continued Research and Innovation: The future directions of Secure Aggregation and Differential Privacy lie in ongoing research and innovation. The evolution of cryptographic techniques, noise calibration methods, and privacy-preserving algorithms will shape the efficacy and versatility of these approaches. Researchers must remain vigilant in their pursuit of advancements that enhance privacy while enabling meaningful insights.

As data privacy takes center stage in the digital landscape, the evolution of Secure Aggregation and Differential Privacy is pivotal. Their fusion with Federated Learning and other cutting-edge methodologies underscores their significance in shaping the responsible, ethical, and secure future of AI research and applications. Adapting to emerging challenges and charting new paths for innovation will ensure that these techniques remain at the forefront of AI's ethical and technological advancement.

32.3 Applications in Healthcare, Finance, and IoT: The fusion of Secure Aggregation, Differential Privacy, and Federated Learning has far-reaching implications across key sectors, including healthcare, finance, and the Internet of Things (IoT). These privacy-centric techniques offer profound applications that leverage data sensitivity, precision, and security in these domains.

Healthcare:

32.3.1 Privacy-Preserving Medical Research: In the realm of healthcare, the synergy between Secure Aggregation, Differential Privacy, and Federated Learning opens avenues for collaborative medical research without jeopardizing patient privacy. This approach empowers researchers to aggregate medical data from diverse sources, ensuring that sensitive patient information remains cryptographically safeguarded. This collaborative strategy expedites advancements in disease prediction, drug discovery, and treatment, all while upholding the sanctity of patient confidentiality.

32.3.2 Personalized Medicine: Secure Aggregation and Federated Learning play pivotal roles in tailoring medical solutions to individual patients. By pooling patient data from various institutions, models predicting personalized treatment responses can be developed. The stringent privacy measures of Differential Privacy ensure that these collective insights uphold patient anonymity and data confidentiality.

Finance:

32.3.3 Enhanced Fraud Detection and Risk Assessment: In the finance sector, Secure Aggregation and Differential Privacy are instrumental in elevating fraud detection and risk assessment capabilities. Financial institutions can collaboratively build robust models to identify fraudulent activities and evaluate risk profiles. Federated Learning empowers these models to evolve through insights from multiple institutions, all while maintaining data privacy.

32.3.4 Informed Market Analysis: Secure Aggregation empowers financial institutions to collectively analyze market trends, fostering informed decision-making. By combining Secure Aggregation with Federated Learning, proprietary trading strategies can remain undisclosed, yet valuable insights can be extracted from a broader dataset. This symbiotic approach enhances predictive accuracy and guides investment choices.

Internet of Things (IoT):

32.3.5 Empowering Edge Intelligence: Secure Aggregation and Federated Learning seamlessly empower the IoT landscape. Devices within an IoT network can collaborate to enhance edge intelligence, allowing localized decisions based on aggregated knowledge while respecting data privacy. This real-time responsiveness is achieved without necessitating data transmission to a central server.

32.3.6 Enabling Smart Cities: Secure Aggregation and Differential Privacy have profound implications for smart cities, enabling data-driven urban planning without compromising individual privacy. IoT devices like sensors and cameras can collectively offer insights into traffic patterns, environmental conditions, and resource allocation. Federated Learning facilitates the development of predictive models for urban planning and resource management through collaboration.

Ethical Considerations: As these applications unfold, ethical considerations are paramount. Adhering to regulations such as HIPAA and GDPR is vital to safeguarding individual rights. Organizations must strike a harmonious balance between deriving insights and upholding privacy. Transparency in data use and obtaining informed consent remain pivotal tenets to ensure ethical utilization of these techniques.

In summary, Secure Aggregation, Differential Privacy, and Federated Learning converge as a transformative trio that bridges innovation with data security. Their applications in healthcare, finance, and the IoT demonstrate their capacity to reshape industries through collaborative insights and decision-making. The trajectory of their impact hinges on responsible adoption and ethical foresight, defining their role in shaping a data-driven future.

32.4 Balancing Model Performance and User Privacy: Achieving a delicate equilibrium between model performance and user privacy is a paramount challenge in the realm of data-driven technologies. The pursuit of powerful AI models capable of extracting intricate patterns from vast datasets must be coupled with unwavering dedication to safeguarding user privacy. This duality underscores the ethical imperative of balancing innovation with responsible data handling.

32.4.1 The Privacy-Performance Trade-off: The intricate dance between achieving exceptional model performance and safeguarding user privacy is a fundamental challenge that shapes the landscape of modern data-driven technologies. This delicate equilibrium involves recognizing the inherent trade-off that exists between the two aspects – model performance and user privacy. On one hand, the pursuit of highly accurate AI models often demands access to vast amounts of detailed data. However, this pursuit raises valid concerns about potential data exposure and misuse, amplifying the need for stringent privacy measures. On the other hand, stringent privacy preservation measures, while essential for protecting users' sensitive information, can potentially hinder model performance by imposing limitations on the availability of data for training and analysis.

32.4.2 Differential Privacy as a Guardian: Amidst this dynamic balance, Differential Privacy emerges as a stalwart guardian. It assumes a critical role in this endeavor by acting as a sentinel that upholds both privacy and performance aspirations. At its core, Differential Privacy introduces a strategic mechanism of controlled noise injection during the aggregation of data. This seemingly counterintuitive addition of noise serves as a powerful safeguard against the re-identification of individuals within aggregated data sets. The controlled noise acts as a shield, ensuring that even with access to the aggregated data, it remains impossible to deduce specific individual contributions. By preserving the privacy of individual data points, Differential Privacy paves the way for the extraction of valuable insights while maintaining a robust level of privacy protection. This dual achievement permits AI models to uphold respectable performance metrics while adhering to the rigorous standards of privacy preservation.

Furthermore, Differential Privacy provides a quantifiable parameter known as epsilon (e). This parameter plays a pivotal role in calibrating the delicate balance between privacy and utility. Epsilon enables stakeholders to make informed decisions regarding the degree of privacy protection they wish to maintain and the level of utility they expect from their AI models. This parameter-driven approach empowers organizations to tailor their privacy-utility trade-off according to their specific needs and requirements.

32.4.3 Secure Aggregation for Collaborative Insights: In tandem with Differential Privacy, the concept of Secure Aggregation further contributes to the endeavor of balancing model performance and user privacy. Secure Aggregation operates as a robust mechanism for data collaboration while ensuring the utmost privacy of individual data contributions. Through cryptographic techniques, Secure Aggregation encrypts the data contributions from various sources before aggregating them. This encryption ensures that sensitive information within individual data points remains cryptographically hidden throughout the aggregation process. While the aggregated data is accessible for collaborative model evolution, the raw and sensitive data itself remains protected.

When combined with Federated Learning – a paradigm that allows models to evolve collaboratively across decentralized devices – Secure Aggregation empowers models to collectively improve without necessitating the transfer of raw data. This cryptographic approach aligns with the overarching goal of striking an equilibrium between model accuracy and user privacy. By enabling models to learn from the collective insights of diverse data sources while obfuscating the underlying data itself, Secure Aggregation aids in achieving this balance.

In essence, the tandem efforts of Differential Privacy and Secure Aggregation exemplify the comprehensive strategies employed to navigate the complex terrain of balancing model performance and user privacy in the evolving landscape of AI technologies.

32.4.4 Contextual Considerations: The intricate task of harmonizing privacy and performance in AI systems demands a nuanced approach that takes into account contextual considerations. This recognition underscores the need for decision-making that is context-aware and sensitive to the intricacies of the data, domain, and potential impact on users' lives. Contextual considerations guide the determination of the appropriate balance between sharing data and achieving optimal model performance. The specific nature of the data being dealt with, the domain it pertains to, and the potential consequences for individuals and society at large must all be meticulously weighed.

32.4.5 A Human-Centric Approach: Central to the endeavor of finding equilibrium is the foundation of a human-centric approach. This approach revolves around valuing and respecting users' preferences, expectations, and rights when it comes to their data. An essential aspect of this approach is the provision of transparent and meaningful choices to users regarding the sharing of their data. Implementing robust privacy-preserving techniques and mechanisms ensures that users' data is treated with the utmost care. Crucially, obtaining users' informed consent becomes pivotal in building trust and striking the right balance between model performance and user privacy.

32.4.6 Continuous Iteration and Learning: The pursuit of equilibrium between model performance and user privacy is not a static achievement: rather, it constitutes an ongoing and evolving endeavor. This dynamic nature underscores the necessity for continuous iteration and learning in the AI landscape. As both AI and privacy technologies advance, new methods for preserving privacy while enhancing model performance will inevitably emerge. The process of striking the balance must be iterative, requiring regular reassessment to remain adaptable to the evolving technological landscape and the shifting norms and expectations of society.

32.4.7 Ethical Imperative: In summary, the journey to attain a harmonious balance between model performance and user privacy transcends mere technical challenges: it is a profound ethical imperative. It calls for collective efforts from organizations, researchers, policymakers, and society as a whole. This collaborative endeavor is not just about innovation but about safeguarding fundamental principles. Transparency, user consent, data protection, and the responsible application of AI technologies are all intertwined in the ethical fabric of this pursuit. Only through this comprehensive and holistic approach can AI's potential be harnessed responsibly and sustainably, ensuring that the benefits of AI are enjoyed while safeguarding individual rights and societal well-being.

32.5 Project

Unsolved Project

Suppose you're developing a project that explores federated learning and privacy-preserving AI, with a focus on balancing model performance and user privacy. To ensure your project is comprehensive and effective, you need to understand the concept of federated learning, secure aggregation and differential privacy techniques, applications of federated learning in healthcare, finance, and IoT, and strategies for balancing model performance with user privacy. Before starting, research the following: the principles and mechanisms behind federated learning, methods for secure aggregation and ensuring differential privacy to protect user data, real-world applications of federated learning in various sectors such as healthcare, finance, and IoT, and techniques for optimizing model performance while maintaining a high level of user privacy. This foundational knowledge will help you develop a project that effectively integrates federated learning and privacy-preserving techniques in practical applications.

32.6 Lab Activity

Unsolved Lab Activity

Implement a federated learning model for a specific application (e.g., predicting patient outcomes in healthcare or fraud detection in finance). Evaluate its performance and privacy benefits.

Task: Use a deep learning framework to implement a federated learning model for a specific application, such as predicting patient outcomes in healthcare or fraud detection in finance. Train the model across multiple simulated devices or institutions and evaluate its performance and privacy benefits. Document the implementation process, including setup, training procedure, and performance evaluation. Provide visualizations of the model's performance and privacy enhancements.

Exercises

Exercise 1 – Multiple Choice Questions

1. What is the key differentiator of Federated Learning compared to centralized methodologies?
   A. Raw data aggregation C. Global data sharing
   B. Decentralized model training D. Data exposure
2. In Federated Learning, what type of devices act as training nodes?
   A. Central servers C. Individual user devices
   B. Cloud servers D. IoT devices
3. What is the advantage of decentralized model training in Federated Learning?
   A. Faster data transmission C. Reduced device storage requirements
   B. Improved data privacy D. Centralized data processing
4. What is the purpose of collaborative model aggregation in Federated Learning?
   A. To centralize all data C. To create a unified global model
   B. To share raw data across devices D. To minimize device participation
5. How does Federated Learning ensure data privacy during model aggregation?
   A. By sharing raw data between devices C. By only sharing model updates
   B. By aggregating data on a central server D. By encrypting all data

Exercise 2 – True/False

1. Federated Learning does not involve the centralization of raw data from individual devices.
2. Applications of Federated Learning are limited to the healthcare industry.
3. Secure Aggregation in Federated Learning ensures that individual device data remains private during the training process.

Review Questions

1. What is the primary focus of Federated Learning, and how does it differ from centralized machine learning methodologies?
2. How does Federated Learning address concerns about data privacy and security in comparison to centralized approaches?
3. Explain the concept of decentralized model training in Federated Learning. What types of devices can act as training nodes?
4. What advantages are associated with decentralized model training in Federated Learning?
5. What is the significance of collaborative model aggregation in the Federated Learning process, and how is it achieved while maintaining data privacy?
6. How does Federated Learning ensure data privacy during the model aggregation phase?
7. List and briefly describe some of the advantages of adopting Federated Learning in machine learning applications.
8. Provide examples of use cases where Federated Learning is applied in different sectors, such as healthcare, smart devices, natural language processing, and autonomous vehicles.
9. What is the primary objective of Secure Aggregation in the context of Federated Learning, and how does it protect sensitive data?
10. What is Differential Privacy, and how does it contribute to preserving individual privacy in machine learning and data analysis?

Answers

Exercise 1- 1. B 2. C 3. B 4. C 5. C
Exercise 2- 1. True, 2. False, 3. True

Online Resources

Online Exam Paper:
Link: https://forms.gle/w4pEnvMX8CvWWbia9
QR Code:

Chapter 32 Videos Playlist:
Link: https://www.youtube.com/playlist?list=PLzlh_31VWEFo7QueD4nQStQMFDQXzW38s
QR Code:

Viva Voce Questions

Q 1: What is Deep Learning?
Answer: Deep Learning is a subset of machine learning that uses neural networks with many layers (deep networks) to model and understand complex patterns in large amounts of data.
Q 2: Why is Deep Learning important in today's world?
Answer: Deep Learning is crucial because it drives many advancements in AI, enabling technologies such as autonomous vehicles, sophisticated natural language processing, and image recognition systems, which significantly impact various industries.
Q 3: Can you describe the historical development of Deep Learning?
Answer: Deep Learning has evolved from neural network research in the mid-20th century. Key milestones include the development of backpropagation in the 1980s, the resurgence of interest in neural networks in the 2000s with increased computational power, and recent breakthroughs in deep architectures like CNNs and RNNs.
Q 4: What are the basics of neurons and activation functions?
Answer: Neurons are the fundamental units of neural networks, modeled after biological neurons. Activation functions, such as ReLU, sigmoid, and tanh, introduce non-linearity to the model, enabling it to learn complex patterns.
Q 5: Explain the structure of Artificial Neural Networks.
Answer: Artificial Neural Networks consist of layers of interconnected neurons: an input layer, one or more hidden layers, and an output layer. Each neuron receives input, applies a weight, adds a bias, and passes the result through an activation function.
Q 6: What is forward propagation in neural networks?
Answer: Forward propagation is the process by which input data passes through the neural network's layers, from the input layer to the output layer, producing a prediction.
Q 7: What is backpropagation?
Answer: Backpropagation is a training algorithm used for neural networks. It calculates the gradient of the loss function with respect to each weight by the chain rule, and updates the weights to minimize the loss.
Q 8: How do you address overfitting in neural networks?
Answer: Overfitting can be addressed through regularization techniques like L1/L2 regularization, dropout, and by using cross-validation and proper data augmentation.
Q 9: What are Convolutional Neural Networks (CNNs)?
Answer: CNNs are a type of deep learning model specifically designed for processing structured grid data like images. They use convolutional layers to automatically learn spatial hierarchies of features.
Q 10: Describe the function of convolutional and pooling layers in CNNs.
Answer: Convolutional layers apply filters to the input data to detect features, while pooling layers downsample the data, reducing its dimensionality and computation requirements, helping to make the model invariant to small translations.
Q 11: Name some famous CNN architectures.
Answer: Famous CNN architectures include LeNet, AlexNet, VGG, and ResNet, each known for their innovative structures and contributions to the field of computer vision.
Q 12: What is transfer learning?
Answer: Transfer learning involves taking a pre-trained model on a large dataset and fine-tuning it on a smaller, specific dataset. This approach leverages existing knowledge to improve performance and reduce training time.
Q 13: What are Recurrent Neural Networks (RNNs)?
Answer: RNNs are a class of neural networks designed for sequential data. They have connections that form cycles, allowing information to persist across time steps, making them suitable for tasks like time series analysis and natural language processing.
Q 14: Explain the purpose of Long Short-Term Memory (LSTM) networks.
Answer: LSTMs are a type of RNN designed to overcome the vanishing gradient problem. They use memory cells to maintain long-term dependencies, making them effective for tasks requiring the understanding of long-term context.
Q 15: What are Generative Adversarial Networks (GANs)?
Answer: GANs consist of two neural networks, a generator and a discriminator, that compete against each other. The generator creates data samples, while the discriminator evaluates their authenticity. This process improves the quality of generated data.
Q 16: How are GANs used in image generation?
Answer: GANs are used in image generation by training the generator to produce realistic images from random noise, which the discriminator evaluates. Over time, the generator learns to create highly realistic images.
Q 17: What is reinforcement learning?
Answer: Reinforcement learning is a type of machine learning where an agent learns to make decisions by performing actions in an environment to maximize cumulative reward.
Q 18: How do Deep Q-Networks (DQN) work in reinforcement learning?
Answer: DQNs use a neural network to approximate the optimal action-value function. The network is trained to predict the reward of actions in given states, helping the agent to choose actions that maximize future rewards.

Q 19: What is the importance of attention mechanisms in deep learning?
Answer: Attention mechanisms allow models to focus on relevant parts of the input when generating output, improving performance in tasks like machine translation and image captioning by effectively handling long dependencies.
Q 20: Explain the concept of transformers in deep learning.
Answer: Transformers are a type of model architecture based on self-attention mechanisms. They allow for parallel processing of sequences and have become the foundation for many state-of-the-art models in natural language processing.

YouTube Link for Viva Voce Questions:
https://www.youtube.com/playlist?list=PLzlh_31VWEFp5RteaX5LIB0VxDN2Jvehw

QR Code:
\

Additional Resources

Deep Learning Whole Book Videos Playlist-
Link: https://www.youtube.com/playlist?list=PLzlh_31VWEFqRk3aFJxqbX5_ScifBp-2e
QR Code:

Chapter 1 Video Playlist Link:
Link: https://www.youtube.com/playlist?list=PLzlh_31VWEFrL_MPjYAT4sqgh-ahzjx6o
QR Code:

Chapter 2 Video Playlist Link:
Link: https://www.youtube.com/playlist?list=PLzlh_31VWEFoF2ylm3_gLGZGj89lSDNp6
QR Code:

Chapter 3 Video Playlist Link:
Link: https://www.youtube.com/playlist?list=PLzlh_31VWEFrMbJxGWnmTNQZQboJfVxNe
QR Code:

Chapter 4 Video Playlist Link:
Link: https://www.youtube.com/playlist?list=PLzlh_31VWEFqaWmuIt0FaKYOnGfwB-mAe
QR Code:

Chapter 5 Video Playlist Link:
Link: https://www.youtube.com/playlist?list=PLzlh_31VWEFpu7ARqlhxr1j4igFbu-wv1
QR Code:

Chapter 6 Video Playlist Link:
Link: https://www.youtube.com/playlist?list=PLzlh_31VWEFqq1Xj4kI4wPe0Z6oHEe--J
QR Code:

Chapter 7 Video Playlist Link:
Link: https://www.youtube.com/playlist?list=PLzlh_31VWEFqDcuCq347CJOJ53pSdv8H0
QR Code:

Chapter 8 Video Playlist Link:
Link: https://www.youtube.com/playlist?list=PLzlh_31VWEFrrjDjyLWypIIpkkt9kRkK
QR Code:

Chapter 9 Video Playlist Link:
Link: https://www.youtube.com/playlist?list=PLzlh_31VWEFrGGGXpOi1SIMeFRo2pMg-C
QR Code:

Chapter 10 Video Playlist Link:
Link: https://www.youtube.com/playlist?list=PLzlh_31VWEFqtOWfUgu46KO0TCkSyHyXi
QR Code:

Chapter 11 Video Playlist Link:
Link: https://www.youtube.com/playlist?list=PLzlh_31VWEFqjY6Py6i6rcFEIBD1Z4ti9
QR Code:

Chapter 12 Video Playlist Link:
Link: https://www.youtube.com/playlist?list=PLzlh_31VWEFo0stlv2Y_9sSBtHfid7ioq
QR Code:

Chapter 13 Video Playlist Link:
Link: https://www.youtube.com/playlist?list=PLzlh_31VWEFoVGOwBkc_B4CbIR0Zen-my
QR Code:

Chapter 14 Video Playlist Link:
Link: https://www.youtube.com/playlist?list=PLzlh_31VWEFolAEMzd64gYh0Sa4_qsemC
QR Code:

Chapter 15 Video Playlist Link:
Link: https://www.youtube.com/playlist?list=PLzlh_31VWEFqzFujVB1fyRrtLRQijacv0
QR Code:

Chapter 16 Video Playlist Link:
Link: https://www.youtube.com/playlist?list=PLzlh_31VWEFoWA6HvdBx7D2LyRuXUXXzd
QR Code:

Chapter 17 Video Playlist Link:
Link: https://www.youtube.com/playlist?list=PLzlh_31VWEFq_uQErBGm5pIfg1qdc6Fuc
QR Code:

Chapter 18 Video Playlist Link:
Link: https://www.youtube.com/playlist?list=PLzlh_31VWEFoBRXgt-MvHWzmbmKrh1wgI
QR Code:

Chapter 19 Video Playlist Link:
Link: https://www.youtube.com/playlist?list=PLzlh_31VWEFpgOq2KvtilNQE7K-bW8OY9
QR Code:

Chapter 20 Video Playlist Link:
Link: https://www.youtube.com/playlist?list=PLzlh_31VWEFoLM-AylnGYzPrqR702cTGV
QR Code:

Chapter 21 Video Playlist Link:
Link: https://www.youtube.com/playlist?list=PLzlh_31VWEFoYaPQl8wzSWbnECgDfNSRP
QR Code:

Chapter 22 Video Playlist Link:
Link: https://www.youtube.com/playlist?list=PLzlh_31VWEFq0HBRLOOwmyfH7dMevkdSN
QR Code:

Chapter 23 Video Playlist Link:
Link: https://www.youtube.com/playlist?list=PLzlh_31VWEFpmzNKd0azl459J43wkukzP
QR Code:

Chapter 24 Video Playlist Link:
Link: https://www.youtube.com/playlist?list=PLzlh_31VWEFofpABLMzfKtSxXzxfxy0Im
QR Code:

Chapter 25 Video Playlist Link:
Link: https://www.youtube.com/playlist?list=PLzlh_31VWEFr6n_Pb_8RzzIEvMS6f9cBA
QR Code:

Chapter 26 Video Playlist Link:
Link: https://www.youtube.com/playlist?list=PLzlh_31VWEFopNzE_ZcVrytKhqOZ-kSvH
QR Code:

Chapter 27 Video Playlist Link:
Link: https://www.youtube.com/playlist?list=PLzlh_31VWEFqEU7thYi0XoexALnwzlHFV
QR Code:

Chapter 28 Video Playlist Link:
Link: https://www.youtube.com/playlist?list=PLzlh_31VWEFp1ElAdAfYZnQ9DyNr_dCOI
QR Code:

Chapter 29 Video Playlist Link:
Link: https://www.youtube.com/playlist?list=PLzlh_31VWEFqSMtOV5WGF5q3Rqzram25h
QR Code:

Chapter 30 Video Playlist Link:
Link: https://www.youtube.com/playlist?list=PLzlh_31VWEFoiZvr62_D67cYCU3-_WsaQ
QR Code:

Chapter 31 Video Playlist Link:
Link: https://www.youtube.com/playlist?list=PLzlh_31VWEFr8VsB3NDJcqzlFPJNPczks
QR Code:

Chapter 32 Video Playlist Link:
Link: https://www.youtube.com/playlist?list=PLzlh_31VWEFo7QueD4nQStQMFDQXzW38s
QR Code: